Worship as Body Language

Elochukwu E. Uzukwu, C.S.Sp.

Worship as Body Language

Introduction to Christian Worship: An African Orientation

A PUEBLO BOOK

The Liturgical Press Collegeville, Minnesota

A Pueblo Book published by The Liturgical Press

Design by Frank Kacmarcik, Obl.S.B.

Library of Congress Cataloging-in-Publication Data

Uzukwu, E. Elochukwu.
Worship as body language : introduction to Christian worship : an African orientation / Elochukwu E. Uzukwu.
p. cm.
"A Pueblo book."
Includes bibliographical references.
ISBN 0-8146-6151-3
1. Catholic Church—Liturgy. 2. Catholic Church—Africa.
3. Gesture in worship. 4. Posture in worship. 5. Gesture—Religious aspects—Christianity. 6. Nonverbal communication (Psychology)
7. Africa—Religious life and customs. I. Title.
BX1977.A35U97 1997
264.02—dc21 96-51705
CIP

Contents

Acknowledgments

The kind of questions Christian communities in Africa were asking before and after Vatican II are responsible for the kind of answers proposed in this book. My students in Nigeria, Zaire, and Congo Brazzaville were participants in the dialogue recorded in this book. Many were enthusiastic about the historical and anthropological approach to questions of the liturgy and the administration of the sacraments. Some expressed concern and dissatisfaction that their lecturer was using no recognizable textbook and challenged the authenticity of both the content and method of my teaching. Others who were interested in passing examinations were distressed when they were obliged to study the anthropological dimensions of the gesture, ritual, myth, and symbol that are not as clear and mathematical as the "matter and form" of the Thomistic-Aristotelian heritage. Their enthusiasm and anxieties urged me to do further research into concepts capable of expressing the reality of the Christian experience and celebration in the African context. I am grateful to the various seminaries and higher institutions in these countries for the opportunity they afforded me to produce this book. Those former students of mine—especially in Zaire—who found it difficult to teach liturgy with the traditional textbooks may find in this book the results of my many discussions with them inside and outside the classroom.

I am particularly grateful to the Episcopal Conference of Zaire for the confidence they reposed in me during the years they had to negotiate with the Sacred Congregation for Divine Worship over the "Zairean rite." The challenges they faced, which were necessary in the dialogue between sister churches, were also a great help in my in-depth research into liturgical history. I am also grateful to the members of the research committee on Igbo Mass (Awka diocese of Nigeria) for the three years of research (1983–1986). We were not given permission to experiment on the Mass, but we acquired a lot of knowledge on the social organization of the Igbo and the sentiments that prevail in their ritual assemblies. The year I spent as associate pastor in Isienu (Nsukka diocese, Nigeria, 1993) was a very fruitful year. My pastor and former student Christopher Mbogu has a lot of experience in reconciling families and groups with a Christian liturgy in tune with the local traditions. His experiments have helped me in reflecting on creative liturgies in Africa.

The proprietors, staff, and students of the Spiritan International School of Theology allowed me to take a year's sabbatical leave (1991/92). Without their assistance I could not have written this book. I am also grateful to the Spiritan Generalate in Rome, the Nigerian Province and the Trans-Canadian Province of the Spiritans, and Missio Aachen for the subsidies given me to facilitate my leave and research. Six months of that leave I spent with my family in Umuzu village, Okofia, Nnewi. The warmth and intimacy enjoyed with my mother and relatives strengthened my optimism in developing a liturgy based on dynamic relationships.

My colleagues, former professors, and friends read parts of the manuscripts, recommended literature, facilitated access to libraries in the Toronto university system, criticized the methodology, or gave support and encouragement during the two years when this book was written (1992–1993). Thus in Toronto Professors T. Horvath, G. Schner, J. Kloppenburg, A. Miklòsházy, and my friend P. Odozor made their contributions to this book. I profited also from the critical remarks and suggestions of J. C. Okoye (Rome), C. I. Ejizu (Port Harcourt), A. Ekwanife, A. Onyeneke, B. Abanuka, and O. Iwuchukwu (Isienu, Nsukka), Professor P. de Clerck and J. Gross (Paris). My friend and Colleague, Breifne Walker, assisted me in preparing an index to this book. Miss J. Itodo was very devoted in typing parts of the scripts. May my many friends in whose house and company I felt very much at home and who made sure I did not give in to discouragement accept singly and collectively my thanks. And may the One who envelops us all in his bosom, the sky in whose center we always find ourselves without ever reaching its fringes, rain his soothing benedictions on us all!

E. E. Uzukwu, C.S.Sp.
Chevilly-Larue, May 25, 1994

Introduction

Worship involves motion: humans move toward God in response to God's movement toward humans. The total human person (embodied spirit) makes this gesture toward God and toward other humans.

The principal argument of this book is that our motions or gestures, and the way we generally interpret human rhythmic movement, are bound to an ethnic experience. Consequently, our praise or thanksgiving, adoration or contemplation, prayer of quiet or measured ritual dance, which display the assembled body of worshipers before God or spirits, have meaning within an ethnic group. Christian worship, as a human expression of the encounter with the God of Jesus Christ, must always be local. The Christian faith is one; its expressions are necessarily many. This is our presupposition in this work. It sets the stage for appreciating the crucial interest of liturgical inculturation in Africa.

The first and second chapters of this book are connected. Chapter one affirms the ethnic basis of all human gestural behavior. As motion of the body, the gesture finds its meaning within the social body. Each human action (body motion) is judged insofar as it is in tune or out of tune with the established patterns of a group. In Christianity, the Greco-Roman patterns of movement predominate. Sub-Saharan Africans who were evangelized by the Latin Church have not fully tuned into African body motions to express the one Christian faith. Chapter two highlights the principal function of gesture as creating or re-creating community. Through its ritual action the community expresses what touches it most; by repeating the familiar ritual gestures it is mobilized to action in its world. In the native African context, any event touching the life of a group or an individual may be an occasion to convoke a ritual assembly. In the Jewish and Christian traditions the crucial foundational events (Exodus and Cross-resurrection of Jesus) dominate the ritual assembly. The impact of native African ritual assemblies on Christian practice is displayed in chapter five, where some experimentations in local African liturgies are examined.

Chapter three is a segment of its own; though it is connected with the preceding chapters. The community in assembly narrates its founding story. Sometimes the narrative is a ritual recalling of the events of the past that are relived in the present. In chapter three the functional properties of sacred narratives (myths) are described. Samples of sacred narratives are taken from the African, Mesopotamian, and Jewish-Christian traditions. In the African foundation narrative (of the Igbo of Nigeria), the sacred history impacts on the political, social, and economic dimensions of life. Life in all its totality becomes ritualized; it is lived under the eyes of God and spirits. The Mesopotamian sacred narrative is ritualized in the domain of politics. The sacred history or myth is narrated in full during the new year *akitu* festival. In the Jewish and Christian stories, which are given more space in our reflection, the sacred history is recalled in ritual celebrations; the daily life of the faithful reproduces the narrative. Indeed, in the Christian tradition, the life of the martyr reenacts the life of Jesus the Christ. The ritual celebration of the Christian sacred history in the Eucharist confirms the one faith of the Christian "commonwealth" against heterodox beliefs. Our commentary on the narrative and its ritual application to life brings out the salient theological dimensions of worship.

The last two chapters are concerned with the practical application of what has been examined in the preceding chapters. Chapter four examines passage and life-crises rituals and their impact on human societies. The focus is on those rites of passage that are initiatory. First of all, the pool of African experience of patterns of initiation is ready-to-hand to influence a contextual celebration of Christian initiation. Second, the array of such passage rites in Africa calls for the creation of more transition rituals beyond those existing in the Roman rite. In the last chapter (chapter five) we have samples of liturgies that are already emerging in the sub-Saharan African region. Experimentation in West, Central, and Eastern Africa are reviewed. While English and French-speaking West Africa have created new Christian initiation and life-crises rituals, Eastern and Central Africa have focused their attention on creating Eucharistic liturgies and liturgies for the consecration of virgins. These emergent local liturgies testify to the validity of the age-old patristic principle that different customs in the Christian Church only confirm the unity of our faith in Christ.

Chapter One

Human Gestural Behavior as Ritual and Symbolic

The African world as humans experience it is a world full of activity: action, reaction, interaction. The gesture that is motion or movement, measured beat or pulse, helps us to grasp the kind of activity recorded in Africa. Africans take note of the pattern of motion which characterizes some animals. They employ these observations to instruct, educate, or entertain. Proverbs, pithy sayings, legends, and myths are full of such observable patterns among animals. The legendary chameleon, for instance, has its measured movement. This gesture goes back to the time of creation when God sent the chameleon to inspect the created earth. The earth was not yet firm; consequently, the chameleon's motions display care. On the other hand, the hen (and fowls in general) has an almost reckless motion of scattering earth when scavenging for food. This is a gesture bestowed on the hen when it was sent down to the earth by Oduduwa or Obatala (the Yoruba creator divinities) at the time of creation. Its motion of scattering earth made firm land appear. This gesture has become part and parcel of the hen's pattern. Animals display particular motions at play or during mating, in asserting territoriality, sensing danger, or expressing aggression. As the Igbo of Nigeria say, when a bird in motion tilts its wing, one knows where it is going to perch.

Among humans, the gesture retains the characteristic of motion. It is the movement of the body; a measured movement. The pattern of this movement depends on place, time, and space. Our interest in the gesture is based on this characteristic of human movement as display of the body. We consider this display vital for the understanding of worship.

THE GESTURE AS BODY LANGUAGE

The gesture that is our concern in this chapter is not limited to the African world. Humans in the universe may rightly be described as "acting-beings." Marcel Jousse may be right in emphasizing that prior to learning what humans were from the fossils of the tools they made (*homo faber*, signaling the dawn of culture),[1] anthropologists should pay close attention to the personal struggle of the species to create meaning through body movement. Men and women made their first tools from their very bodies, i.e., through gestures.[2] The human person is an endless complex of gestures. The fabrication of tools is an extension of human gestures. Therefore, the real birth of culture dates from the time human beings designed their gestures.

The human gesture is a designed movement of the body in time and space. Humans who find themselves in this universe of interaction are sometimes described in such action-laden terms as living energy, life-force, or "life-ing" by Africans.[3] They assimilate bodily the impact that this universe makes on them, and they display, bodily, adequate responses. This adequate corporeal response is a designed and learned pattern of behavior. It is a pattern rooted in ethnic experience of the universe. Thus when two people meet "they will adjust the distance between themselves according to their ethnicity, their level of intimacy, their prior relationship, their business together, and the available physical space and circumstance."[4] A young Yoruba or Nupe person in Nigeria sinks to the ground or prostrates full-length on meeting an elder; also the Urhobo of Nigeria greet the elder or chief by touching the ground with both hands. On the other hand, among the West Niger Igbo of Asaba (Nigeria), young people keep their hands in their pockets when being scolded by elders. This restrains them from hitting back when hit by an elder in the interchange. The Akan of Ghana pull off their shoes when going into the presence of the Asentehene (or king), just as Moslems enter the mosque barefoot. A lay person in medieval Christendom, no matter how elevated in rank, bowed to a clergyman or displayed other gestures of respect whenever they met.[5]

The action and interaction through body movement that humans learn and display are not limited to humans. The universe, as we have noted, is and has always been a theater of action and interaction. The action into which we are implicated is older than the human species. Human gestural activity is therefore designed from existing "inter-activity" in the universe. This shows both the intimate link between us and the universe and the indefinite character of gestures. According to Scheflen and Scheflen: "Some organizations have survived for thousands of years. Architectural structures sometimes last for centuries. Recognized languages may be 50,000 years old. The basic behaviors of courting, dominance, and territoriality may be millions of years old and certain reactions to environmental stress go back as far as mammals."[6]

In an unconscious way things acted on or along with other things in the universe. Human involvement in this measured motion both continues what was there and introduces a difference. Human consciousness makes human gestural activity a design and not a simple instinctual response to external or internal stimuli. There is style or strategy in the rhythm of human body movement. This measured motion is intimately connected with speech (verbal gesture). It is thus a rational activity. Repetition is the law that guides the rhythm of human gesture. All neonates within any given sociocultural area (ethnic group) learn to become human through repeating the group's gestures.

The Hands as the Human Rational Tool

From ancient times it has been perceived that the gesture of standing erect and the natural endowment of hands to humans are the root of human rationality. Aquinas calls the hand the "tool of tools" *(organum organorum)*. He believes that the hand is directly linked to erectness, to language, and to the privilege of reason. It links easily the other parts of the body. Medieval authors depended on the thinking of Plato, Aristotle, and other classical Greek and Roman philosophers to express the paramount position of the hand for human gestural behavior. It is the human rational tool. "Man has hands because he is the wisest of all beings" (Aristotle). And though nature has not provided humans with arms and other arts (skills or deftness), they have hands as their instrument of reason (Galien).

It is therefore not surprising that the definition of gesture in the Middle Ages, and indeed in the Western tradition, according to Schmitt, tended very much to be linked with the gesture of the hand — an organ very prominent in rhetoric. *Gestus in manibus est* (gesture is in the hands). The Carolingian writer Remigius of Auxerre established a difference between movement and gesture by stressing that motion concerns the whole body while gesture concerns strictly the hands and other members. Speech *(pronunciatio)* is in the movement of the voice and in the moderation of gestures. The voice comes from the mouth, movement is in the whole body, while gesture is in the hands.[7] This definition is influenced not only by rhetoric, but particularly by Christian rhetoric (preaching). The Christian preacher is at prayer and not simply at a Roman podium trying to persuade the audience. The definition also censors body movement, particularly gesticulation and the dance. The dance was gradually eliminated from the liturgy in medieval Christendom.[8]

The priority of the hand as the highest tool of human gestures is not limited to the Greco-Roman world. Each sociocultural group documents in its language — action and speech — the role of the hand in communication. For example, among African groups the gesture of helping someone implicates the hand: "giving a helping hand" (*inye aka*, Igbo). Similarly, to be involved in a case either for good or for evil is "to have one's hand in it" (*aka ya di na ya*, Igbo). Among the Bantu of the Zaire region (especially the Yansi, Luba, Yaka, etc.), Hochegger has produced volumes of study in ritual gestures. The gestures involving the hand include making of covenants, love and friendship rituals, rituals of purification, witchcraft, and so on. The hand thus appears to be prominent in the gestures of healing and destruction among these African groups.[9]

In Greco-Roman antiquity, gesture (*gestus* in Latin) generally meant movement or body disposition; in particular it meant the movement of an individual part of the body, especially the hand. *Motus* (movement) is a synonym of *gestus*, especially in the frequent expression *motus corporis* (body movement). But *motus* has the wider meaning of any movement at all (e.g., of the land, stars, animals, soul, etc.). In Greek, *kinesis* is the equivalent of *gestus* and *motus*.[10]

The Gesture Establishes Group Identity

Each human community or ethnic group designs its own gestures to express its experience of life in the universe. From the ordinary and daily routine of greeting, bidding welcome or farewell, to the more complex patterns of making a pact or making war, healing, praying, or dancing, each particular gesture, whether accompanied by words or not, establishes communication among the group and displays the operation of group identity. The newborn assimilate (through a learning process, i.e., enculturation) the motions established as a way of doing by years or ages of repetition. In this way they join the order or rhythm of interaction in the universe as the society (social body) expresses it. Consequently, no individual member of the group sets himself or herself in motion indiscriminately. To do so would amount to acting out of tune. To posit a gesture that is out of tune may bring shame or cause embarrassment. And, depending on the level of interaction involved, such a profanation of a way of doing may require a corrective process (e.g., ritual purification) according to the code of the society. Therefore, there is always a reference to the patterns of interaction set up by the social body.[11]

Similarly, no ethnic group imposes its pattern of communication or its way of doing on another group; nor does any group set aside another's designed response to the impact of the universe arbitrarily. To act in such a way is equally to act out of tune. Such an aggression becomes one more impact of the universe on the aggrieved group. The group reacts with adequate gestures to protect its interest. Rather, human groups may learn, formally or informally (acculturation), from one another's experiences accumulated through repeated interactions.

Briefly, gestural behavior is repetitive; it establishes a way of doing; it is above all a pattern of communication that ensures group identity. When we refer to gestures in this way we are underlining the properties of ritual and symbol. These are two key concepts for any exploration into worship. Ritual, as we shall see in the next chapter, is basically a pattern of action involving body motions (verbal and nonverbal). It is a gesture that establishes communication and identity within a group, thus it is symbolic. The rhythm of gestures and its ethnic roots will later help our explorations into the properties of ritual behavior. In the present chapter we shall concentrate on the rhythmic and symbolic character of body movement. This will help us to highlight the divergent attitudes toward the body and motion in various sociocultural areas. It helps us also to show how these have influenced and may continue to influence the patterns of behavior peculiar to worship.

THE BODY AS PRIMAL SYMBOL

Gestural behavior is body language. Whether verbal or nonverbal, it is a way any community creates meaning. Individuals who belong to the "speech community" (ethnic group) freely function with the gestures of their society (social body).

In African communities, past and present, where oral patterns of communication predominate, gestures are highly developed.[12] While it is likely in Africa to have motions of the body unaccompanied by speech, it is less likely to speak without body movement. The rhythm of body communication along with the power of the word are highly developed in Africa.[13] Jousse underlined three fundamental forms in which any human community expresses the impact of the universe upon it: dance (unity of mime and rhythm), poetry (unity of rhythm and recitation), and music (unity of rhythm and melody).[14] The poetry and music are usually accompanied by the dance in most African communities. This link between music and dance is not limited to Africa. For, as Roger Bacon says, music (with its instrumentation, song, rhythm, and meter) remains incomplete without gestures — the stretching and flexing of the body.[15] The dance, which involves an expansive, rhythmic, nonverbal movement of the body, is one key way of interaction in Africa. In the dance the body is most sharply displayed.

The attitude displayed toward the body and its motions by any social group derives from the group's view of the universe. We shall explore such attitudes as displayed in the Greco-Roman world and in Africa. The Greco-Roman gestures deriving from a particular worldview influenced Christian practice — liturgy, ethics, preaching, and spirituality. The African attitudes, on their own part, derive also from the African worldview and should influence Christian life in Africa.

"Spirit" and "Body" in Greco-Roman Gestures

Greco-Roman antiquity (especially the classical period) projected the image of gestural behavior that prioritized the hand (and the face). The science of rhetoric as expounded by Cicero and adapted by the Fathers of the Christian Church (in particular Augustine of Hippo) outlined the proportionate movements and poise of the orator. The emphasis was on moderation — the ideal gesture reveals the dominance of spirit over matter. While gestures were accepted as reasonable, gesticulation was understood as excessive and was to be rejected. Gradually, from antiquity down to the Middle Ages, the ideal of godlike immobility was preferred by the elite to body movement, the spirit to the body. Immobility was understood as the gesture of "spirit" as opposed to the motions of "body." Peter Brown exposes this pattern in his description of the common climate of opinion shared by two great Egyptians: Plotinus the philosopher and Anthony the hermit. This has reference to their attitude toward the body. Plotinus was ashamed he had a human body while Anthony blushed when he had to eat. Both were admired for "godlike" mastery of mind over body.[16] This is not the body in whose rhythmic movements (gestures) the self becomes manifested according to the African experience (see below). Rather it is a body that has become a problem to the spirit, a burden to the self, a prison for the soul. This displays the Western dualistic perception of humans in the world. In modern times this dualism has been made sharper by the Cartesian reduction of the human being to a thinking machine. This Western viewpoint, based on a set of experiences and philosophical assumptions, is legitimate and has created the Western human type. But it has to be stressed that it is one cultural attitude among many others.

The inculturation of Christianity in the West popularized this cultural type and deeply influenced further developments of the attitude to the body and gestures. More than the influence of Stoicism and Platonism, the doctrine of original sin as finally propounded by Augustine and adopted by the Western Church entrenched the understanding of body as *sarx* (flesh): a thing which is fallen; an instrument of sin. Against the optimistic anthropology of the English monk Pelagius, which claimed that Adam's sin was nothing but a bad example, and, therefore, we were born neither vicious nor virtuous but have the capacity for either though provided with neither, Augustine reacted in disbelief. In his interpretation of the Pauline Adamic midrash (Rom 5:12), he asserted: "all men are understood to have sinned in that first 'man,' because all men were in him when he sinned; and from him sin is derived by birth, and is not remitted save by being born again."[17]

The Augustinian doctrine of original sin was already held in its essential features by Ambrose and Ambrosiaster. It had a profound influence on conceptions of the body in the Western tradition. First of all, bodily gestures are ruled by the presence of sin; second, through the incarnation of the Word the regeneration of humans damaged by sin is realized. Christian morality, liturgy, and asceticism projected continence and modesty as the primary virtues. Thus care is taken to avoid any tendency toward the *commotio carnis* (disturbance or motions of the flesh). In cenobitic life the best antidote against desire *(libido)*, according to the Western tradition (Ambrose, Augustine, Gregory the Great, Cassian), is to merge the individual gestures into the community motions. During training and after profession, the novice is led to renounce individual body (personal) movement in order to assume the community movement (Cassian).[18] This elimination of the individuality of gestures characterizes generally monastic life.

The suspicion in which the body and gestures were held led to the restriction of body motions to levels considered acceptable — the reasonable proportion. Gestures classified as excessive (gesticulation) were denounced. In a medieval Christendom where theological rationality held sway, the opinion of the clergy on gestures within the social (Christian) order predominated. In the footsteps of Ambrose of Milan, references to the dance of David and similar gestures common in the psalms became sublimated. They were reinterpreted as piety and ecstatic union through which the Christian is brought in tune with the cosmic rhythm. References to the liturgical dance of children by Justin the Martyr or the modest dance in the Church mentioned by John Chrysostom and Gregory Nazianzen or the Easter dance of the subdeacons in the twelfth century remain isolated. The stretching and flexing of the body were not considered by the elite as moderate. Consequently, they were proscribed.[19]

It was not only the flexing of the body (dance) which became suspect. Those whose occupations were connected with the theater were judged negatively. Thus minstrels, histrionics, comedians, and so on, became reprobate. Their gestures were a mimicry and thus unnatural. They propagated patterns of behavior unhealthy for the salvation of the society. For example, they put on masks (thereby breaking the boundary between the living and the dead), practiced juggling and performed dances that were lewd or declared obscene. Dances in the church and cemeteries that were put into pastoral use by the mendicant orders were also suspect and were condemned by councils and Church leaders. In particular the dance of death *(danse macabre)*, which became prominent in the fourteenth and fifteenth centuries, did not escape condemnation. This dance, which has its roots in pre-Christian beliefs about the dead appearing and drawing the living into their circular dance and announcing to them their approaching departure, was used to dramatize preaching. In this mime, which was executed in churches and cemeteries, death, which is displayed as the lot of each person (pope or prince, bishop or knight, rich or poor, clergy or laity), draws each dancer in the hierarchical order in making the round. The gestures of the dance of death were considered excessive. In addition, they desecrated holy ground. They were consequently denounced.[20]

However, from the twelfth century a more positive attitude was developing about the body and gestures. By then, according to Schmitt, *gesta* referred to collective or principal actions of a group or key individuals (history); gesture *(gestus)* referred to the characteristic body movements or attitudes of a group (like the Germans or the French, the clergy or the laity, Cistercians or Benedictines); the moral judgment implied in approving or condemning behavior tended to be more individualized. Thus customs and gestures did not necessarily carry a value judgment. Furthermore, the kind of gestures proposed to novices by Hugh of St. Victor in his *De institutione novitiorum* were adapted by royalty and the aristocracy. The mendicant orders (especially the Franciscans) also propagated the acceptable behavior patterns in their preaching to lay people to enable them to attain salvation. In this way the body could be seen as an instrument of salvation.

Developments in the science of medicine and surgery, which were effectively outside the control of the clergy, also led to a different conception of the body. Medical science propagated a mechanical conception of the functioning of the body. This drew attention to the geometrical dimensions of body movement. The impact of this is felt in painting and sculpture, and it contributed in no small way to the development of architecture in the West (especially the Gothic type).[21]

The shift in conceptions of the body did not imply an abandonment of *modestia*. Moderation still revealed the human soul in action — the moral dimension of gestures. However, patterns of gestures in contact with popular folk culture that were reprobated were gradually being tolerated. Liturgical dramas and celebrations came to be influenced by gestures of jugglers to which they were compared. This resulted in the expansion of Christian ritual gestures to proportions unknown in patristic times. Finally, since gestures have reference to groups (an ethnic group, a crowd, monks, clergy or laity, etc.), and the value judgment of behavior (morality) is individualized, the aesthetic dimension of body movement was projected. The Middle Ages may thus be called an age of gestures, not only because of the variety, multiplication, and repetition of gestures, but because, through the genius of the clergy, Christendom held to what it inherited from antiquity and adapted it profoundly to respond to new patterns of body movement that resisted being relegated to the category of the excessive (gesticulation). We shall see below the functioning of some of these gestures in liturgical celebrations.

African Body Attitudes and Gestures

The African experience of body differs from both the Greco-Roman antiquity and its adaptation in medieval Christendom. The profound implications of this difference for an African way of being Christian will be shown in this study. Contrary to the Greco-Roman and Western Christian practice, Africans do not experience the body as a prison for the soul, an indicator of "fallen-ness," and, consequently, an instrument of sin.

The African experience of body and gestures displays humans in the universe grasped as a totality. The body is the center of the total manifestation of person in gestures. In gestures (verbal and nonverbal) the self reveals itself, from head to toe, as one complex reality — visible yet invisible; corporeal-incorporeal; part of, but also the center of a complex universe of interaction. The rhythm of interaction in this universe is discovered, re-created, and expressed bodily by humans.

African sociocultural groups appreciate the difference between the body and the soul. However, in the rhythm of gestures a complex self becomes manifest and defines itself basically in terms of relatedness. The complexity of the African notion of person, instead of leading to a devaluation of the body, reveals itself in bodily gestures. Body motions, whether accompanied by speech or not, embody the group, reveal its universe of beliefs, while not excluding individual responsibility.

Among the Igbo of Nigeria, for example, *mmadu* (the human person) is a plurality of relationships. In the myth of human incarnation,[22] the body *(ahu)* of a newborn is related to the action of intercourse of the parents. The characteristics or potentialities *(agwa)* expected of the newborn are related to recognized and socially approved patterns of behavior (gestures) of revered ancestors, living elders, noncorporeal spirits, or even malignant spirits (*ogbanje*, spoiler-spirits). Then the spiritual self or soul *(mmuo)* is related to a fundamental prenatal choice made in conjunction with a personal creative god or genius *(chi)* who links each individual to his or her destiny. This prenatal choice is manifest physically on one's palms (*akala-aka*, marks on the hand or life-lines). The name or names imposed on a child during the naming ceremony (the social birth of the child) take all these relationships into consideration. But all these components are an apparatus for becoming a person. It is one's achievement in the world of relationship that declares one *mmadu* (human). The Yoruba of Nigeria, Gourmantche and Samo of Bourkina Faso, and the Tallensi of Ghana each have a similar array of components and interactional possibilities to become a human person. No component is devalued; rather through interactional gestures the self, which is manifest bodily, achieves coherence.[23]

The Power of Music and Dance in the Realization of Person in Gestures

The complexity of the social definition of a person among Africans may appear bewildering to the non-African. The Igbo mythic narrative of human incarnation is even less complex than that of the Dogon of Mali. The Igbo recognize one soul while the Dogon have eight principles or souls that are bisexually paired and are not permanently bound to the body. For example, the female soul of a man dwells in the body but is also located in the female waters of the family, which is under the protection of Nommo (the god-of-the-sea). The totemic sanctuary and the taboo clan animal are also places of repose for these principles.[24] Each individual needs to be initiated into the rhythm of interaction in order to arrive creatively at "person-hood." Sound (of speech, prayer or incantation, of song and music, and especially of the talking drum) is an important vehicle or symbol of rhythmic mediation in this complex universe. The creative appropriation of sound leads to a creative reception of the self. We have thus a different set of assumptions with which, as Africans, we experience the self in the universe of interaction.

In a recent article, "Sound as Ultimate Reality and Meaning: The Mode of Knowing Reality in African Thought," Anyanwu has argued that since knowledge is never experienced in total detachment in Africa, sound is a model for expressing the participant-performer dynamics of knowing. The experience of the other, which is also the experience of the self, is in the rhythmic harmony of interaction. To objecting logical positivists Anyanwu replies that the dimension of sound or life-force, and human participation in it, is the way Africans handle (or dance) the ambivalence of life: "There is a rhythmic sharing of experience through music and dance, and dancing is a rhythmical order in the universe of Sound. All activities of life manifest that rhythmical order."[25] In a similar though restricted way Niangoran-bouah has shown that the drum, a unique symbol/instrument of communication in black Africa, is comparable to the Bible or the Koran. It both carries the primordial word and is identical with the primordial word. The language of the Drum accompanied by ritual texts is best revealed in the enthronement of kings, funerals, initiation rites, new year, and new yam festivals in the West African region.[26] The drum and sound both generate and call for adequate gestures (ritual, social, moral, etc.) for the re-creation of the individual and society. Each social group has its pattern of experiencing and expressing the flow of life-force or sound in the universe. At the same time each individual created in a unique way (symbolized, for example, by the *chi* among the Igbo and the *ori* among the Yoruba) follows his or her pattern of tapping or tuning into the rhythmic flow of life in the cosmos. In this way individual gestures are neither submerged in the collective style nor detached from it.[27]

The complex universe of Africans where humans experience life through the rhythm of sound (life-force), through the rhythm of the talking drum, is another legitimate experience based on its own set of assumptions. The rhythm of this universe is best appropriated through the dance where the group mimes the beat of the cosmos in order to tune into it. The rhythm of the dance displays the human grasp of a life full of paradox. Mveng has shown that rhythm in African aesthetics is fundamentally rational. It is self-creation. The discovery of the beat or rhythm of the universe, realized through feeling its pulse in the dance (barefoot), liberates humans to be creative. To grasp the logic of rhythm is to discover the key for the interpretation of the paradox that life is. Rhythm is inserted at the point of the experience of the conflict between life as limited and life as continuity. In other words, rhythm is the primordial resolution of the conflict between life and death, between being and nothingness, between time and eternity.[28]

This complex rhythmic appropriation of the universe ensures that rhythm in Africa is not controlled by any fixed number and quantity as is the European experience. Rather it tends toward dialectical expression, preferring complexity or multiplicity to the logic of regulated determinism. This dialectic is expressed in poetry or prose, in sculpture or painting, in the dimensions of sound or the talking drum. But the most popular place where Africans live the dynamic harmony of the universe is in music and dance. When the drum is struck once with the right hand, the left hand strikes twice realizing one unit of rhythm. If the left hand strikes the drum twice, the right replies by striking thrice, realizing another unit of rhythm. These motions (gestures) come in multiple or combined numbers. Consequently, our native African rhythm (music) defies incorporation into the pattern of the harmony of numbers that guides European meter. Students of African and Afro-American music insist that African percussion rhythm is polymetric (several sorts of basic meter being heard simultaneously) and polyrhythmic (a single basic meter being accented and syncopated in different ways).[29] The African executes bodily in the dance the complex nature of African rhythm as expressed in music. And all these gestures are a realization of human creative freedom that integrates the universe into human destiny.

The harmony Africans seek to live through rhythm displays their preference for the reconciliation instead of the separation of opposites. Basically, nothing stands alone. As the Igbo saying goes, *ife kwulu ife akwudebe ya* (a thing stands and another stands beside it — to confront or complement it). Thus we have the familiar combinations of male-female, left-right, uphill-downhill, north-south, earth-heaven, and so on. The image of the spoiler-godling like Eshu of the Yoruba pantheon projects this struggle for harmony realized through discovering the pulse of the cosmos. Eshu finds a house too small to sleep in, but yet he stretches himself comfortably in a tiny hut. This represents the ambivalence of a universe perceived only through the rhythm of interaction. As Anyanwu remarked:

"Eshu is not just a religious experience but reality as experienced; the personification of the mysterious twinness or opposition, the agitation, conflict, strains, frustrations and tensions provoked by the duality of the self and the other, self and itself. Eshu is a symbol of this ambiguity and conflict in life as lived."[30]

This rhythmic reconciliation of opposites in interaction explains why the Bambara, Dogon, and Malinke of Mali consider the twin model as perfect realization of "personhood" or ontological perfection. The problem of the positive and negative, the certain and uncertain, is not resolved by exclusion, but by harmony.

In Africa the body is the crucial focus of this realization of harmony in the universe through gestures. It is thus *primal symbol*. Through the ritual process of initiation, African social groups ensure the opening up of humans, bodily, to be awake to the pulse or depth of life in the universe. When pressure is brought to bear on the person bodily by way of actions like flogging, facial scarification, incision, exposure to the hazards of nature in forests or bushes, the intention is not simply to instil fear into the "initiand" so as to make him or her assume the movement of the social body. Rather, it is the awakening and schooling of the person as a whole to grasp the cosmic rhythm.[31] That is why among the Igbo the eyes of the diviner are opened *(iwa anya)* to see hidden acts or intentions of spirits and humans; the hands of the priest are opened *(iwa aka aja)* to offer effective sacrifices; the tongue of the *ozo* (elder) is cleansed *(isa ile)* to speak only the truth and thus to do justice. The ritual gestures performed in initiation involve suffering, but the intention is to direct the initiand to be aware of, and thus to internalize, the rhythm of interaction in a complex human universe. The self is opened up for creativity realized in interaction. The focus of this activity is the body, the primal symbol — the primary focus or instrument of human communication or of creating meaning.

BODILY GESTURES AND INCULTURATION OF CHRISTIANITY

The divergent attitudes toward the body as experienced in the African and Western traditions may expose the possible misunderstandings and conflicts in the cross-cultural contacts between the two traditions (formal and informal acculturation). We noted the dualistic tendency of the Western perception of the self; the great influence of the philosophy of Descartes solidified this dualism in modern Western culture. We also indicated the holistic and dialectical experience of the self among black Africans. The pessimism of the West was communicated through the great Greek and Roman classical traditions; the body and movement became more suspect through the process of inculturating Christianity in the West. We argue that such a pattern of interpreting experience, based on legitimate but particular sets of assumptions, may be generalized only by doing violence to other legitimate patterns. Though we recognize that Africans may borrow gestural patterns of the West without doing harm to their fundamental vision of humans in the universe (and the same also applies to the West), we insist that to *impose* a gesture in order to realize a uniform practice of Christianity is harmful.

Gestures are symbolic codes. In worship, rituals and symbols are aspects of gestural behavior. The ritual action as a presentation of the community before God and spirits goes back to the ethnic group for its meaning — like all gestures. Insofar as ritual gestures involve body movement, they are particular; they thus display a particular ethnic pattern of interaction within the universe. The difference we noted between African and Western attitudes toward the body and movement express this particularity. It shows that bodily motions are variously interpreted from one culture area to another. Birdwhistell pointed out that in the field of kinesics, after fifteen years of research, he and his associates have not found any body motion or gesture that has the same social meaning in all societies.[32] A Roman may express compunction by striking the breast, while among most West Africans it may simply be an expression of arrogance. It is thus clear that we may live in the same universe but may not express its impact on us in the same way. Even at the deepest level of the experience of the mystery that life is to all of us (religion), the ritual expression of this mystery (whether verbal or nonverbal) remains particular. Whether the experience is by way of the Jewish-Christian revelation, or through African, Hindu, or other religions, the ritual expression of interaction with God or the Absolute is particular. To deny this particularity is to deny that body motions (gestural behavior) are the principal characteristic of ritual.

Because worship is concerned with body motions or gestures, African Christians see worship as a channel to display their deep experience of the mystery revealed in the Christian story. And since African sociocultural groups have successfully integrated body and spirit into interactional gestures, a healthy expression of the incarnate human in African Christian liturgy should constitute the intent of the inculturation of worship in African Christian communities. Here inculturation is understood as the experience and expression by African Christians of the mutual impact of gospel and culture in their respective sociocultural area.

Indications from the early attempts to bring Christianity in tune with African experience show that the approach of the present study has merits. Those early attempts, though restricted in scope, tuned into the flow of African sound as expressed in the drum, rhythmic hand clapping, swaying, and dancing. The motions accompanied liturgical hymns put to African melody. Those hesitant beginnings asserted the crucial difference in the functioning of body and its gestures in Africa as opposed to the received Western pattern. They tried to say that, instead of being evil and an instrument of sin, the body is rather primal symbol, and thus the center for communication and creating meaning individually and corporately. The task of liturgical inculturation in Africa is to integrate successfully the various dimensions of the gesture into Christian worship. The voice is raised in song and prayer; the hand and the whole body are poised in orientations of prayer, dance, and the execution of liturgical arts and architecture; and the Christian person at prayer, inserted within the wider society, is summoned to display responsible behavior (the ethical dimension of worship). Inculturation becomes one way in which African Christians participate in re-creating the continent, a task consonant with the Christian vocation to re-create the world.

In this section we shall review inculturation by examining some of the gestures adopted within the Western liturgy. The cultural roots of these attitudes will be indicated. Then we shall briefly point out the problems and prospects of liturgical inculturation in Africa.

Brief Survey of Liturgical Inculturation in the Western Church

The impact of Greco-Roman antiquity on the practice of Christianity cannot be overemphasized. Early non-Palestinian Christianity and Church, which flourished during the patristic period, imbibed this world to the full. Even though not all the Fathers will share the optimism of the historian Eusebius of Caesarea, who saw the emergence of the Roman empire (under Augustus) and the birth of Christ as ordained by God to happen in the same period and to work in harmony, there is hardly any aspect of the Greco-Roman pattern of life that did not influence Christianity. The Christians decided either to assume these patterns totally or to adapt or transform them.[33] It is this mutual impact between Gospel and the Greco-Roman life patterns (or culture) that may lead one to assert that the inculturation of Christianity and its liturgy was such a success in the West that it became a founding element of the Western culture.[34]

Biblical and liturgical scholarship admit that Christian worship from the earliest times was dependent on the Jewish antecedents. But the subsequent Western development of gestures in worship, directed by the Christian elite, tended rather toward restriction and sublimation. There was naturally greater dependence on Greco-Roman patterns than on Jewish patterns. Boman paints an imaginative picture of the postures of the Greek and the Jew to underscore the difference in their gestural patterns:

"The matter is outlined in bold relief by two characteristic figures: the thinking Socrates and the praying Jew. When Socrates was seized by a problem, he remained immobile for an interminable period of time in deep thought; when Holy Scripture is read aloud in the synagogue, the orthodox Jew moves his whole body ceaselessly in deep devotion and adoration. . . . Rest, harmony, composure, and self-control — this is the Greek way; movement, life, deep emotion, and power — this is the Hebrew way."[35]

Hebrew patterns had little chance in the interface with the Greek culture that had spread over the Hellenized world. Philo had to present the Old Testament in Greek terms showing the overriding power of Greek culture in the Greco-Roman world. In the West the emergence of upper-class Romans as leaders of the Church, following the decline of the fortunes of the Roman empire, assured the rule of the high culture in the practice of Christianity. Jerome and Augustine struggled with the relationship between the Christian imperative and the culture in which they were reared; the result was inculturation.[36] The decline of the Roman empire created a pessimism that helped upper-class Romans flee the world *(fuga mundi)* into an alternative city (*City of God*, Augustine), where the leaders paralleled those of the doomed city. (Ambrose dressed always as a senator — in alb and chasuble.) Christian moral and sexual life favored the Stoic ideal: Christian asceticism. The four cardinal virtues on which morality is built were adopted by Ambrose from Cicero; three Christian (theological) virtues completed the way of Christian morality.

In Western liturgical practice inculturation was far-reaching. It suffices to compare the sole Roman Eucharistic Prayer (the Roman Canon or Eucharistic Prayer I of the reformed Roman liturgy) with those of other liturgical rites to see the difference. This great prayer is heavily dependent on "pagan" Roman prayer patterns. One may also compare the minimalist and precise approach to bodily gestures characteristic of the "genius of the Roman rite" with even the suppressed Gallic liturgies of the West. The precise Roman pattern proved unacceptable in the Frankish territories and were modified in the reform of Charlemagne. Consequently, the Gregorian sacramentary Pope Hadrian sent to Charlemagne was provided with a supplement by Alcuin.[37] We shall come back to the divergences in liturgical practice in a later chapter. Here we shall address only the issue of body orientation in the Western liturgy.

Body Orientations and Attitudes in Western Christian Prayer

Christian worship in the West, as we noted above, was deeply tuned into the Greco-Roman world. Though the apologists were vociferous in their rejection of "pagan" (Greco-Roman) religion,[38] yet the practice belied these stout denials. Christians were part of the society in which they lived. As a sect, distinct both from the parent Judaism and the Greco-Roman religious world, they had boundaries that marked them out.[39] But they drew freely from the gestures used in these religions without feeling they were betraying their Christian faith. The choice of the hours of prayer and the preference for gestures like orientation toward the east, washing of hands before prayer, taking of baths, erectness and extension of hands in prayer, patterns of kneeling, kissing, etc., were part of the Greco-Roman world before being reinterpreted to embody the Christian experience. We shall discuss briefly some of the most influential of these gestures.

Orientation Toward East. We may start our comments about the patterns of Christian liturgical gestures by noting how the rhythm of Christian prayer and devotion followed the privileged prayer hours linked to the motions of the heavenly bodies. While Jewish prayer revolved around the third, sixth, and ninth hours (i.e., 9 A.M., noon, and 3 P.M., respectively), the Greeks and Romans preferred prayer at sunrise and sunset. Didache (8:2-3), Tertullian (*De Oratione* 25 and 42), Cyprian (*On the Lord's Prayer* 34–36), and Hippolytus (*Apostolic Traditions* 35) bear united testimony to the early Christian appropriation of these periods of prayer. The prayer at sunrise and sunset that Tertullian claimed was obligatory (*De Oratione* 42) later formed the nucleus of Cathedral and Monastic office (East and West). The third, sixth, and ninth hours, which were probably universal points of reference in the ancient world, were later integrated into the basic morning and evening prayers.[40] In a sociocultural area where the sun-cult was popular or where this heavenly body was drawn into the cosmic praise of the creator, the Christian group could hardly escape being drawn into regulating prayer through the rhythm of this heavenly body. The astrological belief that the sun, having completed its daily motions, pauses at midnight to begin a new day influenced Christian prayer at midnight (testified by Clement of Alexandria, Origen, Tertullian, and especially Hippolytus). At midnight the Christian joins a worshiping universe to praise the creator. According to Hippolytus:

"The presbyters have handed down a tradition that at this hour every creature is still for a certain moment to praise the Lord. Stars and trees and waters stand hushed for an instant, and all the host of angels minister to him at that hour together with the souls of the righteous to praise God. That is why it is right for all believers to be careful to pray at this hour; and the Lord bears witness to this when he says, Behold a cry was made at midnight of those who said: behold the Bridegroom has come, rise to meet him; and he adds saying, Therefore watch; for you do not know in what hour he comes."[41]

Thus the motion of the Christian to pray is integrated within the movement of the universe.

The importance of solar symbolism in the Greco-Roman world made its full impact on the Christian group. The pervasive practice of orientation toward east ensured that worshipers faced the rising sun. The risen Christ is now symbolized by this sun. At baptism, during the liminal gesture of rejecting Satan and embracing the Christ, the neophyte in the waters turns toward the west to abjure Satan and then toward the east to confess Christ.

It is from the rising sun that the Lord will return. M. J. Moreton has drawn attention to the practice in the Egyptian Eucharistic celebration where the deacon invites the assembly, before the Sanctus, to stand and turn toward the east *(eis anatolâs blépsate)*.[42] This call sums up both the structural (architectural) orientation of churches (East and West) and, consequently, the orientation of the body during prayer. The Christian at prayer turns toward the risen Lord, represented in the rising sun.

From the earliest Christian place of assembly discovered at Dura-Europos to the basilical structures set up from the Constatinian era, the eastward orientation was adopted as Christian. Thus the Christians followed the common Greco-Roman practice of making the temples face the west so that worshipers would face east.[43] Only in Rome (Lateran Basilica, St. Peter's Shrine and Basilica, etc.) was there a different orientation. The result was that while the Pope or the celebrant faced east the congregation faced west. A practice developed among some worshipers, according to a vexed Leo the Great, whereby before entering St. Peter's Basilica "they turn round and bow themselves towards the rising sun and with bent neck do homage to its brilliant orb."[44] If Leo (in the fourth century) was unaware of solar symbolism in the Roman Church, Clement of Alexandria (d. 215 C.E.) took it for granted that "prayers are made towards the sunrise in the East, in accord with the system of the sun."[45]

The fascination with light among Romans and the Christian conviction that Christ is the light that drives away the darkness probably led Christians to adopt and transform the ancient celebration of light in evening prayer *(lucernarium)*. Tertullian claimed that the practice was borrowed from the Jews by the "pagans." However, Taft may be right in calling it "a baptized pagan rite."[46] The text of this thanksgiving for light (Phōs Hilaron) was provided by Basil of Caesarea (d. 379 C.E.). It still resounds in the Vespers of some Eastern and Western liturgies.

"O joyous light of the holy glory of the immortal Father,
heavenly, holy, blessed Jesus Christ!
As we come to the setting of the sun and behold the evening light,
We praise you Father, Son and Holy Spirit, God!
It is fitting at all times that you be praised with auspicious voices,
O Son of God, giver of life.
That is why the whole world glorifies you!"[47]

We conclude that the Christians followed the dominant Greco-Roman astrological notions to regulate their prayer and to orient themselves and their places of worship in presenting themselves before God-Christ.

The Orante *or Standing Position.* This is the oldest and most persistent Christian gesture at prayer. It is an attitude inherited from the

Greeks and Romans who normally prayed standing with arms lifted up and the palms facing heaven. It is a gesture representing piety; according to Clement of Alexandria, it symbolizes the motion of the soul toward the spiritual realm. The *orante* in Christian iconography sums up the Church at prayer.[48] This has remained the basic gesture of prayer in the East. Tertullian testifies to its predominance in Sunday worship and the paschal season. The posture, according to him, reflects the resurrection of Christ from the tomb on Easter day.[49]

Cassian, who in the fifth century went to instruct himself on Eastern monastic life (Egyptian, Palestinian, and Cappadocian practices), narrated how the standing position was combined with other gestures. Egyptian monks prayed in common twice a day (morning and evening). The *orante* position was the chief posture. The monks were seated for the reading of the Psalm by one of them, then they stood with arms extended for silent prayer, prostrated for a brief period to pray, and finally stood once again for silent prayer. Cassian reproached the Western monks who prolonged the prostration in order to rest and not to pray.[50]

The *orante* posture was naturally adapted by Christians who did not limit it to the typical posture of Greco-Roman piety. Thus the arms were also extended in the form of a *cross* to portray both the imitation and confession of the Christ. For Tertullian the cruciform pattern is reflected in the prayer of Moses (Exod 17:11), in the sculpture of the human structure, and in the motion of flying birds.[51] In the medieval West where kneeling with folded hands was establishing itself as the Christian gesture, the standing position was in retreat. In a thirteenth-century work attributed to Pierre le Chantre *(De Oratione et partibus eius)* about fifty-eight patterns of orientation in prayer are enumerated. The first three, which are the most important, are all in the standing position: hands folded and lifted up, hands spread in the form of a cross, and hands open before the eyes in supplication. The nine positions of the prayer of St. Dominic still preserved the *orante* posture (with hands spread in the form of a cross, and folded and lifted up). But when kneeling asserted its dominance, standing became identified with lukewarmness.[52] However the *orante* position, which projects erectness and the various motions of the hand, has been preserved in the West as the privileged gesture of the presiding priest reciting the Eucharistic Prayer.

Genuflexion, Kneeling, and Prostration. These gestures portray humility. They were more common among ancient Romans than among Greeks. In the New Testament they are considered an attitude of adoration (*proskynesis* — Matt 4:10; Luke 4:8; John 4:21, 23; Rev 3:9; 4:10; 5:14; 7:11; etc). In the patristic period they were adopted mainly for private prayer. Tertullian taught that kneeling (the posture of angels) is suitable for morning prayer. He recommended it also for liturgical prayer in Lent and Ember days.[53]

It is in the Middle Ages that the posture of kneeling, combined with the gesture of folded hands resting at the breast, became decisively the attitude of the Christian at prayer. The Dominican master general Humbert de Romans, in his commentary on the Rule, devoted a chapter to *inclinatio* or mode of prayer. This involved six attitudes: bowing (simple or solemn), genuflexion (kneeling erect or kneeling bowed), prostration (either a more profound bowing while genuflecting or prostrating totally with the whole body). But the combination of this penitential gesture with the folding of the hands (an adaptation of a feudalistic cultural gesture) intensified humility and personal prayer. Schmitt sees this combination as indicative of a particular development in spirituality and religious sensibility characteristic of the Middle Ages. Compared to the ancient "opening out" of the *orante,* this new practice of kneeling with folded hands indicates a "closing in" of the person bodily. This gesture thus reveals a tendency as from the twelfth and thirteenth centuries to seek individual interiorized devotion, at times intellectual, at times emotional. The silent reading of the Liturgy of the Hours crowned this movement by the end of the Middle Ages.[54]

The Sign of the Cross and the Gesture of Blessing. The cross is the unique symbol of Christians: a symbol of the triumph of Christ and of election of Christians (Rev 7:3; 9:4; 14:1; 22:4). The gesture of making the sign of the cross, tracing it on the forehead and other members, is in itself Christian prayer. It demarcates the recipient as a possession of the Christ and ensures protection against satanic powers. This gesture is even more potent when traced with the Eucharistic bread.[55]

In the sign of the cross the motion of the hand becomes most prominent *(gestus in manibus est).* In the Middle Ages, where there was a very strong demarcation between the clergy and the laity, the gesture of the cross became the privileged gesture of blessing (by the priest). In his authoritative study of gestures, Schmitt devoted a chapter to the hand of God *(La Main de Dieu)*. He shows how God the Father is simply represented in painting and sculpture by a hand emerging from the clouds in the familiar form of blessing.[56] Gy has argued that the practice of communion in the mouth may have been occasioned by the emphasis laid on the consecrated hand of the priest at ordination from Carolingian times, and not to the introduction of unleavened bread. The priest's hand blesses, makes holy, and handles holy things; it must not be compared with the hands of lay people. Women were first asked to receive communion in hand covered with cloth, and finally every lay person was obliged to receive in the mouth.[57]

The prominence of the priest's power to bless brings into focus a Christian cultural phenomenon revealed in medieval worship: multiplication of gestures and multiple repetition of a popular gesture (like the sign of the cross). The liturgical reform introduced by the Carolingians tried to propagate an elite and uniform pattern of gestures in the Christian society despite the incorporation of peoples of different backgrounds into the Roman empire. This was in line with their ideology of unity, which saw the unity in the God-head as replicated in unity in the Church and the empire. The official liturgy predominated for the elite; but the need of the majority — rural dwellers and the working poor — ensured the continuation of the paganism and syncretism practiced by this "popular" culture-group. Adjustments became necessary in order to ensure unity. Consequently, the popular culture asserted its influence on the elite. The result was the incorporation into the official liturgy of various blessings, conjurations, and exorcisms to protect humans and beasts, houses and fields, marriages and births, etc. In all these the power of the priest to bless was prominent. Thus the age-old magical attitudes were reintroduced into the dominant culture but now rendered harmless or sanctified.[58]

Some priests felt a pastoral obligation to keep alive the interest of their audience (the faithful). In this effort they tried to out-perform the jugglers and minstrels. Their activities varied from the nonliturgical theatricals performed within the church (liturgical dramas and the dance of death) to the multiplication of gestures or the repetition of the same gesture within the Eucharistic celebration. Those who were not involved in pastoral work, like Aquinas and the monks in monasteries, criticized liturgical and non-liturgical performances which appeared excessive: e.g., multiplication of signs of the cross, kissing of the altar, bowing, and other ridiculous gesticulations during the Eucharistic celebration. But from the eleventh and twelfth centuries these gestures were popularly integrated into Christian practice. They were interpreted, i.e., related to the passion of Christ. The presiding priest became a real tragedian. For the satisfaction of the elite, these gestures were also rationalized. For example, Cardinal Lothaire could give a theologico-mathematical justification for the twenty-five signs of the cross made by the priest during the recitation of the Canon of the Mass. The elite like Albert the Great, Thomas Aquinas, and the monks may fulminate against these gestures and insist on the power of the words for consecration, as their master (Peter Lombard) taught. But the gestures made by the priest (especially the blessing and elevation of the host) impressed on the audience the power of Christ and of the priest who handled these holy objects.[59] The abundance of the gestures and their integration within the official liturgy appear to be the way medieval wisdom struck a compromise with the various subcultures within Christendom. Thus one may agree with Gy that Christian and liturgical inculturation in the West not only drew from the existing culture but even created the Western culture.[60]

The Western Reformation, Acculturation, and Evangelization

The attitude of compromise that allowed medieval Christendom to cater for varied cultural patterns was radically modified by the disasters that befell Europe between the fourteenth and fifteenth centuries: pestilence, famine, wars, the Turkish advance, and above all, the Reformation, which led to the disorganization of the Church. The natural evils and wars, on the one hand, led to an increase in magical attitudes. On the other hand, the reformers (Protestant and Catholic) were intolerant of magic. They fought against paganism, superstition, and idolatry. A gigantic process of acculturation of the masses to the patterns of behavior of the minority elite commenced. To realize this objective Protestants and Catholics established numerous seminaries and schools after the Council of Trent. Catechisms proliferated to help banish religious ignorance, which was the root cause of damnation. The Mendicant Orders perfected the preaching of missions, and through these a sustained pressure was directed at the conscience of the masses. The emphasis on sin produced the expected feeling of guilt and drove the fear of hell into the hearts of the masses. At this time the confessional also made its appearance as the ever present companion of the preacher. State power was used by both Catholics and Protestants to impose the uniform Christian behavior.[61]

This late medieval "Christianization" of Europe was particularly interesting for the rest of the world, because it tallied with the period of growing European contact with Africa, Asia, and America. The attack of preachers against superstition, magic, and idolatry in Europe was exported to the rest of the world. This may explain the negative attitude of Catholic and Protestant missionaries, formed in the post-Reformation West, toward behavior patterns different from European gestures. The line between "us" and "them" may be synonymous with the line between true worship and idolatry. Consequently, the outcome of the controversy over the Chinese rites and the experiments of Roberto de Nobili in India were predictable. It is thus not surprising that the Asian substitutes to European rites were condemned:

"We condemn and detest their practice as superstitious . . . we revoke, annul, abrogate and wish to be deprived of all force and effect, all and each of those permissions, and say and announce that they must be considered for ever to be annulled, null, invalid and without any force or power" (Benedict XIV, *Ex Quo Singularis*, 1742).[62]

The Chinese and the Indians reacted adequately to this imposition of foreign behavior patterns on them: they ignored Christianity.

The Christianization of Europe, especially with its emphasis on guilt, produced great results in the civilization of Europe. However, great multitudes of the poor, the miserable, beggars, etc., who constituted the majority in the society were untouched by this movement. These poor, who were increasing in numbers in the cities, were treated as despicable and unbelievers. To these should be added the rural dwellers who were less touched by the wave of Christianization than city dwellers. These were moving from the over-populated countryside to the cities during the industrial revolution and thus formed the bulk of the proletariat. Since they were marginally touched by the missions in countries like France their condition explains the situation of the so-called de-Christianization of Europe.[63]

As Delumeau asserts, the Church did not lose the working class, rather it never really touched their level.[64]

The Enlightenment put the advance of knowledge very firmly in the hands of lay people. The clergy became more and more marginalized. The influence of the Church waned in the cities. There was a retreat to the countryside normally referred to as pagan. De-Christianization, in the sense of absence of coercive following of Christian behavior resulting in non-Christian populations, became a reality in the West. Another gigantic process of acculturation was thus needed. While the Modernist crisis worsened the self-insulation of the Church, the two world wars sharpened the need for acculturation. The Liturgical Movement, which gathered momentum after World War II, mapped out the channels of this acculturation. Its orientation was to go back to the sources of Christianity, to bring the liturgy back to the people of God, and to update liturgical practice.[65] The Second Vatican Ecumenical Council (1962–1965) put an official stamp on this process. But at Vatican II acculturation was no longer solely a European problem; it had become the concern of the world Church.

The Experience of Liturgical Inculturation in Africa

Pre-Colonial and Colonial Times

The first encounter between Europe and black Africa was traumatic for the Africans. After a brief period of trade in merchandise, the hunting for and the enslavement of the cream of the African youth started. The terror created by this slave-hunting, in which Afro-Arab slave kingdoms and some African chiefs later participated, is well narrated by the slave-raiders. From the first experience of the raiding (fifteenth century), the question uppermost in the mind of black Africans on meeting a European was that of personal security.[66] Christendom persuaded itself that it was saving African souls by dehumanizing African bodies through slavery. Thus it would be strange to talk about adopting adequate African gestures in the liturgy at this stage. Naturally, the mission centers set up by the priests who accompanied the Portuguese traders in the West Coast and Central Africa were simple extensions of their familiar parent sacred space.[67] The priests were not carrying a prophetic message to change their marauding countrymen and the Africans. Elmina (Ghana), Whydah (Benin Republic), Benin City, and Warri (Nigeria) were mainly foreign trade posts. Christianity disappeared from these places when the foreigners left. The evangelization of the Kongo kingdom by the Portuguese Capuchins who tried to tie together the parallels between sixteenth-century Kongo and European cosmologies aroused more hope. However, the growing interest in slavery and the intolerant attitude of Italian Capuchins toward the Kongo "syncretistic" Christianity in the seventeenth century assured its disappearance.[68]

The second encounter during the colonial period was no less traumatic. The continent, which for four centuries was drained of its youthful manpower and retarded in all manner through slavery, found it impossible to cope with a nineteenth-century aggressive Europe that had perfected its war machine through its internal wars and external plunder.[69] The missionaries who followed or preceded the colonizers shared the same climate of opinion with the colonizer — colonize, civilize, Christianize (the 3 Cs). Since the virtues of Europe were absent from Africa, the colonial official, the missionary, the anthropologist, and the explorer cooperated in implanting these virtues through the 3 Cs. And since it was rare to find any institution (civil or ecclesiastical) that asserted its independence of this ideology of European dominance,[70] attempts at adaptation lacked the human basis. Thus the well-intentioned pontifical declarations like *Maximum illud* (Benedict XV, 1919), *Rerum ecclesiae* (Pius XI, 1926), *Evangelii praecones* (Pius XII, 1951), *Fidei donum* (Pius XII, 1957), and *Princeps pastorum* (John XXIII, 1959), and the strong counsels of founders or leaders of missionary congregations like Francis Libermann or Marion de Bressilac, lacked "anthropological" teeth. They certainly helped the missionary, on the microdimensional level, to perform some good works; on the macrodimensional level, they formed part and parcel of European colonial policy. The dignity (and thus humanity) of the African person who should worship in context was not recognized. Both person and context were negated. Mveng could rightly talk about anthropological impoverishment.[71] The racialist attitude that increased at the period of the abolition of slavery to ensure the subjugation of the black people being colonized was entrenched in the behavior of evangelizers of all denominations. African behavior patterns — from sexual and family ethics to sociopolitical and religious practices — were in principle discriminated against. In the war against superstition, magic, paganism, and idolatry, genuine human values were not recognized.

One anecdote drawn from the experience of Sylvia Leith-Ross, who did field work in Nneato (Imo State of Nigeria) in the early thirties, may help to illustrate the impact of the colonial attitude in the liturgy. She participated in a Methodist worship where the Scripture readings, taken from Malachi and Hebrews, were rendered in Union Igbo. Her overall assessment of the worship was negative. It was ugly, alien, and dull. "Religion, as expressed in the service, seemed neither to have grace nor colour, neither mystery, nor joy, nor life." However, the ceremony was to end with collection, roll call, and church accounts. It was at the time of collection that it appeared "as if the wind of the Spirit had at last blown through the building." There was brisk activity when the pennies and cowries were being collected and counted. Gifts in kind were auctioned. "The excitement was intense, the bidding fast and furious." She then concluded:

"All this [i.e., the collection, etc.] they appreciated, it was part of the fabric of their lives, it was a reality they knew and understood. I do not suggest for a moment there was anything unseemly in the scene. It was only curious as representing what appears to be the culminating point of interest in an act of worship. Yet, if the Ibo's highest expression of himself is in finance, then it is no doubt that he should sanctify it in this way."[72]

The Methodists were ahead of the Roman Catholics by adopting Union Igbo in the liturgy: Roman Catholic worship (readings, etc.) was in Latin. But Union Igbo was not understood by the congregation; the songs set to Western tunes in a tonal language failed to establish adequate communication. The Church collection was the only gesture that touched their life-experience. Similar experiences were the rule all over Africa in colonial times. The rare exceptions, like the admission of Congolese religious art from the Kivu region into the Church by Father G. de Pelichy (1920) or the incorporation of *ozo* (title-taking) into the west Niger Igbo Church by Father Zappa (1915, a practice that Shanahan outlawed that same year east of the Niger),[73] only confirm the rule. As a result, all over black Africa, independent Churches (Zionist and Ethiopian or separatist) split from the mainline parent Churches in an attempt to redeem the dignity of the African person and to provide patterns of worship responding to the context insofar as they were able to interpret the received Christian faith. Thus inculturation, as it was practiced in these churches, not only became an interaction between a sociocultural area and a received gospel message, but also a political and liberation affair.[74]

Political Independence and Vatican Council II

Political independence failed to inaugurate the era of consolation promised by the politicians and freedom fighters. The neocolonial arrangement assured that the exploitation of the masses, now directly ruled by their own people, would continue. Political power became linked with economic power; leadership turned into a "self-recruiting oligarchy" that normally did not tolerate opposition. One-party states sprang up all over Africa in the name of African culture.[75]

The withdrawal of the colonial powers and the accession to independence deeply influenced the mainline Churches who did not want their control of the "minds" of the people (especially through the school) to be completely lost. The Churches followed policies similar to the politics of the colonial powers before independence. Timid moves toward adaptation (especially the introduction of vernacular hymns) were increasing. Then on 25 January 1959, Pope John XXIII announced the Second Vatican Ecumenical Council; on 6 June 1960, the president of the preparatory commission on the liturgy was appointed (Cardinal Cicognani, with Father Bugnini as secretary). Membership of the commission was based on nationality (countries in which the liturgical movement was active and prospering), competence, liturgical spiritualities, and pastoral experience. The only African on the commission was Joseph Malula (then auxiliary bishop of Leopoldville, Kinshasa). His experience in the vernacular liturgy and the efforts made on indigenization in Zaire merited him the place.[76]

Vatican II: A Change of Attitude Toward Non-Western Cultures. Vatican II was an assembly of the world Church. With the presence of about 160 African and Asian bishops at the council, the self-image and the behavior patterns characteristic of the Roman Church were deeply affected. From monocultural rigidity, which predominated in the Church since Constantine and Theodosius (313 and 380 C.E.), the Church addressed itself to its pluricultural spread. As the Constitution on the Liturgy stated: "in the liturgy, the church has no wish to impose a rigid uniformity in matters which do not involve the faith or the good of the whole community. Rather she respects and fosters the spiritual adornments and gifts of the various races" (*Sacrosanctum concilium,* no. 37).

Not only was cultural independence taken as a part of the Christian response (see *Ad gentes* 22, *Gaudium et spes* 4–10, 53–62), it was declared that authentic and full humanity comes to humans only through culture (*Gaudium et spes* 53). What this meant was that the discussions among Africans, and between Africans and Europeans, on Africanization, indigenization, incarnation, naturalization, etc., of the Christian faith in the African context have been adorned with the garments of respectability. Thus it was recognized that Africans could exercise power at a certain level in the way they express the reception of the gospel message, for power was at stake in the whole discourse on Africanization, as is natural in a colonial situation. This move has become a responsible preoccupation, not only of the local Church but of the universal Church.

From the impetus given by the Council, experiments in vernacular liturgy and in typically African gestures were promoted. Wider powers or scope for experimentation were presumed by some African local Churches, especially after the publication of the Missal of Paul VI (1969). The Gaba Pastoral Institute (established by the Association of Member Episcopal Conferences of Eastern Africa — AMECEA) produced new Eucharistic Prayers. In the same conference Small Christian Communities were adopted as a pattern of developing a true local Church. In Zaire, a new Mass was composed and was being used *ad experimentum;* rituals for the consecration of virgins and new approaches toward leadership in parishes (*bakambi,* lay leadership or ministry) were being developed. A Cameroonian Mass with strong emphasis on African patterns of assembly and gestures was practiced at Ndzon-Melen. And in French-speaking West Africa, experiments were carried out on Christian initiation.[77]

Score Sheet on Inculturation in African Churches. Three decades after the convocation of Vatican II, the score sheet on inculturation or the localization of the Church in Africa remains unimpressive. Apart from the official Roman approval of the "Roman Missal for the Dioceses of Zaire," official interest in the practical application of inculturation has been very limited. Indeed many bishops have placed obstacles to harmless practices, many have refused permission for experimentation and many more have ignored the whole issue. The kind of control exercised by both local and Roman Church organs dampen the enthusiasm of those involved in experimentation. "This [i.e., the control] is often done in the name of unity and orthodoxy, under the phobia of heresy and schism, with caution of superstition and magic, nationalism and superficiality, and allegations of lack of 'sound' theology and deviation from 'healthy' tradition."[78]

Since inculturation addresses all aspects of life of a given sociocultural region — arts, religion, philosophy, economy, society, and politics — the characteristics of medieval feudalistic patterns of authority that persist in the Church must also come under its gaze. For example, the Small Christian Communities in AMECEA countries had a tremendous effect when it was started in 1976. The communities were set to work on the social implications of the gospel and on inculturation. But the clergy constituted the chief obstacle; they would only tolerate a clerically supervised community. While the service of authority is essential to the very functioning of the Christian community, excessive clerical control constitutes an obstacle to creativity.[79]

Briefly, what has been achieved as inculturation in the African local Churches can hardly compare with the experience of the Eastern and Western Churches, some of whose examples have been given above. It was the hope of some that the special Synod for Africa, which was announced by John Paul II and took place in 1994, would generate a more dynamic pattern of inculturation. In the report at the end of the interventions, Cardinal Hyacinthe Thiandoum of Darkar said:

"It can be said that inculturation emerged as an overriding concern at this Synod. It concerns every aspect of the life of the Christian in Africa; it is the marriage of professed faith and concrete life. Inculturation has nothing to do with seeking a cheap and easy Christianity, rather its final aim is sanctity in an African manner."[80]

Inculturation or Liberation. Among African theologians a lively debate has developed. There is a retreat from a romanticization of the cultural element. Some fear that the cultural element may glue attention only to what Tutu calls "anthropological concerns," which address chiefly "the split in the African soul" and may thus fail to produce "a sufficiently sharp cutting edge" in order to challenge the plethora of problems facing modern Africa. Ela insists that the African cry today is for liberation, and that an Africanization that avoids upsetting the social equilibrium of modern African states may only provide Africans with a liturgy in indigenous African music, enabling them to mount Calvary sustained by the hope of heavenly happiness but oblivious of the oppressive hands laid upon them, as the Negro Spirituals did for black Americans in the past. Some others have warned about the tribalization of Africa through the ethnic implications of inculturation.[81]

The above criticisms and hesitations are producing healthy results among theologians and Church leaders who are addressing more sharply the social context. For example, in South Africa the *Kairos Document* (1985) and the *New Kairos* (1990) call on the Church to abandon its "ambulance ministry" and to descend to the terrain of the liberation struggle. In this connection a new ecumenical pattern of prayer is developing to cope with the complex social context. Mofokeng describes the new prayer as "a religion that brings together and merges elements of traditional African religious practices like dancing and a high emotional spirituality, liberative elements of African culture, such as a strong sense of solidarity and sharing and a theology with a distinct political, economic and social agenda."[82]

The merging of the cultural (anthropological concerns) and the "liberative" in the liberation struggle in modern South Africa shows that an integral approach is necessary for the development of a contextual Christian life in contemporary Africa. In this way a re-created culture emerges. Bimwenyi has asked whether modernity has swallowed up the African peculiarity. He replied that change occurred rapidly on the morphological level (passing modes like dress, etc.), but that change was slower on the level of institutions (sociopolitical) and hardly discernible on the structural level of symbolization where the questions of life, God, and the invisible hierarchies are posed. Inculturation theology, according to Bimwenyi, should concentrate on this third level.[83] Metogo countered that Bimwenyi's purported immobilism on the third level is dependent on Holas' and Thomas' view that African mentality is unchangeable. Bimwenyi tried to correct their view; but, Metogo maintains, he failed to go far enough. Modernity has aroused a total reinterpretation of all African values and doctrines that create the African identity. The religious dimension is not immune from this change. Atheists are also found in Africa.[84]

While the elite argue over change, over the impact of the modern technological culture on African traditions, over the functioning of religion in contemporary Africa, or even over the impact of atheism, contemporary Africa is being turned into a vast religious market and the traders in religion reap a rich harvest. Because of Africa's persistent hunger for the spiritual, and because of its agonizing socioeconomic travail worsened by the postcolonial deception, religious practices of all shades and colors become ways of coping with life in the world. There is the popular movement toward faith-healing and healing centers, there is the increase in the action of the Spirit and the attraction of prayer in the Spirit that fascinate the young (charismatics and fellowships). And, finally, new religious movements, which include fundamentalist Christian groups, nativistic cults, gnostic type spiritualism from the Far East, exert a strong influence on the young, the elite, and the unattached. According to Shorter:

"Society is emerging from one well-defined, traditional form into an altogether new and unfamiliar form. . . . There is a great deal of tension and frustration. People are searching for ways to cope with a new experience. They borrow ideas from their cultural tradition and give them modern application. They turn to neighbouring cultures for extraneous images to express the unfamiliar. They are innovative and syncretist, bringing forth 'treasures old and new.'"[85]

The spiritual hunger among modern Africans is a way the modern Africans reveal their religiosity.[86] The refusal to impose a radical split between the human world and the spiritual world challenges the African theologian to propose patterns of worship that will integrate the whole world of the African. To descend to the terrain of the struggle, to descend to the level of the ordinary African person and assimilate the daily material and spiritual concerns, may be the way the theologian will acquire the experience to propose patterns of living in the world (ritual and ethical), which neither produces a split in the African psyche nor ignores the daily suffering of men and women. Indeed, the more one participates in charismatic prayer, the more one feels close to prayer patterns that have the possibility of responding to the needs of African Christians. The rhythmic interchange of songs, prayers, reflections on Scripture passages, short responses accompanied by instrumentation, tapping, swaying/dancing, and other adequate gestures recommend this pattern of prayer as having the possibility of merging the biblical faith and contextual (modern) experience of African traditions.

Theologians are justified in debating issues related to method, and of the pertinence of the subject matter of African theology. But the task of inculturation must still remain a priority as a practical engagement: providing rituals (verbal and nonverbal) and giving direction for ethical behavior consonant with the present situation in which the African person is living.

NOTES

1. For toolmaking and beginnings of African culture see J. D. Clark, ed., *Cambridge History of Africa, vol. I: From the Earliest Times to c. 500 B.C.* (Cambridge: Cambridge University Press, 1982); see also J. D. Clark, "The Pre-Historic Origin of African Cultures," *Journal of African History* V/2:1964, 161–83.

2. M. Jousse, *L'Anthropologie du Geste* (Paris: Resma, 1969) 46, 49.

3. See E. E. Uzukwu, "Igbo World and Ultimate Reality and Meaning," *Ultimate Reality and Meaning* 5/3:1982, 188–209; K. C. Anyanwu, "The Meaning of Ultimate Reality in Igbo Cultural Experience," *Ultimate Reality and Meaning* 7/2:1984, 84–101; V. Mulago, *La Religion traditionelle des Bantu et leur Vision du Monde* (Kinshasa: Faculté de Théologie Catholique, 1980); P. Tempels, *Bantu Philosophy* (Paris: Presence Africaine, 1959).

4. A. E. Scheflen and A. Scheflen, *Body Language and Social Order* (Englewood Cliffs, N.J.: Prentice-Hall, 1972) 28.

5. J.-C. Schmitt, *La Raison des Gestes dans l'Occident Médiéval* (Paris: Gallimard, 1990) 59.

6. Scheflen and Scheflen, *Body Language and Social Order,* 126.

7. Schmitt, *La Raison des Gestes,* 36–37, 64–65.

8. L. Gougaud, "La Danse dans les Églises," *Revue d'Histoire Ecclesiastique* XV:1914, 5–22, 229–45; Schmitt, *La Raison des Gestes,* 96.

9. H. Hochegger, *Le Langage des Gestes Rituels,* vol. I (Bandundu: Ceeba, 1981).

10. Schmitt, *La Raison des Gestes,* 96–98.

11. See two interesting studies of E. Goffman on patterns of interaction: *Interaction Ritual* (New York: Pantheon Books, 1967); *The Presentation of Self in Everyday Life* (New York: Doubleday, 1959).

12. See Hochegger's *Le Langage des Gestes Rituels.*

13. See, for example, M. Griaule, *Conversations with Ogotemmeli* (London: Oxford University Press, 1965); J. Jahn, *Muntu: An Outline of Neo-African Culture* (London: Faber and Faber, 1961) esp. ch. 5.

14. Jousse, *L'Anthropologie du Geste,* 5–8.

15. Roger Bacon, *Opus Tertium,* cap. LIX, "De Musica," cited by Schmitt, *La Raison des Gestes,* 284.

16. P. Brown, *The World of Late Antiquity* (London: Thames and Hudson, 1971) 96–98; see also his *The Body and Society* (New York: Columbia University Press, 1988).

17. Augustine, *Against Two Letters of Pelagius,* 4.7, in P. Schaff and H. Wace, eds., *Nicene and Post-Nicene Fathers of the Church,* 2nd series, vol. V (Grand Rapids, Mich.: Eerdmans, 1986). The opinion of Pelagius is contained in the introduction to this same volume.

18. See Schmitt, *La Raison des Gestes,* 74–76.

19. See Gougaud, "La Danse dans les Églises," 18–21, 232–4; Schmitt, *La Raison des Gestes,* 86–92.

20. Schmitt, *La Raison des Gestes,* 261–73; Delumeau, *Le Péché et la Peur. La Culpabilisation en Occident XIIIe–XVIIIe Siècle* (Paris: Arthème Fayard, 1983) 85; Gougaud, "La Danse dans les Églises," 230–1.

21. See Schmitt, *La Raison des Gestes,* esp. 133, 139, 235–9; and the whole of chs. 4–6.

22. The myth will be treated in detail in chapter three.

23. See Uzukwu, "Igbo World and Ultimate Reality and Meaning"; E. I. Metuh, *African Religion in Western Conceptual Schemes* (Ibadan: Pastoral Institute, 1985) ch. 7; V. C. Uchendu, *The Igbo of Southern Nigeria* (New York: Rinehart and Winston, 1965). For similar conceptions of the person among sub-Saharan Africans see G. Dieterlen, "L'image du Corps et les Composantes de la Personne chez les Dogon," *La Notion de Personne en Afrique noire,* Colloques internationaux de CNRS, no. 544, 11–17 Oct. 1971 (Paris: CNRS, 1981) 205–29. See also the contributions of Hampate Ba, Y. Cisse, A. Neron de Surgy, and the introduction to the colloquy by M. Cartry in the same volume.

24. See Dieterlen, "L'image du Corps." See also J. Jahn, *Muntu: An Outline of Neo-African Culture,* ch. 5.

25. K. C. Anyanwu, "A Response to A.G.A. Bello's Methodological Preliminaries," *Ultimate Reality and Meaning* 14:1991, 61–69, esp. 67. Anyanwu's principal argument is in his "Sound as Ultimate Reality and Meaning: The Mode of Knowing Reality in African Thought," *Ultimate Reality and Meaning* 10:1987, 29–38.

26. G. Niangoran-bouah, "La Drummologie et la Vision negro-africaine du sacré," *Mediations Africaines du Sacré,* Actes du 3e Colloque international du CERA, 16–22 Feb. 1986 (Kinshasa: Faculté de Théologie Catholique, 1987) 281–95.

27. See Anyanwu, "Sound as Ultimate Reality and Meaning," 34; C. Achebe, "Chi in Igbo Cosmology," in his *Morning Yet on Creation Day* (London: Heinemann, 1975) 93–103; O. B. Lawuyi, "Self-Potential as a Yoruba

Ultimate: A Further Contribution to URAM Yoruba Studies (URAM 7:173–200; 11:233–42)," *Ultimate Reality and Meaning* 14:1991, 21–29.

28. E. Mveng, *L'Art d'Afrique noire: Liturgie cosmique et Langage religieux* (Yaounde: Cle, 1974) esp. 86–103.

29. Ibid.; Jahn, *Muntu: An Outline of Neo-African Culture,* 165, esp. 164–9; Schmitt, *La Raison des Gestes,* 74–76.

30. Anyanwu, "A Response to A.G.A. Bello's," 67.

31. See E. E. Uzukwu, "African Symbols and Christian Liturgical Celebration," *Worship* 65/2:1991, 101–2.

32. R. Birdwhistell, *Kinesics and Context* (Philadelphia: University of Pennsylvania Press, 1970) 81; cited by R. Firth, *Symbols, Public and Private* (London: George Allen and Unwin Ltd. 1973) 307.

33. See *Eusebius: Church History,* 1.4.15 and 4.7.1, in P. Schaff and H. Wace, eds., *Nicene and Post-Nicene Fathers of the Church,* 2nd Series, vol. I.

34. See P.-M. Gy, *La Liturgie dans l'Histoire* (Paris: Cerf, 1990) 59.

35. T. Boman, *Hebrew Thought Compared with Greek* (London: SCM Press, 1960) 205.

36. See *The Confessions of St. Augustine;* Schmitt, *La Raison des Gestes,* ch. 2; see also W.H.C. Frend, *The Rise of Christianity* (London: Darton, Longmann and Todd, 1984) ch. 6, esp. 554–7.

37. See E. Bishop, *Liturgica Historica* (Oxford: Clarendon Press, 1918). See my analysis of the Roman Canon in my Th.D. thesis, *Blessing and Thanksgiving among the Igbo: Towards a Eucharistia Africana* (Toronto: University of St. Michael's College, 1978). See also V. Fiala, "Les Prières d'Acceptation de l'Offrande et le Genre littéraire du Canon romain," *Eucharisties d'Orient et d'Occident,* vol. I, B. Botte et al., eds. (Paris: Cerf, 1970) 117–33; R. A. Keifer, "The Unity of the Roman Canon: An Examination of Its Unique Structure," *Studia Liturgica* XI:1976, 39–58; M. Andrieu, *Les Ordines du Haut Moyen Age. I. Les Manuscrits* (Louvain: Spicilegium Sacrum Lovaniense, 1931) esp. viii, 494–525.

38. For a good summary of the views of the Apologists see R.P.C. Hanson, "The Christian Attitude to Pagan Religions up to the Time of Constantine the Great," *Aufstieg und Niedergang der Römischen Welt,* ed. H. Temporini and W. Haase, vol. II.23.2 (Berlin and New York: Walter de Gruyter, 1980) 910–73.

39. See the authoritative work of W. A. Meeks, *The First Urban Christians: The Social World of the Apostle Paul* (New Haven, Conn., and London: Yale University Press, 1983).

40. See R. Taft, *The Liturgy of the Hours in East and West* (Collegeville: The Liturgical Press, 1986) chs. 1–2; A. Hamman, "La Prière chrétienne et la Prière Païenne, Formes et Différences," *Aufstieg und Niedergang der Römischen Welt,* vol. II.23.2, esp. 1199–212.

41. Hippolytus, *Apostolic Traditions* 36; see also Tertullian, *De Oratione* 13; Clement of Alexandria, *Stromata* 3.82.6; H. Chadwick, "Prayer at Midnight,"

Epektasis: Melanges Patristiques offerts au Cardinal Jean Danièlou, ed. J. Fontaine and C. Kannengiesser (Paris: Beauchesne, 1972) 47–49; Taft, *Liturgy of the Hours,* 21–27.

42. M. J. Moreton, "Eis Anatolâs Blépsate: Orientation as a Liturgical Principle," *Studia Patristica* XVII, part two (1982) 575–90, esp. 588–9. See A. Hanggi and I. Pahl, *Prex Eucharistica* (Fribourg Suisse: Editions Universitaires, 1968) 110, 136.

43. Clement of Alexandria, *Stromata* 7.7.43.6–7; Hamman, "La Prière chrétienne," 1210.

44. Leo the Great, *Sermo* XXVII; see P. Schaff and H. Wace, eds., *Nicene and Post-Nicene Fathers of the Church,* 2nd series, vol XII, 140; T. J. Talley, *The Origins of the Liturgical Year* (New York: Pueblo, 1986; Collegeville: The Liturgical Press, 1991) 99–103.

45. Clement of Alexandria, *Stromata* 7.7.43.6–7; Taft, *Liturgy of the Hours,* 14–15; Hamman, "La Prière chrétienne," 1209–12.

46. Tertullian, *Ad Nationes* 1.13; Taft, *Liturgy of the Hours,* 37.

47. Cited by Taft, *Liturgy of the Hours,* 36.

48. Clement of Alexandria, *Stromata* 7.71.40.1; see also Hamman, "La Prière chrétienne," 1212ff.

49. Tertullian, *De Oratione* 23.

50. Cassian, *Institutes,* books II and III, P. Schaff and H. Wace, eds., *Nicene and Post-Nicene Fathers of the Church,* 2nd series, vol. II; see also Taft, *Liturgy of the Hours,* 58–62; Schmitt, *La Raison des Gestes,* 74–75.

51. Tertullian, *De Oratione* 29.

52. Schmitt, *La Raison des Gestes,* 299–300, 303–14.

53. Tertullian, *De Oratione* 23, 29; Hamman, "La Prière chrétienne," 1217–19.

54. Schmitt, *La Raison des Gestes,* 295–302.

55. See Hamman, "La Prière chrétienne," 1215–6; Tertullian, *De Corona* 3.4; Hippolytus, *Apostolic Traditions* 41, 42; Justin, *Dialogue* 40.1.

56. Schmitt, *La Raison des Gestes,* ch. 3.

57. Gy, *La Liturgie dans l'Histoire,* 205–10.

58. On the ideology of unity of the Carolingians see Y. M. Congar, *L'Ecclésiologie du Haut Moyen Age: De St. Grégoire le Grand à la Désunion entre Byzance et Rome* (Paris: Cerf, 1968) 267–8; see also his "Le Monothéisme politique et le Dieu Trinité," *Nouvelle Revue Thélogique* 103/1:1981, 3–17. For the interrelationship between the popular and elite cultures in the liturgy of the Middle Ages see J. Delumeau, *Leçon inaugurale au College de France,* 13 Feb. 1975, reprinted as annex I in his *Le Christianisme va-t-il Mourir?* (Paris: Hachette, 1977) 179–214, esp. 191–202; see also J. A. Jungmann, *Pastoral Liturgy* (London: Challoner, 1962) esp. part I, "The Overall Historical Picture."

59. Details of these gestures are contained in Schmitt, *La Raison des Gestes,* 273–84, 334–42, 353–5.

60. Gy, *La Liturgie dans l'Histoire,* 59–60.

61. Delumeau, *Leçon inaugural,* esp. 192–202; for a detailed study of the themes of the missions and preaching see his *Le Péché et la Peur,* 3rd section, "La Pastorale de la Peur."

62. Cited by P. Johnson, *A History of Christianity* (New York: Penguin, 1976) 414–5; see also H. Jedin, *History of the Church* (London: Burns and Oates, 1981) ch. 17.

63. See the interesting study of P. Sassier, *Du Bon Usage des Pauvres: Histoire d'un Thème Politique (XVIe–XXe Siècle)* (Paris: Fayard, 1990). The word "proletariat" was already known before the nineteenth century. Montesquieux and Rousseau used it in the sense indicated by the *Encyclopédie:* "A member of the proletariat is a person who belongs to the poorest class," Sassier, 203.

64. Delumeau, *Leçon inaugurale,* 204.

65. Studies on the liturgical movement abound. See, for example, O. Rousseau, *The Progress of the Liturgy* (Westminster, Md.: The Newman Press, 1951); A. Bugnini, *The Reform of the Liturgy* 1948–1974, trans. M. J. O'Connell (Collegeville: The Liturgical Press, 1990).

66. Among the numerous studies of slavery see the two volumes edited by S. Daget, *De la Traite à l'esclavage,* Actes du Colloque international sur la traite des Noirs, Nantes 1985 (Paris: Société Française d'Histoire d'Outre-Mer; Nantes: Centre de Recherche sur l'Histoire du Monde Atlantique, 1988).

67. See the interesting article of J. Helgeland on the impact of space-time dimensions on religious conversion or adherence. "Time and Space: Christian and Roman," *Aufstieg und Niedergang der Römischen Welt,* vol. II.23.2., 1285–305.

68. See L. Sanneh, *West African Christianity* (Maryknoll, N.Y.: Orbis Books, 1983) esp. chs. 1–3; J. Thornton, "The Development of an African Catholic Church in the Kingdom of the Kongo 1491–1750," *Journal of African History* 25 (2, 1984) 147–67; R. Gray, ed., *The Cambridge History of Africa, vol.* 4: *From* 1600 *to c.* 1790 (Cambridge: Cambridge University Press, 1975).

69. See the special issue of Concilium on the Americas, 1492–1992*: The Voice of the Victims* (1990/6), esp. E. Dussel's "The Real Motives of the Conquest," 30–46. See also P. Vallely, *Bad Samaritans: First World Ethics and Third World Debt* (Maryknoll, N.Y.: Orbis Books, 1990) esp. 87, 98–102; R. Fossaert, *Le Monde au 21e Siècle: Une Théorie des Systemes mondiaux* (Paris: Fayard, 1991) esp. ch. 4, "L'Europe marchande et coloniale."

70. See D. Richards, "The Ideology of European Dominance," *Présence Africaine* 111:1979, 3–18; also E. A. Ayendele, *The Missionary Impact of Modern Nigeria* (London: Longmans, 1966).

71. E. Mveng, *L'Afrique dans l'Église: Parole d'un Croyant* (Paris: Harmattan, 1985); see also M. Hebga, "Worthy and Unworthy Churches," *Concilium* 130 (1979/10) 105–112.

72. S. Leith-Ross, *African Women* (London: Faber, 1934) 122–3.

73. See Badi-Banga Ne-Nwime, "Expression de la Foi Chrétienne dans l'Art plastique zaïrois," *Cahiers des Religions Africaines* XVI nn. 31–32 (1982) 135–67; C. A. Obi et al., *A Hundred Years of the Catholic Church in Eastern Nigeria* 1885–1985 (Onitsha: Africana Fep, 1985) 147; A. O. Gbuji, *Pastoral on Title-Taking and Traditional Funeral Ceremonies* (Issele-uku [Nigeria]: 1984) 11.

74. See, for example, B.G.M. Sundkler, *Bantu Prophets in South Africa* (Oxford: Oxford University Press, 1961); R.I.J. Hackett, ed., *New Religious Movements in Nigeria* (Lewinston/Queenston: The Edwin Mellen Press, 1987); O. U. Kalu, ed., *The History of Christianity in West Africa* (London: Longman, 1980); D. Barret, *Schism and Renewal in Africa* (Nairobi: Oxford University Press, 1968).

75. See, for example, R. Anifowose, *Violence and Politics in Nigeria: The Tiv and Yoruba Experience* (New York: Nok, 1982) esp. 21–24; A. Mbembe, *Afriques Indociles* (Paris: Karthala, 1988).

76. Bugnini, *The Reform of the Liturgy,* 14–16.

77. See my *Liturgy: Truly Christian, Truly African,* spearhead no. 74 (Eldoret: Gaba Publications, 1982); and also my "African Cultures and the Christian Liturgy," *West African Journal of Ecclesiastical Studies* 2/1:1990, 59–83. The Concilium charged with the implementation of the reforms of Vatican II did not find the issues of creativity, adaptation, etc., easy to handle. See Bugnini, *The Reform of the Liturgy,* esp. chs. 18–20. See also A. J. Chupungco, *Liturgies of the Future: The Process and Methods of Inculturation* (New York: Paulist Press, 1989).

78. D. S. Amalorpavadass, "Theological Reflections on Inculturation," *Studia Liturgica* 20/1:1990, 40; see also Chupungco, *Liturgies of the Future,* ch. 1.

79. See J. C. Healey, "Four Africans Evaluate SCCs in East Africa," *African Ecclesial Review* 29/5:1987, 266–77; see also E. E. Uzukwu, "The Birth and Development of a Local Church: Difficulties and Signs of Hope," *Towards the African Synod Concilium* 1992/1, 17–23.

80. Cardinal Thiandoum, "Relatio Post Disceptationem," April 22, 1994, in *L'Osservatore Romano,* weekly edition, 21 (May 25, 1994) 9. See also my recent book, *A Listening Church: Autonomy and Communion in African Churches* (Maryknoll, N.Y.: Orbis Books, 1996).

81. D. Tutu, "Black Theology and African Theology: Soulmates or Antagonists," *A Reader in African Theology,* ed. J. Praratt (London: SPCK, 1987) 46–57; J. M. Ela, *De l'Assistance à la Libération,* Les Tâches actuelles de l'Église en milieu africain (Paris: Centre Lebret, 1981) 12–15; idem, *The African Cry* (Maryknoll, N.Y.: Orbis Books, 1986). See also L. Kaumba,

"Impasses d'une Théologie de l'Inculturation," *Philosophie Africaine face aux Libérations religieuses,* Actes de la XIe Semaine Philosophique de Kinshasa, 27 Nov.–3 Dec. 1988 (Facultes Catholiques de Kinshasa, 1990) 199–215.

82. T. A. Mofokeng, "Popular Religiosity: A Liberative Source and Terrain of Struggle," *Popular Religion, Liberation and Contextual Theology,* ed. J. van Nieuwenhove and B. K. Goldewijk (Nijmegen: J. H. Kok-Kampen, 1991) 55. See also *Challenge to the Church: The Kairos Document,* The Kairos Theologians, Braamfontein 23017, 1985; "The New Kairos," *Voices from the Third World* (EATWOT) XIII/2:1990, 142–3.

83. O. Bimwenyi-Kweshi, *Discours théologique négro-africain* (Paris: Présence Africaine, 1981) 376–84.

84. E. Messi Metogo, *Théologie africaine et Ethnophilosophie* (Paris: l'Harmattan, 1985) esp. 45–48.

85. A. Shorter, *Jesus and the Witchdoctor: An Approach to Healing and Wholeness* (London: Chapman, 1985) 61.

86. A study of this hunger is being carried out by C. I. Ejizu, A. Echeagu, and E. E. Uzukwu in their *African Christian Prayer.*

Chapter Two

Ritual-Symbolic Action as Creating and Re-Creating Community

DESCRIBING RITUAL ACTION

Action is the prevailing characteristic of the ritual. Therefore, every ritual is a gesture, though not every gesture is a ritual. The ritual is a medium of communication within a particular group. It is a programmed way of acting that characterizes an ethnic group so that participants express their being part of the group through the ritual gesture. Consequently, every ritual gesture is a symbolic action — ritual symbol. Indeed Turner, in his description of the symbol, connects it immediately with ritual action: "The symbol is the smallest unit of ritual which still retains its specific properties of ritual behaviour; it is the ultimate unit of specific structure in a ritual context."[1]

As a symbol, the ritual generates group identity. It becomes a code through which a particular group expresses its insertion into the world. It may thus reveal the very heart of a society. In addition, the aspect of repetition, which is a fundamental property of ritual gesture, translates ritual behavior into an instrument of social engineering: it routinizes a way of doing, and, because of its rigid or conservative nature, it possesses the quality of revealing the structures that found a particular social group. Rituals can thus be described as unquestionable "source documents" of any society.[2] According to Monica Wilson:

"Rituals reveal values at their deepest level. . . . Men express in ritual what moves them most, and since the form of expression is conventionalized and obligatory, it is the values of the group that are revealed. I see in the study of rituals the key to an understanding of the essential constitution of human societies."[3]

This impact of ritual on the very structure of social groups has aroused questions about its origins. Existentialists, phenomenologists, pragmatists, and so on, believe that the ritual emerged through trial and error as an answer to existential questions. It originated as an action that installed order into chaos — the chaos of estrangement and human life-questioning. That is why they regard ritual as a regulated gesture acquired by way of gesticulation or through making blind affirmations. Through this process, humans finally succeeded in inventing adequate gestures to pacify their distress in the universe. The proven ritual gestures thus constitute for humans the core codes for dealing with a still confused universe.[4] This search for the psychological origin of ritual highlights the interactional pattern of all ritual gestures (social or religious). Like every gesture, the ritual is basically the social body's reaction to the impact of the universe or environment upon it. The social group goes through a learning process to arrive at adequate rituals that confirm its particular insertion into the world. The acquired social and religious rituals become the medium of interaction and further creativity in the universe despite the rigid or repetitive pattern of ritual action.

The rhythm of ritual gestures acquired by humans is the result of human creativity. It also constitutes the base for human self-discovery and further creative actions in the universe. Philologists stress that the Indo-European root for ritual *(dhê)* stands for "to lay down in a creative way, to establish in existence." Thus ritual behavior is a laying down of patterns of action that are creative and normative for existence (ethical and aesthetic).[5]

The emphasis on creativity and providing norms that guide human existence projects the aesthetic and ethical dimensions of ritual behavior. The creation or emergence of social and religious rituals is a work of art. The repetition of these gestures projects a way of doing based on the memory of the past — the way it *was* controls the way it *is*. This highlights the conservative or preservative dimension of ritual. The creativity also indicates the way it *ought to be*. This embraces the normative, dynamic, or transformative aspects of ritual.

We consider these dimensions of ritual as fundamental for explorations into worship. Furthermore, they appear crucial to us for the inculturation of Christian life in Africa. Inculturation is not only preoccupied with patterns of worship, but also with the norms for guiding life in society. A close study of ritual action may reveal to us that religious practice immediately has its ethical implications. And because ritual is an action rooted in ethnic experience, the emphasis today among the oppressed peoples of the world that active "liberative" positions should be adopted in Christian practice (liberation ethics, liberation praxis) should encourage Africans to pay close attention to the dynamic properties of the behavior displayed in ritual.[6] Thus the prominence of ritual in many aspects of African life should not be regarded as a perversion, rather it should be seen as a possible way of social transformation. For, though conservative, the religious ritual is creative of life and imposes on practitioners obligatory patterns of interaction.

In this chapter we shall examine the general characteristics displayed in ritual action. The results of our scrutiny apply to any social or religious ritual gathering and not only to African assemblies. The impact of these ritual properties on liturgies in tune with the African context will be shown in a later section of this study (chapter five). We shall also show how the Jewish-Christian assembly *(qahal* or *ekklesia)* originates from a particular ritual environment. Our detailed illustration of the Christian assembly will draw from the assembly of the Church of the Apocalypse.

RELIGIOUS RITUAL CREATES OR RE-CREATES COMMUNITY

The broadest understanding of ritual connects it immediately with community. Since the rite is a gesture (body movement), it seeks its meaning within a social body. This fundamental reference of ritual to the community indicates how interdependent humans are: humans express by acting together their belonging to a social body. This definition of the human type in relationship, demonstrating interdependence and co-inherence, also defines human "self- and world-limitation."[7] And when one speaks about "limits-of" or "limits-to" our human condition, as Tracy rightly points out, one has entered the domain of the transcendent, the domain of religion.[8]

Religious ritual assembles the community to reaffirm its foundation. It makes the acting community experience the anchor of its existence. The community therefore participates in a transcendent reality. It expresses and realizes this experience of its foundation through ritual action. Religious ritual can thus be called the highest point of ritual action, for in it resides the community's self-discovery. Face to face with its ritual anchor, the community grasps its place in the world. "Ritual action is a means by which its participants discover who they are in the world and 'how it is' with the world."[9] To talk about discovery or recognition is to set aside the spectatorial language of science and to embrace the symbolic language of religion. Religious language is self-involving or participant, as linguistic philosophers like Austin and Evans stress. It is only by celebrating and participating in a community's religious ritual action that the community and individuals renew or experience the foundation of their life. They get in tune with what makes the community what it is. Thus one can correctly say that ritual is the bedrock of public religion. The ritual clearly says that religion is in a category of its own:

"The cultural expression of religion differs. But religion remains itself. And the proof lies in the rite. . . . Theologies differ, but rites remain the same. . . . The grammar of corporate religion, the morphology or outline of the rite, tends everywhere to reproduce itself. In this sense, the rite is the rock upon which public religion is based."[10]

When a community is placed on its foundation in the ritual action, it is placed in relationship with the ritual anchor, the referent of ritual, the Other, which is present in but also outside the normal condition of human existence. This is the sacred, God and spirits. Through signs and symbols, through gestures (verbal and nonverbal), the community is displayed before the sacred, who is invited to see, approve, complete, understand, or recognize the ritual action. In this action of pleading with the "observer" or the ritual anchor, the community is inserted into a life that is more consistent and more complete than the social and everyday life.[11] Africans who like to ritualize activities in the everyday life aim at effectively lifting this life beyond the everyday; they place the everyday on the altar of the transcendent. It is in the ritual context and ritual time that the group is most intensely in touch with its spiritual originators. Consequently, this ritual experience creates and re-creates the community, or, according to Turner, it creates or re-creates the categories through which humans perceive reality.[12]

Ritual Creativity and Certain Sociological Theories of Religion

The intense activity experienced in ritual, the results (effects) expected that far outstrip the physical actions posited, the relationship with the sacred and with a foundation story (myth) not only make the ritual behavior attractive to social scientists. For some the ritual assembly creates the sacred (Durkheim), for others ritual action projects the power of tradition (Malinowski). We emphasize the distinction between the ritual assembly and its anchor; we draw attention to the "play element" of ritual behavior, which ensures creativity in the present without denying the memory of past tradition.

Durkheim, who has greatly influenced the study of religious behavior, ended up identifying the religious with the social. He correctly pointed out that religion is about society and that religious practice (ritual) is the core of religious behavior. It is within the ritual assembly (of the Australian aborigines) that one arrives at "a state of exaltation," one is beside oneself. "So it is in the midst of these effervescent social environments and out of this effervescence itself that the religious idea seems to be born."[13] Durkheim is perceptive in his assessment of the assembly (sacred gathering) and what can happen in the assembly, as well as on the demands and the protections that both society and religion address to humans. But he is mistaken in identifying the totem and the god, in identifying society and the god. Levi-Strauss has pointed out that the totem is a factor in social differentiation, and that, rather than present emotions, the effervescent social surroundings and the effervescence, giving rise to the religious idea, presuppose it. While the ritual context may lead to exaltation, the exaltation does not create the ritual.[14] The ritual anchor (the sacred) outside society founds society (as foundation stories narrate), but it is not the society itself. However, in the ritual action the community identifies itself through words and gestures with the anchor.

A similar reply can be given to Rene Girard's religious anthropology. Girard defines the sacred as that which dominates us but which we, as humans, are incapable of dominating. This sacred, according to him, is violence. The emergence of the human type is realized in the act of killing one of its own kind (the weakest, the scapegoat). Humans are so dominated by violence that the ritual murder was necessary in order precisely to arrest the spiral of violence. That is why sacrificial rituals proliferate in societies without a judicial system in order to maintain the unity of the society and to prevent violence. In modern societies, the judicial process puts reprisals into government hands. Girard claims that ritual, which is the core of religion, is based on the misunderstanding of the primordial act of violence: the scapegoat mechanism is the object of religion; its function is to perpetuate or renew the effects of this mechanism in order to ensure that violence is outside the community, i.e., directed against the sacrificial victim. Ritual activity is to deceive (cover up) or purify violence — dissipating it on the victims who are incapable of taking vengeance and at the same time satisfying the human thirst for violence.[15] Girard's thesis appears to be based on the Freudian claim that religion is a collective neurosis and on Durkheim's identification of society with the sacred. Girard's discovery of "what was hidden since the foundation of the world"[16] remains a claim that appears acceptable only through a religious commitment. One recognizes the spiral of violence in the traditional and modern societies. One knows as well that sacrifice is the highest form of prayer among many peoples of the world.[17] However, patient observation of societies shows that, despite the interrelationship between the sacred and the social, they are not identical. The religious ritual seeks to transform (renew, create, re-create) society and thus to ensure the well-being of humans through the ritual action itself.

It is important to give full value to the creative and re-creative aspect of ritual action within a worshiping community. This has not been sufficiently stressed by Malinowski and the functionalist school despite the accent they laid on ritual and social integration. According to Malinowski, creating an atmosphere of homogeneous belief is the purpose and function of ritual behavior. In this way, especially among illiterate peoples, public ritual performance becomes an indispensable way of conserving, manifesting, and transmitting the "inalterable and inviolable" sacred tradition and codes of behavior. Malinowski is correct in emphasizing that in ritual (especially in rites of initiation) the power of tradition is expressed from generation to generation, and that the lore of the society is transmitted to ensure cohesion and continuity in tradition. We, however, must underline that in the ritual context a dynamic relationship exists between the ritual anchor and the community, between ancestral time and the present time. In the ritual action, through the interchange of words and gestures, the human-divine interaction embodies the ludic — another name for creativity. The pattern of religious ritual celebrations reveals what Hugo Rahner aptly calls man at play, or *homo ludens* according to Johan Huizinga. The play dimension of ritual (a happy combination of earnestness and humor) ensures that ritual (like play) is directed to no other end apart from itself. Ritual-symbol is thus "auto-telic." All actors in the ritual (human and divine) posit gestures full of meaning, yet bound to no mathematical necessity: the human gesture is a prayer (soliciting or seducing the divine anchor), while the divine pleasure to respond to prayer is not a necessity. The divine creation of humans (by which action God becomes the ritual anchor), though meaningful, is not a necessary act.[18] Creativity (as play) is thus part of the internal logic of ritual.

In African communities, the everyday, commonplace needs, both material and spiritual, constitute the purpose of the presentation of the community before God. The power of tradition is active in the present through the ancestral gestures (power of memory of the past). But the present needs are the preoccupation; they are ritually resolved by recalling a past pattern adapted to these needs in order to shape the future. In this way the actions drawn from the past are not "inalterable" in a dogmatic or fixed (static) way. The past is not reproduced numerically, rather it is assumed in a dynamic way to generate such an activity that re-creates the present to shape a better future. Thus change or development is also mediated through ritual behavior (the pace of the change varying from one group to another).[19]

Repetitive Character of Ritual, Change, and Renewal

We have already noted that repetition is one of the principal characteristics of ritual action. The obligatory style of ritual has led some social scientists to accord it minimal or no orientation at all to change. Bloch, for example, asserts that ritual as a language is a "frozen statement." In secular terms, according to him, there is a *"disconnection* between the religious statement and the real world"; thus "religious rituals are misstatements of reality."[20] It is true that ritual communication is different from everyday speech acts, but they are not polar opposites. Bloch states the difference as follows:

EVERYDAY SPEECH ACTS:	FORMALIZED SPEECH ACTS:
Choice of loudness	Fixed loudness patterns
Choice of intonation	Extremely limited choice of intonation
All syntactic forms available	Some syntactic forms excluded
Complete vocabulary	Partial vocabulary
Flexibility of sequencing of speech acts	Fixity of sequencing of speech acts

Few illustrations from a fixed body of accepted parallels	Illustrations only from certain limited sources, e.g., Scriptures, Proverbs
No stylistic rules consciously held to operate	Stylistic rules consciously applied at all levels[21]

Formalized language, according to J. L. Austin, is "illocutionary" or "performative." In other words, its force does not lie in reporting facts but in specifically having the force to influence people.[22] Everyday speech acts have "propositional force," i.e., they are open to discussion, explanation, and contradiction. Ritual communication is not open to this kind of contradiction. It rather opens up an environment where, through participation, ritual passengers experience the depth of their world. The "nonparticipant observer," with a Marxian suspicion of state or religious hierarchy, may describe the symbolic ritual environment as "a kind of tunnel into which one plunges, and where, since there is no possibility of turning either to the right or the left, the only thing to do is to follow."[23] This is partially true. It fails, however, to advert to the multiple ways in which ritual passengers are opened up to interact with nature, fellow participants, and the divinity, leading to creativity.

The creative dimension of ritual is real. Change, even if it is slow, not only occurs with time in the ritual practice itself, but also in the narrative that may form part and parcel of ritual. But the most important aspect of change that ritual may carry is its capacity to become an instrument of ethical and social reform. Radical Moslem and Christian groups prove that this power of ritual to effect reform can operate in any sociopolitical and economic system. The experience of "the past and the present in the present" (Bloch) mobilizes participants to renew and deepen their life and the quality of life of the social group. Traditional African rituals and the rituals of African independent Churches make this abundantly clear. We have already referred to the emergence of independent Churches in Africa as signaling not only the move toward inculturation of Christianity, but also as an assertion of human liberation. By setting up alternative patterns of Christian religious practice these Churches effectively employed ritual as an instrument of this change.

Similarly, traditional rituals in African religion embody this change. For example, in the Swazi kingdom (southern Africa) an annual kingship ritual *(Incwala)* turns out to be an opportunity to renew the kingdom. The politico-religious ceremony takes place during the summer solstice. It begins with the seclusion of the king. At full moon, the king emerges naked from his seclusion. Rites of reversal, which replicate the everyday speech acts, form part of the process: alternatively groups of subjects pity and lament for him; taunt, vilify, and revile him; or extol his strength and triumph. This ritual affirms the established order (kingship/hierarchy) as right and good. The dramatic ritualization of the ambivalence of the order of relations in society specifically heals this relationship, binds the king and subjects to be faithful to the social contract, and ensures the prosperity and progress of the kingdom. In this way ritual shows its possibility to effect change.[24]

We are not saying that ritual could not be or is not manipulated by social and religious hierarchs. Indeed its repetitive pattern leaves it open to the danger of being frozen, robbing ritual action of its dynamic creative potential. When this happens emphasis is on ritualism, formalism, rubricism. There is a concern for excessive purism and an obsession with performing the rites according to the rules. This spills over into social life in forms of ethnic purity and xenophobia. This pathological tendency (Freud) derogates from the symbolic intentionality of ritual behavior. Instead of seeing the ritual as creating the environment, through words and gestures, for interaction between the human and the divine, between this earth and the unseen world — bringing out the ludic and creative dimension of ritual — there is rather an insistence on imposing on humans a sacredness that irrupts from the outside, that defines itself solely by the discontinuity between humans and gods.[25] Living cultural elements become suspect. There is a preference for a fixed ancestral past as interpreted by the ruling ritual elite. Ritual practice becomes esoteric, and the religious gathering turns into a spectacle where the ritual experts act and the spectators watch.

This pathological threat calls for ongoing renewal in ritual practice. The renewal centers principally on reestablishing the symbolic intent of ritual behavior. It insists that the eternal is manifest in the temporal and that both interact in the ritual context, that the ordinary is the vehicle for the transcendent — neither being made null by nor identified with the transcendent. Furthermore, the temporal (cultural, passing worldly) constitutes a vital test for the eternal (time of ancestors, tradition) and vice versa. While both times are distinct, they are not utterly discontinuous. Therefore, rituals that are "other-worldly" or "anti-worldly" become rejected as escapist. Such rites shy away from the problems of this world that participants bring to their worship. While maintaining their distance (difference) from this passing world, through memory of ancestral gestures, rituals provoked by the problems of this present time use symbols drawn from this passing world to respond to the problems of life. In this way ritual action is not insulated from the real human world. Its character as gestural behavior (interaction in an environment) saves it from this insulation, and its structural ethical dimension assures its relevance in a world where humans and spirits interact for the well-being of humans.

THE RITUAL DISPLAY OF HUMANS IN AFRICA

The African is generally described as being incurably religious. This is supposed to be a derogatory assessment. However, the attachment of Africans, yesterday and today, to religious practice may display their grasp of the aesthetic and ethical dimensions of ritual behavior. In Africa there are periodic rituals to mark the seasons and rituals of transition: passages from childhood through adolescence to adulthood and old age. Any event of life — success or failure, health or sickness, arrival or departure — is marked by ritual. Instead of this practice diminishing with cross-cultural contact and modernity, religious rituals appear to be on the increase. Foreign patterns are being merged with local African ones. On the one hand, the "normal order" transmitted from time immemorial is repeated in rituals (old and new); on the other hand, the changes in structures of society caused especially by the colonial and postcolonial experience lead to rituals adapted to respond to these changes. The intent of these ritual performances is the well-being of humans located in their universe.

The predominance of what Zeusse calls the "structure" over "salvation" in African religious practice is still pervasive all over Africa today. Everyday, commonplace reality and the need to be delivered from material wants or to achieve material contentment are very much the intent of ritual behavior today.[26] "The people respond to God in and because of particular circumstances, especially in times of need. Then they seek to obtain what he gives, be that material or spiritual."[27] There is no aspect of everyday life that does not come under the influence of religious ritual. This has led Horton to argue that African religion is a kind of science, located in the "closed" system as opposed to the "open" system of Western science. According to him, the intent of ritual is not communion with God; rather, like science, religious ritual seeks to explain, predict, and control the human universe:

"People want a coherent picture of the realities that underpin their every day world. They want to know the causes of their fortunes and misfortunes in this world. They want to have some way of predicting the outcomes of their various worldly projects and enterprises. They want, above all, to have the means of controlling events in the space-time world around them."[28]

What Horton says about "ritual man" in Africa is part of African ritual behavior. But his insistence that African religion is a science insulated in the "closed" predicament is a rehashing of the outmoded thesis that "primitive religions" are magic (pseudoscience). According to this view, these religions are as preoccupied with ritual effectiveness as Christianity is concerned with communion with God. However, in the African world integrally perceived, the rhythm of ritual pervades all departments of life. Patient observation and empirical data resist the ease with which traditional societies are declared "closed." Openness to change (as is characteristic of the Igbo world), acceptance of the elasticity of knowledge (as in the Yoruba *ifa* divination) not only indicate another point of view, but are all taken up into the rhythm of the social group's ritual.[29] The utilitarian or materialistic tendency of African ritual behavior does not negate the spiritual reality of ritual. Rather, it projects the integral unity of the universe: the material and spiritual needs are intimately linked and are displayed before the spiritual originators of a group, without whom they may not be realized. Thus, instead of putting religion and science in separate compartments (Horton), the human person in the particular environment is a subject of both. Through ritual both science and religion ensure human well-being.

Illustration of How Religious Ritual Display Renews African Communities

The dynamic aspect of ritual (linking past to present to shape the future) characterizes ritual activity in African communities. Divinities, ancestors, or events, which established the communities in the past, are still experienced in the present ritual time. They form one dynamic whole with the community to shape its actions in the future. This can be seen in the way religious assemblies are convoked in African communities.

Any aspect of African life may attract religious ritual performance. A religious ritual assembly may be provoked by political, social, economic, or purely religious reasons. For example, the practice of initiating traditional chiefs assumes a religious ritual dimension because the king/chief is a link with the ancestors of the group. Their initiation or enthronement becomes an occasion to reenact the foundation stories of the group, thereby renewing the basis of the existence of the group. Such initiations and periodic festivals provoke assemblies where the life of the community is renewed, and the community's commitment to the moral order on which it is founded is reaffirmed.[30] We shall examine initiation rites in detail in a later chapter. Here, we shall discuss one recorded case of an assembly provoked by a crisis experienced by an African village-group in the normal day to day life. It is a case of land dispute between two clans among the Kongo ethnic group. The case shows that the community is renewed in the common and everyday life routine, that the social (profane) and the religious (sacred) overlap or merge with relative ease. It supports what Zeusse calls the sanctification of the everyday in life. In other words, ritual shows that the transcendental is actual and that the sacred is ordinary in the African world.[31]

Two clans *(bivumu)* in a Kongo village were involved in a land dispute.[32] Clan heads *(ngudi makanda)* assembled to make peace. They looked into the case. But before they passed sentence they imposed taxes on both parties: rams, pigs, cocks, heads of bananas, etc. (The tax covers the seating fee of the judges.) One party to the conflict could not afford the ram. The clan-chief was in great distress. He called a meeting of his council to present the case to the ancestors. The men of the clan gathered in the evening in the ancient site of the village (*kuedi bwala,* a holy ancestral site; in such a case the cemetery would equally suffice). They came with palm wine and kola nuts. Libations were poured and the kola was offered. Then the clan-chief went on his knees and pleaded with the ancestors. He narrated the history of the land dispute, explained how the situation had become desperate because the clan could not afford the ram, and told them that the clan under his care would be ruined since the clan had no other arable land. He prayed to the ancestors to remember the love for their descendants and to provide them with the ram. He told them to look kindly on the clan's prayer and come to their aid because it was a legitimate defense of their own ancestral land. Further libations followed the prayer. The assembly dismissed and the men returned to the village.

The clan-chief received a reply in a dream that same night: the ancestors would not abandon their descendants, their descendants would win the case; the chief should go to the ancient village square early in the morning to collect the ram. The chief woke up. He roused the people and narrated the reply received through the dream. A victory celebration was declared. Early in the morning the chief returned to the square with his council. In front of a large red mantle, visible from the village, stood a tied ram. The chief prostrated, then collected both the ram and the mantle. He offered the ram and the other requirements to the judges. The clan won the case. The whole community participated in the victory celebration. The chief kept the mantle as a symbol of the new vigor given to his authority by the ancestors *(bakulu).*

The clan was confronted with an economic and political problem. Legal processes were available to resolve the issue according to native law and custom. But the cost of the legal process threw the clan into a crisis. It was normal for the clan-chief to convoke an assembly, and normal for him to lay the problem at the feet of the clan-ancestors. The following steps were adopted in the religious assembly: convocation of the assembly by the clan-chief (the ancestral representative and thus the chief priest of the clan); pouring of libation and offering of kola nut (gestures of communion); invocation of the ancestors by the chief, who pleaded with them to intervene in favor of their descendants; awaiting the reaction of the ancestors who replied through a dream; and, finally, victory celebrations in which the renewal of the life of the community tied to the ever present ancestors was ritually displayed.

This ritual process is the popular pattern in the Central African region where ancestral cult is very strong. In other places the principal spirits that may be involved in such a crisis vary. For example, among the Igbo, though ancestors will be involved, Ala (the earth deity who presides over the land and over law and order) will be prominent. But it is common practice to convoke a religious assembly involving the community or a cross section of it to resolve issues affecting everyday life. In this way life is lived under the eyes of God and the spirits. In the Kongo example, the invocation of the ancestors and their miraculous answer renewed the community and assured it of the presence of its spiritual founders. It is the awareness of this presence that guides life in the present and shapes it in the future. The material need of the land ensures well-being to the living and the living-dead. The possession of the land (which is also spiritualized) also guarantees the survival of the memory of the ancestors with whom the living keep daily communion through prayers and libations. For the land of the living and that of the ancestors, though different, are warmly linked.

JEWISH-CHRISTIAN RITUAL AND THE ORIGIN OF THE COMMUNITY (CHURCH)

What we stated above as the framework for ritual and its renewal or creation of community is applicable to the Jewish-Christian experience. The main difference between ritual in the African sociocultural area and in the Jewish-Christian tradition lies in the different emphasis laid on the action of the ritual anchor, or, more concretely, on the functioning of the foundation story. While both groups would assert that God and/or the spirits intervene in their history, the Jewish-Christian practice concentrates its ritual attention chiefly around the apprehension of the divine saving activity as contained in their foundation story. Among the African groups the story may be celebrated periodically (annually, like in the new year festival) or occasionally (for example, at the coronation of chiefs or kings or during initiation ceremonies). In the Ancient Near East, according to Albrektson, divine intervention in history was a common phenomenon. What remains unparalleled in the experience of Israel is how the foundation story dominates ritual activity.[33] This issue will be fully addressed in the next chapter when we come to consider the foundation story (myth). We are obliged to mention it here to insist on the intimate connection between the foundation story and ritual in the birth of the Jewish-Christian community or Church.

The Jewish Experience

Historians still argue on how many groups of peoples, who later came to be called Israel, left Egypt. There are many opinions on their settlement processes and the generalization of a common belief in

Yahweh. But there appears to be some measure of consensus that there was a historical escape from Egypt and that there was a group that practiced the Yahweh cult (probably the house of Joseph). This cult was later generalized, and Yahweh was proclaimed the liberator of Israel.[34] We shall discuss this in detail under Israel's foundation story (chapter three).

Old Testament faith and theology insist that the totality of the Exodus experience created Israel and that the birth of Israel was ritually enacted. This experience controlled Jewish life through the liturgy in which the Exodus event is ritually remembered. The prominence of the Exodus in Jewish worship did not have the force of law before the Deuteronomic reform in the time of King Josias (622 B.C.E.). Only in the situation of a centralized cult with a strong priestly-prophetic control would Israel's foundation story dominate all worship. Ritual activities before this time were carried out principally in the sanctuaries.

Sanctuaries as Ancient Places of Worship

Before the Deuteronomic reform, the twelve families (tribes) presented themselves before God (and before Yahweh) for mercy and thanksgiving in the numerous shrines whose foundation is attributed to one patriarch or another as its founder. The rituals in these sanctuaries were not necessarily the Yahwistic (Exodus) cult. The motive for assembling to worship may be provoked by any life event. The prophets and Deuteronomic preachers were to condemn worship in these sanctuaries as tainted with paganism. However, it was the ritual at the sanctuaries that dominated Israelite cult before the construction of the Jerusalem Temple.[35]

There are sanctuaries that preexisted the settlement in the land of Canaan, and there are others established after the merger of the peoples (or tribes) to form one Israel. Shechem, Bethel, Mamre, and Beer-sheba were places of worship attached to the patriarchs; Gilgal, Shiloh, Mizpah of Benjamin, Gabaon, Ophrah, Dan, and Jerusalem came into prominence after the entry into Canaan. The story about each place of worship moves from the founder (ancestor) to the descendants. For example, the Yahwist and Eloist attribute the sanctuary of Bethel to both Abraham and Jacob (Gen 12:28; 28:10-22). Jacob had his famous vision at Bethel, and there Yahweh renewed the promise made to Jacob's ancestor, Abraham. It later became a pilgrimage center (1 Sam 10:3; Amos 4:4). In this sanctuary, there is an assembly before Yahweh, sacrifices are made to Yahweh, Yahweh is consulted through the priest, and the ark of the covenant was once deposited at Bethel. Here, after his schism, Jeroboam installed a cult to rival that of Jerusalem. But Bethel was originally a place of Canaanite worship: "How awesome is this place *[maqôm]!*" (Gen 28:17). The name given to it by Jacob — Bethel, house of God — is significant. El is the head of the Canaanite pantheon.[36]

Each sanctuary is under the charge of a priest *(kôhen),* or father, who lives there (1 Sam 1:7, 24; 3 Shiloh). The people consult him (Judg 18:5-6; Dan), and make their offering through his intermediary, but the offerer slaughters the victim. Though most of these sanctuaries were condemned by the prophets who propagated orthodox Yahwism, Deiss is correct in insisting that they were places where sacred narrators recounted the wonders of Yahweh — either as accomplished at the Exodus or in the land of Canaan.[37] However, one could not settle in a land without coming into contact with the patterns of behavior of the land (formal and informal acculturation). The Hebrews were thus deeply influenced by patterns of Canaanite sociopolitical and religious behavior. (We shall see this in greater detail in the next chapter.) The prophets, on their own part, insisted on faith in Yahweh alone and in no other divinity, a faith expressed in a mono-Yahwistic cult. But, up to the time of the Deuteronomists, the sanctuaries were the accepted places of worship (Deut 26:1-11). It was only later that the Exodus motif was generalized as the foundation story of a united Israel and the principal feasts became pilgrimage feasts to be celebrated in the one sanctuary (Temple) of Jerusalem.

A ritual that may be even older than the cult at the sanctuaries and figured prominently in the Deuteronomic liturgical propaganda is the Pasch. It is a ritual common to all pastoral peoples. Its archaic form, as recorded in Exodus 12:3-4, shows that it is a family ritual:

"On the tenth of this month they are to take a lamb for each family, a lamb for each household. If a household is too small for a whole lamb, it shall join its closest neighbor in obtaining one; the lamb shall be divided in proportion to the number of people who eat of it."

The elder (father of the family) slaughters the lamb and roasts it. The ritual is performed before the shepherds strike camp (as is also common among Arab pastoral groups). In addition, there is another ancient ritual whereby a family or a group of peoples make a sacrifice to God after a three-day pilgrimage (Gen 22:4ff.; Exod 5:3; Num 10:33).[38] This ritual, as well as the Pasch, has been integrated into the liberation story of the Hebrews from Egypt. In the experience of the Jewish people as a nation and a religious group, the prominence of the liberation story in the ritual renewal of the bond with Yahweh ensured the creation and re-creation of the community.

The Ritual Constitution of Israel into a People

The description of the process of the ritual creation of Israel by the later editors of the Pentateuch takes the Exodus experience, made up of the liberation from Egypt and the Sinai covenant, as the key experiences that constituted Israel into a people. Critical scholarship may not accept this later edition as historical. Some, like von Rad, argue that the covenant did not form part of the primitive creed contained in Deuteronomy 26:1-11. But it may be that the Sinai covenant was a ritual performed independently of the myth-narrative of the escape from Egypt along with the merger of the various groups into one people in the land of Canaan.[39] Thus the Sinai ritual may contain a very ancient ritual model of assembly in Israel — an assembly, the story claims, created on Sinai itself.

There are three steps in the process of this ritual creation of Israel as a people: Yahweh calls the people to assemble, the will of Yahweh is revealed, and Yahweh concludes the covenant with the people.

The convocation of the Sinai assembly was the initiative of Yahweh. It was made through the intermediary of Moses, to whom Yahweh was revealed in the burning bush. Moses and Aaron went to Pharaoh and said to him:

"Thus says the LORD, the God of Israel, 'Let my people go, so that they may celebrate a festival to me in the wilderness.' . . . The God of the Hebrews has revealed himself to us; let us go a three days' journey into the wilderness to sacrifice to the LORD our God, or he will fall upon us with pestilence or sword" (Exod 5:1-3).

All the events narrated — from the interaction between Moses and the Egyptian leadership, through the crossing of the sea of Reeds, the trials in the wilderness, up to the arrival at Sinai — were interpreted in Israel as designed by Yahweh their God.

The narrative of the revelation of the will of Yahweh at Sinai is unique. We not only have tradition — histories laid one on top of the other dealing with only one subject, the revelation of the divine will on Sinai — but, as von Rad stresses, this very lengthy narrative (covering Exod 19:1 to Num 10:10) failed to penetrate the ancient Jewish creed. It thus guarded its independence and entered the salvation history narrative at a later date. The two dominating traditions in the narrative are the Yahwistic tradition (Exodus 19–24; 32–34) and the priestly record (Exodus 25–31; 35 / Num 10:10). There are common features as well as differences. Both traditions display the revelation of Yahweh on Sinai and the establishment of fundamental laws guiding a people. But while the Yahwist presents the Decalogue (the ten words) as a law establishing divine lordship over all the domains of life, the priestly tradition insists on the revelation of a sacred order legislating over the ritual life and cult objects. The high point of the priestly narrative is, naturally, the descent of the glory of Yahweh.[40]

Finally, the conclusion of the covenant is a celebration. It is, of course, a covenant of unequals.[41] The Eloistic narrative (Exod 24:3-8) is more integral than the Yahwistic story, which omits even the word covenant (Exod 24:1a, 9-11). Moses read the book of the covenant and the people responded in agreement: "All that the Lord has spoken we will do, and we will be obedient" (Exod 24:7). Even in this kind of covenant of unequals, where the weaker party is mainly passive, the word of agreement is indispensable. After the response, Moses threw the blood of the covenant upon the altar and on the people saying, "See the blood of the covenant that the Lord has made with you in accordance with all these words" (Exod 24:8). The blood containing life (*nefes,* Gen 9:4; Lev 17:11-14) is a material symbol demonstrating the establishment of community of life between Yahweh and Israel. The ritual gestures of Moses (or rather, the actions of God — the ritual anchor — and the participating assembly), which are replete with symbolism, create a completely new order: God takes Israel as child in the strongest of terms, gives the people a share of his life, and thereby establishes a blood relationship with them.

In the minds of the later editors of the Pentateuch, and indeed of the prophets, who were the greatest influence on the evolution of Hebrew tradition (memory), the Exodus event, which reached its climax at the Sinai covenant, is the creation of Israel. This fact may be suggested by the meaning attached to the word *qahal* (assembly or gathering) in the edition of the Pentateuch and its further developments. The more primitive term for the ad hoc convocation of Israel and/or its leaders is *ʿedah*. But, according to Milgrom, *ʿedah* fell out of use probably during the period of the monarchy and was replaced by *qahal*.[42] The Hebrew lexicon assigns two fundamental meanings to *qahal:* convocation and congregation. First of all, it is used to denote an assembly specially convoked for various purposes: e.g., evil counsel (Gen 49:6) or civil affair (1 Kgs 12:3), war or invasion (Num 22:4), and the company of returning exiles (Jer 31:8). Still, in the primary sense *qahal* denotes an assembly convoked for religious purposes. Most of the more primitive use of assembly in this religious sense is concerned with gathering to hear the words of Yahweh at Horeb (Deut 4:10; 9:10; 10:4; 18:16), to hear the words of Jeremiah (Jer 26:17), and for feasts, fasts, and worship (2 Chr 20:5; 30:25; Neh 5:13; Ps 107:32, etc.). In this primary sense of the use of *qahal,* 72 out of 111 occurrences are for religious purposes. It is a gathering or assembly in the presence of Yahweh, the ark, or the Temple involving the recalling of the covenant or Torah, accompanied by prayers and sacrifices. There is also a secondary sense of *qahal* meaning a congregation as organized body. This secondary sense is dependent on the primary meaning.

The Deuteronomists deeply influenced the evolution and understanding of *qahal* in Israel. For them the day of the assembly *(hayôm ha-qehal)* has creative ritual implications. We cite two passages from Deuteronomy to show this ritual interest:

> "And the LORD gave me the two stone tablets written with the finger of God; on them were all the words that the LORD had spoken to you at the mountain out of the fire on the day of the assembly" (Deut 9:10).
>
> "Then he wrote on the tablets the same words as before, the ten commandments that the LORD had spoken to you on the mountain out of the fire on the day of the assembly; and the LORD gave them to me" (Deut 10:4).

The day of the assembly refers to the covenant ritual at Sinai between Yahweh and Israel (Exodus 19; 24). In the ritual experience Yahweh became the God of Israel, the chosen people (cf. Jer 31:31-34). The Deuteronomists (Levitical preachers operating probably within the context of the cult) and the prophets were most instrumental in the propagation of Yahwism in Israel (cf. Joshua 24). Thus Israelite religious assemblies became a ritual memorial of the covenant on Sinai (the ritual aspect of the Exodus experience). All further assemblies — Sichem in 1200 B.C.E. (Josh 24:1-28), Josias in 621 B.C.E. (2 Kings 22–23), Ezrah in 398 B.C.E. (Nehemiah 8) — have to recall the Exodus event as the core of Israel's religious ritual. The same applies for feasts in Israel. Thus without this convocation, in ritual context, Israel, as a constituted body or congregation, would not exist.

In the Septuagint *qahal* is translated *ekklesia*.[43] But its meaning goes beyond the Greek sense of assembly of citizens convoked by the voice of the herald to deliberate on public affairs. The Septuagint rather gives *ekklesia* a predominantly religious meaning: an assembly of the children of Israel, convoked by God, with the primary purpose of listening to the word of God at Horeb (Deut 4:10; 9:10; 18:16):

"How you once stood before the LORD your God at Horeb, when the LORD said to me, 'Assemble the people for me, and I will let them hear my words, so that they may learn to fear me as long as they live on the earth, and may teach their children so'" (Deut 4:10).

Israel is therefore assembly *(qahal-ekklesia)* through living the Exodus event displayed in ritual (its creation). Israel is maintained in existence through ongoing renewal or reenactment of this foundational experience. Ritual-memorial and the prophetic ministry maintained this event in the consciousness of Israel and marginalized other patterns of religious ritual.

The Ritual Constitution and Sustenance of the Christian Church

When one pays close attention to the social context of the New Testament writings, the story of the beginnings of what later came to be called Church *(ekklesia)* and its worship may lack clarity. Jesus and the movement that took its rise from him were radically rooted in the Jewish way of life. He was a Jew; his followers, who confessed him as the Christ, were Jewish-Christians. Thus, their practices, no matter how influenced by the social context of the Greco-Roman world, were deeply rooted in the Jewish antecedents. The privilege granted to Jews by the Roman government to assemble in their socioreligious clubs or fellowships was enjoyed by Christians whose associations could be classified at the early period as sects of Judaism. Even when other gatherings were banned by imperial decree, Jewish meal fellowships were permitted. According to Josephus:

"For even Caius Caesar, our imperator and consul, in that decree where he forbade the Bacchanal rioters to meet in the city, did yet permit these Jews, and these only, both to bring in their contributions, and to make their suppers. Accordingly when I [Julius Caesar] forbid other Bacchanal rioters, I permit these Jews to gather together, according to the customs and laws of their forefathers, and to persist therein."[44]

Nevertheless, the influence of the Greco-Roman surroundings (felt more by Hellenistic Christians than by Palestinian Jewish-Christians) must be presumed in the various patterns of experiencing assembly in the New Testament (apostolic and post-apostolic) communities.

In our survey of the constitution of the Church in the New Testament period we emphasize two points: the variations in the experience of assembly in the New Testament and the ritual establishment and/or renewal of the Christian community. The key function of ritual in the emergence and self-definition of any New Testament community is finally the principal preoccupation of this section. The churches in the book of the Apocalypse will be used to demonstrate this in detail.

Various Experiences of Assembly in the New Testament

Jesus proclaimed the coming of the kingdom of God. He made a prophetic-eschatological call to *metanoia* (repentance) in continuity with the prophetic ministry of John the Baptist. There is, however, a distinctive emphasis in the ministry of Jesus: the kingdom comes with his proclamation (Matt 11:4-6; 12:28; Luke 10:23; 17:20ff.). Situated within his Jewish society Jesus is presented by the New Testament tradition as challenging the society in order to change it. In his preaching, the messianic times dawned as foretold by the prophets (cf. Isa 2:2-5; Mic 4:1-3). He thus comes across as a prophet-reformer of Judaism and a teacher in the Jewish wisdom tradition. His prophetic role created conflict within Judaism. This conflict ended in his shameful execution. But his pattern of preaching and living the kingdom ensured that this disgraceful crucifixion was not to be the last heard of the prophet-reformer.[45] His death had eschatological consequences:

"Caiaphas, who was high priest that year, said to them, 'You know nothing at all! You do not understand that it is better for you to have one man die for the people than to have the whole nation destroyed.' He did not say this on his own, but being high priest that year he prophesied that Jesus was about to die for the nation, and not for the nation only, but to gather into one the dispersed children of God" (John 11:49-52).

The miraculous resurrection of Jesus and/or the confession of his being alive in his words and deeds in the assembled community are continuous with his practice of the kingdom during his life in the flesh. As Schillebeeckx puts it:

"The messianic 'must suffer' of Jesus is not a 'divine' must. It is forced on God through Jesus by human beings, yet God and Jesus are not thwarted by it, not by virtue of the resurrection as such, which would then be regarded as a kind of compensation for the historical failure of Jesus' message and praxis, but because his 'going around Palestine doing good' was itself already the beginning of the kingdom of God, of a kingdom in which death and injustice no longer have a place. In Jesus' practice of the kingdom of God his resurrection is already anticipated."[46]

The followers of Jesus became a distinct group by assembling in his name to continue his kingdom praxis.

Meal Assembly to Remember Jesus Radically Open to All Initiates. The social conflict that the preaching and the kingdom praxis of Jesus created within Judaism, while not creating a new religious movement during the earthly life of Jesus, already set in motion the emergence of such a division. In other words, if Jesus did not found a Church (as a distinctive sect within Judaism), he certainly laid the foundation for its emergence.

The situation of conflict existing between the followers of Jesus and their Judaistic opponents testifies to the emergence of boundaries. It also gives us the key indication of the type of assembly that Jewish-Christians were evolving. In Q, a source shared by Luke and Matthew, there is a record of the praxis of Jesus and his disciples that drew sharp criticisms from their opponents (Luke 7:31-35; Matt 11:16-19).[47] It is the issue of sharing table (eating and drinking) with publicans and sinners. The intention of the passage is to debunk the criticism directed against Jesus (and later against his followers) that he was a glutton and drunkard. The source contrasts Jesus and John the Baptist (who was also criticized as having a demon because he fasted). But this tradition (Q) positively approves Jesus and John as children of wisdom. It emerges from the passage that a key pattern of assembling in early Jewish Christianity is around meals. These are fellowship meals.

Smith and Taussig present the common meal traditions found in the Greco-Roman world, which could have been adapted by Jews and Christians to suit their needs. These include family gatherings, funeral banquets, sacrificial banquets, philosophical society meetings, trade guild meetings, and religious society meetings. They suggest that philosophical society meetings, which included a tradition of a symposium, were adapted for use in the Jewish and Christian communities. The symposium coming at the end of the meal is a philosophical (learned) conversation. The philosopher or Jewish sage discusses a significant topic. A text from the Mishnah confirms the practice:

"R. Simeon says, 'Three who ate at a single table and did not talk about teachings of the Torah while at table are as though they ate from *dead sacrifices*. . . . But three who ate at a single table and did talk about teachings of the Torah while at that table are as if they ate at the table of the Omnipresent, blessed is he'" (*Abot* 3:3 A and C).

In Christian meal assemblies this kind of learned discussion took the form of instructions (cf. Acts 20:7).[48] It is likely that the Christian groups that were setting up boundaries even within Judaism may have been similar to these philosophical assemblies. Indeed Josephus calls the Christian movement a "philosophical school."[49]

The distinctiveness of the gatherings of the Christian movement is its openness to those considered as outsiders by Judaism (especially of the pharisaic tradition). This conflict in praxis started in Jesus' lifetime and continued in the assemblies of early Christianity. "Look, a glutton and a drunkard, a friend of tax collectors and sinners!" (Luke 7:34; Matt 11:19). The Jesus movement, while worshiping in the synagogue, kept its own gathering where the meal is the central action. But it differed from the synagogue tradition (or from the pharisaic tradition) by being open to questionable characters; it thus distanced itself from the Jewish practice. It referred to the authority of Jesus for its action (as the preservation of the story by Q proves). The break with the synagogue became permanent when the Christians were finally expelled with a curse (the *birkat minim* of the Jewish Tefillah, cf. John 10).[50]

Meals are social boundary markers. To share a meal is to share a relationship, to share life. The practice of Q entrenches a pattern of relationship in assembly that breaks down discrimination on the level of the constitution of membership and, consequently, on the level of interaction. This experience of Q, based on the authority (sayings) of Jesus, is a fundamental experience of assembling as Christians. This is demonstrated by the pre-Pauline baptismal hymn recorded in Galatians 3:26-28:

"For in Christ Jesus you are all children of God through faith. As many of you as were baptized into Christ have clothed yourselves with Christ. There is no longer Jew or Greek, there is no longer slave or free, there is no longer male and female; for all of you are one in Christ Jesus."

The hymn quoted by Paul, which has its full force in the baptismal liturgical assembly, ritualizes (thus routinizes) the way of Jesus as a way of freedom and liberation (Gal 5:1; 5:13; 2 Cor 3:17).[51] First of all, membership in the Christian movement is open to anybody who so desires. Then, through baptism (as opposed to circumcision), all discrimination based on race and religion (Jew/Greek), social ranking (slave/free), social definition of gender roles (male/female), are abolished. The washing of baptism, which draws a line between "the unwashed world and the washed Christians," establishes a new group of humans called, in Pauline theology, "the Body of Christ."[52] This experience has not only mystical but also social (and thus ethical) consequences. It is a rejection of all structures of dominance within the Christian community. Thus the hymn in Galatians 3:28 is best understood as a "communal Christian self-definition."[53]

Assembly with Divergent Ecclesiologies. The radical practice of assembly enshrined ritually in the baptismal liturgy is not understood by all to apply always to sharing *(koinonia)* at all levels. The meal comes in again as a prominent indicator of difference. Even though Christian meals establish social bonding and mark out the community, the Jerusalem Church (under James) also followed pharisaic dietary rules: they were Jews (not dining with Gentiles) and Christians (not dining with the synagogue). Thus they were a Jewish-Christian sect that took the circumcision and the Sinai covenant seriously. Peter, while not sharing their views, had no problem in sharing meals with Gentiles and meals with Jewish-Christians who excluded the Gentiles. He leaves the impression that local conditions should prevail on the issue of meals; he could then defer to the sentiments of the visitors from James (Gal 2:11-13). Thus, there emerge three ecclesiologies: assembling around a meal to remember Jesus where all discrimination breaks down (Q); assembling around a meal to remember Jesus but maintaining pharisaic ritual purity excluding Gentiles (James); and assembling around a meal to remember Jesus while the meal itself is organized according to local sentiments (Peter). Each of these ecclesiologies is influenced by a different pattern of interactional ritual in the Christian assembly.

For Paul, however, the meal assembly not only marks out Christians, but the bonding caused by this ritual action is demonstrated to be rooted in the kingdom praxis of Jesus. Meal sharing is a liturgical experience that witnesses to the confession that justification is through faith in Jesus, not through the law, not through circumcision (Galatians 2–3). The practice of the meal assembly is a foundational theological (ecclesiological) issue. It touches the very essence of the community as Christian. The social differences in the wider Greco-Roman world are outlawed in the Christian assembly. The Christian meal-assembly "as a zone under taboo" abhors discrimination.[54] Therefore, Paul could boldly reproach Peter, Barnabas, and other Jewish-Christians for withdrawing from sharing table with the Gentiles because they "were not acting consistently with the truth of the gospel" (Gal 2:14).

Paul disagreed with Peter and Barnabas, and this difference may have led to the parting of ways between him and Barnabas (Acts 15:39-40).[55] However, it does not appear as if Paul's opinion prevailed. This divergence in the perception of the meal assembly indicates a plurality of viewpoints that should only be expected in the social setting that spawned the Christian assemblies.

Recent scholarship has shown that the earliest Christian experience of assembling in the name of Jesus was in the form of house-churches. The characteristics of these house-churches reflect the features of clubs or associations within the context of the Greco-Roman world. Pauline letters and Acts of the Apostles make frequent references to these house-churches.[56] Such churches assembled in the houses of Prisca and Aquila (1 Cor 16:19; cf. Acts 18:18-19), Mary the mother of John Mark (Acts 12:12), Chloe (1 Cor 1:11), and Philemon. These are probably wealthy householders (some of whom are slave owners) who have large living-rooms to accommodate such an assembly. It is the actual gathering (assembling) in such houses to keep the memory of the Lord that gave the name church-assembly *(ekklesia)* to these gatherings. In these meal gatherings the Eucharistic rite, instruction, conversion-initiation, etc., were practiced. From this we underline that the church-assembly is an actual gathering of Christians in the house of one of their members.[57] This links the New Testament usage of *ekklesia* to the Old Testament religious meaning of *qahal-ekklesia*. Thus when Paul addresses letters or makes references to the churches in Galatia (Gal 1:2; 1 Cor 16:1) and the churches in Macedonia (2 Cor 8:10), he could hardly be referring to a regional assembly. Rather he is referring to the house-churches that occasionally may have had the habit of meeting as a regional grouping.[58]

A variety of house-churches may have arisen in the major Christian centers, and, predictably, may not necessarily be in agreement with one another. Brown suggests that there may have been, for example, a house-church of Christian Jews attached to the Mosaic law, a house-church of mixed Jewish and Gentile Christians that did not impose circumcision on Gentiles but did not relativize the value of the law in Christian life, a house-church from Pauline mission consisting mostly of Gentiles completely liberated from the law, and the Johannine house-church characterized by the insistence on being children of God and disciples of Jesus, who is present through the Paraclete.[59] The divergences in the understanding of meal assemblies and the different theologies and ministerial roles in these assemblies may have arisen, as Galatians indicate, from racial-religious background, social ranking, and gender differentiation. But they are all Christian assemblies insofar as they gather around a meal to keep the memory of Jesus.

The Role of Ritual in the Constitution and/or Renewal of the New Testament Assembly

The simplest form of the Christian assembly in the New Testament is the house-church. It is the gathering to remember the Lord, who died and is confessed as raised or as alive through the Spirit active in the community, that makes the church. The action of assembling is a gesture replete with meaning. The assembling in itself is a Christian ritual action because it is an action tied to or anchored in the Jesus event. Its purpose is to experience through assembling the presence of the risen Jesus.

We therefore emphasize that gathering-in-assembly is a ritual action. However, the action performed in the gathering displays more strongly the nature of the assembly. The point Luke makes about the breaking of the bread *(he klasis tou artou),* the fellowship *(koinonia),* and the attention to the instruction *(didachē)* of the apostles may be illuminating about the role of Christian rituals in structuring the assembly. "They devoted themselves to the apostles' teaching and fellowship, to the breaking of bread and the prayers. Day by day, as they spent much time together in the temple, they broke bread at home and ate their food with glad and generous hearts" (Acts 2:42, 46).

These assemblies are house-churches (*kat ᾿oikon,* from house to house). They revolve around meals like all such clubs or free associations in the Greco-Roman setting. The apostles' teaching *(didachē),* like the symposium in the philosophical clubs, centers around the event of the Lord Jesus, narrated during the meal gathering. Luke attaches a special importance to the action he calls the breaking of the bread. This expression, which occurs once in the Old Testament (Jer 16:7), is unknown to the Greek tradition. It is rather the habitual rabbinic expression for Jewish meal practice.[60] The breaking of the bread follows the "benediction" of the father of the family over the food: "Blessed be Thou, (Yahweh our God), who bringest out bread from the earth" (*t.ber*. iv:6). The table members reply, "Amen."

Luke is thus using Jewish (rabbinic) table vocabulary to describe a Christian ritual action that marks out the Christian assembly from all other clubs and associations. This ritual is the Christian Eucharistic action. The practice of these house-churches may have centered around the simple breaking of bread with its prayers rather than the regular use of bread and wine.[61]

The practice of the breaking of bread is so prominent in Lucan communities that the evangelist links it intimately with the very origin of the Church. In the apparition of Jesus to the two disciples on the road to Emmaus (Luke 24:13-35), they realize who he was (i.e., that he was alive) at the breaking of the bread:

"When he was at the table with them, he took bread, blessed and broke it, and gave it to them. Then their eyes were opened, and they recognized him; and he vanished from their sight. Then they told what had happened on the road, and how he had been made known to them in the breaking of the bread" (Luke 24:30-31, 35).

It is the resurrection faith that creates the Church. The narrative of the vision at Emmaus insists that this faith (i.e., the recognition of Jesus of Nazareth, who died, as alive) is experienced (as opening of the eyes) in the community's Eucharistic rite. This rite, made up of the four gestures of taking bread, blessing and breaking it, and then giving it to his disciples, has been simply called the breaking of the bread. The action of breaking bread (and the thanksgiving over the cup) is a ritual-symbol in which the authority (competence) of the Lord (Christianity's foundation) is recognized by the community. It is thus not questioned (like all performative acts). This makes the full effect of the symbol-covenant to be operative. We thus have a creative (constitutive or institutional) and exemplary narration of an action, so that when repeated it renews the community.[62] In this way one may say that the Church's Eucharistic rite creates and re-creates the community.

Experts suggest that Luke may have idealized the community life among the early Christians. He may have introduced some of his personal views into the interpretation of the community's praxis of following the Way. His insistence on the community being in accord or being of one heart and one soul may never have been realized, but his emphasis on the Eucharistic rite and its creative function in the community is not simply his creation. We noted that the basic structure of the assembly (from Q source and Pauline communities) is gathering around a meal. The meal reaches its peak in the Eucharistic rite where the memory of Jesus is kept alive. The correct way to participate in the meal (without discrimination) was so important for Paul that he saw the whole Christian praxis threatened by Peter's action at Antioch.

In his letter to the Corinthians Paul established an internal connection between the life (praxis) of the Church and the narrative of the institution of the Eucharist. This is in a context where he was emphasizing the correct way of celebrating the Lord's supper *(he kyriake deipnon).* In house-churches made up of the poor and the rich, the supper of the Lord, correctly partaken, must overcome all differences (1 Cor 11:20-22). To entrench this Eucharistic ecclesiology, Paul narrated the story of the institution at the Last Supper (1 Cor 11:23-26), a tradition that he received; a tradition he uses to underline that the Lord is recognized at the Eucharistic celebration made up of the seven crucial gestures over the bread and wine. This recognition is the beginning of the life of the community. This life of the community displayed in the Eucharistic rite is dynamically prolonged (eschatology) by keeping this memorial: "For as often as you eat this bread and drink the cup, you proclaim the Lord's death until he comes" (1 Cor 11:26).

The synoptic writers create a similar effect by incorporating the supper narratives into the most primitive New Testament corpus (the passion narratives). This succeeds in interpreting the death of Jesus as a total self-gift (sacrifice, dying the way he lived). But the narrative style entrenches the establishment (institution) of a way of doing (ritual-symbol), a way that links the Eucharistic rite to the birth of the Church. It may be true, of course, that since these are foundational narratives (of originating actions, *in illo tempore*), they may reflect practices that are structural to the constitution of Christian assemblies. In other words, the narratives may not be pure historical accounts, since a Eucharistic rite founding the Church before the resurrection would be impossible. However, one must insist as well that the praxis of Jesus before his death, and through his death, is prolonged into the praxis of the community where he is recognized as alive. In this way the ritual-symbol makes the Church, which celebrates the living savior in its assembly. We now explore this creative and re-creative dimension of the Christian ritual in the liturgical assembly described in the book of the Apocalypse.

The Liturgical Assembly of the Apocalypse: A Display of the Church in a Transformed Universe

The book of the Apocalypse provides us with more liturgical texts than any one single book of the New Testament. This book of visions and images is unique in its own way: the visions extend "beyond local politics to global issues and beyond global issues to cosmology."[63] It is addressed, as the author says, to Christian Churches in Asia. In this way we have an "apocalyptic" literature with a difference: in addition to its being visionary and "apocalyptic," it is firmly grounded in a specific time location in the human world.[64] Many authors today are led by internal and external evidence to date the writing of the book after the destruction of the Temple (70 C.E.) and during the reign of Emperor Domitian (81–96 C.E.). Domitian was reputed to have claimed such titles as "our Lord and God" *(dominus et deus noster),* titles that Christians (as the Apocalypse shows) reserve for God alone.[65] The addressee of the Apocalypse is the ecclesial assembly. It is not accidental that the visions were revealed to the seer on the "Lord's day" (Rev 1:10), a very important day for liturgical assembly. And, as Ugo Vanni suggests, such a reading elicits a reaction from the assembly.[66] Vanni even identifies a "liturgical dialogue" taking place in the book. For example, the lector proclaims in Revelation 1:3: "Blessed is the one who reads aloud the words of the prophecy, and blessed are those who hear and who keep what is written in it; for the time is near." The reply of the worshiping assembly comes in Revelation 1:5b-6 in the form of a doxology: "To him who loves us and freed us from our sins by his blood, and made us to be a kingdom, priests serving his God and Father, to him be glory and dominion forever and ever. Amen."

Many commentators underline the importance of the liturgy in the Apocalypse. Thompson insists that the "language of worship" gives unity to the whole book. The hymnic-hieratic opening doxology (1:4-6) has a corresponding closing acclamation, "Amen. Come, Lord Jesus!" (22:20). Then the motif of worship comes in at strategic points in the narrative of the visions.[67] If one agrees with Fiorenza that "eschatology" is the proper horizon for understanding this book, then the prominence of worship at strategic points in the book becomes very interesting. If eschatological concern, that is, "the breaking-in of God's kingdom and the destruction of the hostile and godless powers," is the preoccupation of Apocalypse,[68] then the "heavenly liturgy" (Revelation 4–5; 7; 11; 15; 19, etc.) is already a foretaste of victory. The victory is not to be understood in purely anthropological terms (liberation from sin through the blood of the Lamb, Rev 1:5b-6), but also in sociopolitical terms (cf. Rev 5:9-10). Worship succeeds in setting the stage for the eschatological drama and at the same time in celebrating the dramatic finale of the eschatological narrative.[69] Thus worship (ritual) shapes and reshapes the categories through which the church-community perceives its world. Indeed it creates and re-creates the community.

Though liturgical elements permeate the whole book, they are more explicit in chapters four and five and in the last seven chapters of the book. We shall restrict our analysis to the first segment of the heavenly liturgy (Revelation 4–5). In this liturgy we are not only shown a "realized eschatology," but we also see the gradual Christianization of the Jewish liturgical tradition. The background to the liturgy described by John the seer is thus interesting for the historical study of liturgical inculturation in Asia Minor.[70]

The Liturgy of Revelation 4–5. The letters to the seven churches are completed (Revelation 2–3). The seer is taken "in spirit" into heaven to witness "what must take place after this" (Rev 4:1). What he saw was, first of all, the worship of the "one seated on the throne" by the "four living creatures," and the adoration of the same God by the "twenty-four elders" (Rev 4:1-11). Second, the liturgy continued and climaxed with the ritual enthronement of the Lamb (Revelation 5). It is a heavenly (indeed cosmic) liturgy full of song and gestures.

THE COSMIC LITURGY (REVELATION 4). The vision of chapter 4 is inspired by the vision of Ezekiel 1: the throne and the one seated on it, etc. (Rev 4:2-3; Ezek 1:26-28); the four living creatures with four faces and four wings (Rev 4:6b-8; Ezek 1:5c-10; though in Apocalypse the creatures have six wings instead of four). These four creatures in Ezekiel may represent the four principal constellations of the zodiac, the symbols of the four pillars supporting the earth, or the four cardinal points and the four seasons. Rabbinic exegesis interprets the four creatures as the foundation, the pillars, or the constitutive elements of creation.[71] The vision thus shows God enthroned amidst his creation and all creation (through the creatures) singing in worship: "Holy, holy, holy, / the Lord God the almighty, / who was and is and is to come" (Rev 4:8). The author has modified the Isaian cosmic chant: "Holy, holy, holy is the LORD of hosts; / the whole earth is full of his glory" (Isa 6:3). The phrase "who was and is and is to come" recurs in the Apocalypse (1:4, 8; 11:17). The author probably borrowed this term from the Jewish tradition where the Targum (the Aramaic version of the Old Testament for use in the Synagogue liturgy) explains the divine name as "he who was and is and will be."[72] The God presiding over the created natural order is the Lord of history; history is the terrain of ongoing creation (re-creation), a phenomenon now displayed in the life of the Christian Church.

The seer who was taken up to heaven did not abandon familiar categories to describe his visions. The heavenly liturgy (centering in the *Trisagion,* which has formed part of Christian worship in Asia Minor) was influenced by Jewish practice. Bouyer, Cothenet, and Prigent suggest that the *Qedushat* of *Yozer* of the synagogue morning liturgy must have influenced the liturgy from which the Apocalypse derived its model for the heavenly liturgy. *Yozer* is the first of the three benedictions in the synagogue morning worship preceding the *Shema.* It blesses God the creator of the luminaries and ends with the angelic hymn *(Qedushat),* "Holy, holy, holy."[73] The text of *Yozer* as recorded in the most ancient Jewish liturgical book (*Seder Rav Amram Gaon,* 875 C.E.) is as follows:

"Blessed be thou, YHWH, our God, king of the universe who formest light and createst darkness, who makest peace and createst all things: Who in mercy givest light to the earth and to them that dwell thereon and in his goodness renewest the creation every day continually. How manifold are thy works, YHWH. In wisdom has thou made them all, the earth is full of thy possessions. King who alone wast exalted from aforetime, praised, glorified and exalted from days of old. Everlasting God, in thine abundant mercies have mercy upon us, Lord of our strength, Rock of our stronghold, Shield of our salvation, thou stronghold of ours. The blessed God, great in knowledge, prepared and formed the rays of the sun: it was a boon he produced as a glory to his name. He set the luminaries round about his strength. The chiefs of his hosts are holy beings, they exalt the Almighty, continually declare the glory of God and his holiness. Be thou blessed, YHWH, our God, in the heavens above and on the earth beneath. Be thou blessed, our Rock, our King and our Redeemer, Creator of holy beings, praised be thy name for ever, our King, Creator of ministering spirits, and all of his ministering spirits stand in the height of the universe, and with awe proclaim aloud in unison the words of the living God and everlasting King. All of them are beloved, all of them are pure, all of them are mighty, all of them in dread do the will of their master, all of them open their mouths in holiness and purity and praise and glorify and sanctify the name of the great King, the mighty and dreaded One, holy is He. They all take upon themselves the yoke of the kingdom of heaven, one from the other, and give leave one to another to hallow their Creation: in tranquil joy of spirit, with pure speech and with holy melody they respond in unison in fear, and say with awe: HOLY, HOLY, HOLY, IS YHWH OF HOSTS: THE WHOLE EARTH IS FULL OF HIS GLORY. And the Ophanim and the holy Chayoth with a noise of great rushing, upraising themselves towards them praise and say: BLESSED BE THE GLORY OF YHWH FROM HIS PLACE. To the blessed God they offer pleasant melodies, to the King, the living and ever-enduring God they utter hymns and make their praises heard, for he alone performeth mighty deeds and maketh new things, the Lord of battles, he soweth righteousness, causeth salvation to spring forth, createth remedies, is revered in praises, the Lord of wonders who in his goodness reneweth the creation every day continually, as it is said: (Give thanks) to him that maketh great lights for his grace endureth for ever. Blessed be thou, YHWH, Creator of the luminaries."[74]

The twenty-four elders of the Apocalypse participate in this cosmic liturgy. They constitute a choir responding to the angelic hymn of the four creatures. They sink to the ground before the throne and, offering their crowns, they acclaim:

"You are worthy, our Lord and God,
  to receive glory and honor and power,
for you created all things,
  and by your will they existed and were created" (Rev 4:11).

In the gesture of prostration and liturgical acclamation the twenty-four elders "collapse into one the human spheres of politics and religion." In other words, the regal elders are political figures doing obeisance before their king: they offer him their crowns, as in the Roman imperial cult; they declare him *axios* (worthy), acclaiming him as "Lord and God," evocative of the imperial cult of Domitian. Finally, they state the reason for the dignity accorded him, as is customary in the Jewish *berakah*- (praise-)acclamation or doxology. The reason for the honor is that he is the Creator.[75]

The liturgical action described above is a Christian adaptation of a Jewish praise-liturgy. It is presented in a language suited to the sociopolitical setting of Asia Minor. But it radically rejects the state religion. The fallen Jewish Temple provides the sacred space (heaven) for the worship. The twenty-four elders are Old Testament saints. They perform a legitimate priestly function (see Rev 5:8), since they represent the twenty-four divisions of priests (*maʿamadot* — courses), as they were organized for cult in the second Temple after the Exile.[76] The exultant acclamation that "our Lord and God" is worthy *(axios)* of glory *(doxa)* ritually marks out the boundary between the Christian and the non-Christian. This Jewish-Christian liturgy is a heavenly liturgy that has sociopolitical implications in that part of the earth inhabited by Roman Asians. A liturgy replicating a cosmic drama where Christians are summoned to join forces with God against demonic forces. A liturgy where worship (prostration, offering of crowns and hymns) is addressed to the originator of the universe (the sole ritual anchor) as a hostile rejection of the imperial cult.[77] There is hardly any doubt that the Church of the Apocalypse is born on the altar of this liturgy and is renewed and kept alive by its ritual celebration.

THE ENTHRONEMENT OF THE LAMB (REVELATION 5). The first part of the heavenly liturgy praises God for creation. The second part, which forms a unit with the first, praises God and the Lamb. The vision in Revelation 5 opens with the scroll having seven seals that "no one in heaven or on earth or under the earth was able to open" (5:3). This tripartite division (cf. Phil 2:10) makes for fullness. The Christ or the Lamb who will open the scroll will be exalted above the angels (cf. Heb 2:5-9): "the Lion of the tribe of Judah, the Root of David, has conquered, so that he can open the scroll and its seven seals" (Rev 5:5).

The inspiration of the enthronement liturgy is the image of the Son of Man in Daniel 7:13-14. In both cases there is an investiture with a messianic rule that has universal and worldwide dimension. The messianic titles recalling the glorious times of David have both political and religious overtones. But the messiah in the Apocalypse is the suffering servant. He is sacrificed ("a Lamb standing as if it had been slaughtered"). His sacrifice is depicted as the perfect sacrifice (symbolized by the figure seven: "having seven horns and seven eyes, which are the seven spirits of God sent out into all the earth" [Rev 5:6]). It is this Lamb (possibly evoking the image of the Paschal Lamb in a paschal liturgy)[78] who "went and took the scroll from the right hand of the one who was seated on the throne" (Rev 5:7). The symbolism utilized in the narrative, according to Thompson, is "unambiguously Christian."

"The sealed scroll remains closed to all except the slain Lamb and his followers. The closed book that reveals and realizes 'the things which are to come' is a Christian book — one could almost say a Christian book of liturgy disclosed only in the worship of the Christian community (whether in heaven or on earth)."[79]

Exegetes interpret the scroll as the Old Testament. But it is a true Christian book of liturgy. It is within the Christian assembly, where the Lamb stands as though it had been slain (sacrificed and risen), that the true meaning of the Old Testament can be revealed. This Christianization of the Old Testament writings in the Christian assembly is typical of the resurrection faith-praxis: "Were not our hearts burning within us while he was talking to us on the road, while he was opening the scriptures to us?" (Luke 24:32; cf. Luke 24:27, 45; 2 Cor 3:14-16).

The reaction of the Christian assembly in this heavenly liturgy where the Lamb is recognized as redeemer and liberator is an outburst of joyful song called the "new song" (Rev 5:9). This Christian hymn opens with the adoration of the Lamb by the four creatures and the twenty-four elders who become harpists. It gathers momentum when myriads of angels join in the worship of the Lamb. Finally, it reaches a crescendo in the great symphony of praise where every creature in heaven and on earth and under the earth and in the sea sing the concluding *berakah*-acclamation (or doxology). The praise is sealed with the "Amen," as in every liturgy of Jewish inspiration. In our context it is pronounced by the four living creatures (Rev 5:14).

In the first place, the liturgical prostration, instrumentation (with harps), and offering of incense accompany the hymn of praise that narrates the reasons for the enthronement worship of the Lamb:

"You are worthy to take the scroll
 and to open its seals,
for you were slaughtered and by your blood you ransomed for God
 saints from every tribe and language and people and nation;
you have made them to be a kingdom and priests serving our God,
 and they will reign on earth" (Rev 5:9-10).

It is typical of Hebrew praise *(berakah)* tradition to state the reason for the praise of God.[80] In the "new song," *axios ei* (worthy art thou) introduces the praise that is really a narrative-memorial of the victorious work of the Lamb who was slain. The imagery of the narrative derives from the Old Testament and Jewish Liturgy (e.g., the Paschal Lamb of the Jewish-Christian paschal liturgy) and from the Greco-

Roman world (the lamb as "purchasing agent" who pays ransom for slaves or prisoners of war). The victory of the lamb is of universal application and has eschatological consequences. The liberated are constituted into a "kingdom and priests" (see Exod 19:16) and they exercise their kingship on earth in the eschatological future.[81]

Second, the myriads of angels add their voice to the creatures and elders in the congregational refrain acclaiming: "Worthy is the Lamb that was slaughtered / to receive power and wealth and wisdom and might / and honor and glory and blessing!" (Rev 5:12). The Lamb with seven horns and seven eyes (perfection of sacrifice) has been bestowed with seven titles (fully worshiped as God). The worship concludes with the sung doxology: "To the one seated on the throne and to the Lamb / be blessing and honor and glory and might / forever and ever!" (Rev 5:13).

The Lamb is not only projected as the Lord of the Christian assembly, but also as Lord of the universe. Christian worship in its full dimension is a cosmic liturgy. Thus the Apocalypse takes this earth seriously despite the sharp boundary it establishes between Christians and their tormentors. In their worship, the exercise of freedom and kingship on earth, anticipated as future (eschatology), is realized (celebrated) especially through the "evocative power of the hymnic word."[82] This hieratic-hymnic narrative of the great achievements of the Lamb justifies the community's worship of the Lamb and, consequently, their rejection of emperor's cult. No creature is worshiped, not even the revealing angel who is only a fellow servant (*syndoulos*, Rev 19:10; 22:8-9). All members of the assembly (including ministers) are priestly and kingly. They collapse into one level (*communitas* or camaraderie according to Turner) to offer worship to the Lamb.[83]

The author of the Apocalypse, however, does not allow worship to become an illusion. The eschatological reserve is maintained. What is tasted in worship is real and yet points to the future. The marriage of the Lamb is yet to come (19:7), and the Christian assembly (bride) must get herself ready to be clothed with fine linen, bright and pure (19:8). The Christian assembly (the seven churches, i.e., all the churches) gathered in worship reads the letter of John, is instructed and challenged in worship, and is thus prepared for the coming of the Lord (the Lamb). There is no possibility of defining this assembly (church) of the Apocalypse outside of or without reference to worship.

Conclusion: Gathering in Assembly Makes the New Testament Church

One may conclude from the New Testament experience that the gathering or coming together as assembly is a ritual act that creates the Church *(ekklesia).* This experience has influenced the use of the term *ekklesia* in the New Testament, principally by Paul and then by Luke. The frequent Pauline reference to house-churches supports this position.

Luke, who tells the story of the birth of the Church as arising from the out-pouring of the Spirit on the day of Pentecost (Acts 2), pays particular attention to the ritual context of this experience. In the upper room, the apostles "were constantly devoting themselves to prayer, together with certain women, including Mary the mother of Jesus, as well as his brothers" (Acts 1:14). Being in accord or in unanimity (one heart and one soul) is a favorite expression of Luke in the first part of his story of the Acts of the Apostles, and he uses the term within liturgical context. In the oneness of heart and in prayer, they gathered together in one place *(epi tō autō)* on the day of Pentecost (2:1). *Epi tō autō* is another characteristic term describing the Christian liturgical gathering (Acts 1:15; 2:44-47), a term used in a similar sense by Justin the Martyr *(kata autō).*[84] During the New Testament period, the feast of Pentecost had become for the Jews the celebration of the gift of the Covenant and Law on Sinai. It was thus suitable that the Holy Spirit should be given to the Christian assembly on the memorial day of the Sinai covenant. The outpouring of the Spirit on the gathering on that particular day transformed the gathering in the upper room into a new *ekklesia:* the eschatological continuation of the *ekklesia* in the desert (see Acts 7:38). Luke's use of "gathering in one place" *(epi tō autō)* confirms the New Testament experience that gathering to remember the Lord (now present in the Spirit) makes the Church. As Grelot says, it is the assembly effectively gathered that gives name to the group. This gathering creates the possibility of the assembly being convoked or being referred to corporately as Church susceptible to being convoked, and not the other way round. Thus a church that does not gather as assembly would be a contradiction.[85]

Second, the communities' theologies and ecclesiologies may have assumed distinct characteristics not only because of race and religious backgrounds, social standing and gender differentiations, but also because of a hostile sociopolitical environment within which they are located (Apocalypse). Despite these differences, there is unanimity in keeping the memory of Jesus the Christ. This memory is the intent of each Christian assembly gathered around a meal.

Finally, the New Testament material rejoins what is generally stated about ritual action as creating and re-creating community. It is in the ritual-gesture that any community's awareness of itself and its place in the universe is experienced and expressed. The community assembled to worship dwells in the environment (ritual-symbolic context) where it is intimately bonded to the key symbols of its story (myth-symbol) and relates to the symbols in an appropriate style (ritual action). We shall now turn to these narratives or foundational stories to explore their impact on the community and its ritual action.

NOTES

1. V. Turner, *The Forest of Symbols: Aspects of Ndembu Ritual* (Ithaca, N.Y.: Cornell University Press, 1967) 19; see also R. Didier, "Des sacrements, Pourquoi," *La Maison Dieu* 119:1974, 36.

2. J. Cazeneuve, *La Sociologie du Rite* (Paris: Presses Universitaires de France, 1971) 14; see also Hochegger, *Le Langage des Gestes rituels*, vol. 1 (Bandundu: Ceeba, 1981).

3. Cited by V. Turner in *The Ritual Process: Structure and Anti-Structure* (Chicago: Aldine, 1973) 6.

4. P. Oliviero and T. Orel, "L'Expérience Rituel," *Recherches de Science Religieuse* 78/3:1990, 329–72, esp. 331–4.

5. Ibid., 334–5.

6. See T. W. Jennings, "On Ritual Knowledge," *Journal of Religion* 62/2:1982, 111–27, esp. 111.

7. R. Grainger, *The Language of the Rite* (London: Darton, Longman and Todd, 1974) 21; see also his *The Message of the Rite: The Significance of Christian Rites of Passage* (Cambridge: Lutterworth Press, 1988) 12–13.

8. D. Tracy, *Blessed Rage for Order* (New York: Seabury Press, 1975) 93.

9. Jennings, "On Ritual Knowledge," 113.

10. Grainger, *The Language of the Rite,* 19–20.

11. Jennings, "On Ritual Knowledge," 113; Grainger, *The Language of the Rite,* 10.

12. V. Turner, *The Drums of Affliction* (Oxford: Clarendon Press, 1968) 16; see also his *Dramas, Fields and Metaphors: Symbolic Action in Human Society* (Ithaca, N.Y., and London: Cornell University Press, 1974) 55–57.

13. E. Durkheim, *The Elementary Forms of the Religious Life,* 2nd ed. (London: George Allen and Unwin, 1976) 218–9.

14. C. Lévi-Strauss, *Totemism* (Boston: Beacon Press, 1963) 71; see also A. de Waal Malefijt, *Religion and Culture: An Introduction to the Anthropology of Religion* (New York: Macmillan Co., 1968) 58–63.

15. R. Girard, *La Violence et le Sacré* (Paris: Grasset, 1972) 59, 135; see also his *The Scapegoat,* trans. Y. Freccero (Baltimore: John Hopkins University Press, 1986).

16. See R. Girard, *Des Choses cachées depuis la Fondation du Monde,* written in collaboration with J. M. Oughourlian and G. Lefort (Paris: Grasset, 1978).

17. It is the experience of Greeks and Romans, of Jews and Igbo. See R. K. Yerkes, *Sacrifice in Greek and Roman Religions and Early Judaism* (London: Adam and Charles Black, 1953); F. A. Arinze, *Sacrifice in Ibo Religion* (Ibadan: Ibadan University Press, 1970).

18. The points of ritual as play is well developed by H. Rahner in his *Man at Play,* trans. B. Battershaw and E. Quinn (New York: Herder and Herder, 1967) esp. 7, 11–17. See also J. Huizinga, *Homo Ludens* (Boston: Beacon Press, 1953); J. J. MacAloon, "Sociation and Sociability in Political Celebrations," *Celebration: Studies in Festivity and Ritual,* ed. V. Turner (Washington, D.C.: Smithsonian Institute Press, 1982) 255–71.

19. For the views of B. Malinowski, see his *Magic, Science and Religion* (Garden City, N.Y.: Anchor Books, 1954) esp. 40, 67–68; see also Turner, *Dramas, Fields and Metaphors,* esp. chs. 1 and 7; M. Bloch, *Ritual, History and Power: Selected Papers in Anthropology* (London: Athlone Press, 1989) especially his treatment of "the past and the present in the present."

20. Bloch, *Ritual History and Power,* 42–43.

21. Ibid., 25.

22. J. L. Austin, *How to Do Things with Words* (Cambridge, Mass.: Harvard University Press, 1962) 234; cited by Bloch, *Ritual, History and Power,* 32. See also F. Marty, "Signe, Symbole, Sacrement," *Recherches de Science Religieuse,* 75/2:April–June 1987, esp. 223–5.

23. Bloch, *Ritual, History and Power,* 41–42.

24. See MacAloon, "Sociation," 255–6. See also T. O. Beidelman, "Swazi Royal Ritual," *Africa* 36/4:1966, 373–405; H. Kuper, "A Ritual Kingship among the Swazi," *Africa* 14/1944, 230–56.

25. See A. Vergote, *Dette et Désir* (Paris: Seuil, 1978) 136–7.

26. E. M. Zeusse, *Ritual Cosmos: The Sanctification of Life in African Religions* (Athens: Ohio University Press, 1979) esp. ch. 1. See also C. Gaba, *Scriptures of an African People: The Sacred Utterances of the Anlo* (Maryknoll, N.Y.: Orbis Books, 1973) 3–4.

27. J. S. Mbiti, *African Religions and Philosophy* (London: Heinemann, 1969) 67.

28. R. Horton, "Judaeo-Christian Spectacles: Boon or Bane to the Study of African Religions," *Cahiers d'Etudes Africaines* 96/24–4:1984, 391–436. See also his "Ritual Man in Africa," *Africa* 34:1964, 85–103; "African Traditional

Thought and Western Science: Part I: From Tradition to Science," *Africa* 37:1967, 50–71; "Part II: The 'Closed' and 'Open' Predicaments," *Africa* 37:1967, 153–87; "African Conversion," *Africa* 41/2:1971, 85–108.

29. For the openness to change among the Igbo see S. Ottenberg, "Ibo Receptivity to Change," *Continuity and Change in African Cultures,* ed. W. R. Bascom and M. J. Herskovits (Chicago: University of Chicago Press, 1959) 130–43. See also V. C. Uchendu, *The Igbo of Southeast Nigeria* (New York: Holt, Rinehart and Winston, 1965); Uzukwu, "Igbo World and Ultimate Reality and Meaning," *Ultimate Reality and Meaning* 5/3:1984, 84–101. For the elasticity of Yoruba perception of knowledge see W. Soyinka, *Myth, Literature and the African World* (London: Cambridge University Press, 1967) 53–54. H. S. Levinson debunks Horton's picture of traditional religion in his "Traditional Religion, Modernity and Unthinkable Thoughts," *Journal of Religion* 41:1981, 37–58.

30. See J. La Fontaine, *Initiation: Ritual Drama and Secret Knowledge Across the World* (Middlesex: Penguin, 1985) 125.

31. Zeusse, *Ritual Cosmos,* 3.

32. This information was supplied in a study on *liturgical assembly* collectively done by the students of the Kongo ethnic group in 1982, Grand Seminaire Jean XXIII, Kinshasa, Zaire.

33. B. Albrektson, *History and the Gods: An Essay on the Idea of Historical Events as Divine Manifestations in the Ancient Near East and in Israel* (Lund: CWK Gleerup, 1967) 113; see also J. Barr, "Story and History in Biblical Theology," *Theology Digest* 24:1976, 265–7.

34. See, for example, J. H. Hayes and J. M. Miller, eds., *Israelite and Judaean History* (Philadelphia: Westminster Press, 1977) esp. ch. 4.

35. R. de Vaux did a detailed study of the ritual in the sanctuaries in his *Ancient Israel: Its Life and Institutions* (London: Darton, Longman and Todd, 1961).

36. Ibid., 291–2; F. M. Cross, *Canaanite Myth and Hebrew Epic: Essays in the History of the Religion of Israel* (Cambridge, Mass.: Harvard University Press, 1973) chs. 2–3.

37. L. Deiss, *Vivre la Parole en Communaute* (Paris: Desclee de Brouwer, 1974) 32; English translation: *God's Word and God's People,* trans. M. J. O'Connell (Collegeville: The Liturgical Press, 1976) 9.

38. See H. Cazelles, "L'Assemblée liturgique et les différents Rôles dans l'ancien Testament," *L'Assemblée liturgique et les différents Rôles dans l'Assemblée,* 131–42, esp. 131.

39. N. K. Gottwald proposes this line of interpretation in his *The Tribes of Yahweh: A Sociology of the Religion of Liberated Israel* 1250–1050 B.C.E. (Maryknoll, N.Y.: Orbis Books, 1979) esp. 77, 88–99. We shall explore Gottwald's interpretation in greater detail in the next chapter.

40. G. von Rad, *Old Testament Theology: Vol. I: The Theology of Israel's Traditions* (Edinburgh: Oliver and Boyd, 1962) 187–90.

41. See D. J. McCarthy, *Treaty and Covenant: A Study in Form in the Ancient Oriental Documents and in the Old Testament* (Rome: Pontifical Biblical Institute, 1963).

42. J. Milgrom, *Studies in Cultic Theology and Terminology* (Leiden: Brill, 1983) esp. ch. 1: "Priestly Terminology and Social Structure in Pre-Monarchic Israel."

43. For the lexicographical analysis see *"Qahal," A Hebrew and English Lexicon of the Old Testament*, ed. F. Brown, S. R. Driver, and C. A. Briggs (Oxford: Clarendon Press, 1972) 874–5. See also L. Deiss, *Vivre la Parole en Communauté*, 57–59; A. Medebielle, "Église," *Dictionnaire de la Bible*, ed. L. Pirot, Supplement II (Paris: Letouzey et Ane, 1934) esp. 487–90.

44. Josephus, Antiquities 14.10.8.

45. See the concise theological statement on Jesus' resurrection by E. Schillebeeckx in his *The Church: The Human Story of God* (New York: Crossroad, 1990) 127–32.

46. Ibid., 129.

47. See the analysis of the passage by D. E. Smith and H. E. Taussig, *Many Tables: The Eucharist in the New Testament and Liturgy Today* (London and Philadelphia: SCM and Trinity Press International, 1990) 44–50. For a recent work on Q see J. S. Kloppenberg, *The Formation of Q: Trajectories in Ancient Wisdom Collections* (Philadelphia: Fortress Press, 1987).

48. Smith and Taussig, *Many Tables*, 21–28. See Plato, *Symposium* 176E; Sirach 9:14-16. Citations from the Mishnah are taken from J. Neusner, *The Mishnah: A New Translation* (New Haven, Conn., and London: Yale University Press, 1988).

49. Schillebeeckx, *The Church*, 147. See also R. Banks, *Paul's Idea of Community: The Early House Churches in their Historical Setting* (Grand Rapids, Mich.: Eerdmans, 1980) 22; Meeks, *The First Urban Christians*, esp. ch. 3.

50. The *Tefillah* is the eighteen or nineteen prayers of petition that conclude the synagogue worship. *Birkat ha-minim* is the twelfth benediction. We shall refer to the *Tefillah* in greater detail in the next chapter.

51. E. S. Fiorenza makes an incisive analysis of this passage in her *In Memory of Her: A Feminist Theological Reconstruction of Christian Origins* (New York: Crossroad, 1988) ch. 6; see also Banks, *Paul's Idea of Community*, ch. 2.

52. See W. A. Meeks, *The First Urban Christians: The Social World of the Apostle Paul* (New Haven, Conn., and London: Yale University Press, 1983) 154–7.

53. Fiorenza, *In Memory of Her*, 213.

54. Meeks, *The First Urban Christians*, 159. Meeks cites the work of G. Theissen, *Studien zur Soziologie des Urchristentums* (Tübingen: Mohr [Siebeck], 1979) 312.

55. Smith and Taussig, *Many Tables*, 62.

56. See Meeks, *The First Urban Christians;* Banks, *Paul's Idea of Community;* R. E. Brown, "New Testament Background for the Concept of Local Church,"

Proceedings of the 36th Annual Convention of the Catholic Theological Society of America, 10–13 June 1981, 36:1982, 1–14; Fiorenza, *In Memory of Her,* ch. 5; Schillebeeckx, *The Church,* 144–54.

57. Banks, *Paul's Idea of Community,* 36.

58. Ibid., 36–37; Brown, "New Testament Background," 5.

59. Brown, "New Testament Background," 8–9; see also his detailed and suggestive description of the ecclesiologies of these churches in his *The Churches the Apostles Left Behind* (New York: Paulist Press, 1984).

60. See J. Jeremias, *The Eucharistic Words of Jesus* (London: SCM Press, 1973) 175–6 and footnotes.

61. The issue is controverted. H. Lietzmann is of the view that the celebrations were mainly with bread ("bread Eucharists"); see his *Mass and Lord's Supper,* introduction and supplementary essay by R. D. Richardson (Leiden: Brill, 1953) 200–1. Dix rejects Lietzmann's thesis in his *The Shape of the Liturgy* (London: Dacre, 1975) 61–63. Jeremias and Achtemeier support the view of the practice of simple breaking of bread. See Jeremias, *The Eucharistic Words of Jesus,* 52, 115; P. J. Achtemeier, "The Origin and Function of the Pre-Marcan Miracle Catenae," *Journal of Biblical Literature* 91:1972, esp. 213–7.

62. The Lucan narrative has been analyzed in detail by L. M. Chauvet in his *Du Symbolique au Symbole* (Paris: Cerf, 1979). See also H. Denis, "Les Sacrements font l'Église-Sacrement," *La Maison Dieu* 152:1982, 13. M. Eliade's definition of myth is applicable to our type of narrative. See his *Myths, Dreams and Mysteries* (London: Collins, 1974) 16. Credit goes to G. Dix for insisting that the seven principal gestures of Jesus influencing the structure of the Eucharistic rite of the Church be reduced to four. See his *The Shape of the Liturgy,* 48.

63. L. L. Thompson, *The Book of Revelation: Apocalypse and Empire* (New York and Oxford: Oxford University Press, 1990) 5.

64. Ibid., 56. C. J. Hemer more than any recent author has tried to locate the social-historical setting of the references in the Apocalypse. See his *The Letters to the Seven Churches of Asia in their Local Setting,* Journal for the Study of the New Testament, Supplement Series 11 (Sheffield: JSOT Press, 1986).

65. Thompson, *The Book of Revelation,* 16–17.

66. U. Vanni, "The Ecclesial Assembly 'Interpreting Subject' of the Apocalypse," *Religious Studies Bulletin* 4/3:1984, 79–85. See also J. A. Grassi, "The Liturgy of Revelation," *Bible Today* 24/1:1986, 30–37.

67. Thompson, *The Book of Revelation,* 53ff.

68. E. S. Fiorenza, *The Book of Revelation: Justice and Judgment* (Philadelphia: Fortress Press, 1985) 46–47.

69. Thompson, *The Book of Revelation,* 63–69; Fiorenza, *The Book of Revelation,* 68–81.

70. Ashamani, "The Orthodox Liturgy and the Apocalypse," *Patristic and Byzantine Review* 9/1:1990, 30–37.

71. See P. Prigent, *Apocalypse et Liturgie* (Neuchatel: Delachaux et Niestlé, 1964) 49–55.

72. Ibid., 57.

73. See L. Bouyer, *Eucharist: Theology and Spirituality of the Eucharistic Prayer* (Notre Dame: University of Notre Dame Press, 1968) 66; E. Cothenet, "Liturgie terrestre et Liturgie céleste d'après l'Apocalypse," *L'Assemblée Liturgique*, 143–66, esp. 154–7. For the text of the *Qedushat* see R. Hedegard, *Seder Rav Amram Gaon: Part I: Hebrew Texts with Critical Apparatus, Translation with Notes and Introduction* (Lund: a.-B.Ph. Lindestedts Universitets-Bokhandel, 1951) 48–49. See also E. R. Goodenough, *By Light, Light: The Mystic Gospel of Hellenistic Judaism* (New Haven, Conn.: Yale University Press, 1935) esp. ch. 11: "The Mystic Liturgy."

74. Hedegard, *Seder Rav Amram Gaon*, 46–49.

75. Thompson, *The Book of Revelation*, 58. See also D. E. Aune, "The Influence of Roman Imperial Court on the Apocalypse of John," *Biblical Research* 28:1983, 5–26.

76. See 1 Chr 24:1-19; Mishnah *Taanith* (On Fasting) 4:1-2.

77. See Ashamani, "The Orthodox Liturgy and the Apocalypse," 31–33.

78. M. H. Shepherd does not hesitate in calling the liturgy of the Apocalypse a paschal liturgy. In his view Revelation 4–5 is the liturgy of the paschal vigil. See his *The Paschal Liturgy and the Apocalypse* (London: Lutterworth Press, 1960) esp. 77–84, 87–89. This view is shared by Prigent in his *Apocalypse et Liturgie*, 69–79. However, Aune rejects the widely held view that the heavenly liturgy of the Apocalypse is a projection of a liturgy celebrated by Christians. He rather argues that Roman imperial court ceremonial exerted the preponderant influence. See his "The Influence of the Roman Imperial Court on the Apocalypse of John."

79. Thompson, *The Book of Revelation*, 59.

80. The *Berakah* characterizes Jewish synagogue worship. See chapter three below.

81. See Fiorenza, *The Book of Revelation*, 72–74.

82. Thompson, *The Book of Revelation*, 71.

83. See Thompson, *The Book of Revelation*, 69–71; V. Turner, *The Ritual Process*, 94ff.

84. *The Martyrdom of Justin*, Recension A.3.1, in *The Acts of the Christian Martyrs*, introduction, texts, and translations by H. Musurillo (Oxford: Clarendon Press, 1972).

85. P. Grelot, "Du Sabbat juif au Dimanche chretien," *La Maison Dieu* 124 (1975) 14–54, esp. 17.

Chapter Three

Foundation Stories (Myth-Symbols) and the Theology of Worship

The previous chapters indicate to us two major dispositions of an assembled religious community or of a body susceptible to being convoked in assembly for religious purposes: the ritual-gesture of gathering together to perform certain rites (verbal and nonverbal) and the projection of the central story of the group that may be narrated or reenacted during the liturgical assembly. Sometimes the story may simply constitute a background for linking the assembly to its ritual anchor (the sacred or referent of ritual). These two dispositions are intimately connected. In the Kongo (African) assembly the clan ancestors form the key referents to which the ritual action of the community is bound. In the Jewish and Christian gatherings, life is woven around the foundational stories of the Exodus-settlement and the cross-resurrection of Jesus the Christ.

The foundation stories and the referents of ritual are symbolic. They are collective representations that shape the world for the group and shape behavior (ritual and ethical) to respond in an ordered pattern.

In this chapter, we will explore the impact of the foundation stories on the community highlighting their intimate relation to the community's ritual action. This will be followed by samples of these stories. Our sample stories are the Nri myth of origin that comes from the Igbo of Nigeria, the *Enuma Elish* of ancient Babylonia, and the Jewish and Christian Exodus-settlement and cross-resurrection stories. It is true that there are differences in the way the foundation story is perceived among Jews, Christians, and other groups. But we use myth (or myth-symbol) to describe all these stories, knowing that in the

Christian story, for example, there is a historical core. But insofar as it is symbolic history, as opposed to documentary history, the story functions as myth (though a broken myth).[1] The examples will show how the stories shape and are shaped by worship. Our reflection will draw out the theological implications of the action of the community in relationship to the foundation story.

MYTH-SYMBOL AS RELATED TO RITUAL-SYMBOL

Describing the Myth

The basic thing one may say about the myth (*mythus* in Greek), which will command unanimity among the various disciplines (e.g., classics, literary criticism, religion, sociology, etc.), is that the myth is a tale. The difference between the myth-story and other kinds of stories, and the function of the myth within any social group, remains a matter of controversy.[2] The classicist and literary critic interested in the content of the myth in Greek classics and other literary texts (oral and written) prefer a wide definition of myth. They are not preoccupied with its social and religious functions. Rather, they like to highlight its character as tale, its tendency to fantasy, and, consequently, the facility with which it dislocates the logical order of things. They relate myth to legends, fables, folktales, etc., from which the myth differs not in nature but in quality. This underscores the aesthetic and imaginative dimension of the myth. Thus Okpewho, after a critical review of the various theories, defines myth as

"simply that quality of fancy which informs the creative or configurative powers of the human mind in varying degrees of intensity. In that sense we are free to call any narrative of the oral tradition a myth, so long as it gives due emphasis to fanciful play. It is the quality of fanciful play that provides one solid structural link between several generations of the concept of myth, first as oral narrative and now as fanciful idea (even a dominating one)."[3]

On his part Kirk, a classicist, after a thorough survey of the theories of myth, settled for the minimal definition: "Myths are at the very least tales that have been passed down from generation to generation, that have become traditional." And a tale is traditional by its narrative quality, functional quality, or both. Kirk lays special emphasis on the quality of fantasy and dislocation, which is the distinguishing mark of myths that have developed into a tradition. This quality may arise from the storytelling itself, from making use of material drawn from dreams, and from concern with the supernatural.[4]

One may then appreciate the complaint of the classicist or the literary critic about the way philosophers, ethnologists, psychoanalysts, historians of religion, etc., work with universalizing theories of the myth. For example, the myth has been defined as allegorical, aetiological, or as "charters of social facts and beliefs" by the nineteenth-century nature-myth school, Andrew Lang, and Malinowski, respectively. Robertson Smith propagated the idea that myths are an account for rituals misunderstood. Psychoanalysts (Freud and Jung) elaborated them as reflections of unconscious fears or the collective unconscious determined by archetypes, and Lévi-Strauss described them as a reproduction of the common structures of mind and society. Whatever the merits of these theories, they all err by their dogmatism.[5]

More dogmatic and prejudicial to our grasp of the myth are those theories that are ethnocentric. Ethnographic material drawn from non-Western peoples (enslaved, colonized, or both) has been harnessed to bolster the Western ideology of dominance, leading to a cultural definition of the non-Western human as a radically different type. Darwinian biological evolution was clothed with racial characteristics to invent the savage.[6] The myth (story) lost its symbolic character, and attention was focused on mythic ("mythopoeic") mentality (Tylor, Levy-Burhl). Ethnologists, psychoanalysts, and philosophers talked with little restraint about "savage races" who reproduce a pattern of life and thinking comparable to European antiquity. These "savages" deify their dead (Euhemerism); they live in a twilight state of consciousness where dreaming and experiencing are indistinguishable. Consequently, "the primitive does not think *consciously*," rather, for him, "thoughts appear." "The primitive mentality does not *invent* myth; it *experiences* them" (Jung). In this way Jung's primitives are distinct from the civilized West. The famous Jungian *archetypes* that exert positive influence today in the interpretation of symbols and myths are tainted with racism. The archetypes are general symbols that manifest themselves through the unconscious mind in myths, dreams, delusions, and folklore. There is an instinctive trend in humans to form these representations, as birds have the impulse to build nests. But since the archetypes throw a bridge between the consciousness of the present and the unconscious and instinctive primeval past, there is no doubt that archetypes differ, as to their formation, in the "primitive" and "civilized" minds.[7] Jung and others may have toned down their excessive language, but "mythical mentality" and "humanity in its infancy" are still current in some quarters.[8] We draw attention to such exaggerations by stalwarts like Jung to caution against a narrow approach to the myth and to emphasize the benefits of an interdisciplinary approach.

The appreciation of the myth as literature in which the imagination and fantasy are fully deployed is certainly a very helpful way of interpreting it. After all, the myth is basically a story (oral or written literature). But the variety of views expressed on the characteristics of the myth show that aesthetics is not the only attraction of myth. The myth says something about the universe, about people living in the universe, about human societies that delight in reciting these myths. There are certain fundamental qualities of the myth that have been highlighted by the human sciences. Without absolutizing any one of them, a brief outline of these qualities may help us appreciate the surplus meaning encountered in myth.

Qualities of the Myth

We have already referred to the various theories of the myth. When we talk about the qualities of myth we try to integrate the various facets that may have been absolutized in one theory or the other. In this way we hope to expose the richness of myth. Following Campbell's categories,[9] while not always following his elaborate arguments, we describe the qualities under four special functions: the metaphysical-mystical, the cosmological, the social, and the psychological functions.

In the metaphysical-mystical aspect, the religious function of the myth predominates. Not all myths are religious. However, the supernatural figures prominently in many myths and constitutes the background for most myths. When the fabulous events of the beginning are recounted (primordial history), the gods move in and out; they are other but the same with the dynamic cosmos. Founding ancestors and heros are drawn larger than life. And the human species, in the elementary form, is shown to be dependent. To the *homo religiosus* the myth necessarily incorporates the divine structure: the theophany that calls for awe, humility, respect, and, consequently, worship. For the *homo religiosus*, the myth-symbol implicates ritual as a necessary complement.[10]

Second, the fabulous narrative projecting the divine or prompted by the divine ground is about cosmic origins. Eliade has argued that the cosmogonic is the fundamental myth: the emergence of the reality called the cosmos and its mode of being. All other myths share, in one way or the other, in the cosmogonic myth. The importance of creation myths as protomyths becomes manifest when one narrates the origin of any single type of being in the universe. All these prolong the story of how the cosmos came into being and the very order of being. Thus, according to Eliade, all mythology is also ontophany.[11] Campbell, no doubt, makes a point in insisting that it is not the archaic religious texts, but science that gives us cosmology today.[12] But the language of these narratives, insofar as it is about origins, continues to differ from science and to maintain its value as we shall see below.

Third, the cosmogonic narrative, and other narratives of origin (like the theophany narrated in *Enuma Elish*), have impact on society: they not only show that something has happened *in illo tempore,* but this event is exemplary, establishing a pattern of human behavior. Again Eliade, drawing from Malinowski, has emphasized this paradigmatic aspect of the myth: "It relates how things came into being, providing the exemplary model and also the justifications of man's activities."[13] In this way the myth roots ethics and ritual into the very structure of being. It ensures, as Campbell says, "the enforcement of a moral order: the shaping of the individual to the requirements of his geographically and historically conditioned social group."[14] This social dimension of the myth, which science cannot replace, has far-reaching implications for the evolution of cultures and civilizations. As Schelling states, "It is not by its history that the mythology of a nation is determined, but, conversely, its history is determined by its mythology."[15] This paradigmatic quality of the myth will be illustrated in detail in the examples presented below.

Finally, while ideals of the group are renewed through ritual memorial of the myth or through the application of these ideals in ethical, political, or economic domains, the *myth addresses each individual personally (consciously or unconsciously).* Jung's archetypes, i.e., the general symbols rooted in the unconscious mind, are revealed in this aspect of the myth. The individual thus arrives at an emotional, psychical, and spiritual satisfaction. This psychological function of myth is, for Campbell, the "most vital, most critical function of mythology":

"to foster the centering and unfolding of the individual in integrity, in accord with d) himself (the microcosm), c) his culture (the mesocosm), b) the universe (the macrocosm), and a) the awesome ultimate mystery which is both beyond and within himself and all things:

'Wherefrom words turn back,
Together with the mind, not having attained.'"[16]

The kind of myth that addresses the individual person, as described above, creating harmony in the self (conscious-unconscious), must be a dynamic and living myth. Something that operates not only on the individual unconscious, but also on the collective unconscious. Jung is thus correct in insisting that we need such myths to "frame a view of the world which adequately explains the meaning of psychic wholeness, from the cooperation between conscious and unconscious."[17] Such a myth becomes a foundational symbol so powerful as to carry us away, embody us in itself, and move us so deeply as we surrender ourselves to it.[18] In their quest to produce this kind of effect in human life, all sciences (natural and human) meet and show themselves to be cultural systems (Polanyi). While Jung calls this symbol archetypes, Polanyi refers to it as tacit dimensions of our knowing, and Kuhn talks about paradigms.

The satisfaction the myth-narrative brings to the individual and the group is experienced in all religious systems. As Jung says, the worst evil that may befall an individual or a society is the loss or collapse of myth.[19] The need is as vital in a modern high-tech society as it is in societies with simple technology. No kind of esoteric mentality, society, or culture generates mythic thoughts. The operation of the human mind is basically the same (Lévi-Strauss). Though Polanyi amplifies: "the cognitive process in both the primitive and the modern mind . . . is rooted in the same principles, but the results differ because archaic thought tends to be based *on more far-reaching tacit integrations* than are acceptable to the scientific mind of modern man."[20] This caveat notwithstanding, the living myth is dynamic, moving peoples and cultures to venture beyond the familiar and to embrace the depth and mystery that life is to all of us.[21]

Myth and Its Relationship to Ritual

Myth and ritual belong together. This statement does not overlook the insistence of classicists and literary critics that some myths are narrated for amusement and entertainment, while others are narrated for intellectual edification.[22] Again, the statement does not imply that myth derives from ritual, nor ritual from myth. There are certainly stories that have no ritual counterparts, and many rituals are not reenactments of myths. But the two belong together because they represent human primordial expressions of the experience of the impact of the universe. Both are a representation of beliefs about the cosmic order; a part of the distress of humans in exploring and expressing the great mystery the world (and life in the world) is to all of us.[23] Thus it is not surprising that at the most intensive narration by any community of its sacred history, which gives it identity in the universe, the recitation takes place in ritual assembly; sometimes, there is a ritual execution (reenactment) of the foundation story.

Myths are also narrated for entertainment and intellectual edification. But insofar as these tales belong to the community (even if invented by poets, Plato), they elicit adequate gestures when narrated in a gathering. This is very much the case in African communities where word and gesture are happily integrated. Oftentimes it happens that the gestures or responses of the audience exercise an influence on the story leading to further amplifications. The imaginative dimension of the myth anticipates such amplifications.

It is important to insist that adequate gestures accompany storytelling in assemblies (even if such a gesture is immobility or intense listening). Such gestures (body movement) and the story belong together. The style of the body movement assumes more or less regularity (consistency) depending on the type of story and kind of gathering. But in those gatherings that are religious in nature, the rhythm of the movement and the narrative assume a definite style (ritual). Thus in affirming that myth and ritual belong together, we draw attention first of all to the tendency to act out a story being narrated — action being the reverse side of the narrative and in no way inferior to the narrative. Then in the context of the religious assembly, the merging of the myth and ritual within the one liturgical action shows how ritual and myth are profoundly concerned with the same subject: the dialectics of the human condition experienced in relation to the sacred, and the successful presentation of the whole picture of human life in the universe in a way that makes sense to the assembled participants.

SAMPLES OF SACRED NARRATIVES AND THEIR IMPACT ON THE LIFE OF THE COMMUNITY

We have shown that the myth is a story. It is about the life of the community inserted within its universe. Depending on the type of narrative, the community's self-definition is more or less exposed in the myth. But in religious myths (foundation stories or sacred histories), there is a profound display of the "self" of the community: a display where the language of gesture merges with the verbal narrative to generate (regenerate) the social body. Here the word becomes flesh — the story *(mythus)* is ritualized or gives voice to the assembly's ritual action. The narrative, which is by nature retrospective, merges the past with the present through memory. It makes the assembled community relive those actions that established it as community.

As we noted above, our samples of myths will be drawn from (1) an African community (the Igbo of Nigeria), (2) the Babylonian past *(Enuma Elish)*, and (3) the Jewish and Christian traditions. The purpose is to demonstrate how living religious myths, reflecting a primordial experience of the cosmos, shape (and are shaped by) the life of the community (especially in the domains of worship and ethical behavior). Our commentary on the primordial experience as contained in each narrative and as applied especially to the ritual life of a given community displays the theological dimensions of worship.

The choice of an African myth is guided not only by the interest to show the dynamics of myth-making in African communities, but also to clearly maintain the African orientation in our description and exploration of Christian worship. The Babylonian story *(Enuma Elish)*, though no longer practiced, exercised a considerable influence in the Mesopotamian world. Peoples of the Ancient Near East (including Semites) lived under mutual influence, a situation of acculturation. Thus Hebrew religion will be shown to form part and parcel of the environment that spawned it. The Jewish practice, needless to say, has fundamental influence on the Christian way. Similarly, New Testament communities and Christian communities of all times read their sacred history as a new Exodus (Passover) that Jesus achieved through his death-resurrection. Each of these narratives shapes and is shaped by life in a given community. Allowing each to speak within its context helps us to examine the connection between the story and its application to life.

The Nri (Igbo) Myth of Origin and Its Reenactment in Igbo Life and Worship

Situating the Igbo

The Igbo constitute one of the three major ethnic groups of Nigeria (West Africa). They number between fifteen and twenty million. They live on both banks of the Niger between five and seven degrees north latitude and six and eight degrees east longitude. Their neighbors are the Tiv, Igala, and Idoma (to the north), the Ekoi and Ibibio (to the east), and the Ijaw and Edo (to the south and west respectively). In addition to the river Niger (and its tributaries like the Anambra river), the Igbo country is watered by the Imo, Cross, and Ulasi rivers. It falls within the rain forest belt. However, demographic explosion and the long period of human habitation in the Igbo country have led to the disappearance of the rain forest and the deterioration of the land.

Recent archeological finds in Ugwuele (Uturu, Okigwe, Abia State) strongly suggest that Stone Age humans inhabited the Igbo country between 200,000 and 250,000 years ago. The discoveries revealed "the largest handaxe factory in Nigeria if not in the world," and may have provided "the earliest evidence of man in Nigeria."[24] Excavations in the Cross River (Afikpo) and northern Igbo (Nsukka) areas yielded tools and ancient pottery carbon dated to about 4,500 years ago. The similarity between the ancient pottery work and those found today in Nsukka suggests a degree of ethnographic continuity.[25] Finally, the results of archaeological work in Igbo-ukwu (Anambra State) revealed a highly developed practice of priest-kingship (Nri culture) and a facility with bronze existing before the ninth century C.E.[26] All these go to show that humans have been interacting with the environment for thousands of years in the key culture centers of the geographical area inhabited today by the Igbo.

The Igbo, who belong to the Kwa linguistic group of the Niger-Congo language family, lack a collective oral tradition of migration and settlement.[27] There is no common ancestry. Rather, each village-group (a community of kindreds with or without a common ancestor) is aware of its identity as a political unit. However, the language, customs, cosmological ideas, and religious practices are features common to all Igbo (though with local variations). Two centers have been marked out by historians as the core culture areas from which the Igbo dispersed to all the areas they occupy today: Nri-Awka in Anambra State and Amaigbo-Orlu in Imo State. Oriji, in his recent study, accepts these primary core centers and argues for secondary and tertiary core areas whose traditions are also of great antiquity.[28]

The Nri-Awka axis is the most popular culture center in Igboland. During the colonial period, Nri practically eclipsed the Amaigbo-Orlu area, which has little or no experience of Nri hegemony.[29] Leonard, tickled by Nri ritual ascendancy over a large segment of Igboland, could find only one proverb to support this religious domination: "The street of Nri family is the street of the gods, through which all who die in other parts of Iboland pass to the land of the Spirits."[30] Nri is holy land! It gives protection to fugitives and abhors bloodshed. The privileged role it plays in Igbo life is rooted in its myth of origin. Since the excavated site at Igboukwu revealed religio-political and economic artifacts of Iron Age strain, historians believe that settlements around the Nri-Awka axis were completed before the migrations to other centers. These migrations are estimated to have taken place between 500 B.C.E. and 500 C.E.[31]

The Nri Myth

The myth reproduced below was narrated by Nwaokoye Odenigbo and recorded by M. A. Onwuejeogwu (in 1966 and 1968). It is thus not a tale narrated in a cultic or liturgical setting. It suffers from the limitations of all such tales narrated to anthropologists — the narrator being inclined to the dramatic in an effort to impress the researcher. However, Odenigbo's narrative compares well with earlier observations by N. Thomas (1913–14) and M.D.W. Jeffreys (1935–36).[32] Parts of the narrative (italicized) are commentaries by the narrator reflecting beliefs and practices of the Nri and Igbo people. These amplifications (unavoidable in myth-narratives) may be regarded as part of the myth. The numbering of the paragraphs is introduced to facilitate commentary.

"1. The father of all Nri was Eri. No one knows where he came from. Tradition *[odinani]* says he came from God [Chukwu]. *He was a great man sent by God to rule all the people of Anambra. Before he came to the Anambra the people were living in scattered huts. They had no king.*

"2. It is said that the earth was not firm, as it is today, when he was on earth. He got Awka smiths to use bellows to dry the flooded land. *The Anambra at times floods its banks.*

"3. When he came there was no food for the people. He prayed to God *[Chukwu]* to send food to his people. God demanded that he should sacrifice his first son and daughter to him. He did the sacrifice and buried his children. Yam and palm tree grew out of the spot where he buried his son, and vegetables and cocoyam grew out of the spot where he buried his daughter. *This is why the first son and daughter of Eze Nri after his coronation have* ichi *marks made on their faces seven days after birth. This is also why all male children of Nri must take the* ichi *title. Eri brought yam and all food. The earth produces it. The 'earth force' is great.*

"4. *Thus there was a covenant between earth and man. The earth produces the food that man eats. The earth becomes the greatest supernatural force* [alusi]. *Eri controlled yam and other food and the earth that grows them. No person should defile the earth by spilling human blood in violence on it. This is the covenant. It must be kept. We Nri keep it. We told other Igbo to whom we gave yam to keep it.*

"5. Eri was rich and had two wives. The first bore Ifikuanim, the father of the founder of Aguleri, the father of the founder of Igboariam, the father of the founder of Amanuke, the mother of the father of the founders of Awkuzu, Nteje, Nnando. His second wife bore Onoja Oboli, who left the Anambra and founded Igala.

"6. It was Eri who brought the great supernatural beings *[alusi]* of Eke, Afo, Nkwo and Oye. These four *alusi* visited him in the form of a person and concealed their names. In the night Eri's messenger sent rats to enter the baskets of fish of these *alusi.* When the rat has entered that of Eke, Oye called 'Eke! Eke! A rat has entered your basket.' They slept. Then the rat entered that of Oye, and Afo cried out 'Oye! Oye! A rat was in your basket.' The rat entered that of Afo, and Nkwo cried out 'Afo! Afo! A rat has entered your basket.' The rat finally entered that of Nkwo, and Eke cried out 'Nkwo! Nkwo! A rat has entered your basket.' In the morning Eze Nri greeted his *alusi* friends by calling their names one after the other. They were surprised. They established four market days which are found in all Igbo settlements. Then they disappeared. *Eke, Oye, Afo, and Nkwo are all the market supernatural beings today. I am Isi Nze of Uruoji and I am the chief priest of Anwoye. I shall tell you about Anwoye next time.*

"7. You can see that Eri was a great man from God. He communicated with Chukwu. He brought yam and other food. He brought the days of the week. He told blacksmiths to go around doing things for the Ozo title. Igbo had no yams and he brought yams to them. Igbo had no titles and he brought titles.
"8. Eri lived and died. . . ."

Interpretive Commentary[33]

It is already noted that the storyteller included commentaries in the myth-narrative. In this way he shows how the myth is being lived by the Nri and Igbo communities. The narrative is also not within the context of cult. Indeed there is no evidence that there is a recitation of the Nri myth during any ritual celebration. Rather the myth proclaims a sociocultural and cosmic order that is reenacted in the life of the Nri priest-king, who is a reproduction of the founding hero; it is also reenacted in the various dimensions of Nri and Igbo life (ritual, political, social, and economic).

Eri is presented as the civilizing hero of Nri and Igbo world. His appearance in Nri (the world) is miraculous. Other oral histories may show evidence that the Nri migrated from Igala land (northern neighbors of the Igbo). But the fabulous in the myth would convert the migration into a miracle ("No one knows where he came from") and tie it to creative (cosmic) action: "Chukwu sent Eri to this earth" (§1). Instead of linking his descent to Igala land, as oral history suggests, he is projected as the ancestor of the Igala: "His second wife bore Onoja Oboli who left Anambra and founded Igala" (§5).

Arriving on earth the hero encountered two kinds of disorder (chaos): sociopolitical — "They had no kings" (§1) — and cosmic (telluric) — "The earth was not firm" (§2). Here two stories may have been merged. The myth about the resolution of the cosmic disorder may have antedated the myth of kingship. However, since kingship is an ancient practice in Nri it may be difficult to say exactly when both motifs were merged. In the report of N. Thomas, the founding myth is introduced as the story about the origin of kingship:

"The traditional account of the origin of kingship is that Ezenri and Ezeadama came from heaven and rested on an ant heap; all was water. Cuku asked who was sitting there and they answered, 'We are the kings of Nri and Adama,' therefore Cuku and the kings talked. After some conversation Cuku gave them each a piece of yam; yams were at that time unknown to man, for human beings walked in the bush like animals."[34]

The sociopolitical disorder shows that people already lived on earth before the arrival of the hero. But they were not fully human (civilized): they had no king and there was no agriculture. As the account of Thomas puts it, "Human beings walked in the bush like animals." The establishment of kingship is uppermost in the mind of the myth-makers as the mark of civilization (§7). In Thomas' narrative Ezenri and Ezeadama (Ezeadama is king of the original inhabitants of Nri land) descended from heaven already as kings.

The cosmic chaos was resolved in collaboration with Awka smiths who used their bellows to dry up the flooded land (§2). It is possible that the experience of flooding caused by the Anambra river may have influenced this section of the myth. Nwaokoye Odenigbo's commentary points to this direction. But the myth insists that Eri took firm control of the land. It is at this stage that Eri (i.e., *mmadu*, the human type) settled on earth (Nri land). Eri is the ideal human. This differentiates him from the previous inhabitants of the land. This is what Ricoeur calls concrete universality in the myth: "Through the figure of the hero . . . experience is put on the track of existential structures: one can now say man, existence, human being, because in the myth the human type is recapitulated, summed up."[35]

The next challenge the hero faced was famine: "There was no food for the people" (§3). The solution to this problem taxed the creative genius of the hero. He prayed to God (his sender). Chukwu conceded to him the creative act by demanding a violent ritual action: fatal attack on his children — the sacrifice of his first son and daughter. It is not stated why Chukwu wanted the bloody human sacrifice, which is in a sense a type of self immolation. Other accounts of the coming of yam do not talk about violence. Thomas' story simply said that Chukwu gave yams to Ezenri and Ezeadama after their conversation. However, after this sacrifice the land was opened up to drink the sacrificial blood and to receive the remains of the sacrificed children. This marked the beginning of culture (agriculture), a beginning whose story is tied to violence. The group could settle and spread (§4) because this primordial ritual act of violence (Girard) had given them identity by binding them to the land. It was not simply ordinary land or earth. Rather they were now bound to a supernatural reality (deity *alusi*) that made itself manifest in Nri land. Consequently, they were assured of peaceful settlement (taboo against bloodshed), of nourishment (yam, cocoyam, and other plants), and of a place to bury their dead (a ritual process that is the originator of peace and prosperity).

The last founding act of the hero was the establishment of the four-day week *(eke, oye, afor,* and *nkwo).* It is a penetration of the mystery of time accomplished through a shrewdness that reflects the behavior patterns of the legendary *mbe* (tortoise). This shrewdness is reproduced in Igbo markets.

This brief commentary on the Nri myth draws out the key achievements of the civilizing hero. More important for our reflection on the theology of worship is the way this myth of origin shapes the life of the Nri and Igbo communities: in other words, the relationship between the story and the practice of life. Equally important is the way the practice of life has contributed in shaping the myth.

Life in Nri (and Igboland) as Controlled by the Myth

The way Nri religio-political and ritual life is organized shows the impact of myth in life. A people's history, according to Schelling, is shaped by its myth. Nwoga has cast doubt on the truth-value of Nri myth. Its claim that Chukwu sent Eri from heaven does not tally with oral documentary history that states that the ancestors of Nri migrated from the upper Anambra waters. In addition, according to Nwoga, the pattern of the Nri myth-narrative is influenced by colonial interest. Finally, the reference the myth makes to Chukwu should not be read as a reference to an omnipotent God, but to the oracular deity of Arochukwu.[36] It is our view that Nwoga fails to appreciate the power of fantasy in the myth. The myth lays no claim to bland documentary history. It narrates Nri origin. And, indeed, Nri myth is shown to be a true cosmogony because not only does it talk about the founding of a community and culture, but it is enfleshed in ritual and other aspects of the life of Nri and Igbo people. There is certainly a cognitive (and rational) aspect to the myth. But the power of the myth (as living myth) lies in its ability to sustain a way of living in the universe.[37] About the referent Chukwu, we do not doubt that the concept acquired amplifications through contact with Igbo neighbors, Igbo subcultures, and even with the various Christian missions. This is healthy acculturation. But it suffices for our analysis that Chukwu functions as originator of Nri and is recognized as omnipotent in the Nri-Awka culture area.[38]

The principal areas of life dominated by the Nri myth that we shall explore in this detailed reflection are (1) the religio-political (priest-kingship in Nri as a reenactment of the life of the founding hero of Nri), (2) morality and the cult of the earth deity, Ala, in Nri and Igboland, and (3) the economic life of the Igbo (especially as related to the markets).

Priest-Kingship in Nri. The priest-king in Nri is the link between the past, as established by the hero, and the present. Between the eleventh and twentieth centuries there were about fifteen kings who occupied the ancestral throne.[39] Each king traces his origin back to the founding ancestor, Eri. Each king is a ritual reproduction of Eri. The initiation rite of a new king shows that the ritual process of becoming Ezenri (Nri priest-king) follows closely the path traced by the hero in establishing the Nri kingdom. The following parallels from the ritual process make our claim clear:[40]

ERI	EZE NRI
1. No one knows where he comes from; he came from Chukwu.	1. His father must be dead; he must be shown to be the choice of Chukwu, Eri, Ancestors, and Spirits through revelations and visions confirmed by diviners; he must get the approval of the state leadership (Nze and Nzemabua) and the public.
2. The earth was not firm (flooded), but Eri took firm hold of the land.	2. He must experience the return of chaos (e.g., through deaths in his family, collapse of his compound walls in the dry season); he travels to Aguleri to obtain the lump of clay from the bottom of the Anambra river for making the ritual pot *(odudu)* for the shrine of Nri Menri (giving him a solid place in the ancestral line). He interprets, enacts, and

	abrogates laws touching the sacredness of the land *(nso ala)*; he presides over and sends priests of Ala to Igbo to supervise purificatory rituals, thereby taking firm hold of the land.
3. He introduced agriculture through violence: sacrifice of his son and daughter.	3. He performs *ichi* (facial scarification) ritual on his son and daughter born after his coronation; he has mystical powers over crops, especially the yam; he guards the yam medicine *(ogwu ji)*; he causes the miraculous ripening of a head of palm fruit.
4. He introduced the four-day week and the markets.	4. He stays four days in Aguleri to receive the blessing of Eri; he influences the passage of time by drawing the calendar of feasts and opening the new year by special proclamation.
5. Eri is spirit *(muo)* with a cult.	5. Eze Nri goes through a ritual death, is mourned and buried; he is *muo*, a living *alusi;* he is saluted as *igwe* (sky); he neither sees a corpse nor offers sacrifice.

Eze Nri is thus a ritual reproduction of Eri, the ideal human. This is very strongly expressed in the address of the presiding priest when the candidate is about to be buried in a shallow grave:

"You who are about to enter the grave, rise up again with a vivid shining body. May no sickness or harm befall you: Rise up as previous *eze* (king) Ndri have done. Rule your people with truth and justice. Go to Aguleri, obtain your *odudu*, and may you return safely to rule your people."[41]

The kind of power that Eze Nri and his lieutenants exercise over Nri and the rest of Igboland under their influence is ritual and not political. But the functioning of religion in Igbo life creates a situation where a purely religious ritual, like purification, assumes sociopolitical characteristics. The Nri are feared because of this kind of power. But they are not abhorred like the cult-slaves *(osu)*, who are totally the property of the spirits. Their ascendance is demonstrated in the way their *ofo* is given priority over that of any other village-group in their area of dominance. *Ofo* (a branch cut from the *detarium senegalense* tree) is not only a symbol of truth and uprightness, but also a symbol of authority and agnatic hierarchy. *Nri ji ofo* (Nri holds *ofo* or authority) is a popular saying. They are given preference in splitting kola-nut. The nut, which comes from the kola tree *(kola acuminata)*, is a symbol of hospitality and commensality. It is an important factor in kinship differentiation and in determining social status. When various titles *(ozo)* are conferred, in those communities where sociopolitical status is enshrined in titletaking, the presence of an Nri representative is required.[42] In this way Nri people and their king continue the civilizing mission of the founding ancestor, Eri.

Morality and the Cult of the Earth Deity (Ala). The ritual ascendance the Nri enjoy in Igboland (especially within the Nri-Awka axis) is based on their special relationship to the earth deity (Ala). The clearing of the morass (chaos) that Eri achieved when he arrived on earth was done in collaboration with Awka smiths. But the importance of the land as spirit-force *(alusi)* did not become manifest until there was need for food. The recognition of Ala as spirit-subject began to emerge through the action of Chukwu, who demanded human sacrifice. Eri brought this to fruition through the sacrifice (priestly action) of his son and daughter. The action of Eri is a primordial priestly act creating the recognition of the sacredness of the land (Ala). The burial of the sacrificial victims was the primordial act of presenting sacrificial offering. If the offering was made to Chukwu, it was the mouth of the land that was opened to receive the victims. From this founding act it emerges that spirits are fed when gifts are presented to them.

But the more important point is the exalted position of Ala in worship. The result of the extreme and violent act of Eri is the consecration of the land — it became a spiritualized subject intimately bonded to the community. She protects her people as mother by providing them with food (principally yam) and by establishing a covenant of peace whereby bloodshed is outlawed. But the fact that the land receives the dead creates awe and dread in regard to this deity. At the burial of young people or notables, the exclamation is still heard today: *chei! ihe ala na-eli!* (Behold what the land eats!).

Ala is a popular and noncontroverted deity in Igboland. She may even be the most popular deity, a deity "beyond the capriciousness of Igbo man."[43] The field of morality is under her care. Each segment of Igbo society has a shrine and sacred space of Ala; the kindred, the village-group, and the town (a cluster of village-groups) each have a sacred grove and space of Ala. All laws, from the simple *iwu* (rules) to the *odinani* (tradition; vital laws and customs of the land), are enacted in the presence of Ala, who sanctions the same. All abrogation of laws and all alienation of land in perpetuity require a reference to this powerful deity. Abominations *(alu)* are *nso ala* (forbidden by the land or touching the sacredness of the land). Homicide (willful or unwillful), stealing of yam, incest, etc., are abominations: they desecrate the land consecrated in mystical time in the sacrificial blood of the children of Eri. Such abominations require ritual purifications to prevent the menacing anger of Ala.[44]

The shedding of blood is an invitation to chaos to re-cover the land. The person who sheds such blood is expected to commit suicide or to flee from the village, an exile that may last for seven years.[45] His or her family must also leave the village for at least seven native weeks (twenty-eight days). The person's property is destroyed (normally by burning). After the exile a sacrifice of expiation is offered to reestablish order. The final ritual of expiation normally takes place at the shrine of Ala. Priests of Ala perform such sacrifices; in those areas where Nri has dominance, Nri priests are invited to perform the ritual. In a situation where the murderer commits suicide, an expiatory sacrifice precedes the murderer's burial. In one such instance at Owele (near Enugu), Meek recorded that the brother of the murderer took eight yams and one chicken to the priest of Ala, who made the offering and prayed:

"Ala, this chicken and these yams have been given to you by the brother of the man who killed your child and then hanged himself. He beseeches you to accept these gifts and to refrain from pursuing the brothers and children of the murderer. He who killed a fellow-man has also killed himself. Let his crime, therefore, follow him to the next world."[46]

The claim of the Nri myth is that the establishment of this moral order is based on the cosmic order (or civilization) revealed in the story about the civilizing hero. This cosmic order supervised by the earth deity and ancestors is scrupulously guarded within the Nri group. They claim that they try to persuade other Igbo to guard the same sacredness *(nso)* of human life as *nso ala* (touching the sacredness of the land). Even during the period of slavery when human life was cheapened, slaves were neither bought nor sold in Nri markets or the markets of the Nri colonies. This does not mean that some Nri, especially those living in colonies outside Nri land, did not participate in such a trade. But to practice such a trade in Nri markets would be an abomination. Furthermore, throughout that turbulent period of slavery and colonialism, it is on record that for once in Nri history an Nri king took up arms to fight a war. And that was to resist the Abam mercenaries who were hunting for slaves for the Aro group. An Nri historian called the action of the king "a mushroom attempt"; for, after all, "it is an abomination to kill any human being even in war."[47] One may thus appreciate the full weight of the statement: "Thus there was a covenant between earth and man. . . . No person should defile the earth by spilling human blood in violence on it. This is the covenant. It must be kept. We Nri keep it. We told other Igbo to whom we gave yam to keep it" (§4). The theological commentary by Nwaokoye Odenigbo is stated as an ethical imperative flowing from the violent sacrifice narrated in the founding myth. The ritual of expiation that follows bloodshed is the reverse side of the ethical imperative, and both are drawn from the Nri religious experience.

There is much more rhetoric among various religious systems today. Some religions claim superiority over others. In the recent collective study *The Myth of Christian Uniqueness,* John Hick maintained that the crucial test for uniqueness should be rested on how far each religion upholds the dignity of the human person.[48] The Nri have persisted in upholding this principle rooted in their founding myth. Some Igbo village-groups created or borrowed practices that dehumanize people. Some of these heinous practices include slave trade, cult slavery (*osu*-caste system), and human sacrifice to bury dead chiefs or to make annual expiation for the accumulated evil of the society. The practice of human sacrifice increased when slavery was at its height.[49] But the Nri rejected *osu*-caste system and human sacrifice, and they forbade slave markets within their enclave. Furthermore, a wanted murderer was also given sanctuary within the confines of Nri dominion.

Today we live in more violent times and in a violent world. In such times, the reflection of Nwaokoye Odenigbo (in 1968) on the service of authority in Nri may be food for thought for the rest of the Igbo and, indeed, for all humans.

"When the white men came, they asked us to abrogate the codes of abomination and taboos. They said that they had brought peace based on different ideas. We agreed and decided to watch them. Today, we see war everywhere; we see brothers have sex with their sisters, we see people strangulate others to acquire their wealth. The white men brought many good things; they brought peace between Igbo communities but they have not brought peace within the communities. We Nri brought peace within communities when we ruled. We are doing all we can to bring peace between communities but the slave trade did not allow us to, and the white men came and stopped us from ruling. White men have arms and we do not believe in fighting. Fighting spills blood on the earth and this is an abomination. The white men that came started by killing those who did not agree with their rules. We Nri never did so: we tried to persuade and convince people not to do so. Okoli Ijeoma of Ndikelionwu and the Edo did what the white men did — they killed people. We Nri condemn it."[50]

There may be exaggerations in this reflection. But this is a clear case of myth shaping the behavior (and history) of a people, and the people's behavior has also influenced the story. The political pretensions of the founding story may not appeal to certain Igbo groups. However, the moral code that guides the conduct of the Igbo and the reparations and ritual imperatives that follow the shedding of blood confirm the vitality of the Nri myth. The persistence of these behavior patterns in varying shades and forms into our own day may in a way support Schelling's view that consciousness may resist the myth process, but consciousness is unable to impede this process, much less annul it.[51]

Nri Myth and the Economic Life of the Igbo. AGRICULTURE. It was the search for food that led to the blood-bond between the Nri and the earth deity. The gift of food (yam) originated from Chukwu, who taught Eri plant domestication. But the yam emerged from the bowels of the earth creating a filial intimacy between humans and the earth deity: "When a man is born, he drops on the ground and Ala looks after him"; "most things that we have come from her, and without her gifts we should be lost indeed."[52]

All foods come from the land, but the chief in the list given by the myth is yam. The Igbo domesticated and have continued to plant the various types of *dioscorea* from Neolithic times: *dioscorea rotundata, dioscorea cayenensis*, and *dioscorea dumentorum*. These crops were domesticated in the West African yam belt between 3,000 and 5,000 years ago.[53] According to the Nri myth the appearance of the yam, which closely followed taking firm hold of the land, signified the emergence of culture.

Yam cultivation must have been at the root of the further development of Nri culture. The crop had to be accumulated in sufficient quantity to allow for the leisure of creating a kingship and title-taking. There is evidence, not only in the Nri-Awka axis but also in the Amaigbo-Orlu area (in other words, all over Igboland), that the Igbo passionately applied themselves to the production of yam. Coursey describes the Igbo as one of the "most enthusiastic yam cultivators" not only in West Africa, but indeed all over the world.[54]

The Nri myth thus shows how the achievement of humans influences myth-making: life shapes the myth. The storyteller (Nwaokoye Odenigbo) suggests this in paragraph three. When the desired crops germinated from the graves of the sacrificed children he comments: "This is why the first son and daughter of Eze Nri after his coronation have *ichi* marks made on their faces seven days after their birth." The *ichi* (facial scarification) is the seventh or eighth title taken by Nri boys. It is at the lower level of titles in those areas of Igboland where achievement is socially and ritually recognized. The abundance of yams produced by an individual or his parents (accumulation of wealth) is a necessary condition for taking a title. In the Amaigbo-Orlu axis, one of the coveted titles is *ezeji* (king of yam). To join the *ezeji* society one must own at least one hundred stacks of yam — no mean feat.[55] One could thus say that yams created kingship and titles leading to a hierarchization of society to project human industry. This life experience later influenced the myth and formed part of the story.

But the myth is intended to shape human life. It is told in order to found human industry and struggle with an undomesticated (chaotic) earth within the cosmic order. Eri faced chaos. He prayed to God, begging for food so that human life would not be wiped out. Chukwu asked him to commit his whole life — industry (symbolized in his children) — in order to produce food and develop culture. Thus the founding myth teaches the importance of prayer, as well as the importance of an aggressive embrace of life (i.e., the industry and technology needed to produce the food). The ritual recognition of success in Igbo societies is a testimony of how such a myth has continued to shape human life. (In Igbo tradition this dimension of success is best revealed in the myth of preexistence and creation of each individual human — the myth of the personal *chi* or creative genius.)

The importance of yam in the development of religion and culture is shown in the harvest festival, which revolves around the yam spirit *(Ahiajoku)*. The celebration opens with family and kindred rituals at the beginning of harvesting and reaches a climax with the village-group and town thanksgiving. The thanksgiving is marked by adequate sacrifices, song, dance, and merriment. Among the Oratta (Owerri) each homeowner, at the beginning of the harvest, kills a cock and sprinkles the blood on the cult symbols of the spirit saying: "I and the members of my household are now ready to eat the new yams. May they give us health and cause no injury. Accept, we beseech you, our gifts of yams, and may you not be defiled thereby."[56]

The most solemn communal rite is called *iro ofo* or *ofala* in many Igbo communities. Among the Onitsha Igbo it is a solemnity tied to the annual emergence *(ofala)* of the king. The ceremony is preceded by a period of "dreaming" *(nlo)*. The king retreats for four days (one native week). He communes with Chukwu, with Onitsha land, with other spirits and ancestors. His emergence follows the celebration of the yam festival by all the clans except his own.

"He demonstrates that he has survived another year as a living atonement for the sins and misdeeds of the Onitsha people, that he has mourned the community's dead and has been shown guiltless of their deaths, that he and the community have been filled with strength, fullness and richness of life, and that he has foreseen the events of the year and found them good."[57]

Sacrifices are offered followed by ritual dancing and merriment. Then the royal clan celebrates the yam festival, followed by the king's ceremonial eating of the yams.

This thanksgiving harvest has become a national festival among the Igbo. The Imo state government has converted this annual festival into a forum for the Igbo to assemble and reflect on their cultural heritage. This state-organized festival peaks with the Ahiajioku Lectures, in which the relevance of Igbo culture in various areas of human endeavor is explored.[58]

The activities mentioned above (industry and thanksgiving festival) prove the relevance of the gift of yam story as a living myth. Today, most Igbo perform the thanksgiving in the Christian Churches instead of doing so at the shrine of Ahiajioku, Ala, and the ancestors. In this way the Christian God (Chukwu) appropriates not only the attributes of the Igbo Chukwu, but also the fertility characteristics of Ala and Ahiajioku. This is also how the Jewish-Christian tradition took over festivals of the Canaanite and pastoral peoples. The social context and the Christian message have merged.

TRADE AND MARKET ECONOMY. No section of the Nri myth is so close to Igbo life-experience as the story of Eri's encounter with his mystical visitors (fishmongers); an encounter through which he established the four-day week. It is possibly because the account is so true to life and reflects the commonplace and everyday reality that Nwoga dismisses its claims to revelation. Since the four-day week is a practice common to West African peoples Nwoga concludes that "there was no special revelation of the four days by the Eze Nri and the test motif relates to the oracular Chukwu of Arochukwu."[59]

The segment of the myth on the days of the week (§6) may have developed independently to fuse later with the sections on agriculture and kingship. It is so vital to Nri life that a new Eze Nri inherits the power to re-create time (see the parallels). The myth shows Eri grappling with the mystery of the passage of time. This materializes in the symbol of the supernatural force guarding the secrecy of time (*ubosi-nano*, four days). This symbolic force of time *(ubosi-nano)* has a special cult among the Igbo. Locked in the struggle to pierce through this secrecy, the hero sought the assistance of mythical forces symbolized in the rat. In the first place no creature knows better how to introduce itself into a basket of fish *(nguga azu)* than the rat. But in the realm of myth time has not yet been regulated. So, the hero's ingenuity in establishing creative relationships is being projected. These relationships stretch from Chukwu (sender, creator) to humans (Awka smiths) in order to create dry land; then they swing back to Chukwu, who directs Eri to Ala (earth deity and provider) to receive the produce of the earth (yams, etc.). In order to regulate time and its movement, the motions of Eri encircle the animal world. Eri comes across as an astute business hero. As soon as he pierced through the mystery of time, thanks to his messengers, he named the four days that are the four markets supervised by the four spirits: *eke, oye afor,* and *nkwo.* The market is bound to the emergence of trade, for which the Igbo are well known.

But before Eri counted the four days (i.e., before he saluted his guests by their names) he penetrated the density of time, the eventfulness of each day *(ubosi)*, time as opportunity. This is the revelation that Eri bestowed on Nri and Igbo communities: to grasp what lies in store for progress each day so that the linear and cyclical passage of days, weeks, and seasons may be eventful. The market and trade (economy) not only afford opportunity to exchange goods and learn from the other, they are cosmic realities revealed in mythic time. Conversely, the practice of trade in everyday markets among the Igbo may have influenced the narrative details of the myth.

It is not an exaggeration to say that the market is the nerve center of every Igbo village-group. The industry characteristic of the Igbo is displayed in their local markets, in the Nigerian market, and in the facility with which they move around all over Africa and other continents looking for new markets. The Igbo-ukwu excavations show that by the ninth century C.E. trade may have been well established with North Africa and Asia (Israel). The characteristic trait of the Igbo to struggle is well known all over Nigeria and West Africa. While Igbo culture may accommodate failure (despite its competitive and success-oriented features), it rejects indolence. In 1789 Olaudah Equiano, an Igbo ex-slave, wrote that "everyone contributes something to the common stock; and as we are unacquainted with idleness, we have no beggars."[60] This cultural pattern arouses jealousy and bad feelings, especially when the Igbo apply the shrewdness reflective of the way Eri penetrated the secrecy of time in their dealings with other competitors. For, the world is a marketplace, and to succeed one has to haggle and bargain shrewdly. Without such shrewdness life may remain at its dreaming level, and the myth would remain unactualized.

If the economic activity is derived from the myth it is also related to ritual. Ritual precedes any economic enterprise in the form of prayers and sacrifices. Thanksgiving follows any successful business — prayers and sacrifices. Since success or failure in business touches each human personally, the divinities or forces that come into prominence would not be time, but *chi* (the personal creative genius) and *ikenga* (for men alone — a two-horned carved object representing a man's strength and will to succeed).[61]

Myth-Making in Nri (Igbo) Community and Creation

The Nri myth analyzed thus far is not a creation myth as such. It is rather a sacred story whose roots probably lie in historical recollections of a migration. It is a myth of origin: origin of a people, its culture, and the core elements of its universe (divinities, the land and its products). That is why we prefer to call it a cosmogony and anthropogony.

The Igbo do not really have a myth of creation in the sense of *creatio ex nihilo*. In a 1968 interview Nwaokoye Odenigbo said that "Nri people believe and taught Igbo people that *Chukwu* is *Okike*, that is, Creator."[62] However, apart from local village-group myths (like the Nri myth) that tell about the community's origin, there is no myth of creation of the whole universe. There is an understanding that Ala constitutes the whole earth created by Chukwu. Two very important heavenly bodies, *anyanwu* (the sun) and *onwa* (the moon), which are messengers or eyes of Chukwu, are sent to traverse the sky *(igwe)* over the land *(ala)* in intersecting paths, and to divide the world into four quarters giving rise to the four-day week. But there is no social unit in practical relationship with this whole earth; thus, the cult and myths of Ala remain local.[63] Even the widespread myths about the unique creation of individual humans through the act of the personal *chi* (personalized creative genius) remain further limited. Each preexistent "self" (soul) meets with the individual *chi* assigned to the person by Chukwu. He or she negotiates with the individual *chi*, who defines in a pact the broad outlines of the person's destiny. And through a creative act of *chi* he or she enters the already-formed physical body in the womb and is born as the infant whose destiny has been traced on the palm of the hands *(akala aka)*.[64]

The universe is the creation of Chukwu and not a part of Chukwu, despite the fact that Chukwu is also invoked as Chi n'uwa (*chi* in the world), or simply Uwa (the world). The purpose of the universe is intimately linked to human interest (full realization of life). The universe, which includes the world of the dead and the world of the living, is a theater of interaction. The concern of humans is not when the universe began or when it will come to an end, rather, there is a positive embrace of the universe as the theater where humans struggle to realize life's destiny (in the world of the living), so that when they pass over to the world of the dead they may continue to influence human affairs as ancestors who have achieved fullness of life.

Concluding Remarks: Nri Myth — An Example of African Pragmatic Approach to Religion

Our reflections in this first sample of the myth, the Nri myth of origin, may help us to appreciate the cultural root of the Igbo person's pragmatic approach to life and religion. Religion is valuable only when it leads to the enhancement of life of humans in the world. Religion is not perceived as an end in itself, and yet religion permeates all of life. Local divinities are invited to or expelled from families and villages to the extent that they help or impede the positive harvesting of the opportunity that time stores in its mysterious heart. Chukwu, Ala, and the personal *chi* are always begged to help the individual, family, or community. Ancestors who are very powerful may even be rebuked and threatened with starvation if they do not act in favor of their families. Uchendu is right to draw attention to the contractual pattern *(do ut des)*, which pervades Igbo ritual attitude.[65] The spirits are invoked and/or fed daily or on a regular basis. Great love and intimacy may develop between humans and spirits (especially with the personal *chi*). But the intentionality of religious practice or belief is clear: the integral welfare of humans. If this attitude is truly proved to be characteristic of African religious experience (as some studies appear to indicate),[66] then the *homo religiosus africanus* may have the key to the solution of the crisis of religious practice in the contemporary world: religion is made for "man" and not "man" for religion (cf. Jesus' attitude to the Sabbath). The social, political, and economic spheres of life can be so informed by moral imperatives and ritual practices as to lead to the enhancement of human life. This is the story of Nri myth that is shown as shaping and being shaped by life in the Nri-Awka axis of Igboland and beyond.

Enuma Elish: *Babylonian Exaltation of Marduk in Cosmos, Ritual, and History*

Enuma Elish is a hymn to the head of the Babylonian pantheon Marduk. It is recorded in seven tablets and narrates the exaltation of Marduk, who vanquished Tiamat, enemy of the gods. This poem displays the energy, courage, and shrewdness of Marduk, who converted the distress and timorousness of the gods to his own advantage. If he would be avenger of the gods, the rest of the gods must be subject to him. He must assume absolute authority. He must preside over the destinies, and his words must be unalterable. When the proposal to be avenger of the gods was made to him by Ansar, Marduk replied:

"O Lord of the gods, Destiny of the great gods,
If I, your avenger,
Conquer Tiamat and give you life,
Appoint an assembly, make my fate pre-eminent and proclaim it;
In Upsukkinaku seat yourselves joyfully together,
With my word in place of you will I decree fate.
May whatsoever I do remain unaltered,
May the word of my lips never be changed nor made of no avail" (II, 133–40).[67]

One is not surprised that, after the resounding victory over Tiamat, the gods honored him with fifty names, titles that assemble the names and qualities of the gods (probably an elaboration of an older god list).[68]

History of the Text

Enuma Elish (literally "when on high") is both the opening phrase and the title of this poem. It has been considered often as the "standard cosmogony," the most thorough treatment of the theme of creation that any people in the ancient world has preserved. An epic (or rather a hymn) whose substance goes back to ancient Sumerian prototypes of the third millennium B.C.E., though the actual texts may have been composed in the middle or late second millennium B.C.E.[69] However, Lambert has argued strongly that *Enuma Elish* is anything but typical or standard cosmogony. It is rather aberrant: "The *Epic of Creation* is not a norm of Babylonian or Sumerian cosmology. It is a sectarian and aberrant combination of mythological threads woven into an unparalleled compositum. In my opinion it is not earlier than 1100 B.C."[70] Lambert may have modified his ideas about the sources of the composition that, according to him, included a West Semitic strand, but his dating of the composition in the second millennium B.C.E. has found favor with expert opinion.[71]

The principal argument in support of a late dating of *Enuma Elish* is the intention of the poem: the enthronement of Marduk. Marduk was a local deity in Babylon, a city that came into prominence in the time of Hammurabi (eighteenth century B.C.E.). Gods like Anu, Enlil, and Ea dominated the scene in the Mesopotamian region before this time. But before the end of the second millennium B.C.E., Babylon and its god, Marduk, sat on top of the Mesopotamian world. Marduk, called Lord or Bel, was on top of the gods. The usurpation of power in the pantheon did not occur suddenly, despite the middle Babylonian date now accepted for the composition of *Enuma Elish*. Rather, the popularity of the divinity grew gradually, starting from the Old Babylonian period.[72] The first indication that Marduk was on the ladder of fame is seen in the promulgation of the Code of Hammurabi. In the prologue Anu and Enlil (his superiors) gave him power over all peoples, made him great among the Igigi-gods, and established an enduring kingship for him in Babylon:

"When lofty Anum, king of the Anunnaki,
(and) Enlil, lord of heaven and earth,
the determiner of the destinies of the land,
determined for Marduk, the first born of Enki,
the Enlil functions over all mankind,
made him great among the Igigi,
called Babylon by its exalted name,
made it supreme in the world,
established for him in its midst an enduring kingship,
whose foundations are as firm as heaven and earth —

at that time Anum and Enlil named me
to promote the welfare of the people,
me, Hammurabi, the devout, god-fearing prince,
to cause justice to prevail in the land,
to destroy the wicked and the evil,
that the strong might not oppress the weak,
to rise like the sun over the black-headed (people),
and to light up the land. . . .
When Marduk commissioned me to guide the people aright,
I established law and justice in the language of the land,
thereby promoting the welfare of the people.
At that time (I decreed). . . ."[73]

Thus the new political climate initiated by Hammurabi, which pushed Babylon into prominence making it the capital of Sumer and Akkad, favored the local deity (Marduk).

But it was at the reign of Nebuchadnezzar I (late twelfth century B.C.E.) that the supremacy of Marduk over the gods was complete. Nebuchadnezzar overthrew the Cassite (non-Mesopotamian) dynasty. He waged war against Elam and recovered from them the statue of Marduk that was plundered by them from Babylon. All the victories scored by Nebuchadnezzar were attributed to the benevolence of Marduk. Some inscriptions within this period referred to Babylon as "the holy city" and to the victories of Nebuchadnezzar as willed by Marduk: "O Marduk, Lord, Wise One, Great God, Splendid One, you created me, you entrusted to me the kingship over the totality of people." Or again: "The widespread people, with whom Marduk filled my hand, I made subject to Babylon."[74]

It was at this favorable time that the priests of Marduk and the king of Babylon promoted Marduk to his supreme position. Lambert believes that *Enuma Elish* was perhaps composed at this period as "a product of the very campaign that resulted in the official promotion of Marduk in the reign of Nebuchadnezzar I."[75]

Enuma Elish *as a Foundation Story*

Enuma Elish is generally referred to as a creation epic. Conford insists, however, that it is not an epic but a hymn: epics do not reflect ritual action, nor are they recited as incantations to reinforce the efficacy of a rite every time it is performed.[76]

As a creation myth that is recited within a given context or which shapes the lives of humans within a given community it gives foundation to human existence. Scholars are unanimous in asserting that the exaltation of Marduk in this hymn completely overshadows the cosmogonic and anthropogonic segments of the story. Instead of the normal anthropocentric world we are presented with a theocentric narrative. Thus this myth may legitimately be called the "creation of the gods": "As for us, by however many names we pronounce, he is our God! / Let us then proclaim his fifty names" (VI:138–43, ANET).[77] The opening lines underline that the poem is preoccupied with the affairs of the gods.

"When in the height heaven was not named,
And the earth beneath did not yet bear a name,
And the primeval Apsu, who begat them,
And chaos, Tiamat, the mother of them both —
Their waters were mingled together,
And no field was formed, no marsh was to be seen;
When of the gods none had been called into being,
And none bore a name, and no destinies [were ordained];
Then were created the gods in the midst of [heaven]" (I:1–9).

The period being described is primeval and thus not within time; the waters (Apsu and Tiamat) do not replicate known "sweet" and "salt" waters. Rather they are mythic: the upper and the lower world in complete diffusion. "A sort of hydrological variant on the theme of the primeval union of Chaos-heaven and Chaos-earth."[78]

The poem proceeds to narrate the conflict among the gods (theomachy), which was exacerbated by the slaying of Apsu by Ea through magical incantations. It was then that Tiamat decided to create real chaos by destroying the gods; in other words, to cause the extinction of life (activity) in the heavenly realm, to create the notion of gods as *miti* (dead, IV:154; VII:26).[79] But Marduk, assuming absolute power, triumphed over Tiamat. He then proceeded to organize the cosmos in an absolute way: he used half of Tiamat's body to establish a covering for the heaven, which was vaguely conceived as already existing (IV:138; I:19);[80] he secured a peaceful habitation for the gods; he created the constellations, the moon, and the sun; he formed the earth with outflowings from Tiamat's body (her spittle, her "poison," and effluences from her eyes, etc.; V:47–57); from divine blood he formed man to be slave of the gods;[81] finally, Babylon was made the house of the gods. A god who provides for his kind in such a way merits full praise from them (the fifty titles).

Let us then proclaim his fifty names:
(1) Marduk, as Anu, his father, called him from his birth;
Who provides grazing and drinking places, enriches their stalls,
Who with the flood-storm, his weapon, vanquished detractors, (And) who the gods, his fathers, rescued from distress.
Truly, the Son of the Sun, most radiant of gods is he.
In his brilliant light may they walk forever!
On the people he brought forth, endowed with *life*,
The service of the gods he imposed that these may have ease:
Creation, destruction, deliverance, grace
Shall be by his command. They shall look up to him! (VI:122–33, ANET).
Father Enlil called his name (50) "LORD OF THE LANDS" (VII:136, ANET).
With the title "Fifty" the great gods
Proclaimed him whose names are fifty and made his way supreme (VII:143–44, ANET).

Lambert has shown how the extraordinary interest in the fortunes of Marduk made *Enuma Elish* a composite poem, a poem that he argues borrowed from two other Akkadian myths (Anzu and Labbu). Saggs, on his own part, sees in *Enuma Elish* a conflation of a number of myths (six in all), which were originally separate and distinct.[82] These expert observations and historico-critical analyses help our understanding of the myth. They lead to a greater appreciation of the sociohistorical climate that favored the production of such a myth — a myth that, nevertheless, shaped people's lives. Temple poets (priests) put together the hymn. Babylonians (Mesopotamians) experienced it as a bridge between their conscious experience and their collective unconscious (serving as archetype). It is a story about the becoming of the gods and about human life. The narration of the poem on the fourth day of the new year *(akitu)* festival reenacts and reaffirms the dynamics of the cosmic order.

Enuma Elish as Shaping and Being Shaped by Cult and History

The hymn to the gods has as its high point the divine battle (theomachy) and the enthronement of Marduk. The formation of humans out of divine blood and earth has as its purpose ministration to the gods in order to liberate the gods from the burden of service. Humans are puppets (*lullu*, savage), slaves (VI:6–7). The story is foundational and establishes this as the way it was and ought to be. Humans fulfill this function in the temple of the gods. They reenact the whole cosmic order in the new year festival, whose peak is the procession of the gods, the celebration of Marduk's supremacy, and the proclamation of the destinies (of the gods and of the king).

But are humans mere puppets? We need to answer this question in order to fully appreciate how human history shapes the cosmos. Humans do not simply experience "cosmos as history" in the eternal return of things as reenacted in the new year festival.[83]

In the creation of humans, the blood of a god was mixed with earth to form them. According to Berossus, Bel (Marduk) used his own blood mixed with earth. Thus King's translation reads: "My blood will I take and bone will I (fashion), / I will make man" (VI:5–6).

Further evidence indicates that the "blood" was that of the rebel Kingu, the consort of Tiamat.[84] The slaughter of Kingu and the use of his blood followed the advice of Ea, who wanted to prevent undue oppression of all the rebel gods.

"Ea answered him, speaking a word to him,
Giving him another plan for the relief of the gods:
'Let but one of their brothers be handed over;
He alone shall perish that mankind may be fashioned.
Let the great gods be here in Assembly,
Let the guilty be handed over that they may endure'" (VI:11–16, ANET).

"'It was Kingu who contrived the uprising,
And made Tiamat rebel, and joined battle.'
They bound him holding him before Ea.
They imposed on him his guilt and severed his blood (vessels). Out of his blood they fashioned mankind" (VI:29–33, ANET).

In another Mesopotamian myth *(Atra-hasis)*,[85] humankind is created in a similar way to minister to the gods. A god is slaughtered and all the other deities bathed in his blood (ritual purification). Then Nintu (the birth goddess) mixed the blood with clay and fashioned humankind. The goddess Mami addressed the divine assembly:

"You have commanded me a task and I completed it.
You have slaughtered a god together with his personality.
I have removed your heavy work.
I have imposed toil upon mankind."

In both cases, in order to form humankind it was important to sacrifice a god. This establishes an unbreakable bond between gods and humans. According to Michalowski: "In order to create mankind the gods must sacrifice one of their own. The rite of passage that is depicted here, with a scapegoat motif, . . . provides a reciprocal bond between gods and men. Such a bond means that although mankind must serve the gods, the gods also needed them."[86]

The gods need humankind to feed them and to maintain their shrines. We noted a parallel experience in the Nri myth in which the sacrifice of the son and daughter of Eri created a covenant between the deity (Ala) and humans. The deity forbade further blood-letting after being fed with (or rather, being recognized in) the blood of the primeval children of Eri. The earth protects and nourishes her children, who in turn worship her and other divinities through feeding and feasting them.

Another dimension to the relationship of humankind and the gods in Mesopotamia is brought out in the reasons given for the flood in the *Gilgamesh* epic. The noise *(rigmu* or *huburu)* of humankind disturbed the god Enlil. Michalowski has argued for a positive and creative interpretation of the noise. The noise of humankind is responsible for the flood in the myth of *Labbu,* just as the noise of the gods troubled Tiamat and Apsu in *Enuma Elish.* They decided to destroy the gods in order to lie down in peace (I:23–52). Noise represents activity or creativity, while the repose desired by Tiamat and Apsu was death. Chaos (noise) as used in Mesopotamian myths does not mean only disorder. According to Hollenbach, "disorder still implies the existence of determinate things which are in disorder." The more radical chaos (the wish of Apsu and Tiamat) "is the idea of nonexistence of anything, not only in the static sense of no things being, but in the dynamic sense of nothing acting."[87] The price of their "death-wish" was the loss of their lives. They passed through the chaos of divine combat so that the gods, heavens, constellations, earth, and humans would be created. But in the case of the flood, the gods (led by Enlil) failed to appreciate the interactional (gestural) dynamics of the bond between them and humankind. To silence the noise (creativity, chaos of humankind) is to destroy creation. Humans are bonded to the gods, but the bond is rooted in a basic primeval freedom enjoyed both by divine and human beings. The expression of this freedom is mythically described as noise or chaos.[88]

The flood in the *Gilgamesh* epic put the survival of both humans and gods in question. While humans perished, the gods were frightened and ascended to the heaven of Anu. When the waters receded and the rains stopped, the human survivor, Uta-napistim, offered sacrifice on Mount Nimus. He mused:

"I poured out a libation on the top of the mountain,
Seven and seven cult-vessels I set up,
Upon their pot-stands I heaped cane, cedarwood, and myrtle,
The gods smelled the savor,
The gods crowded like flies about the sacrificer."[89]

Just as humans need the gods, the gods need humankind. Thus the place of humans in the universe is not expressed as that of "a blind slave of the gods, but as an independent creative being": "The harmony and hierarchical arrangement of the world does not require that mankind be passive. The creation of these creatures, as well as the clash which resulted in the flood, serves as an etiological charter which affirms the independent status of mankind."[90]

The New Year (Akitu) Festival: A Ritual Affirmation of Babylonian Cosmic Order. The information we have about the new year *(akitu)* celebrations is incomplete. The ritual edited by F. Thureau-Dangin dates from the period that Greek rule was imposed on the Mesopotamian region.[91] But the conservative nature of ritual ensures that the substance of ancient practices may still be identified despite the layers of accretions that accumulated through the centuries. The new year festival occurs at the beginning of the first month of the year (Nisan) and lasts for twelve days. Our ritual contains only the events of the second, third, fourth, and fifth days. What happened on other days can be deduced from historical records and secondary material.[92]

The festival contained in the ritual is certainly a new year festival soliciting the protection of Marduk, pleading for his mercy, asking for his blessing, and proclaiming his universal supremacy. But this forms a second layer that dates from the second millennium B.C.E. There are records of agricultural festivals in Ur, Nippur, and Babylon dating to the third millennium B.C.E. They are called *akitu* (plural, *akiti)* festivals, a word that stands both for the building in which the festival takes place and the festival itself. The building is normally erected in farmlands and there is a procession with the god from his temple ("taking the god by the hand") to the *akitu*. In Ur and Babylon the *akitu* takes place in the first month, and in Nippur in the twelfth month. There is also an *akitu* held at Ur in the sixth month at sowing time. This has features of a fertility cult with a sacred marriage (hierogamy).[93]

Thus in historical order there is (1) the harvest festival in which the god is taken by the hand from the temple to the *akitu* building, (2) the fertility ritual involving a hierogamy, and (3) the festival of Marduk (Bel) who decrees destinies both for the gods and for the land. The *akitu* is thus not a reenactment of *Enuma Elish.* However, it certainly became a reaffirmation of the cosmic order in which Marduk is celebrated as supreme, the gods are honored, and humans are subordinate. It reaffirms the covenant bond between gods and humans: gods are to be fed and worshiped; humans are to be protected and blessed.

The first five days of the festival constitute a preparation for the departure of Marduk from his *Esagila* (temple). The rites include ritual purification of shrines and the confession of innocence by the king. Praise, petitions, and penitence are the forms of prayer. These project the supremacy of Marduk and the dependence and weakness of humans. For example, on the second Nisan the high priest *(sesgallu,* also written *urigallu)* rises two hours before dawn (4:00 A.M.), bathes himself with river water, presents himself before Bel (Marduk), and pronounces the following prayer:[94]

"O Bel, who has no equal when angry,
O Bel, excellent king, lord of the countries,
Who makes the great gods friendly,
O Bel, who fells the mighty with his glance,
Lord of the kings, light of mankind, who divides the portions —
O Bel, your dwelling is the city of Babylon, your tiara is the [neighboring] city of Borsippa,

Broad heaven is the 'totality of your liver.'
O Bel, with your eyes you see all things,
[With] your oracles you *verify* the oracles,
[With] your glance you hand down the law,
[With] your . . . you . . . the mighty;
When you look [at them], you grant them mercy;
You show them the light, [and] they speak of your valor.
Who does not speak of your glory, does not glorify your sovereignty?
Lord of the countries, who dwells in the temple Endul, who grasps the hand of the fallen,
Grant mercy to your city, Babylon!
Turn your face to the temple Esagil, your house!
Establish the 'liberty' of the people of Babylon, your subordinates" (ll:5–32).

This is a praise-invocation of Marduk, universal lord and god; a narration of his supreme power over the gods, destinies, and humankind; a pleading with him for mercy over Babylon his city. This prayer celebrates (acknowledges in praise) the cosmic order as expressed in *Enuma Elish.*

The liturgical activities on fourth Nisan are also preparatory, though still expressing the cosmic order: intercessory prayers or "raising of the hands" are addressed by the *sesgallu* first to Bel and then to his consort Beltiya (my lady, the goddess Sarpanitu). Both prayers begin with praise-invocation and end with a plea for mercy. Beltiya is requested to "give life to the children of Babel, her clients" and to "intercede for them before Marduk, the king of the gods" (ll:264–5). Late afternoon that same day, after the second meal (the gods are served two meals a day), the high priest recites the hymn *Enuma Elish* with his hands lifted up. The front tiara of the god Anu and the throne of Enlil are covered while the *Enuma Elish* is recited (ll:280ff.). No reason is given for this rubric. The covering of Anu's tiara and Enlil's throne during the ritual recital may indicate a ritual build up to score the importance of Marduk, which will reach its climax on the eighth day when all the gods will be assembled, with Marduk as supreme, decreeing destinies. Smith even establishes a connection between this last act of day four and the humiliation of the king on day five. If the king was a foreigner (and Smith believes that the ritual was put together when foreigners ruled Babylon), then

Enuma Elish and the humiliation of the king may be part of a nationalistic religious propaganda — asserting the supremacy of Marduk and Babylon.[95]

The ceremonies of the fifth day of Nisan begin four hours before dawn. Marduk is again invoked, but under the title of various stars. According to *Enuma Elish* Marduk created the stars and the constellations. This ritual invocation may be a way of delineating the calendrical aspects of the year.[96] Two hours after sunrise the high priest invites a sorcerer to purify the temple of Bel and the shrine *(Ezida)* of Nabu, the son of Bel. A decapitated sheep is used for the ritual cleansing. The sorcerer does not enter the sanctuary of Bel, but that of Nabu, whose statue will arrive later in the day in procession from Borsippa.

When Nabu arrives, the king is there to welcome him. He accompanies Nabu to the temple and is offered water to cleanse his hands. Then the king passes through a ritual process of humiliation. In the presence of Bel, the high priest takes all the insignia of office away from the king and places them before the god, Bel. The priest strikes the king on the cheek, drags him by the ear, and makes him bow down to the ground. Then the king makes the following confession of innocence:

"I did [not] sin, lord of the lands,
  I was not neglectful of your godhead,
[I did not] destroy Babylon, I did not order her to be dispersed.
[I did not] rain blows on the cheek of a subordinate, . . .
  I did not humiliate them.
[I watch out] for Babylon; I did not smash its walls" (ll:424–8).

The high priest addresses the king in the following words: "Have no fear. . . . The god Bel [will listen to] your prayer. . . . He will magnify your lordship. . . . He will exalt your kingship. . . . The god Bel will bless you for ever. He will destroy your enemy, fell your adversary" (ll:434–46).

The political dimension of this ritual passage undergone by the king has been noted by many commentators.[97] The ritual shows the interplay between the cosmic and the political orders. The king of Babylon receives his kingship from Marduk and is thus the chief servant (priest) of the gods. Through him the divine plan is carried out in history. Any failure in his duties toward humans and toward the gods threatens the cosmic order, leaving an open invitation for chaos to take over (i.e., death for gods and humans). The hierarchical structure among the gods is reproduced in society. In other words, the supremacy enjoyed by Marduk among the gods is also enjoyed by the king among humans. This makes the king's function as chief servant crucial. He must act in such a way that the blessing of the gods toward humankind be realized so that humans, led by the king, may serve the gods. Black may be right in insisting that the king's humiliation is a personal humiliation and that the ritual atonement is between the king and the god, not for the whole people.[98] No other person enjoys his exalted position. But it is for this very reason that the fortunes of the king (as supreme, despotic?) leader affects the people. This converts his ritual confession of innocence into a national affair without limiting in the least his personal responsibility. His supremacy is, however, limited. He is not a ritual reproduction of the god who decrees destinies. Marduk who shepherds the gods is equally the shepherd of humankind. He can take the throne away from a king who is unfaithful to his purpose in history. This is indicated in the second ritual striking of the king by the high priest:

"The scepter, circle, and sword [shall be restored] to the king. He shall strike the king's cheek. If, when [he strikes] the king's cheek, the tears flow, [it means that] the god Bel is friendly; if no tears appear, the god Bel is angry; the enemy will rise up and bring about his downfall" (ll:448–52).

The blessing of the tears may signal rainfall in the new year, which would be a more primitive meaning of the ritual. Later experience may have led to the additional general oracle of political success and prosperity.[99] But insofar as the king's behavior has impact on the natural and political climate of Babylon, so much does he carry Babylon into his ritual process. His personal ritual has community implications.

The ritual covering the events of sixth to twelfth Nisan is lost. It is known from other sources that on sixth Nisan the statues of other gods arrive in Babylon from their home sanctuaries for the *akitu*. On the eighth days the king "takes Bel by the hand," inviting him to leave his temple for the *akitu*. Bel first moves to the shrine of destinies to determine the destiny of the gods. According to *Enuma Elish,* decreeing destinies indicates overlordship by Marduk. After overcoming

Tiamat, Marduk faced Kingu and took the Tablet of Destiny from him:

"Moreover, Kingu, who had been exalted over them,
He conquered, and with the god Dug-ga he counted him.
He took from him the Tablet of Destiny that were not rightly his,
He sealed them with a seal and in his own breast he laid them" (IV:119–22).

The Tablet of Destiny is the means by which power is exercised, and wearing them in one's breast is for the victor an emblem of power.[100] The gods thus called Marduk, who controlled the destinies, Lugal-dimmer-an-kia (Divine king of heaven and earth) as one of his fifty titles:

"Lugaldimmerankia is his name which we proclaimed in our Assembly.
His commands we have exalted above the gods, his fathers.
Verily, he is Lord of all the gods of heaven and underworld
The king at whose discipline the gods above and below are in mourning" (VI:138–43, ANET).

In his inscriptions Nebuchadnezzar II attested that on the eighth day of the new year festival Lugaldimmerankia went to the shrine of destinies to decree the destiny of the gods, and on the eleventh day to decree that of the king: "They determine in there the destinies of distant days, the destinies of my life."[101] Destinies may be oracular utterances about the land and about the king on whom the fate of the land depends. The rite of decreeing destinies during the *akitu* is a reenactment of the supreme power of Marduk as it was in primeval times.

It is after proclaiming the destinies on the eighth day that the procession of the gods and people move in joyous celebration to the *akitu*. To begin the procession, the doors of Marduk's shrine are flung open and the priests cry out: "Go forth, Bel! O king, go forth! / Go forth, Our Lady, the king awaits you!"

Bel and his consort go forth. The king takes Bel by the hand, escorts him into his chariot, and leads the procession. The procession of the rest of the gods and goddesses and all the jubilating populace follows along the splendidly garlanded Procession Street. The procession includes prisoners of war, foreigners who pay tribute, and a display of the armed forces. It was a very popular (harvest) festival, with the king taking charge of the entertainment.[102] On eleventh Nisan, the gods reassemble at the shrine of destinies in the temple of Nabu, Marduk's son. The destiny of the land was proclaimed in the destiny of the king. On the twelfth Nisan the festival comes to an end.

The *akitu*, Babylonian, festival brings together ancient agricultural practices and the later enthronement festival of Marduk, patron of Babylon, as supreme in the cosmos. The festival is not a ritual reenactment of *Enuma Elish*, but its dominant motif is a faithful reaffirmation of the cosmic order outlined in the *Enuma Elish*.

THE COSMIC ORDER IN MESOPOTAMIAN POLITICS. This question has been partially handled in the ritual passage of the king of Babylon. His dominion over the kingdom is assured by his fidelity to the order established in primeval times. The annual *akitu* festival becomes a check on the king's behavior. The decree of destinies not only reenacts the primeval universal powers of Marduk, but also demonstrates that his will (plan) is carried out in history.

We already noted that Marduk achieved his supremacy when the fortunes of Babylon turned for the better during the reign of Nebuchadnezzar I; before then Anu and Enlil were heads of the pantheon. Lambert believes that the projection of Marduk to this supremacy may have been resisted by priests of other divinities in other cities. For example, during the reign of Nebuchadnezzar I in Nippur, an unusual inscription on the boundary stone projected the supremacy of Enlil: "Enlil, the lofty Lord, the aristocrat of heaven and underworld, the noble, the lord of all, king of the great gods, who has no god who can rival him in heaven or underworld, at the giving of whose command the Igigi show submission and reverently heed. . . ."[103] Of course in the *Enuma Elish* one of the fifty names given to Marduk is Enlil: "Because he created the spaces and fashioned the firm ground, Father Enlil called his name [50] 'LORD OF THE LANDS'" (VII:135–6).[104]

A stronger resistance to Babylonian religio-cultural pretensions came from their northern neighbors (cousins), Assyria. While Babylon was the center of learning and the treasury of the old Sumerian tradition, Assyria was militarily superior. The Assyrian patron god, Assur, shared the same name as the city — something like a holy city deified.[105] The closeness of city and god was such that the king of Assyria was practically a viceroy of Assur. Assyrian kings wrote periodic reports to the god about state affairs.[106] The prerogative of Assur in history is recognized. Sargon II saw his succession as a favor from Assur so that he would

"renew the cultus of the temple, to make the ritual perfect, to make the cult-centre splendid, he steadfastly gazed on me amongst all the black-headed [people] and promoted me. He fully made over the land of Assyria into my hands for administration and direction; he made my weapons bitter over the four [world] regions."[107]

Kings saw their militarism and imperialism as a fulfilment of the plan of Assur in the world and history. This extended to their southern Babylonian neighbors.

Babylon was sacked twice by two Assyrian kings, Tikulti-Ninurta I (ca. 1210 B.C.E.) and Sennacherib (689 B.C.E.). When Ninurta invaded Babylon the Cassite dynasty was still in power. An epic dedicated to Tikulti-Ninurta's victory reveals the mingling of the cosmic and the political (historical) order and the dominance of Babylonian culture despite their humiliating defeat in the hands of Assyria.[108] Ninurta is pictured as the agent of the gods sent to punish Kastilias (Kastilias IV, the Babylonian king), who broke the terms of the treaty with Assyria. The Babylonian gods, angry with Kastilias, abandoned their native sanctuaries:

"Of the lord of all the lands, his Enlilship was distressed with
Nippu[r].
To the habitation of Dur-Kurigalzu he does not approach. . . .
Marduk abandoned his august sanctuary, [the city]
He cursed the city of his love, Kar. . . .
Sin left Ur, [his] cult centre. . . .
With Sippar and Larsa S[amas was angry]."[109]

But this Assyrian claim that military victory over Babylon was the will of the gods of Assyria and Babylon hides what Machinist calls a culture war *(Kulturkamf)*. This is evident from the events that followed the sacking of Babylon: there was a cultural shift from Babylon to Assyria (among the Assyrian loot were major literary collections transferred to Assur); Babylonian gods said to have abandoned their homeland to join Ninurta in his campaigns up north were alleged to have led him down south to conquer Babylon; the god Assur assumed characteristics of the chief Babylonian god, Enlil; the chief statue of Marduk was plundered and installed in Assur where he was held in honor with a new year festival.[110] The issue is not simply to settle once and for all Babylonian territorial claims, but to overcome the cultural domination of Babylon in the Mesopotamian region. The solution of the cultural threat was to absorb as much of Babylonian patterns as possible. And these politico-cultural decisions were theologically interpreted as the plan of the gods.

Michalowski has argued that the Assyrian threat to Babylonia may have caused the promotion of Marduk as the supreme deity with universal powers. In the period under review, Assur was supreme in Assyria, while no god within the Babylonian pantheon enjoyed such supremacy. With the threat of Assyria, Babylonian priests of Marduk started the religio-cultural propaganda symbolized in the *Enuma Elish,* which made Marduk supreme like Assur.[111] Michalowski's thesis is rendered difficult by the notorious Assyrian propensity to clothe their gods in borrowed Babylonian characteristics. Even Sennacherib, who detested Babylon and Marduk, did not escape this borrowing. In one of his historical annals he narrated how he changed the face of the city of Babylon. One of his acts of desecration is narrated thus: "I removed the debris of Babylon and piled it in heaps in that *akitu*-temple as a sight for future generation." But no sooner did he get back to Assyria than he started transforming Assur into a Marduk: the theomachy of *Enuma Elish* became a battle between Assur and Marduk; Assur replaced Marduk in *Enuma Elish;* the statue of Marduk repatriated after the death of Ninurta was installed again in Assyria with its feast; and, above all, the Assyrian god took over the Tablet of Destiny. An inscription of Sennacherib describes this Tablet of Destiny:

"The Tablet of Destinies, the bond of supreme power, dominion over the gods of heaven and underworld, the kingship of the Igigi and anunnaki, the secret of the heavens and the netherworld, (5) the link of the Canopy of Anu and Gansir, the leash of the [multitudes?], which Assur, king of the gods, took in his hand and held [at his breast] — a representation of his form, the replica of his proper appearance, [is depicted] on it; he grasps [in his] hand the leashes of the great heavens, the bond of the [Igigi] and Anunnaki. (10) [In] front of the representation of Assur, his lord, he [Sennacherib] stood a representation of Sennacherib, king of the entire world, king of [Assyria], who fashioned the images of Assur, Anu, Sin, Samas, Adad, Beleti-ili and Istar of the Bit Kitmuri temple, the shepherd who makes humble obeisance, the agent of Assur, his lord. (15) [O Assur, father?] of heaven, king of the gods, determiner of destinies, you alone hold in your hands the Tablet of Destinies of the gods; look after the reign of Sennacherib, king of Assyria, and determine [?] as my destiny a fine destiny, a destiny of good health [?] [and] kingship! Exalt my head among all who reign, and (20) let the base of my throne be secure as a mountain for long days to come! For me, your provisioner, from east to west subject [all the foreign lands?] to my yoke! Let the human race beseech [you that my sons], my grandsons, my dynasty (25) [and my descendants?] endure among humanity [for all] eternity!"[112]

This inscription testifies to the universal dominion of Assur as opposed to Marduk. It bears testimony to the common feature of Mesopotamian life embedded in the *Enuma Elish*; namely, the gods are supreme, humans serve them, and the chief servant or agent is the king. Worship, providing for the gods, ensures protection by the gods. Political propaganda and military campaigns are directed by the gods who determine destinies. But the destinies are not as deterministic as to allow no room for change or freedom, as Hollenbach alleges.[113] Rather, insofar as the gods wish the good of humans who are formed from their blood and stay alive in order to feed them (twice a day), humans are allowed to exercise their freedom within the limits of the relationship. The ruler who is unjust to humans, and therefore to the gods, is overthrown. Sennacherib was thus overthrown by his son (Esarhaddon) and his nobles. They hastened to undo his crime by rebuilding Babylon and reestablishing the *Esagila*, temple, of Marduk and the gods. The gods are supreme; they must be obeyed.

The struggle for political dominance in the Mesopotamian region is given a theological interpretation. *Enuma Elish,* as a hymn that narrates in fabulous style the struggle in the Babylonian pantheon, necessarily shaped human behavior to respond to primeval patterns. It is a myth that acquired new elements by reason of sociopolitical events and through frequent narrative within the *akitu* festival. The greatest influence in its amplification is the political struggle in the Mesopotamian region where life, in all its dimensions, is not simply lived under the eyes of the gods, but its broad outlines are annually decreed by the lord of lords (Marduk). Myth, ritual, and life fully belong together. In the epilogue to *Enuma Elish* the scribes direct that this pattern be handed down from generation to generation:

"Let them be kept in mind and let the leader explain them.
Let the wise and the knowing discuss [them] together.
Let the father recite [them] and impart to his son.
Let the ears of shepherd and herdsman be opened.
Let him rejoice in Marduk, the Enlil of the gods,
That his land may be fertile and that he may prosper.
Firm in order, his command unalterable,
The utterance of his mouth no god shall change.
When he looks he does not turn away his neck;
When he is angry, no god can withstand his wrath.
Vast is his mind, broad his sympathy,
Sinner and transgressor may come before him. . . .
He wrote down and [thereby] preserved [it] for the future.
The [dwell]ing of Marduk which the gods, the Igigi, had made,
. . . let them speak.
. . . the son of Marduk,
[Who] vanquished Ti[iamat] and achieved the kingship" (VII:145–62, ANET).

Jewish Foundation Story (Myth-Symbol) as Creating and Re-Creating Israel

Our analysis so far in this chapter has shown how each community is displayed in its story of origin. Each foundation story is intimately related to cult. Either it functions as a narrative within a festival *(Enuma Elish)* or it is reenacted fully or partially in a socioreligious activity (Nri myth and *Enuma Elish*).

In the Nri myth we pointed out that the story of the civilizing hero may have developed out of a historical migration from the upper Anambra river. The need for food, land, etc., may have influenced the development of other segments of the story, thereby projecting further the creativity of the founding hero. The sacred (Chukwu, the sacralized Ala, and other spirits) is recognized as a reality on which the hero and community depend. The sacred is thus an integral part of the story, recognized as the initiator of the story of the origin of the community, which has also become its own story. In *Enuma Elish* the historical activators for the development of the various parts of the story, and especially for the projection of the Babylonian patron deity (Marduk) into the headship of the pantheon, have been noted. The possible ways in which segments of older agricultural festivals fused with the celebration of the politico-religious triumph of Marduk in the one *akitu* festival were also highlighted.

When we come to the Jewish story we hesitate. A different set of criteria is insinuated in assessing the Jewish religious, political, economic, and social life. The story and its various layers come from "historical events," which should not be confused with the "nature myths" of their neighbors in the Ancient Near East. Some claim that one should not classify this multi-layered story as myth. However, we shall retain the term myth (myth-symbol) for all the foundation stories. The Jewish story, like the Nri myth of origin or the *Enuma Elish,* may have at its core a relationship with historical events, but the narrative structure is nothing like a historical documentary. It is popular and symbolic history, like other foundation stories. The events narrated are primordial or originating events. And, rooted in the cult, there is an interest that narratives of the past shape the life of the assembled community. The cult becomes part of the story, expanding it at strategic points.[114]

In this section, therefore, we will outline (1) the Jewish foundation story, the story of Israel's creation, (2) the Jewish ritual as memorial of the foundation story shaping and being reshaped by Israel's life, and, finally (3), we will explore how the merging of this "historical creation" of Israel with the Jewish story of the origin of the universe impacted on Jewish cult. Our reflection at each stage tries to bring out the theological dimensions of worship in Israel.

The Jewish Foundation Story and the Origin of Israel

Deuteronomy 26:1-11 contains the shape of a thank-offering ritual of the first fruits of the agricultural harvest. The Israelite carries the first fruit in a basket to a priest at a designated sanctuary. The presenter says, "Today I declare to the LORD your God that I have come into the land that the LORD swore to our ancestors to give us" (Deut 26:3).

The priest receives the gift and sets it before the altar. Then the presenter makes the following narrative-confession:

"A wandering Aramean was my ancestor; he went down into Egypt and lived there as an alien, few in number, and there he became a great nation, mighty and populous. When the Egyptians treated us harshly and afflicted us, by imposing hard labor on us, we cried to the LORD, the God of our ancestors; the LORD heard our voice and saw our affliction, our toil, and our oppression. The LORD brought us out of Egypt with a mighty hand and an outstretched arm, with a terrifying display of power, and with signs and wonders; and he brought us into this place and gave us this land, a land flowing with milk and honey. So now I bring the first of the fruit of the ground that you, O LORD, have given me" (Deut 26:5-10).

The above narrative contains two fundamental elements of the Jewish founding story: an escape from Egypt (liberation) and a settlement in the land of Canaan (the Promised Land). It is significant that such a narrative would take place in the context of a cult of Yahweh, the liberator. Indeed the narrative-confession turns out in the end to be an address of gratitude to the Lord. This converts the narrative into an instrument of praise (thanksgiving). The preoccupation of the narrative is not documentary history. Rather, we have a speech-act within the cult expressing the reality of a community bonded together by its faith in Yahweh. The bond is strengthened by the ritual action in which the story is told.

We already noted in the second chapter that Old Testament scholars admit that there was a group (of Israelites) who escaped from Egypt and that the cult of Yahweh may have been known by this group. Beyond this, any other reconstruction of Israel's early history is conjectural. Extrabiblical information about the early period of Jewish history is very scanty. Egyptian sources mention a group called *ʾApiru* (see Exod 1:11), an itinerant socially marginal people who were in Egypt between the fifteenth and twelfth centuries B.C.E. There is mention of "Israel" in the stele of Merneptah (ca. 1220 B.C.E.) celebrating Egyptian victories in Palestine. There is also evidence of Semitic influence in the north-eastern delta region of Egypt, probably the "land of Goshen" where the ancestors of Israel lived (see Gen 45:10; 46:28).[115] This scanty extrabiblical material limits the reconstruction of Israel's history mainly to internal evidence.

Old Testament scholars work with three hypotheses to tell the history of Israel's origins: (1) the pan-Israelite exodus and invasion hypothesis, which takes the canonical accounts of Scripture as basically reliable; (2) the independent-migrations and separate-settlement hypothesis, which argues that a careful analysis of older traditions embedded in Numbers and Joshua reveals an ignorance of any initial pan-Israelite conquest. It was only when the various groups merged into one Israel that their independent conquest traditions became combined and telescoped within the careers of Moses and Joshua.[116] Those who share this second viewpoint — Albright, Alt, Noth, etc. — follow Albright's interpretation of the archaeological material to date the conquest in the thirteenth century B.C.E. Finally, (3) Mendenhall proposed the hypothesis of a sociopolitical upheaval (peasant revolt) against Canaanite city-states. In other words, the liberation was an internal affair within the land of Canaan. Gottwald developed this hypothesis and calls it a social revolution instead of a peasant revolt. There was probably an enslaved group that fled from Egypt. They brought with them the story of liberation and the cult of Yahweh. These two dominant symbols, according to Gottwald's elaboration of the hypothesis, drew together all those in bondage. Canaan was then a part of the Egyptian empire. Gottwald not only reorganized Mendenhall's thesis, he also applied a strict sociological method in his interpretation of Israelite religion. This distanced him from Mendenhall.[117]

Each of these hypotheses accepts that the talk about Israel necessarily implies a talk about liberation from bondage and settlement in the land of Canaan. But the crucial question is how the tribes that were separate before the settlement in Canaan (Noth) realized their self-identity and became united in the one cult of Yahweh.[118] There are again various attempts to answer this question, but since it is a question of origins (rooted in ancestral time, *in illo tempore*), all narratives of this self-identity are layered with theologico-liturgical material. The real grasp of the historical event thus becomes a matter for speculation. Wellhausen's theory is that the Israelite tribes came into contact with one another and developed mutual bonds at Kadesh-Barnea, from where they staged various entries into Canaan. Another opinion is that the concept of Israel as a composition of a number of Yahwistic tribes emerged from the monarchy of Saul and David. A third theory is the amphyctyonic hypothesis developed by Alt-Noth and favored by many historians and theologians (e.g., von Rad, Bright, Weiser, Kraus, Mowinckel, etc.). It is based on the Greek and Old Italian experience: a confederacy that gave the Israelite tribes a common sense of identity after entering into Canaan. This confederacy is renewed annually, and Joshua 24 is supposed to be the ancient ceremony establishing and/or expanding the confederacy to non-Yahwistic tribes.[119]

The key attractions of the amphictyonic theory are the tribal confederacy and the common religious ceremony that are part of Israel's experience. But the weakness of the comparison lies in the fact that Israelites did not settle around one focal point, nor did they have a central sanctuary. Schechem, Bethel, Shiloh, and Gilgal were cult centers that were never clearly stated as national shrines. It appears that wherever the portable ark was housed, there stood the central sanctuary. There was also no central feast like the covenant festival that, as Weiser claims, continued a practice of covenant renewal similar to the one recorded in Joshua 24. Gottwald, who leans heavily on Noth's historical works, did not find Noth's amphictyonic hypothesis convincing. In addition to the deficiencies listed above, the twelve-tribal pattern so crucial to Noth's amphictyony cannot be proven to have existed in pre-Davidic Israel; it is also not found among Greeks and Italians.[120]

All these hypotheses, however, keep on affirming certain key points as constitutive of the Jewish foundation story: the confession of Yahweh as liberator of Israel and the settlement of Israel on the land of Canaan; the creation of a people, which has the consciousness of being the one people of Yahweh, drawn into a confederacy, as Joshua 24 suggests, through Yahwism (the covenant religion of the Exodus group).[121]

Gottwald, whose *Tribes of Yahweh* has been hailed as a paradigm shift in Old testament studies,[122] proposed a sociological (materialist) interpretation of the symbolic history of Israel as revealed in the narratives. He argued for a critical historical-sociological approach in order to answer adequately Noth's question about the self-consciousness of Israel as a federation (which could not have happened before the occupation of Canaan) and to justify her united cult of Yahweh.[123] Yahwism cannot be understood apart from the socio-political community that articulated, transmitted, and practiced the religion of Yahweh. Gottwald follows Noth in stressing that the tradition of the

Pentateuch presupposes the existence of the historical phenomenon "Israel." Consequently, he accepts that the deliberate arrangement of diverse peoples into the social system called Israel and their self-conception as the people of Yahweh are preconditions for the formation of Israel's traditions. On the other hand the cult, within which the basic themes of the story of Israel are narrated, is the setting of the traditions that recount the bringing together of peoples into the social system called Israel. "It was the cult, with its complex of religious exercises aimed at establishing and maintaining right relations with the sacred, i.e., the realm of Yahweh, which formed the institutional subset in the Israelite social system directly responsible for setting forth the nuclear themes around which traditions gathered."[124]

The themes proclaimed in communal worship in various contexts (sanctuaries) were also narrated in other areas of social life for entertainment or intellectual formation (as is characteristic of the myth-narrative). These grounded the self-consciousness of Israel as the redeemed people of Yahweh, a people settled in the Promised Land, a people having as ancestors Abraham, Isaac, and Jacob (originally three independent groups), a people who moved from Canaan to Egypt and then back to Canaan. These independent stories were accepted in the process of merging, and they formed part of the cult-narrative before the traditionists (JEDP) gave them their present shape in the Pentateuch. In other words, the actual process of uniting peoples hitherto unrelated into one people, liberated from bondage to become the people of Yahweh, happened before the emergence of the monarchy. The most foundational themes of their story — Exodus-settlement (epic, history) and theophany-covenant-law (Sinai tradition, cult) — are not separate themes connected by J only during the monarchy, as von Rad claimed. Rather, Gottwald argues (following Noth and Weiser) that they perform different functions and that they grew out of original and integral cultic and ideological functions in ancient Israel.

The historical recital (Exodus-settlement) within the cult, celebrated in an already constituted or reconstituted community, looked back at what Yahweh had done in Israel's past. This was really the past of different tribes that became adopted into the historical cultic recital to form the past of a united Israel. The theophany-covenant-law segment presupposed by the historical recital was immediately celebrated in the cult where Yahweh manifests himself to the people, binds himself to them, and shows himself as the sovereign whose will is to be followed. According to Gottwald, the Sinai tradition later became objectified to assume narrative form at a time when the generation that established a united Israel had died out, when the southern kingdom of Judah joined the federation (eleventh century B.C.E.), and when the threat of Philistine city-states necessitated a closer unity in the confederation (close to the time of the monarchy). This conversion of the Sinai cult material into a story, and its placement at a strategic position before the actual entry into Canaan (i.e., as if the theophany-covenant-law actually happened in that desert), increased its sacredness and ensured a standardized cult program for a united Israel.[125]

The advantage of Gottwald's reconstruction is that it takes seriously the social setting of the groups that merged to form a united Israel. There was a situation of bondage demanding liberation and yielding an egalitarian confederacy. Their religion (Yahwism) emerged from this social crisis and was not simply something imposed from the outside (sociology and religion). The biblical narratives are accepted as serious source materials, but careful attention is paid to the historico-critical method (Noth being the main inspiration). One may not accept all the conclusions Gottwald arrived at through the sociological method (e.g., giving the social process of the tribal merger a priority over Yahwistic religion, as if the latter derived from the former though energizing the former),[126] however, the main thrust of his reconstruction, which situates Israel's foundational story (Exodus-settlement) within human (historical) experience (bondage, revolt, and process of uniting in egalitarian tribal confederacy), may help us explore how their life was shaped by the story. If we take seriously the social dimensions of their experience, we will be saved the trouble of making false claims about their religion and life; rather, the common factor they shared with their neighbors will help sharpen the distinctiveness of their experience.

The Jewish Foundation Story Reenacted in Cult Through Ritual Memorial

The historical reconstruction of the functioning of the Jewish foundation story within the cult may be as tentative as the reconstruction of the history of Jewish origins. But from the interplay between the story and the ritual in the gestation of the tribal confederacy, it is probable that the context of the cult continued to provide the environment for communicating the reality of a united Israel and the one faith in Yahweh.

Deuteronomy 26:5-10 has been described by von Rad as an example of Israel's ancient creed. Though the view of a primitive Israelite creed has lost favor among Old Testament scholars, the Deuteronomists in their liturgical sermons may be drawing from more ancient commonplace themes, which were later expanded in Jewish history.[127] This prayer of offering of first fruits may indicate an earlier effort (by Levitical priests) to shape, within the cult, the consciousness and praxis of a united Israel liberated by Yahweh.

The most remarkable impact of the foundation story on the consciousness of Israelites through the channel of the cult is the transformation of pre-Israelite festivals. Just as the birth of a united Israel came as a gradual process, the transformation of pre-Israelite family, tribal, or national rituals into a Yahwistic cult must have been gradual. There was no sudden leap to convert Canaanite festivals into a memorial of the central story of Israel. In the process, the patient ideological work of Levitical priests in various sanctuaries and the intervention of the prophets and Deuteronomists must be acknowledged.

In order to explore the impact of the core story of Israel (Exodus-settlement) on life and worship (theophany-covenant-law), we will show (1) the conversion of festivals into a memorial of liberation by Yahweh (in some cases the transformation was total while in others the original motifs predominated) and (2) the recalling of these events to Yahweh and to Israel within and outside the cult in situations of national crisis.

Israelite Festivals as a Memorial of Liberation by Yahweh. There are three pilgrimage festivals *(hag)* celebrated by a united Israel in the land of Canaan, according to the most ancient liturgical calendar reproduced in the Pentateuch (Exod 23:10-19; 34:18-26; see Deut 16:1-7). These pilgrimage feasts (Unleavened Bread, Harvest or feast of Weeks, and Ingathering) are celebrated in central sanctuaries. They require every male to appear before the Lord (an opportunity for a national census):

"Three times in the year you shall hold a festival for me. You shall observe the festival of unleavened bread; as I commanded you, you shall eat unleavened bread for seven days at the appointed time in the month of Abib, for in it you came out of Egypt. No one shall appear before me empty-handed. You shall observe the festival of harvest, of the first fruits of your labor, of what you sow in the field. You shall observe the festival of ingathering at the end of the year, when you gather in from the field the fruit of your labor. Three times in the year all your males shall appear before the Lord GOD" (Exod 23:14-17).

This information may reflect agricultural rituals commonly performed before the merging of the various tribes, at least before the group from Egypt settled in Canaan. The addition of the escape (liberation) motif (23:15) may be late. Thus the principal feasts of a united Israel were Canaanite (pre-union) agricultural festivals. Therefore, the Israelites of Canaanite origin who overthrew their rulers in a social revolution celebrated these feasts before the recognition of Yahweh as their God, and those liberated from Egyptian bondage appropriated these feasts when they settled in Canaan. The general rubric suggested by the context of these three pilgrimage feasts is that they are celebrated for Yahweh and not before any other divinity.

The Yahweh motif in these festivals produces a double effect: an agricultural thanksgiving festival (a nature-festival) is interpreted (transformed or "historicized") as a celebration of Exodus-settlement; in the cult where the celebration takes place the covenant-law of Yahweh is renewed. Second, Yahweh, who was recognized as liberator of Israel from bondage (a warrior deity Yahweh Sabaoth), is transformed into a divinity who not only bestows the Promised Land, but also makes it yield fruit for the nourishment of Israel. Yahweh assumes the characteristics of a fertility deity. These two theological ideas may be clarified as we analyze some of the festivals.

The dominant impact of the Exodus-settlement motif on the festivals is immediately evident in the feast of Unleavened Bread. Under the influence of the Deuteronomist and priestly traditions, this feast became merged with the nomadic Passover, which was a family festival. Since both feasts fall within the first month of the Jewish calendar (Nisan, Babylonian; Abib, Canaanite), the merger was an easy affair. However, since the Pasch attracts the liberation motif more readily than the feast of Unleavened Bread does, the paschal theme predominates in the fused celebration. We will examine this combined feast in greater detail after looking at the harvest festival and Ingathering.

THE HARVEST FESTIVAL OR FEAST OF WEEKS. The harvest festival (*gasir*, Exod 23:16) is more popularly known as the feast of Weeks (*hag shavuʿot*, Exod 34:22; Deut 16:10; or simply *shavuʿot*, Num 28:26).[128] It is an agricultural feast celebrated by confederated Israel in a central or designated sanctuary. It is a festival that retained its agricultural character and even resisted being interpreted in terms of the liberation motif. The detailed prescription of Leviticus highlights the fact that farmers are concerned:

"And from the day after the sabbath, from the day on which you bring the sheaf of the elevation offering, you shall count off seven weeks; they shall be complete. You shall count until the day after the seventh sabbath, fifty days; then you shall present an offering of new grain to the LORD. You shall bring from your settlements two loaves of bread as an elevation offering, each made of two-tenths of an ephah; they shall be of choice flour, baked with leaven, as first fruits to the LORD. On that same day you shall make proclamation; you shall hold a holy convocation; you shall not work at your occupations. This is a statute forever in all your settlements throughout your generations" (Lev 23:15-17, 21).

The Levitical calendar presupposes the feast of Unleavened Bread as a new year festival marking the beginning of the barley harvest (Lev 23:6), while *shavuʿot* brings the harvest season to the end (celebrated on the fiftieth day; LXX, *pentecostê*). The bread offered to God is the leavened bread that a farming population was already eating during the fifty days of harvest. This is the only context where leavened bread (often associated with corruption) is offered to Yahweh. The highly developed ritual of Leviticus (practiced in the second temple) includes holocausts, sin offerings, and peace offerings.

As a harvest festival, it is marked by a joyous celebration. Indications of the joy experienced in this festival can be found in phrases like the following:

"May those who sow in tears
  reap with shouts of joy.
Those who go out weeping,
  bearing the seed for sowing,
shall come home with shouts of joy,
  carrying their sheaves" (Ps 126:5-6).

"You have multiplied the nation,
you have increased its joy;
they rejoice before you
as with joy at the harvest" (Isa 9:3).

This festival, though celebrated in a designated sanctuary where Yahweh is invoked, lacks the liberation motif. It did not become explicitly the feast of the Covenant-Torah until the intertestamental period (see the book of Jubilees). Kraus suggests that its being grounded in agrarian rites, which left it open to the influence of Canaanite fertility rituals, may explain the lack of early connection between this feast and the core story of Israel.[129] The fertility dimension, it is claimed, endangered the Yahwistic cult. Such arguments are not convincing. The same danger can also be shown to exist for the feast of Ingathering (feast of Booths), which some have compared to the cult of Bacchus (see below). Rather, insofar as this festival is celebrated in the sanctuary of Yahweh, this deity is now thanked (feted) as the provider of the fruit of the earth. Consequently, he functions as a fertility deity. Philo, who is noted for spiritualizing Old Testament practice, retained the agricultural dimension of this pentecost festival called the feast of the first fruits:

"The feast is called the feast of the first-fruits either because before the year's grain is used by man, the first produce of the new harvest and first fruit are to be presented as first-fruits — for indeed it is right and just, when we have received prosperity from God as the greatest gift, not to enjoy the most necessary food, . . . before having offered the first-fruits to Him Who has given it to us; not that we give Him anything, for all things, riches and gifts belong to Him — but because, by this humble sign, we show an attitude of thanksgiving and of piety towards Him Who is not sparing with His graces, but Who extends them continually and liberally — or because the sheaf of wheat is par excellence the first and best produce."[130]

Even when the book of Jubilees and the Essenians connected the feast to the foundation story of Israel, they retained the agricultural motif. It emerges, therefore, that Yahweh cannot be equated with Baal (the god of fertility), yet one should not deny Yahweh the acquired fertility character. Mono-Yahwism or radical monotheism, the distinctive characteristic of the Israelite God, translates itself into an assimilation by the one deity of the qualities predicated of divinity in the Ancient Near East. Thus the harvest festival proves that Yahweh is a fertility divinity insofar as he blesses his people by making the land productive. The blessing *(berakah)* has at its very root fertility or fertilization.[131]

The book of Jubilees (dated second century B.C.E. by Charles) gives great prominence to the harvest festival. While not losing its agrarian motif *shavuᶜot* is transformed into a celebration of the gift of the Covenant. For Jubilees, it is the one covenant concluded with Noah, Abraham, and Moses that is being celebrated or renewed. Moses is instructed to command all Israel to celebrate the feast of Weeks so that they may not forget the covenant:

"And the Lord smelt the goodly savor, and He made a covenant with him that there should not be any more a flood to destroy the earth; that all the days of the earth seed-time and harvest should never cease; cold and heat, and summer and winter, and day and night should not change their order, nor cease for ever. . . . For this reason it is ordained and written on the heavenly tables, that they should celebrate the feast of weeks, in this month once a year, to renew the covenant every year. And this whole festival was celebrated in heaven from the day of creation till the days of Noah — twenty-six jubilees and five weeks of years; and Noah and his sons observed it for seven jubilees and one week of years. . . . But Abraham observed it, and Isaac and Jacob and his children observed it up to their days, and in thy days the children of Israel forgot it until you celebrated it anew on this mountain. And do thou command the children of Israel to observe this festival in all their generations for a commandment unto them; one day in the year in this month they shall celebrate the festival. For it is the feast of weeks and the feast of first-fruits" (VI:4, 17–21).[132]

Among the group from which the book of Jubilees emanated and among the Qumran Covenanters the feast of Weeks became the celebration and renewal of the covenant. It was the feast of feasts. It was celebrated on the fifteenth day of the third month (Sivan) and was also linked with oaths. The inspiration for linking *shavuᶜot* with the covenant was derived from Exodus 19:1: "On the third new moon after the Israelites had gone out of the land of Egypt, on that very day, they came into the wilderness of Sinai." The celebration narrated by the Chronicler on the third month during the reign of Asa may also be the feast of Weeks. It involved a renewal of the covenant and the taking of oaths to walk on the way of Yahweh (2 Chr 15:8-15). Rabbinic tradition reveals, in the second century C.E., that the feast of Weeks celebrates the giving of the Torah, thus linking it to the Sinai event.[133] Christians were familiar with this interpretation of *shavuʿot* (Pentecost) as the feast of Covenant/Torah (Acts 2, etc.).

We conclude that the evidence for the transformation of the harvest pilgrimage feast into a festival commemorating the core of Israel's experience of Yahweh was late. The feast was celebrated in a sanctuary where Yahweh alone was invoked. In this way the thanksgiving rendered to Yahweh as the cause of fertility divests the Canaanite divinity of his power over fertility and projects unto Yahweh attributes he did not have.

THE FEAST OF INGATHERING (FEAST OF BOOTHS). Ingathering is the third of the pilgrimage feasts requiring a gathering at a central sanctuary (*hag ha-ʾasiph,* feast of Ingathering, Exod 23:16; 34:22). It is the harvest festival that brings the agricultural year to an end: "You shall keep the festival of booths for seven days, when you have gathered in the produce from your threshing floor and your wine press" (Deut 16:13). *Sukkot* (Booths or Tabernacles), according to the Deuteronomic calendar, is also the name of this festival; later it became the dominant appellation.

Sukkot is the most popular and prominent pilgrimage festival celebrated in Israel, which should not be surprising since it falls at the end of the agricultural year and at the beginning of a new planting season. Some call it the fall new year (following the Canaanite and Egyptian calendar).[134] It is a thanksgiving autumn festival celebrated in the seventh month. It is marked by joy and dance, eating and drinking, and general merry-making. This merriment can be seen in the action of the kindred of Gaal of Schechem, who were opposed to the regime of Abimelech: "They went out into the field and gathered the grapes from their vineyards, trod them, and celebrated. Then they went into the temple of their god, ate and drank, and ridiculed Abimelech" (Judg 9:27). For young girls it served as an annual opportunity to display and to secure suitors. In one such annual festival, the decimated Benjaminites were allowed by the confederacy to snatch wives from among the dancing daughters of Shiloh (Judg 21:19-23).

Up to the time of rabbinic Judaism the song and dance were maintained in this agricultural festival. As they danced, the young girls of Jerusalem sang:

"Fellow, look around and see — choose what you want!
Don't look for beauty, look for family:
Charm is deceitful and beauty is vain,
but a woman who fears the LORD is to be praised" (Prov 31:30).[135]

The practice of the joyous liturgical dance continued in the Temple into the time of Christ. The joy reaches its summit at the ritual of water libation. This may have been an ancient Temple practice. It was opposed by conservative elements among the Sadducees because it lacked a biblical foundation. However, the Mishnah (*Taanit* 1.1–2) calls it a prayer for rain: "When do they include the mention of *the powers of rain* [in the Prayer]? R. Eliezer says, 'On the first day of the Festival [of Tabernacles].' R. Joshua says, 'On the last day of the festival.' . . . They ask for rain only near [the time of] rain."

The ritual of water libation is preceded by the ritual of drawing water (called *Beth ha-She'ubah*) from the spring of Siloam. The preparation for this generates popular joy: "Anyone who has not seen the rejoicing of *bet hashshoebah* in his life has never seen rejoicing."[136] At cock-crow the priests sound a trumpet. A solemn procession moves down to the fountain of Siloam. A golden jar is filled with water. Then the procession, accompanied by trumpet blasts ("a sustained, a quavering, and a sustained note on the *shofar*"),[137] moves back to the Temple through the water gate. The presiding priest mounts the steps leading to the altar, pours the water libation into the basin of offering from which the water flows into the bottomless depths. After this there is a procession around the altar accompanied by cries of Hosanna. Flutes, harps, lyres, cymbals, trumpets, and other musical instruments feature in this festival: "pious men and wonder workers would dance before them with flaming torches in their hand, and they would sing before them songs and praises."[138] This procession in song and dance occurs once per day for the first six days, but seven times on the Seventh day.[139]

The Deuteronomic legislation about this festival is replete with the joy that marks the celebrations. It is a feast to the Lord, with ethical implications — the joy of the festival should be shared especially with those in need:

"You shall keep the festival of booths for seven days. . . . Rejoice during your festival, you and your sons and your daughters, your male and female slaves, as well as the Levites, the strangers, the orphans, and the widows resident in your towns. Seven days you shall keep the festival for the LORD your God at the place the LORD will choose; for the LORD your God will bless you in all your produce and in all your undertakings, and you shall surely celebrate" (Deut 16:13-15).

This feast was so popular in attracting pilgrims to sanctuaries that it formed the natural occasion for the dedication of the Temple of Solomon (1 Kgs 8:1ff.). King Jeroboam, who seceded with the tribes of the North in the face of Solomonic innovations and who chose the famous sanctuary of El at Bethel as the new center of the league (confederacy) traditions, inaugurated the Bethel cult during the festival of *Sukkot* (1 Kgs 12:25-33).[140] Even Zechariah believed that when the day of Yahweh comes, the survivors of the nations "shall go up year after year to worship the King, the LORD of hosts, and to keep the festival of booths"; drought and plagues "shall be the punishment of Egypt and the punishment of all the nations that do not go up to keep the festival of booths" (Zech 14:16, 19).

The Levitical calendar (Lev 23:39ff.), which links the festival directly with the central story of Israel, gives a fixed date for this solemnity whose date would normally depend on the nature of the crops. It will be celebrated for seven days starting on the fifteenth day of the seventh month *(Tishri)*, with an additional day of rest. But its connection of the booths with tents in the wilderness appears somewhat unusual.[141]

"You shall live in booths for seven days; all that are citizens in Israel shall live in booths, so that your generations may know that I made the people of Israel live in booths when I brought them out of the land of Egypt: I am the LORD your God" (Lev 23:42-43).

The Israelites in the wilderness did not dwell in booths (or huts), but in tents. The Targum got around this by interpreting *Sukkot* as the *Shekinah*, the cloudy glory (or presence) of Yahweh that covered the Israelites when they came out of Egypt.[142] In this way a sedentary agricultural festival is theologically interpreted as a ritual representation of a nomadic experience. While not losing its agricultural character, *Sukkot* also carried the key symbols of Israel's story and worship.

PASCH AND UNLEAVENED BREAD AS ACTUALIZATION OF JEWISH REDEMPTIVE EVENT IN RITUAL AND LIFE. The Passover *(pesah)* is a nomadic or semi-nomadic festival. If a group of Israelites were involved in animal husbandry before and/or after the settlement and union, then they celebrated the Pasch as their principal festival. In the Jewish tradition, this springtime festival has been fused with the feast of Unleavened Bread. And more than *shavuᶜot* or *Sukkot*, it became identified with the liberation motif of the Jewish story.

In the postexilic period Passover was the most popular of all Jewish festivals. This feast has given the Jewish people the greatest energy to survive. In the tradition-history, recorded in the Pentateuch, the rites of this festival were already being interpreted allegorically. The story that is transmitted contains layers of tradition. The ritual of the Exodus *pesah* (Exodus 12) has been recognized by literary (tradition) critics as containing traditions of JE and P. The post-Exodus rituals (in Exod 12:24ff.; Deuteronomy 16; Leviticus 23; Numbers 9, etc.) also contain the traditions of JEDP. It will be difficult to reconstruct the most primitive *pesah* story by breaking up Exodus 12 into its various traditions. Segal, who closely examined the various opinions about this primitive segment (Exodus 12), is probably right in concluding that the Passover and its traditions, as the documents show, stand in a particular class:

"The age and sanctity of the festival and the popular esteem in which it was held placed these early documents beyond the reach of the would-be reformer — even though the practices which they enjoined had been amended with the passage of time. Whether these or other Passover texts passed through the hands of later redactors is therefore of little importance. They contain material considerably older than the date at which — according to the Source hypothesis — they were redacted. . . . It follows that to attribute portions of the text to schools of redactors on the grounds of their literary composition is lacking in both force and value."[143]

In the Exodus ritual (Exod 12:1-14) the feast occurs in the first month of the year (Nisan). The ritual consists of the selection of a victim by each family, household, or group of neighbors on the tenth day of the month — a one-year-old male lamb without blemish. The victim is slaughtered on the evening of fourteenth Nisan, and some of the blood is smeared on door posts and the lintel of houses. It is roasted and eaten with unleavened bread and bitter herbs. It is eaten in haste. Whatever remains of the meat is burnt. Later narratives amplified this core, which happens in tales of this kind that are narrated in assembly and ritually enacted.

The narrative of the Passover is followed by that of the Unleavened Bread (*massot;* LXX, *azyme,* Exod 12:15-20). It is a festival that consists of eating only unleavened bread and putting away all leaven in the houses. The leaven is viewed as a pollutant, endangering the new crops. Any introduction of leaven is punishable by excommunication; this law later extended to include sojourners (Exod 12:19). The feast of Unleavened Bread, the first among the pilgrimage festivals in the primitive calendar (Exod 23:15; 34:18), is a harvest festival that was probably drawn from the Canaanite agricultural practice. It is celebrated at the beginning of the barley harvest and lasts for seven days. It marks the beginning of the seven weeks preceding the feast of Weeks (Harvest, cf. Deut 16:9).[144] Segal disagrees with most informed opinion that the unleavened bread eaten on the feast of *massot* comes from the new grain harvested. The parched corn that is eaten, he claims, is from the previous year's harvest. He interprets the *pesah* and *massot* (Exodus 12) as one new year festival comparable to the new year festivals in the Ancient Near East and the Mediterranean lands.[145] The primitive Passover, he argues, is one festival celebrated for seven days, beginning with *pesah* and continuing with the *massot.* "It is not that two festivals have been merged to form a single festival; but a single festival has been divided into two in the Bible narrative, because only one group of ceremonies, the Pesah, appeared to have full relevance to the circumstances of the Exodus."[146]

The idea of Passover as a new year festival is defensible, since the first month *(Nisan* or *Abib)* is the Passover month. But the distinctions made in the sources favor the hypothesis of two different festivals. This is more so when Unleavened Bread appears elsewhere as a pilgrimage feast unconnected with *pesah* (a household festival). We thus take the Passover as originally one festival *(pesah).*[147]

The blood ritual in the Passover and the myth of the passing of the exterminator *(masshit)* lends credence to the interpretation of the pre-Israelite model as a festival of redemption. The sprinkled blood protected the household from the exterminator. It may thus have been practiced by nomads or semi-nomads to secure fecundity in the flock and to drive away evil forces. Arabs, in recent times, have been known to smear the entrance to their house with blood when they are threatened with cholera, or to smear blood on their cattle to ensure the good health of the herd.[148] Unleavened bread and bitter herbs are used in the Passover because they are the normal food and seasoning of bedouins. Some believe that their use excludes the contagion of decay (fermentation) in a new year festival. The medicinal herbs may also serve as protection against evil spirits.[149] It is taken in haste to secure blessings of the deity before shepherds strike camp to move to areas of better pasture. Such a festival, which existed among nomads and semi-nomads, lends itself easily to reinterpretation among oppressed Israelites as the myth-ritual vehicle of the Exodus-settlement tradition.

THE PASSOVER AS FESTIVAL OF NATIONAL LIBERATION. The liberation motif was dominant in this festival from premonarchic times, as the Pentateuchal traditions appear to indicate. However, its transformation into a national pilgrimage feast, combining two independent festivals, was begun during the reign of Josias (622/621 B.C.E., 2 Kgs 23:21-23) and must have been completed by the time of the prophet Ezekiel (Ezek 45:21). The Deuteronomic reform, under Josias, projected onto the national consciousness this festival as carrying the foundation story, along with the faith in Yahweh. A family festival was converted into a national pilgrimage feast held in a central sanctuary, Jerusalem.

"Observe the month of Abib by keeping the passover for the LORD your God, for in the month of Abib the LORD your God brought you out of Egypt by night. You shall offer the passover sacrifice for the LORD your God, from the flock and the herd, at the place that the LORD will choose as a dwelling for his name" (Deut 16:1-2).

The theological interest of the Deuteronomistic school and the political pretensions of Josias to rule over a united southern and northern kingdom[150] are merged in this ideology of a central sanctuary where a very popular springtime festival will attract all of Israel. The feast that celebrates national liberation is now an instrument of national unification.

The interpretation of the Passover in terms of national liberation from bondage of Egyptian slavery was already integrated into the primitive sources. In Exodus 12, the details of the ritual, which were probably the same in any nomadic *pesah*, are followed by the Passover myth reinterpreting a pre-Exodus sacrifice:

"It is the passover of the LORD. For I will pass through the land of Egypt that night, and I will strike down every firstborn in the land of Egypt, both human beings and animals; on all the gods of Egypt I will execute judgments: I am the LORD. The blood shall be a sign for you on the houses where you live: when I see the blood, I will pass over you, and no plague shall destroy you when I strike the land of Egypt" (Exod 12:11-13).

The story of the escape of an enslaved people is retold in a myth-symbolic drama pitching Israel's Yahweh against the Egyptian oppressor and their gods. Whenever the *pesah* is celebrated it becomes a reactualization (sacrament-symbol) of the founding experience:

"You shall observe this rite as a perpetual ordinance for you and your children. When you come to the land that the LORD will give you, as he has promised, you shall keep this observance. And when your children ask you, 'What do you mean by this observance?' you shall say, 'It is the passover sacrifice to the LORD, for he passed over the houses of the Israelites in Egypt, when he struck down the Egyptians but spared our houses'" (Exod 12:24-27).

Cross has argued very strongly that there was a springtime festival celebrated in the sanctuary at Gilgal (*pesah* or *massot*). This was a reactualization of the original liberation drama as a "march of conquest." From Joshua 3–5 materials, this Passover festival, which may date to the twelfth century, is reconstituted by Cross as follows: the people sanctify themselves, the ark is borne in solemn procession (Yahweh in battle array), the Jordan serves as Reed Sea, twelve stones are set up at the Gilgal sanctuary as Moses did in the desert (Exod 24:4), and the angelic general of the host of Yahweh appears (Josh 5:3-15; Exod 3:2ff.; 14:19). The victory song of Exodus 15 has its roots, according to Cross, in this springtime liturgy of "ritual conquest." The victory song projects the imagery of the warrior god (Exod 15:13-18), whose exploits are reactualized in the ritual march of conquest with the ark. This took place in the league sanctuary at Gilgal where the twelve tribes may have united.

The importance of the sanctuary at Gilgal is noted by commentators. In the victory songs the ritual factor has also been recognized as having a role in linking the Jordan crossing and the Reed Sea traditions. However, Childs disagrees with the Cross' dating of Exodus 15. He considers the claim by Cross and Kraus of a Passover celebration reenacting the march of conquest highly questionable.[151]

No matter how interesting Cross' theory of an early Passover celebration by the league may be, it appears that the Joshua texts he relates to the covenant tradition (Joshua 3–5) may go back to the priestly editor. But it also appears defensible that the Deuteronomist and the priestly traditions used older material to entrench a novel interpretation of *pesah* and Unleavened Bread, detaching both feasts from their pastoral and agrarian moorings. This interpretation is more radical than what happened with *Sukkot* and *shavuʿot*. A fixed salvation-history view became entrenched in the cult and was propagated through a popular festival that succeeded in giving identity to a people beset by the difficulties of existence.[152] The Deuteronomist, who accepted the foundation story of the past as ideal measure for action in the present, employed ritual recalling *(zkr)* as a key to the actualization of the liberation motif of the festivals. "For seven days you shall eat unleavened bread with it — the bread of affliction — because you came out of the land of Egypt in great haste, so that all the days of your life you may remember the day of your departure from the land of Egypt" (Deut 16:3).

The priestly tradition more than D sacralizes this actualization. P employs the term *zikkaron* (memorial; LXX, *anamnesis* or *mnemosunon*) to underline the actualization (though here we may be dealing with postexilic material). The interest of P is to project the theophany-covenant-law of the past as an expression of the one gracious purpose of God through which an eternal order has been established. The preoccupation is not to relate present Israel with a past event, since in P's view "there is no tension between past and present because the past mediated an eternal order. Rather the concern is to maintain an eternal order and relate Israel to it."[153] "This day shall be a day of remembrance for you. You shall celebrate it as a festival to the LORD; throughout your generations you shall observe it as a perpetual ordinance" (Exod 12:14).

The "children's question" that D built into the Passover story in Exodus 12–13 as a technique of communicating traditional belief is placed by P in the context of crossing the Jordan (Josh 4:6-7; 4:20ff.). Joshua asked twelve selected men, each from a tribe of Israel, to pass before the ark in the midst of the Jordan and pick a stone. The stone becomes

"a sign among you. When your children ask in time to come, 'What do these stones mean to you?' then you shall tell them that the waters of the Jordan were cut off in front of the ark of the covenant of the LORD. When it crossed over the Jordan, the waters of the Jordan were cut off. So these stones shall be to the Israelites a memorial forever" (Josh 4:6-7).

Pilgrims who attended the pilgrimage festivals (including the Passover, according to Cross and Segal) are instructed by the priests in the sanctuaries (in this case Gilgal) on how to transmit the central events of the liberation to their children.[154] P converts the significant cultic objects into a memorial: a sacred and eternal order proclaiming Yahweh's blessing (grace) on Israel. The stone monument at Gilgal creates for the Israelite the possibility of identifying with crossing the Jordan, which ritually reproduces crossing the Reed Sea, to finally assure the Israelite of his or her identity.

"Those twelve stones, which they had taken out of the Jordan, Joshua set up in Gilgal, saying to the Israelites, 'When your children ask their parents in time to come, "What do these stones mean?" then you shall let your children know, "Israel crossed over the Jordan here on dry ground." For the LORD your God dried up the waters of the Jordan for you until you crossed over, as the LORD your God did to the Red Sea, which he dried up for us until we crossed over'" (Josh 4:20-23).

It is perfect or complete memorial that puts the Israelite in immediate relationship with the events that created Israel. This catechesis, when carried on in the family and in the centralized places of cult (northern and southern kingdoms), during and after the Exile, maintained these central events in the consciousness of the people. One may follow Farby in seeing this quasi-institutionalized *anamnesis* as having its long distance effect in all the traditions connected with the

Israelite central story: the passage through the Reed Sea (Exodus 12ff.) is realized in the passage through the Jordan (Joshua 4), in the return from the Exile (Isaiah 43), by the entry into the community of the covenanters at Qumran (1 QS 2:19ff.), in the confession of faith in Jesus (John 6), in baptism in the name of Jesus (1 Cor 10:1ff.), and in baptism into the Church (liturgy of Easter Vigil).[155]

In the Jewish paschal liturgy we see this crucial expression of relating a present assembly to a past order to mobilize worshipers to action. According to Mishnah *Pesahim* 10.5E:

"In every generation a person is duty-bound to regard himself as if he personally has gone forth from Egypt. . . . Therefore we are duty-bound to thank, praise, glorify, honor, exalt, extol, and bless him who did for our forefathers and for us all these miracles. He brought us forth from slavery to freedom, anguish to joy, mourning to festival, darkness to great light, subjugation to redemption, so we should say before him, Hallelujah."[156]

In the Passover liturgy, the *Passover Haggadah,* which embodies the tale of the Passover, is prompted by the four questions asked by the youngest participant in the dinner (the "children's question"). The questions address the issue of why the Passover night is different from all other nights. The father "begins [answering the questions] with disgrace and concludes with glory."[157] The story is a midrash or commentary on Deuteronomy 26:5-8: "A wandering Aramean was my ancestor."

The midrashic commentary centers on Exodus-settlement and omits the Sinai covenant. The Sinai motif enters into the celebration later during the grace (the *birkat ha-mazon*), as happens in all Jewish dinners. The *birkat ha-mazon*, whose text is identical in every Jewish meal, is a vital instrument for reliving the Jewish foundation story. It is made up of three blessings: blessing for the food, thanksgiving for the land and the food, and petition in favor of Israel. This grace recaptures the principal themes of the Jewish story: liberation from bondage, covenant, and settlement in the land that produces the daily bread. As a result in the course of a meal around the family table (a crucial context of Jewish education), "ritual, liturgy, and even culinary elements are orchestrated to transmit a vital past from one generation to the next."[158]

Because the Passover is a high festive day, an embolism is introduced at the thanksgiving and/or petition pericope of the *birkat hamazon* to project the main intention of the festival. The embolism of the Passover celebration is added to the third benediction. The memory motif dominates this embolism, which is the same on every festive day except for the insertion of the feast being celebrated:

"Our God, and the God of our father, may the remembrance of ourselves and of our fathers and the remembrance of Jerusalem, thy city, and remembrance of the Messiah, the son of David, thy servant, and the remembrance of thy people, the whole house of Israel, arise and come, come to pass, be seen and accepted and heard, be remembered and be mentioned before thee for deliverance, for good, for grace, for lovingkindness and for mercy on this *the Festival of Unleavened Bread.* Remember us, JHWH, our God, on it for good and visit us on it for blessing and save us on it unto life by a word of salvation and mercy, and spare, favour and show us mercy, for thou art a gracious and merciful God and King."[159]

The frequent call on God to remember is characteristic of the complaint pattern of prayer (as we shall see in the Psalms). The imagery of key events and personages is brought before God so that God would act in favor of Israel. On the basis of the foundational deeds of the past, God is asked to act in the future in a way that will upset human forecasts though gratifying desires to the fullest.[160] Every pilgrimage festival became a security risk for a colonial government in Israel. This is very much so in the Passover because the Messiah is expected to appear in the course of the celebration. Indeed, the paschal liturgical text is crafted in such a way that this eschatological dimension is unmistakable. It opens with, "This year we are here; next year may we be in Israel"; it concludes with, "Next year in Jerusalem."[161]

In the Passover celebration (pre- or postexilic) the motif of liberation has imposed itself decisively to reduce to an inconsequential minimum the original myth-narratives of the *pesah* and *massot.* The plight of a small nation amidst very powerful neighbors and the frequent experience of exile ensured that the issue of liberation would be the perduring cry of Israel in its face to face with Yahweh. It became natural to point back to the captivating story of escape from

Egypt as the paradigm for measuring God's and Israel's action now and in the future.

The Recalling of Foundational Events to Yahweh and to Israel in Situations of National Crisis. We have been exploring in the last section how Canaanite agricultural festivals (Unleavened Bread, feast of Weeks, and Ingathering) and the nomadic or semi-nomadic celebration of *pesah* have been transformed in the practice of life in Israel to be the carriers of the founding story. In these celebrations, Exodus-settlement and theophany-covenant-law are recalled and, thus, actualized within the cult.

The recalling of the foundation story is not presented to God by the people only during the periodic pilgrimage festivals. This recalling penetrates many aspects of life and experience, within and outside the cult. We shall limit ourselves here to how the re-presentation of the foundation story functions in situations of national crisis as a bond between Yahweh and his people, necessitating the intervention of Yahweh, and how it functions as a challenge to and even as an indictment of Israel so that Israel may repent and follow the way of Yahweh as its ancestors did.

RECALLING PAST EVENTS OF YAHWEH TO ENCOURAGE ACTION — THE PSALMS OF LAMENT. The context where this re-presentation of the foundation story is best demonstrated is in the psalms of lament. The psalms of lament (Westermann) or complaint (Gunkel) depict the woeful plight of the people, who bewailed and lamented with copious tears. They are the cries of a tormented people affronted in that which they consider most holy.[162] The lament can be individual or communal. Here we focus on the community lament set within the cult. In the lament the verb *zkr* may be used with God as subject, or the narrative of the past saving deeds turns into arguments amassed as memories to stimulate God into action. When *zkr* is used it appears in the jussive or imperative mood: "Remember your congregation, which you acquired long ago, / which you redeemed to be the tribe of your heritage. / Remember Mount Zion, where you came to dwell" (Ps 74:2).

The primary subject to whom the lamentation is addressed is Yahweh. The community (subject two) cries to Yahweh (subject one) to liberate them from the enemy or from the disaster (subject three).

According to Westermann, the lament takes the following structure: address (and introductory petition), lament, turning toward God or confession of trust, petition, and vow of praise.[163] But in the psalms of lament where the history of Yahweh's past deeds or foundation story is re-presented (e.g., Psalms 44; 74; 77; 80; 83; 85; 126; Isaiah 63), a sharp contrast is drawn between the past and the present. "The past forces itself into the present precisely in its contrast to the present. What *has* happened is heard as the antithesis of what *is* happening."[164]

The contrast can be seen in Psalm 80.[165] It opens with an address and a call for help (vv. 1-3). The lament that recounts the present woes of the people follows:

"O LORD God of hosts,
  how long will you be angry with your people's prayers?
You have fed them with the bread of tears,
  and given them tears to drink in full measure.
You make us the scorn of our neighbors;
  our enemies laugh among themselves" (Ps 80:4-6).

The nostalgic looking back on God's earlier deeds in Psalm 80 is put in the imagery of the vine:

"You brought a vine out of Egypt;
  you drove out the nations and planted it.
You cleared the ground for it;
  it took deep root and filled the land.
The mountains were covered with its shade,
  the mighty cedars with its branches;
it sent out its branches to the sea,
  and its shoots to the River" (vv. 8-11).

The Exodus-settlement motif is the core of this "looking back." The vine imagery helps introduce further amplifications into an already fabulous founding narrative ("filled the land," "mountains were covered with its shade," "sent out its branches to the sea"). Such hyperbolic recalling tries to put God on the spot and make God react for the good of Israel.

In some laments the looking back to deeds of the past weaves creation into history. The creation (cosmogonic) is depicted as a struggle with and a victory over chthonic forces: chaos is slain by God to establish order. This is very well depicted in the lament of second Isaiah:

"Awake, awake, put on strength,
  O arm of the LORD!
Awake, as in days of old,
  the generations of long ago!
Was it not you who cut Rahab in pieces,
  who pierced the dragon?
Was it not you who dried up the sea,
  the waters of the great deep;
who made the depths of the sea a way
  for the redeemed to cross over?" (Isa 51:9-10, cf. Ps 77:13-17).

In second Isaiah the order established is kingship. In the march of conquest toward this order, "the myth is penetrated by historical memory; the battle with the dragon sea becomes the redemption from Egypt."[166] This demonstrates that in Israel creation and redemption belong together.

It is in the context of the fabulous narrative of the wonders of the past that the warrior God, Yahweh, should reconsider what is being done in the present, as the lament in Psalm 80 stresses:

"Why then have you broken down its walls,
  so that all who pass along the way pluck its fruit?
The boar from the forest ravages it,
  and all that move in the field feed on it" (vv. 12-13).

Yahweh is petitioned to change in a recurring refrain: "Restore us, O [LORD] God [of hosts]; / let your face shine, that we may be saved" (Ps 80:3, 7, 19). Then Yahweh is requested to act in accordance with the past events recalled; in other words, to destroy the enemy and liberate Israel.

"Turn again, O God of hosts;
  look down from heaven, and see;
have regard for this vine,
  the stock that your right hand planted.
They have burned it with fire, they have cut it down;
  may they perish at the rebuke of your countenance.

But let your hand be upon the one at your right hand,
  the one whom you made strong for yourself" (Ps 80:14-17).

This retelling of God's action, which has become the key confession of faith in a situation of national crisis, has the unique power of mobilizing Yahweh to action and bringing consolation to the people. As Westermann says:

"The events of history, remembered by Israel within a confessional setting, were kept alive on those various occasions not only in such a way that an individual could remember and cause others to remember; but also in a way that enabled the congregation to remind God of his acts of deliverance in the past. From the shock of contemporary (national) experience, what once had happened suddenly emerged as that which was now to be held up before God, in the assumption that by forcing God to remember, he might heal the ruptures in the present. Recalling history had the immediate purpose of influencing history."[167]

Commentators agree that the psalms have their setting, generally, in the cult.[168] It is in the familiar setting of Israel's worship that the community in distress recalls the past so that God may remember it in their favor. Then the community makes a vow to God promising to change its behavior: "Then we will never turn back from you; / give us life, and we will call on your name" (Ps 80:18). This vow is not the usual sacrifice of praise (Pss 27:6; 51:15-19; 54:6; 66:13-16; 69:30-31), but a new kind of behavior pattern (faithfulness) born out of the confrontation between the past and present.[169]

An answer to the lament comes from God. This answer, according to Gunkel, "was proclaimed by the priest in God's name" on the days of lamentation. Those who argue for a "covenant festival" (Mowinckel and Weiser) interpret the divine response in the lament as a sure knowledge that participation in the communal festival cult would bring salvation to the community and the individual.[170] However, this response from Yahweh is lacking in most of the psalms (cf. Ps 60:6-8), but appears more frequently in the laments of the prophets.[171] In Isaiah 51:21–52:2, the reply of Yahweh is very well developed:

"Therefore hear this, you who are wounded,
  who are drunk, but not with wine:
says your Sovereign, the Lord,

your God who pleads the cause of his people:
See, I have taken from your hand the cup of staggering;
you shall drink no more
from the bowl of my wrath.
And I will put it into the hand of your tormentors" (Isa 51:21-23).

It is this response motif of the lament style that the prophets adapted outside the cult, twisted, and hurled back on the very people who put their trust in the sacred tradition. In this situation, the famous prophetic disdain for sacrifices, sacrificial hymns (Amos 5:23; 1 Sam 1:15), and sacred usages is projected.[172] The prophet insists on ethical behavior; consequently, Yahweh recalls Israel's sins instead of recalling the saving deeds of the past: "But they do not consider / that I remember all their wickedness" (Hos 7:2a; see also Hosea 6–7). This violent break with cultic tradition is clear in the oracle at the end of the communal lament prompted by a great drought recorded in Jeremiah 14. The oracle declares:

"Thus says the LORD concerning this people:
Truly they have loved to wander,
they have not restrained their feet;
therefore the LORD does not accept them,
now he will remember their iniquity
and punish their sins" (Jer 14:10).

The foundation story and the sole faith in Yahweh (monotheism) are the ground of existence, but this has ethical implications. In certain situations the faith of Israel has been tried beyond the limits of endurance. The response or lack of response from Yahweh (especially since the destruction of the second Temple in 70 C.E.) has been distressing. Antisemitism, which culminated in Auschwitz, cannot be justified by blaming it on the Jewish failure to uphold the ethical consequences of the faith in Yahweh. But for the Old Testament prophets and the Deuteronomic tradition, the ethical grounding of the faith yields blessings and curses. In Deuteronomy *memory* is employed to demonstrate this in history and cult.

AN APPEAL TO ISRAEL'S MEMORY IN CULT AND ITS ETHICAL IMPLICATION — DEUTERONOMY. The Old Testament has been called a book of memorial. Farby has argued that the memory motif as a theological strategy, which makes Israel aware of and grounds it into salvation history, found its way into the Pentateuch (and into most preexilic writings) through Deuteronomy.[173] The monarchy robbed the centralized cult, according to Gottwald, of that creative force that empowered it to generate new schemes for interpreting history. Deuteronomy represents a belated rescue effort.[174] D performs this operation in a way that is different from P. While P regards the land as a gift, D insists that Israel must observe the commandments in order to enter into it. It did not matter that the preachers were operating in the seventh or sixth century B.C.E. They simply threw Israel back six hundred years into the past and left her in the land of Moab to listen directly to the voice of Moses.[175] This direct address is in the form of cultic preaching.

"In Deuteronomy we get a clear picture of how the centralized cult, when it tried to renew itself in monarchic times, did so not by developing new themes, but by embroidering the old basic themes in sermons and hortatory addresses which aimed at closing the historical and social gap between ancient canonical Israel and contemporary monarchic Israel."[176]

The theological devise for bridging this gap between the past and the present is Deuteronomy's appeal to memory.[177] For example, Israel is prompted to recall the servitude in Egypt (Deut 16:12), its deliverance (5:15), the gift of the covenant at Horeb (4:9-13), and Yahweh (4:39ff.). The remembrance bridges the historical gap and makes the covenant offer the direct concern of the present generation.

"This entire commandment that I command you today you must diligently observe, so that you may live and increase, and go in and occupy the land that the LORD promised on oath to your ancestors. Remember the long way that the LORD your God has led you these forty years in the wilderness, in order to humble you, testing you to know what was in your heart, whether or not you would keep his commandments" (Deut 8:1-2).

The issue, however, is not simply to make a historical connection; it is rather to internalize and practice the tenets of the founding story that is narrated "today" in the preaching at the sanctuaries. The theological devise thus links history, liturgy, and ethics together:

"Remember that you were a slave in the land of Egypt, and the LORD your God brought you out from there with a mighty hand and an outstretched arm; therefore the LORD your God commanded you to keep the sabbath day" (Deut 5:15).

"Remember that you were a slave in Egypt, and diligently observe these statutes [Unleavened Bread and feast of Weeks]" (Deut 16:12).

"You shall not deprive a resident alien or an orphan of justice; you shall not take a widow's garment in pledge. Remember that you were a slave in Egypt and the LORD your God redeemed you from there; therefore I command you to do this" (Deut 24:17-18).

"When you gather the grapes of your vineyard, do not glean what is left; it shall be for the alien, the orphan, and the widow. Remember that you were a slave in the land of Egypt; therefore I am commanding you to do this" (Deut 24:21-22).

This evocation of memory is not an empty recollection of past events or a matter of pure intellection. The events ground Israel in existence. Memory, in being evocative of these events, hooks the social laws to the events and invites the present community to identification. Since the story anchors the community to Yahweh, personal practice makes both Yahweh and the story transparent in present life. It is a type of actualization, this time in ethical gesture (which, as we have shown above, is the opposite of ritual gesture). Thus D's concern is not simply humanitarian. Israel's treatment of aliens or keeping the Sabbath or eating unleavened bread (Deut 16:3) is to remember the enslavement in Egypt. In this way Israelites actualize "today" the decisive events in their "history."[178] Sociopolitically, their empowerment manifests the power of the liberating Yahweh of their story only when they restore the dignity of the weak. This emphasis of Deuteronomy, as Farby points out, grounds the entire Decalogue in liberation-*anamnesis:*[179] "I am the LORD your God, who brought you out of the land of Egypt, out of the house of slavery" (Exod 20:2; Deut 5:6).

Deuteronomy therefore shows how the past (foundation story) and the present are yoked together in a living tradition. History continues in this view as sacred history insofar as present Israel establishes continuity with the past through a memory that motivates creative action. If Israel fails to do so, if Israel fails to take the opportunity being offered, the result will be curses and oppression by its enemies (book of Judges) and subsequent exile (Prophets).

D's interpretation of history emphasizes that Israel was sent into exile because it failed the test of the measure: abiding by the tenets of its founding story. But within the exile, and outside the cult, the story continued to function as a paradigm for creation and new creation (P and Deutero-Isaiah).

Israel's Foundation Story, Creation, and Worship

Our analysis of the Jewish foundation story favors the existence of multiple groups (tribes) that formed a league to become one Israel. The cult, theophany-covenant-law, created the environment for the fusion through the recognition of Yahweh as the only God (monotheism or mono-Yahwism). One group in the league had an experience of oppression outside Palestine (Egyptian slavery). It migrated into Palestine (Canaan, then under Egyptian rule), carrying its story of liberation from bondage by Yahweh (the Exodus story). Other groups in the league may have revolted against oppression within the Canaanite city-states. They identified with the Exodus story in addition to their ancestral stories of origin (Exodus-settlement). At the merger, united Israel accepted the various ancestral stories, but with an overriding bonding to a monotheistic faith in Yahweh, their liberator — hence the dominance of the Exodus-settlement motif as exemplified in the cult.

The three main pilgrimage festivals that provided the occasion for the ritual renewal of the league are all agrarian based (feast of Unleavened Bread, feast of Weeks, and Ingathering). The feast of Unleavened Bread was a springtime festival that fell at the same time as Passover, which was a nomadic or semi-nomadic family festival. The Passover possibly afforded an opportunity for covenant renewal (especially at the sanctuary of Gilgal, Cross) and for a reenactment of the Exodus-settlement story. Its importance waned during the monarchy, but was revived during the reform of Josias when it became fused with the feast of Unleavened Bread into a sole new year festival. This new year festival, celebrated in the month of Nisan in the Babylonian calendar, is dominated by the liberation motif. The feast of Weeks retained its agrarian character and was not connected with the Exodus-settlement motif until the second century B.C.E. Ingathering also retained its agrarian character, but since it was an autumn new year festival (Canaanite and Egyptian calendar) it became the most popular festival during the period of the monarchy. The kings naturally adopted Canaanite royal patterns.

We thus see a similar weaving and interweaving of traditions within the cult as happened in the political merging of the groups. We have on the one hand Passover-Unleavened Bread with very strong emphasis on liberation. On the other hand are Canaanite agricultural festivals that retained their agrarian motif and were loosely connected with liberation. There was, however, a clear boundary despite the frequent backslidings, as the prophets testify. Yahweh alone is God. But it is a Yahweh God who sets aside the fertility role of Baal and provides for the fertility of the fields and the flock; a Yahweh warrior-God is depicted as going to war against Egypt and other enemies with the elemental forces of the universe. In the poetic recital of the war against the historical enemies, one glides into a recital of Yahweh's struggle against the force "Sea," or Rahab/Leviathan. This results in weaving the song of victory over these forces into victory over the historical enemies destroyed in the sea (and vice versa; cf. Psalms 29; 74; 78; Exodus 15; Judges 5). There was little hesitation in clothing Yahweh with the mythic qualities characteristic of Marduk, who overthrew Tiamat, or Baal, who overthrew Zebul Yamm.[180] This is perfect inculturation. The enthronement psalms, which were very much influenced by kingship in Israel, drew freely from Ancient Near Eastern models.[181]

Our explorations indicate to us that redemption from bondage, which marks out Israelite consciousness and religion, did not relegate creation and the blessing deriving from it to a secondary place. Von Rad's contention that in the Old Testament the doctrine of creation was subordinated to historical redemption is seriously questioned by scholars.[182] The opposition to von Rad's thesis has also sometimes gone to the other extreme of claiming that creation theology has predominance over redemption in the Old Testament. The two themes predated the union of one Israel, but since the social setting for the fusion of the tribes and the recognition of Yahweh as the only God was that of bondage demanding liberation, the liberation motif had an edge over the declaration of the work of God in creation. However, since God the liberator had to make himself manifest (theophany) and declare his will (covenant-law) in the cult, the conservative nature of the cult ensured the predominance of the settled

Canaanite ritual gestures (verbal and nonverbal). This is not only manifest in the festivals, but also in the hymns (psalms of praise and lament). The two themes (creation and redemption) do not exist in conflict. Rather, the rhythm of cultic practice ensured the fusion of the two in the worship of the one Yahweh.

In this last section of the study of the story and its impact on Jewish worship we will explore: (1) the praise of Yahweh, who is acknowledged as both creator and liberator of Israel from historical enemies and from chthonic forces called Sea; (2) the worship of Yahweh in the postexilic Temple and synagogue, which is a recognition (in thanksgiving) of Yahweh's creation and redemption, a worship that bathes in the awareness of the historical failure of Israel to be faithful to its covenant God (requiring sacrifices for sins and prayer of repentance); and, finally, (3) the specificity of Israel's story and cult in the Ancient Near East.

Praise of Yahweh, Creator-Liberator. The emergence of one Israel anchored in one faith in Yahweh its liberator is the creation of Israel. Second Isaiah, writing during the Exile, made it clear that Yahweh's activity in Israel's history enjoys the quality of the unparalleled work of the Creator-God. Humankind is created by God, but of all human groups, only Israel is said to be created by Yahweh (Isa 45:12; 43:1, 7, 15).

"I made the earth,
  and created humankind upon it;
it was my hands that stretched out the heavens,
  I commanded all their host" (Isa 45:12).

"But now thus says the LORD,
he who created you, O Jacob,
  he who formed you, O Israel:
Do not fear, for I have redeemed you;
I have called you by name, you are mine" (Isa 43:1).

"I am the LORD, your Holy One,
  the Creator of Israel, your King" (Isa 43:15).

This is not *creatio ex nihilo*, but a primordial event of overcoming chaos, inaugurating order, and setting out the nonnegotiable terms on which the community has to live in the cosmos.[183] The narrow definition of creation by Kapelrud — "when something new which was not there before is produced" — will not admit Israel's redemption as creation. For, "ordering of chaos is thus not creation."[184] If this definition is strictly followed, neither the Genesis narrative nor the classic *Enuma Elish* would qualify as a creation story. Clifford has argued (against Kapelrud) that the ancient perception of creation in the myths is not the modern "impersonal interaction of physical forces extending over eons;" rather, it is imagined as "a conflict of wills in which one party is victorious."[185] This is the picture painted in the hymns of Yahweh's victory over Egypt and over the monster Sea to bring the chosen people into the Promised Land. There are thus two categories of creation prevalent in the Ancient Near East (following Fisher and Cross): the cosmogonic and the theogonic. Israel and its Canaanite neighbors preferred the cosmogonic.[186] But they also consider evil political or military actions as possible channels for chaos to recover the land, as is the case in Mesopotamia. This chaos must be overcome through a ritual process in order to sustain a wholesome world for the gods and humans. "In Mesopotamia, Ugarit, and Israel the *Chaoskampf* appears not only in the cosmological contexts but just as frequently in political contexts. The repulsion and destruction of the enemy, and thereby the maintenance of political order, always constitute one of the major dimensions of the battle against chaos."[187] Thus in the hymns or songs of victory that may be used in cultic thanksgiving celebrations, both the historical and the suprahistorical elements of Israel's experience of life in Yahweh are interwoven. Exodus 15 demonstrates this:

"I will sing to the LORD, for he has triumphed gloriously;
  horse and rider he has thrown into the sea.
The LORD is my strength and my might,
  and he has become my salvation;
this is my God, and I will praise him,
  my father's God, and I will exalt him,
The LORD is a warrior;
  the LORD is his name
"Pharaoh's chariots and his army he cast into the sea;
  his picked officers were sunk in the Red Sea.
The floods covered them;
  they went down into the depths like a stone.

Your right hand, O LORD, glorious in power —
  your right hand, O LORD, shattered the enemy.
In the greatness of your majesty you overthrew your adversaries;
  you sent out your fury, it consumed them like stubble.
At the blast of your nostrils the waters piled up,
  the floods stood up in a heap;
  the deeps congealed in the heart of the sea.
The enemy said, 'I will pursue, I will overtake. . . .'
You blew with your wind, the sea covered them;
  they sank like lead in the mighty waters.

"Who is like you, O LORD, among the gods?. . .
The peoples heard, they trembled;
  pangs seized the inhabitants of Philistia . . .
until your people, O LORD, passed by,
  until the people whom you acquired passed by.
You brought them in and planted them on the mountain of your own
  possession,
  the place, O LORD, . . . that your hands have established.
The LORD will reign forever and ever" (15:1-18).

This victory song and similar victory songs and psalms of enthronement (e.g., Judges 5; Psalms 29; 78; 89; 135) proclaim Yahweh's violent impact on the forces of nature and on Israel's hostile neighbors. When Yahweh appears (Epiphany), Yahweh overcomes the oppressors of the chosen people (whether historical or suprahistorical forces). Then Yahweh leads the rescued ones into the dwelling place where he is king.

In these victory songs, Canaanite hymn patterns (and even Canaanite hymns to Baal like Psalm 29) are appropriated with ease into Israelite cult. They were models ready to hand and were creatively utilized by people freely interacting with their environment. They used these patterns to exalt Yahweh their creator-liberator, the one who saves them in a dangerous universe.

As the enthronement psalms show, the mythic motifs (fabulous narratives) were favored during the monarchy (see especially Psalm 89, which exalts the covenant with David). In the psalms of lament, as stated above, the "looking back" in order to liturgically recall the deeds of Yahweh fused the historical and the suprahistorical.

The merging of these two motifs into Israelite cult (especially during the monarchy) had its dangers. The threat of Baalism to Yahwism was real. The "Elijah cycle" of narratives was a clear statement by the growing prophetic tradition of its rejection of Baalism in favor of orthodox Yahwism: it was either Yahweh or Baal. And, as Cross shows, the whole confrontation at Carmel between Elijah and the priests of Baal and the subsequent theophany at Horeb were a projection of the Sinai covenant in which Yahweh's mode of appearing is shed of the characteristics of the storm god. It was a veritable polemic against Baal.[188] However, in Second Isaiah the merging of the historical and the suprahistorical imposed itself once again in the effort by the prophet to paint a poetic picture of the return of the exiles — a new exodus, a new creation.

The utilization of the cosmogonic language by Second Isaiah has been noted above. The prophet, who was operating within the exilic context (as from ca. 540 B.C.E.), introduced a novelty into the recital of Israel's foundation story. The presuppositions of the prophet are, according to Clifford, a perception of Israel's history in three stages: Israel's sin (announced by preexilic prophets; e.g., Amos 2:6-16), Israel's punishment (the Exile, stretching from the destruction of the Temple in 587 B.C.E. to Cyrus' capture of Babylon in 539 B.C.E.), and Israel's restoration (from the time of Cyrus).[189] In trying to persuade his difficult audience (second generation exiles who have acquired a settled pattern of life) to march back to Israel from Babylon, he not only employed the Exodus-settlement model, but pictured the whole process as a new creation. Israel ceased to exist through sin and exile. Israel will be made anew through a restoration (new creation). The exiles participate in the event by an Exodus from Babylon.[190]

The prophetic eschatology of Second Isaiah is peculiar. Cross calls it proto-apocalyptic. Yahweh is portrayed as "approaching Israel with a new action which made the old saving institutions increasingly invalid since from then on life or death for Israel was determined by this future event."[191] The saving actions of the past ("the former things of old") are recalled so that offending Israel may become Yahweh's witness of his lordship in history. Israel, as Yahweh's witness (Isa 43:9-13; cf. 43:9–44:5), is Yahweh's image (icon) in contradistinction to the statues used by the nations (e.g., Babylon) to represent their gods (Isa 41:1–42:9).

The creativity of Second Isaiah may be highlighted further by comparing the handling of creation material in it with that of the priestly tradition. P, in reordering his material on creation, calls the human type "image" (icon) of God (Gen 1:26-28). In this way P wants to say that humankind is seen as a correspondence to God: humans are defined in fundamental orientation to God. They are creative intermediate beings between God and other creatures. Humans' "very existence is intended to be their relationship to God" (Westerman). Second Isaiah, on the other hand, sees Israel as the quintessence of humankind, the key witness and image of Yahweh. Israel is made to participate in the eschatological future through recalling the past deeds of Yahweh:[192]

"Remember this and consider,
  recall it to mind, you transgressors,
  remember the former things of old;
for I am God, and there is no other;
  I am God, and there is no one like me,
declaring the end from the beginning
  and from ancient times things not yet done,
saying, 'My purpose shall stand,
  and I will fulfill my intention'" (Isa 46:8-10).

But the eschatological future will be so different (apocalyptic) that the "former things," i.e., the entirety of Yahweh's interaction with Israel, or her very foundation story (Exodus-settlement, theophany-covenant-law), is rendered irrelevant.[193]

"Do not remember the former things,
  or consider the things of old.
I am about to do a new thing;
  now it springs forth, do you not perceive it?
I will make a way in the wilderness
  and rivers in the desert" (Isa 43:18-19).

In other words, the foundation story "will no longer serve as the national script; it will be replaced by the new story," an element of blasphemy.[194]

The "new things" will be such a novelty that no one could imagine or anticipate it on the basis of any earlier story (48:6b-7). It is the narration of the new creation of Israel in which the prophet utilizes both historical and suprahistorical imagery (cf. Isa 51:9-11). As Cross says: "A new Exodus was described in terms of the language of the old Exodus, and with bold mythological language which dissolved both old and new Exodus into the language of the battle with Yamm and Leviathan, dragon chaos. The myths of creation, in short, were given an eschatological function."[195]

Second Isaiah clearly calls the first redemption (or Exodus) "creation." Israel remembers this as an "active response of faith,"[196] but this is done outside cultic actualization. Recalling the first creation becomes the basis for participating in the new creation, an action of Yahweh that, though described in the old symbols, cannot be predicted from the old patterns.

In the poetic description of the old and the new creation, Second Isaiah not only uses the term *zkr* (remember), which we saw above in Deuteronomic cultic preaching, he also introduces another term, *bara*ʾ (create), which P uses in his creation account (Gen 1:1–2:4). In the forty-nine occurrences of *bara*ʾ in the Hebrew Scriptures, Second Isaiah accounts for seventeen, while P uses it ten times. According to Bernhadt, the term certainly entered the Old Testament as a theological idea during the Exile. The uses in Second Isaiah, Third Isaiah, and the Psalms could favor the assumption of an origin in the cultic language.[197] It means, in Second Isaiah, an unparalleled action of Yahweh the lord of history, in favor of his people. In his use of *bara*ʾ as a special theological word P wanted to underline the difference between God's creation and human invention: unconditionally, through God's command, something comes into being (without necessarily implying *creatio ex nihilo*).[198] This manner of narrative, which is influenced by exilic experiences, carries an open invitation to all creation to praise the lord of history. The universe was created in an unparalleled way (P), as God created Israel, the chosen people (Second Isaiah). "Let them praise the name of the LORD, / for he commanded and they were created" (Ps 148:5).

Worship of Yahweh, Creator-Liberator in Temple and Synagogue. The ancient songs of victory may have been executed in the sanctuaries. Furthermore, there may be a thanksgiving sacrifice (holocaust or communion sacrifice) offered to Yahweh (cf. 1 Sam 15:15). Before the Exile, the Jerusalem Temple was the cult center. It attracted pilgrims for the major festivals involving sacrifice. The earliest sacrificial rituals are the *zebah* or *selamim* (communion sacrifices) and the *ʿola* (holocaust). The sin offering *(hattʾat* and *ʾasham)* may have existed in the Solomonic temple, but the detailed legislation by P is postexilic.[199]

The position of the critical school (Wellhausen) that the sin offering made its entry into the Pentateuch during the exilic and postexilic period may be difficult to defend today. Comparative study of the Mesopotamian ritual reveals a highly developed expiatory ritual (cf. the Babylonian *akitu* festival). But P's detailed and sometimes confusing prescriptions of ritual expiations are outstanding. Almost half of the sacrificial code of the second Temple deal with the expiatory sacrifices: *ʾasham* (guilt offering, e.g., Lev 6:1-7) and *hattʾat* (sin offering, e.g., Lev 6:24-30).[200] This emphasis on sin, remorse, and repentance in exilic writings and the postexilic Temple worship is intimately connected with Israel's historical experience, as preexilic prophetism shows. This awareness appears to have imposed itself on the priestly narrative of the origin of the nations (*goyim*, Genesis 1–11), which set the stage for the real story, the origin of Israel set apart from the nations as image of God. Human rebellion is shown to be responsible for the cycle of creation-flood-new creation (cf. the Babylonian *Atra-hasis* myth).[201] Thus the necessity for repentance *(swb)*, which was the crucial prophetic call, became integrated into the story of origin (the Adamic myth). Humankind was blamed for the rebellion — a movement from personal and community remorse to universal penitence. As Ricoeur says: "the myth in naming Adam, man, makes explicit the concrete universality of human evil; the spirit of repentance gives to itself, in the Adamic myth, the symbol of that universality."[202]

The priestly doctrine of repentance shows a distinction between voluntary and involuntary sins, even if their expiation *(ʾasham)* bears the same name. In the case of an involuntary sin, a simple *ʾasham* (remorse sacrifice, e.g., Lev 4:1ff.) suffices, but if the sin is intentional, *htwdh* (acknowledgment, confession, and, thus, the acceptance of blame) must accompany the *ʾasham* (Lev 5:1-6). Thus: "the repentance of the sinner, through his remorse *(ʾsm)* and confession *(htwdh)*, reduces his intentional sin to an inadvertence, thereby rendering it eligible for sacrificial reparation."[203] Therefore, in the context of sin and repentance, the experience of Yahweh as creator-liberator of Israel and Lord of humankind is also made manifest.

The *zebah* and *ʿolah* sacrifices are more directly linked with praise-thanksgiving and celebrative memorial. The *zebah* is essentially a joyous celebration, a religious service of thanksgiving with a festive meal. Part of the victim (the fat) is burned, and the rest is eaten. It is sacrificed during national and solemn events (e.g., the coronation of Saul, 1 Sam 11:15; bringing the ark into the temple of Solomon, 1 Kgs 8:5; the Passover, Exod 12:27; 23:18; 34:25). These solemn events narrate Yahweh's liberation-creation of Israel using the normal historical or suprahistorical language. The *zebah* is sacrificed also as a fulfillment of vows (Prov 7:14) and at the arrival and departure of friends (Exod 18:12; Gen 31:54). It is the principal sacrifice Israel had in common with its neighbors. It does not appear to differ from the specifically Hebrew sacrifice named *selamim* (also called *zebah selamim*). In later times, its importance diminished probably because of a centralized cult and the prophetic invective against the excesses of such celebrations.[204]

The *ʿolah* was also a sacrifice common to Israel and its neighbors. The victim is completely burned (burnt offering). It is sacrificed for thanksgiving (Gen 8:20; 1 Sam 6:13-14), fulfillment of vows (Judg 11:31; Ps 66:13), reinforcement of prayer (1 Sam 7:9; 2 Kgs 3:27), devotion and reverence (Genesis 22; Judg 6:26). On Sabbaths and high festive days (e.g., New Moon, Unleavened Bread, Pentecost, Atonement) there are additional *ʿolah* sacrifices in the second Temple (Num 28:27; 29:8; Lev 23:8). While the narrative of the communal *zebah* recounts Yahweh's deeds in favor of Israel, it is not clear which narratives, prayers, and responses of the assembly accompany the *ʿolah.* Stevenson suggests that "prostrations and habitual ejaculations, if not hymns, would be the natural expressions of their emotion" (cf. Lev 9:24).[205] Sirach, whose reports reflect the highly organized postexilic courses of Temple service, indicates that toward the end of the sacrifice the priests sound a trumpet, the people prostrate, Levitical chants follow, the people cry in prayer before the Merciful, the priests pronounce the Aaronic blessing, and people prostrate again (Sir 50:14-21).

It is in this postexilic Temple liturgy that the sacrifice as praise of the creator-redeemer of Israel is exemplified. The praise of the creator has already been noted in those psalms that specifically call for this praise. These psalms may be part of the Levitical chants. But explicit information about the *ʿolah* sacrifices and the accompanying praise come from late extrabiblical sources — the Mishnah (second century C.E.) and the Talmud (third century C.E.).

In Mishnah *Tamid,* which deals with the Daily Whole-Offerings, the priests are said to interrupt the morning sacrifice to recite the *Shemaᶜ* (Hear! O Israel):

"Then they came down and came to the office of hewn stone to recite the *Shema.* The superintendent said to them, 'Say one blessing.' They said a blessing, pronounced the Ten Commandments, the *Shema . . . And it shall come to pass if You shall hearken . . . ,* and *And the Lord spoke to Moses. . . .* They blessed the people with three blessings: *True and sure, Abodah,* and the blessing of priests. And on the Sabbath they add a blessing for the outgoing priestly watch" (*m. Tamid* 4:3T–5:1D).

As is usual with rabbinic studies that depend only on oral sources, it is not clear which benedictions precede the *Shemaᶜ* and which come after it.[206] The Babylonian Talmud says that the blessing preceding the *Shemaᶜ* is the *Yozer,* which praises Yahweh the creator of lights, and the Jerusalem Talmud says that it is the blessing of the Torah, while other rabbis say that it is the *Ahabah* ("with abounding love," which blesses Yahweh for the illumination by the Torah).[207] Concerning the benedictions coming after the *Shemaᶜ* some scholars favor the benediction for the Law, the temple sacrifices *(Abodah),* and the thanksgiving *(Hodah)* instead of those in Mishnah *Tamid* 5.1. The reason is that on the Day of Atonement *(Yom Kippur),* after reading from the Torah, the high priest (according to Mishnah *Yoma* 7.1) pronounces eight benedictions: "for the Torah, . . . for the Temple service, . . . for the confession [thanksgiving], . . . for the forgiveness of sin, . . . for the sanctuary [by itself], for Israel [by themselves], . . . and for the priests by [themselves], and for the rest of the Prayer."[208]

Despite the uncertainty about which benedictions are recited, it is clear that the daily Temple sacrifices are accompanied by the *Shemaᶜ*. There is, therefore, a merging of the sacrificing with a profession of faith in the Yahweh of the covenant. The benedictions are possibly preceded by a blessing that praises Yahweh as the creator of the luminaries *(Yozer),* a praise that climaxes in the angelic hymn "holy, holy, holy." The three benedictions following the *Shemaᶜ* may be the *Abodah* (for the Temple sacrifices) and benedictions for the Torah and for thanksgiving *(Hodah).* This indicates that the Temple sacrificial liturgy was dominated by the praise-thanksgiving motif that the Synagogue practice continued. The texts of the prayers possibly used can be deduced from prayers recorded almost a millennium after the destruction of the Temple and within the context of the synagogue nonsacrificial worship. These prayers are better examined within the synagogue liturgy.

PRAISE OF YAHWEH IN THE SYNAGOGUE. If the Temple is dominated by the sacrifice, the synagogue is marked by the blessing *(berakah).* But just as the Temple worship is not a simple nonverbal ritual, the praise of the synagogue has reference to the sacrifice of the Temple. This shows that, despite the fact that the laws regulating the blessing (Jewish prayer) were settled around the third century C.E. (by the Amora'im) and that the prayerbook containing the synagogue and home liturgies did not exist before the ninth century C.E., these prayers were ancient compositions.

The blessing *(berakah),* by which name prayer is known in the Jewish tradition, is an ancient expression of the Jewish way of interacting with Yahweh. In its most basic and original meaning the blessing confers the power of fertility or is fertilization. Westermann sees as explicative the command, "Be fruitful and multiply" (Gen 1:22), which follows the blessing in P's creation story. For "the blessing which God confers on the creatures which he has created is the power to reproduce, multiply and fill the earth." Therefore, according to Westermann:

"The connection between blessing and creation remains basic to all further uses of the word. When God blesses, it is the creator who blesses and the blessing itself works itself out effectively in the life of what is blessed or of the one asking the blessing. Blessing implies creation and is effective as the work of the creator. To speak of life and its dynamism is to speak of the effective action of the creator."[209]

When humans pronounce blessings on other humans — parents over children, superiors over inferiors, priests in the context of organized cult — they are transmitting an active fertile blessing that comes from God the creator, the source of all blessing. This is clearly depicted in the blessing of Joseph by his father, Jacob:

"Joseph is a fruitful bough,
a fruitful bough by a spring;
his branches run over the wall. . . .
By the hands of the Mighty One of Jacob,

by the name of the Shepherd, the Rock of Israel,
by the God of your father, who will help you,
by the Almighty who will bless you
with blessings of heaven above,
blessings of the deep that lies beneath,
blessings of the breasts and of the womb.
The blessings of your father
are stronger than the blessings of the eternal mountains,
the bounties of the everlasting hills;
may they be on the head of Joseph,
on the brow of him who was set apart from his brothers" (Gen 49:22-26).

But the peculiarity of the blessings referred to in the Temple cult, the synagogue, and home liturgies is that God is declared blessed *(baruk)*. It is not that humans now impart blessings on God. Rather, the experience of a divine prodigy prompts the declaration *Baruk Ywh* (Blessed be Ywh). This is followed by a narration of the reasons for declaring Yahweh blessed (e.g., Gen 24:26-27; Exod 18:10, etc.). Sometimes, especially in the Psalter, the reasons for the blessing of Yahweh in the third person are not stated. This converts *brk* into a praise verb (e.g., Pss 41:13; 72:18-19; Ezek 3:12, etc.). The address of Yahweh in the third person was later modified (before and especially after the Exile) into an address in the second person (the thou-style: *baruk ʾatta Ywh,* blessed art thou Yahweh). *Brk* becomes not only an instrument of praise, but also an introduction to prayers of petition where there is a recalling of the founding story, a remembrance of the sins of Israel not only during the period of the Judges and the monarchy but even during the period of the desert wanderings, and a petition for mercy in view of the present misery. Nehemiah is the best example of this use of *brk* (Neh 9:5-37; cf. 1 Kgs 8:56; 1 Chr 29:10, etc.). *Brk* comes close to verbs of confession and acknowledgment (especially *hdh,* deriving from *ydh,* which implies not only confession and acknowledgment of sin but an open declaration as the LXX *exomologein* implies). The impact of prophetism and the experience of the Exile caused by human rebellion (cf. P's creation narrative, Genesis 1–11) have thus left their imprint in the prayer *(berakah)*. While the thou-style became the rule in the synagogue, the Temple retained its benedictions in the third person.[210]

We see then that in the blessing, in Israel's communal worship, the creative power of Yahweh is praised and the experience of this blessing as redemption (Israel's foundation story) is narrated (actualized). The decision of the Amora'im concerning the *berakah* ensured that every prayer (praise-thanksgiving and petition) is a blessing (i.e., filled with Yahweh's creative power). Ledogar summarizes their decisions as follows:

"a) the mention of the name of God.
b) the mention of his Kingship.
c) *baruk* at the beginning when it was a one-sentence formula; at the end, at least, when longer;
d) when several *berakot* followed one another, only the first begins with *baruk;*
e) when, in a longer *berakah,* the thought departs from that of the first phrase, the final sentence is to bring the thought back to that of the beginning."[211]

These rules apply to prayer in the synagogue.

The origin of the synagogue is wrapped in obscurity. It may have started after the Exile and may have been connected with the Temple. The practice of the twenty-four provinces *(maamadôt)* sending representatives to the Temple to participate in the worship and the gathering of those at home in the city square to accompany the Temple cult in prayer could also be linked with the origin of the synagogue.[212] Mishnah *Taanith,* which regulates issues about fasting, says of these gatherings:

"On three occasions in the year priests raise up their hands [in the priestly benediction] four times a day: (1) at the dawn prayer, (2) the additional prayer, (3) the afternoon prayer, and (4) the closing of the gates: on the occasion of fasts, on the occasions of [prayers of members of the] delegation *[maamad]*, and on the Day of Atonement. . . . When the time for a watch came to go up to Jerusalem, its priests and Levites go up with it to Jerusalem. And Israelites who belong to that watch gather together in their towns and study the story of the works of creation" (*M. Taan.* 4:1-2).

The great prayer for which the synagogue is known is the *Teffilah.* It is preceded by three benedictions and followed by another three benedictions. The *Shema*ᶜ, which was a key proclamation in the

Temple worship, is also part of the synagogue prayer. It is preceded by two benedictions, *Yozer* and *Ahabah*. *Yozer,* as we have seen, praises Yahweh the creator of the luminaries; *Ahabah* praises Yahweh for the illumination through the Torah. The *Yozer* has a *Qedushat* (angelic proclamation: holy, holy, holy). It may have had more importance in the synagogue worship before the introduction of the *Shemaᶜ*.

The *Teffilah,* to which all synagogue worship moves, simply means prayer. It is also called the *Shemoneh esreh* (the number eighteen) or the *Amidah* (because it is recited standing). The Palestinian version of the *Teffilah* maintains the number eighteen, while the Babylonian version has nineteen. This is because of the addition of a benediction against Christians (no. 12), which may be a reformulation of an old petition. The benedictions are listed here according to their names to give an idea of the intentions prayed for:

1. *Abot:* God who remembers the pious deeds of the *Fathers* and who will send a redeemer.
2. *Geburot:* God who *quickenest* the dead.
3. *Qedushat ha-Shem: Holiness* of God.
4. *Bina:* For *Intelligence* and knowledge.
5. *Teshuba:* Return to God; *Repentance.*
6. *Selicha: Forgiveness* of sins.
7. *Geulla: Redemption* from affliction.
8. *Refua: Healing* from illness.
9. *Birkat ha-shanim:* Prayer for the good years.
10. *Qibbus galuijot:* Gathering together the dispersed.
11. *Birkat mishpat:* Prayer for justice.
12. *Birkat ha-minim:* Prayer against the heretics.
13. *Birkat saddiqim:* Prayer for the righteous.
14. *Birkat Jerusalem:* Prayer for Jerusalem.
15. *Birkat David:* Prayer for David.
16. *Teffilah:* Petition that God may hear the entire prayer of the people.
17. *Abodah:* Prayer for the acceptance of the service/worship.
18. *Hoda:* Thanksgiving for grace and favor.
19. *Birkat kohanim:* Priestly blessing.

The majority of these benedictions concern the needs of the people of Israel. But these petitions are inserted within the praise that is the rule of all organized prayer in Israel (nn. 1–3; 17–19). On the days when the Torah is read in synagogue worship (Sabbath, Monday, and Thursday) these benedictions form part of the reaction of the people to the word that is announced — a plea that God may listen to their prayer as God listened to the prayer of the Fathers *(Abot)*. On New Moon, an embolism is inserted at the *Abodah* asking God to remember the chosen people. And on Purim and Hannukah, the embolism is inserted at the *Hodah* to thank God for establishing these festivals.

In summary, this core synagogue worship, along with the *Shemaᶜ* and readings, celebrates (praises) the Creator-Redeemer. By placing creative and redemptive work before God and the assembly (especially the *Yozer, Abot, Geburot,* and *Hodah*) the people ask for God's mercy (petitions 4–16). The synagogue worship is thus firmly rooted in Israel's foundation story in both its historical and suprahistorical dimensions.

Concluding Remarks: The Specificity of the Israelite Foundation Story and Worship

We have explored the Israelite story of origin (myth-symbol), its application to certain areas of worship, and its function in noncultic prophetic preaching. Our approach has been sociohistorical: locating Israel in its familiar geographical setting of the Ancient Near East.

The emergence of one Israel is intimately linked with Egyptian and Canaanite oppression. Thus, Israel's recognition of Yahweh as liberator happened in a real sociohistorical struggle for liberation. This kind of narrative is possible because in the Ancient Near East the gods intervene in history to shape human affairs. But for Israel, this "historical" experience of being liberated was so momentous (foundational) that it constituted the key to the creation story: it was Israel's very creation. Israel's warrior god, Yahweh, is depicted as overcoming Israel's historical and suprahistorical enemies in terms that evoke the fabulous. Thus, despite the concentration of narrative on a specific "historical" experience, Israel reveals its Canaanite implantation in the poetic-mythic dimension of the story. Prophetism was incapable of uprooting this cultural environment.

Israel is particular not because its God intervened in history (El, Marduk, Assur, Baal, and the Igbo Chukwu do exactly the same thing),[213] but because Israel recognized itself as *this particular people of*

Yahweh in its *particular story.* Israel distanced itself from the Canaanite pantheon by the effort (not without tears, i.e., the Exile) to recognize exclusive monotheism or mono-Yahwism. If, as Cross suggests, the name Yahweh derives from a causative epithet of El — *el zu yahwî saba'ot* (El who creates the armed hosts, i.e. the heavenly hosts and the hosts of Israel)[214] — then our argument for the creative dimension of this originating and liberating experience is strengthened.

Second, the agricultural and nomadic festivals that preexisted the emergence of one Israel were creatively appropriated by the new nation. Redeemed Israel felt at home in the Promise Land that the creator-redeemer blessed it with. Israel clothed Yahweh with the qualities of the agrarian divinity (fertilizer of the land), while at the same time linking these festivals to its story. The nomadic festival of *pesah* was completely transformed into a liberation celebration.

Third, this small nation that was unable to maintain internal unity (breaking into northern and southern kingdoms) was always a prey to its stronger neighbors (Egypt, Babylon, Assyria). The prophets utilized the threat of the nations to point to the imminent punishment from Yahweh because of Israel's sins. This is a common model in a social setting where priestly oracles and prophetism revealed the will of the divinity. In Israel, prophets and cult experts (Deuteronomic and Priestly) integrated the sinfulness of Yahweh's people into the declaration of oracles, into the nation's story, and into hymns, prayers, and sacrifices. They drew from their experiences and those of their neighbors. Thus in the postexilic Temple and synagogue worship the narrative of the deeds of Yahweh called up the story of the disobedience and evil deeds of the people and concluded with a plea of mercy from Yahweh. The mercy was expected from the prayers and from the expiatory sacrifices that were offered.

The distinctiveness of Israel's story and interaction with Yahweh in its life and worship should not be sought in a unique view of history, in its laws and ethics, or in the habit of placing the interest of its own people over that of any ruler. These ideas are fertilized, with local modifications, in the Ancient Near East. Rather, Israel's distinctiveness may lie in what it rejected from its neighbors: polytheism or henotheism. With prophetism and the cult, the boundary was sharply drawn between Yahweh and the gods. And there was a creative clothing of Yahweh with the qualities of the Ancient Near Eastern divinities as they were experienced in cosmos and history.

These conclusions are not incidental to the role of the African context — sociohistorical, cultural and religious — in the development of African Christian worship. When one pays close attention to the African social setting and compares it with the Jewish-Christian setting, the continuities and discontinuities may be more creatively worked out.

The Christian Foundation Story (Myth-Symbol) as Reenacted in Christian Life and Cult

The Christian foundation story is interwoven with life and cult. In this way it manifests the general qualities of the myth that we applied to the Nri myth, the Mesopotamian myth, and the Jewish story. There is a historical core to the story of Jesus the Christ as lived and narrated by Christians, but it is a story in which as narrators we are involved, bow in worship, and sing songs of praise, and as listeners we are provoked to commitment. It is therefore not a detached historical documentary. It is not a discourse about Jesus as the Christ. It is a talking to our Lord. The story becomes the vehicle of the meaning of our life as Christians.[215]

When we explored the manner of Christian assembly in chapter two we saw that gathering around a meal memorializes Jesus and that the gathering was caused by the recognition of Jesus as alive. The resurrection of Jesus, which is in continuity with his kingdom praxis culminating in his death on the cross, created the Church. The whole narrative about Jesus' life, death, and resurrection shapes and has been shaped by Christian life. Our interest in this segment is to show how the core passage of Jesus — from this life through death into becoming a life-giver — is dramatized in early Christianity, and how the Eucharist functioned as a key vehicle of communicating the memory of Jesus. We break the section into two sub-divisions: (1) the proclamation of Jesus as the Christ in the personal sacrifice unto death of the martyrs (Christian life as supreme act of worship) and (2) the Christ Bread as indispensable and sufficient food to nourish the Church in crisis, thus keeping the Church alive through the memory of Jesus.

Christ Proclaimed in the Martyr's Personal Sacrifice — A Christian Reenactment of Christ's Sacrifice and Redemption

New Testament writings are not known for using existing sacral terms to describe Christian worship, despite the implantation of

Christians into the Jewish and Greco-Roman milieu. For example, the Christian Eucharist was not called sacrifice (despite sacrificial insinuations), and the Christian minister (presbyter-bishop or deacon) was not called priest despite his or her presidence at the Christian assembly. The sacral language gradually became part of the Christian ritual terminology, especially from the second and third centuries C.E. What preoccupied the Christian assembly was the impact of the "Christ-event" in their worship, life, and world. Thus their worship, which is a gathering in assembly to commemorate in story form (myth-symbol) the living Jesus Christ, and their life, which proclaims Jesus as alive in word and behavior, are interwoven. Paul appears to indicate this linkage in a parenetic plea: "I appeal to you therefore, brothers and sisters, by the mercies of God, to present your bodies as a living sacrifice, holy and acceptable to God, which is your spiritual worship" (Rom 12:1-2).

The measured display of the Christian person in ethical life is a *thysia* (sacrifice), which is the spiritual, reasonable, or perfect worship of the Christians. Philosophers, poets, and prophets — Greek, Roman or Jewish — have stressed the greater value of the condition of one's heart over sacrifices. The gods have no need for the blood of sacrifices. Paul brings this spiritualization to its peak: life lived for God or the whole self dedicated to God is perfect sacrifice or worship.[216] Christians in the Greco-Roman world absorbed this spiritualization of sacrifice. Thus in the development of the Christian Eucharistic tradition, from Didache and Justin to the Syrian, Egyptian, and Roman Eucharistic Prayers, there is an insistent reference in this great prayer to the celebration as reasonable, or perfect (Greek, *logikos;* Latin, *rationabilis*), sacrifice. It is seen as a fulfillment of the perfect sacrifice prophesied in Malachi 1:11.[217] The Christian assembly's perfect worship is the Eucharist, where all discrimination is abolished. Then Paul and the tradition after him taught that the Christian's personal appropriation of the memory of the Lord in conduct is also perfect worship (the ethical side of the assembly's ritual).

In the period of crisis, when the Christian way became an opprobrium in the Roman empire, this sacrificial/Eucharistic terminology was seen as the best description of the Christian's witness (bodily), even unto death. Ignatius of Antioch, in his face to face with martyrdom, wrote to the Romans:

"This favour only I beg of you: suffer me to be a libation poured out to God, while there is still an altar ready for me . . . pray leave me to be a meal for the beasts, for it is they who can provide my way to God. I am His wheat, ground fine by the lions' teeth to be made purest bread for Christ . . . so intercede with Him for me, that by their instrumentality I may be made a sacrifice to God."[218]

The "Christ-Bread" that is the focus of the gathering as Church, the vehicle of the memory of Christ, is materialized in the bishop-martyr who was nourished by it all through his life.

Martyrdom, Supreme Proclamation (Making Present) of Christ, and Worship: The Prayer of Polycarp. In its original meaning martyr *(martus)* signified a witness at a tribunal or to a fact. Christians adopted the term and applied it to witnessing to the kerygma. However, to bear witness sometimes involves death. Thus Jesus is witness (*martus,* Rev 1:5), as is Stephen, who shed his blood in bearing witness (Acts 22:20). The following of Christ gradually started to carry sacrificial overtones (shedding blood or being poured out as libation, cf. Romans 8; Phil 2:17). By the time of Ignatius of Antioch the following of Christ was certainly understood in such sacrificial terms.[219]

The idea of religious martyrdom was foreign to Greeks and Romans. Christians inherited it from the Jewish practice, and Frend shows that the descriptions of the *Acts of the Martyrs* depended on the accounts of the Maccabean experience (2 Macc 6:18–7:41).[220] Like the Maccabean experience, the outbreak of persecution may be blamed on the refusal of the Roman authorities to grant freedom of worship to the Christians — a religious freedom only enjoyed by the Jews in the empire. Thus the burning issue during the time of the martyrs — a crucial period of Christian gestation and consolidation — was clearly the issue of cult. The drama of martyrdom proves that cultic participation is the clearest expression of the bonding of a community to its ritual anchor. In the *Acts of the Scillitan Martyrs* — the first clear indication of the implantation of the Christian Church in North Africa (180 C.E.) — Speratus and his companions confess that they have been living in accordance with the rites of the Christian *(ritu christiano se uiuere confessos)*; thus they refused the opportunity to return to the usage of the Romans *(ad Romanorum morem redeundi).* The proconsul, Saturninus, consequently pronounced the death penalty over them.[221] The concentration of interest on the cult as a test of one's fidelity to Roman tradition may have been started by Pliny the Younger and popularized through his letters.[222] In his letter to Trajan he narrated the process of his test:

"An anonymous pamphlet was issued, containing many names. All who denied that they were or had been Christians I considered should be discharged, because they called upon the gods at my dictation and did reverence, with incense and wine, to your image which I had ordered to be brought forward for this purpose, together with the statues of the deities; and especially because they cursed Christ, a thing which, it is said, genuine Christians cannot be induced to do."[223]

The Christians conducted their rites in secret. By excluding noninitiates from their "secret society"[224] they naturally aroused suspicion and attracted the hatred of those excluded in Rome and in the provinces. Those who remained faithful during the test made an open admission of the Christ (i.e., confession, acknowledgment, or praise; LXX, *exomologesis*). This confession was reprehensible to the Roman state. But this proclamation under pressure (the test of Pliny) turned out to be the only rite performed by Christians in the view of all; a rite that climaxed in their public execution (also interpreted by them as sacrifice). But how could the Roman government, reputed for fairness, punish Christians in such a brutal way? The explanation must be sought in the Roman perception of religion. We explore briefly this Roman idea of religion in order to situate the life and worship of Christians in their social context.

ROMAN RELIGION ROOTED IN PIETY AND EXPERIENCE OF DIVINE PROVIDENCE AND OPPOSED TO SUPERSTITION. The writings of the Christian apologists, from Justin to Augustine, may not be considered a sympathetic assessment of Roman religion. These apologies are already a defense of the Christian religion (or rites) against the demands of the Roman society. Romans classified the practices of the Christian association or club *(hetaeria)* as superstitious. Pliny called them a depraved and extravagant superstition. Christian behavior was particularly despicable, according to Tacitus, because Christians were misanthropes, haters of the human race (an accusation that arose from the secrecy of their rites and from the apocalyptic predictions of some groups).[225]

Wilken considers Augustine's presentation of Roman religion in *The City of God* as misleading.[226] Romans took religion and the social order as intimately connected. In this way they were not different from the Nri, the Mesopotamians, the Jews, or even the Christians. Deep religious sensibility is expressed by Romans as *pietas* (piety): a sense of reverence for the traditions of the family; loyalty and obedience to the customs and traditions of Rome, to inherited laws, to those who lived in previous generations; reverence and devotion to the gods and to the ritual and cultic acts by which the gods are honored, e.g., the offering of sacrifices. The public or civic character of this religion ensures the preservation of interpersonal relations and the survival of society and morality.

Piety toward the gods is rooted in the notion that the gods exercise influence in the affairs of humans. Cicero writes the following about this divine providence:

"There are and have been philosophers who hold that the gods exercise no control over human affairs whatever. But if their opinion is the true one, how can piety, reverence or religion exist? For all these are tributes which it is our duty to render in purity and holiness to the divine powers solely on the assumption that they take notice of them, and that some service has been rendered by the gods to the race of men. But if on the contrary the gods have neither the power nor the will to aid us, if they pay no heed to us at all and take no notice of our actions, if they can exert no possible influence upon the life of men, what ground have we for rendering any sort of worship, honour or prayer to the immortal gods? Piety, however, like the rest of the virtues, cannot exist in mere outward show and pretense; and with piety, reverence and religion must likewise disappear. And when these are gone, life soon becomes a welter of disorder and confusion."[227]

There thus exists a genuine religious sensibility in Roman religious practice as opposed to Augustine's insinuations that one could lie about the gods to bring advantage to citizens.[228] In this sense Romans consider themselves very religious, and, indeed, the most religious people the world over. One could then understand the sharp retort of Saturninus the proconsul over the claims and arrogance of the Scillitan martyrs on the issue of religion:

"Saturninus the proconsul said: 'We too are a religious people, and our religion is a simple one: we swear by the genius of our lord the emperor and we offer prayers for his health — as you also ought to do.' Speratus said: 'If you will give me a calm hearing, I shall tell you the mystery of simplicity.'

'If you begin to malign our sacred rites,' said Saturninus, 'I shall not listen to you. But swear rather by the Genius of our lord and emperor.'"[229]

Saturninus presents the normal test of fidelity to the Roman state. Both the Roman and Christian religions have sociopolitical dimensions. But while the Roman religion ensures social order in the human world, the Christian lays claim to an imminent kingdom into which the martyr is welcomed through his/her sacrifice.

It is this kind of belief that Roman religion rejects as superstition. Jewish, Egyptian, and other Eastern religious practices are classified as superstition by the Romans. Among Christians this superstition has been exaggerated. The superstitious person, according to Plutarch, fails to use intelligence in thinking about the gods. Rather he or she delights in fearful images — horrible apparitions that lead to bizarre and extreme behavior. There is an exaggerated feeling of awe toward the gods; one's lot in life no longer depended on what one did — human responsibility — but rather on fate and fortune over which one has no control.[230]

Critics of Christians, like Lucian, Celsus, Galen, Marcus Aurelius, Porphyry, etc., considered the Christian emphasis on *pistis* (belief or faith) irrational. The difference between the view of life of a "cultivated pagan" of the second century and that of the Christian, according to Dodds, is "the difference between *logismos* and *pistis,* between reasoned conviction and blind faith."

"To any one brought up in classical Greek philosophy, *pistis* meant the lowest grade of cognition: it was the state of mind of the uneducated, who believe things on hearsay without being able to give reasons for their belief. St Paul, on the other hand, following Jewish tradition, had represented *pistis* as the foundation of the Christian life. And what astonished all the early pagan observers . . . was the Christian's total reliance on unproved assertion — their willingness to die for the indemonstrable. For Galen, . . . the Christians possess three of the four cardinal virtues: they exhibit courage, self-control and justice; what they lack is *phronesis,* intellectual insight, the rational basis of the other three."[231]

These irrational ideas about the gods breed atheism (according to Plutarch) and should be rooted out. The erosion of piety toward Rome and the gods was the cause of disaster. The threatened Christians, bonded together by their common danger and thus forming a state within the Roman state (Celsus), were blamed for all these disasters because they rejected piety to the gods. This was made painfully clear to them. According to Tertullian: "If the Tiber floods the town or the Nile fails to flood the fields, if the sky stands still or the earth moves, if famine, if plague, the first reaction is 'Christians to the lion!'"[232]

This, however, is only part of the story. The impact of foreign religions (superstitions) was felt on all levels of Roman society by the second century C.E. According to Gager, the bloody purges of the old Roman aristocracy under the regime of the Julio-Claudians (Tiberius, Caligula, Claudius, and Nero) created a vacuum filled by senators of non-Roman and non-Italian origin. These brought their cults into Rome. Hadrian and Marcus Aurelius became initiates of the Eleusinian mysteries, Antoninus Pius legalized the cult of Cybele, and senatorial participation in non-Roman Mithras or Dionysus cults, etc., was on the increase.[233] Among the commoners participation in cults introduced by foreign settlers since the days of the republic was even more widespread. "I cannot abide a Rome of Greeks," says Juvenal, "and yet what fraction of our dregs comes from Greece? The Syrian Orontes has long since poured into the Tiber, bringing with it its lingo and manners."[234] Christians were mainly drawn from the Greek-speaking urban dwelling lower classes in the early centuries.

The official permission to worship foreign gods, nevertheless, remained bound to the Roman perception of the link between religion and the social order. The *pax deorum,* the guarantee for immediate and collective happiness of the populace, is tied to the society supplicating the gods.[235] Whether a god is annexed through ritual *evocatio* (summoned to abandon a city about to be destroyed by Romans) or through *exoratio* (induced to change sides and not homes); or whether mystery cults are embraced by emperors, these have to be practiced on Roman terms. Religious associations or clubs with a possible political agenda were not tolerated. The Bacchic rites, which enlisted members through oath-taking and possessed a common treasury, a hierarchy of lay officials, and a priesthood, were suppressed in 186 B.C.E.[236] Only the Jews, through effective political maneuvers and because of their well-known propensity for religious wars, were conceded the right to practice a religion that was not immediately adapted to the Roman way. But they were not allowed to proselytize. Christians, on the other hand, not only made converts but rejected the efforts made by Romans to adapt Christ to Roman religion. They pitched themselves against all patterns of Roman religious practice.

CHRISTIAN REBELLION AGAINST ROMAN RELIGION — CHRIST ALONE IS LORD, THE MARTYR IS HIS RITUAL REPRESENTATION. In a context where cults and philosophies abound, where one could adhere to many patterns of worship at the same time, the Christians adopted a purposeful and intransigent position: no compromise with Roman society and its religion. This intransigence brought them persecution, but it also explains the great success of Christianity:

"Its very exclusiveness, its refusal to concede any value to alternative forms of worship . . . was in the circumstances of the time a source of strength. . . . There were too many cults, too many mysteries, too many philosophies to choose from: you could pile one religious insurance on another and yet not feel safe. Christianity made a clean sweep. It lifted the burden of choice from the shoulders of the individual: one choice, one irrevocable choice, and the road to salvation was clear. Pagan critics might mock at Christian intolerance, but in an age of anxiety any 'totalist' creed exerts a powerful attraction."[237]

Some may have tried Christianity and abandoned it for other cults, as Pliny's evidence shows. But many who chose this 'totalist' way, mainly men and women who came from the lower classes, felt bound together more firmly by the common threat of persecution. Leaders of the Church and apologists encouraged members to choose martyrdom and not to renounce Christ. Sometimes the choice may cause incredible psychological agony and shatter family piety (as Celsus accused). Vibia Perpetua from North Africa describes this pain in a moving way:

"While we were still under arrest . . . my father out of love for me was trying to persuade me and shake my resolution. 'Father,' said I, . . . 'I cannot be called anything other than what I am, a Christian.' At this my father was so angered by the word 'Christian' that he moved towards me as though he would pluck my eyes out. . . .

'Daughter,' he said, 'have pity on my grey head — have pity on me your father. . . . Think of your brothers, think of your mother and your aunt, think of your child, who will not be able to live once you are gone. Give up your pride! You will destroy all of us!' . . . I tried to comfort him saying: 'It will happen in the prisoner's dock as God wills; for you may be sure that we are not left to ourselves but are all in his power.' And he left me in great sorrow."[238]

The readiness with which Christians faced death became in itself an attraction to non-Christians (Justin was so converted). And yet certain reckless self-denunciations made some (even among Christian apologists) suspect that their boldness may amount to nothing but a death-wish (*thanatôtês,* Clement of Alexandria; *libido moriendi,* Seneca): death to a world perceived as a mere shadow of reality. Clement of Alexandria, among others such as Seneca, rejected this suicidal posture. The *Acts of the Martyrdom of Polycarp* did not "approve of those who come forward of themselves," because "this is not the teaching of the Gospel."[239] The suicidal exaggeration, though uncomfortably widespread, was not the rule. The Christians believed, as Justin argued, that "God did not make the world aimlessly, but for the sake of the human race. . . . If then we kill ourselves, we would be acting in opposition to the will of God."[240]

Christian bloodshed was, nevertheless, seen as a participation in the sacrifice of Christ, forming with the verbal confession of Christ one unbroken living reality.[241] This sacrifice (which is a worship of God rather than demons) is an imitation of Christ, and, like the sacrifice of Christ, it has salvific value. The effect is not only felt by the martyr (remitting all his/her sins) but also by the Church as a whole.

The acts of the model martyr in Asia Minor (Polycarp of Smyrna) show how martyrdom ritually dramatizes the power of the living Jesus who speaks and dies in the martyr.[242] The connection between this narrative and the passion of the hero (the Christ) is unmistakable. The bishop was a beloved leader who was sent to the flames because of the wickedness of "pagans" and Jews. When thrown into the flames, the privileged Christians ("those of us to whom it was given to see") beheld a miracle. The martyr was like bread that is baked, like gold or silver being refined, and emitted a delightful scent like incense or perfume.[243] The martyr was thus an acceptable sacrifice like Jesus Christ. Indeed in some acts of the martyrs, like those of two

Donatist bishops, Marculus and Maximianus, the martyr is assimilated into the Christ himself. When Marculus was stretched on the rack of tortures, a special miracle was granted him: he no longer felt pain, Jesus himself was stretched full-length on his members as if incarnate once again in his tortured body.[244] Many acts of the martyrs recount dreams (a privileged means of revelation) in which the martyr is given a cup to drink (sharing in the cup of Jesus).

The narrative of the martyrdom of Polycarp avoids excessive exaggerations found in some accounts of apocalyptic tendencies in Asia Minor.[245] But it is a clear account of the martyr as witness: a bloody and acceptable sacrifice corresponding to the pattern of the sacrifice of the cross. In addition, the imagery of the Eucharistic sacrifice is prominent in the narrative; a story probably recounted within the Eucharistic setting during the martyr's anniversary. For the martyr, like Christ, has become a personality around whom (at whose tomb) there is a Christian "gathering . . . in joy and gladness . . . to celebrate the anniversary day of his martyrdom, both as a memorial for those who have already fought the contest and for the training and preparation of those who will do so one day."[246] The acts interpret the life of the martyr as a reenactment of the life of Jesus Christ as contained in the Christian foundation story in both the bloody passage and its effects. But, since the reenactment of the Christian story takes place normally in the Christian Eucharistic context, the narrative of the martyr's passage is colored with motifs of the Eucharistic thanksgiving — a case of ritual imposing itself on the story.

Polycarp's prayer sums up the ideal of the life of the martyr despite the terrible passage he was about to undergo: the martyr's passage is a Eucharistic (thanksgiving) Prayer offered to the Father through Christ his child.

"O Lord, omnipotent God and Father of your beloved and blessed child Christ Jesus, through whom we have received our knowledge of you, the God of the angels, the powers, and of all creation, and of all the family of the good who live in your sight: I bless you because you have thought me worthy of this day and this hour, to have a share among the number of the martyrs in the cup of your Christ, for the resurrection unto eternal life of both the soul and body in the immortality of the Holy spirit. May I be received this day among them before your face as a rich and acceptable sacrifice, as you, the God of truth who cannot deceive, have prepared, revealed, and fulfilled before-hand. Hence I praise you, I bless you, and I glorify you above all things, through that eternal and celestial high priest, Jesus Christ, your beloved child, through whom is glory to you with him and the Holy Spirit now and for all ages to come. Amen."[247]

Martyrdom could rightly be described with Dionysus of Alexandria as the celebration of the most brilliant of all festivals — the participation in the heavenly festival.[248]

MARTYRDOM AS INTERCESSION AND EXPIATION. It is this close link between martyrdom and the life of Jesus Christ that prompted Christians to see in the martyr a living intercession and expiation — a prolongation in time of the priestly function of Christ in his Church.

When Polycarp was arrested he requested an hour of prayer. His prayer was prolonged for two hours. The prayer was a "calling to mind all those who had come into contact with him, both important and insignificant, famous and obscure, and the entire Catholic Church scattered throughout the world." This is the normal daily intercession of the bishop.[249] But the martyr's intercessions were believed to have a salvific effect on others. Perpetua was in this way described as an intercessor for her younger brother, Dinocrates, a non-Christian, who died of cancer at the age of seven. When she uttered his name one day when they were at prayer in prison, she realized that she "was privileged to pray for him."

"I began to pray for him and to sigh deeply for him before the Lord. That very night I had the following vision. I saw Dinocrates coming out of a dark hole, where there were many others with him, very hot and thirsty, pale and dirty. . . . There was a great abyss between us: neither could approach the other. Where Dinocrates stood there was a pool of water; and its rim was higher than the child's height, so that Dinocrates had to stretch himself up to drink. I was so sorry that, though the pool had water in it, Dinocrates could not drink because of the height of the rim. Then I woke up, realizing that my brother was suffering."[250]

Perpetua's picture of the underworld and the dead suffering from thirst was probably drawn from her Roman upbringing. These images are common in Homer and Virgil. Indeed some would see in the image of her brother not the later theological struggle between Augustine and Pelagius over original sin (the cancer) and purgatory, but the personal struggle of Perpetua to renounce her Roman religious background in order to embrace Christianity.[251] Her new belief in Christ, which matured in the struggle, strengthened her to pray insistently for her brother with tears and sighs. Then the day they were kept in chains she had another vision, her brother was redeemed, "the pool that I had seen before now had its rim lowered to the level of the child's waist. And Dinocrates kept drinking water from it."[252]

This belief in the power of the martyr's intercession for the benefit of those stung by the devil's snakebite and laboring under the power of sin is very strongly argued by Origen in expiatory sacrificial terms. Origen shared with the current Catholic tradition the view that martyrdom is a (second) baptism (of blood) that purifies one of sins committed after water baptism. But he went further to show that shedding the blood of the noble martyrs is of the same nature as shedding the blood of the lamb who purchased us by his own blood and has us under his power. Thus martyrdom remits the sins of other people. The ritual passage of the martyr is an imitation of the baptism of Jesus (i.e., his death, Luke 12:50): through it they drink his cup (Mark 10:38) and thus obtain the place of privilege at the heavenly altar (Rev 6:9). Consequently, in Origen's theology, the martyrs are defined as priests without blemish because they did not renounce their master, they humbly endured their suffering, and they were detached from the world.[253]

We find in Origen, according to Rordorf, a dynamic conception of redemption. The death of the martyr is closely related to that of Jesus, both of which are an expiation for sins. This is clear in his *Exhortation to Martyrdom:*

"Note also the baptism of martyrdom, as received by our Saviour, atones for the world; so, too, when we receive it, it serves to atone for many. Just as they who assisted at the altar according to the law of Moses seemed to procure for the Jews remission for sins by the blood of goats and oxen, so the souls of believers that are beheaded for the testimony of Jesus, do not assist in vain at the altar of heaven, but procure for them that pray the remission of sins. And likewise we learn that as the High Priest Jesus Christ offered Himself in sacrifice, so the priests, whose leader He is, also offer themselves in sacrifice;

for this reason one sees them at the altar as their proper place. But while some of the priests were without blemish and offered victims without blemish and so performed the divine service, others had blemishes such as are listed by Moses in Leviticus, and were kept away from the altar. Who then is the priest without blemish who can offer a victim without blemish, if not he who bears witness to the last and fulfills every requirement of the concept of martyrdom?"[254]

One may then appreciate Origen's regret of the halt to the Christian persecution. It negatively affected the remission of sins, the clear dramatization of victory over the demons. For Tertullian martyrdom is the only sure means of salvation; only martyrs were seen in prophetic visions of paradise.[255]

Christian apologists believed that the struggle of the martyrs was against demonic powers. Justin, for example, was firmly convinced that the persecutors of the Church were worshipers of the fallen angels who mated with the daughters of men, resulting in dire consequences for the peace of society. Tertullian is of like mind.[256] Thus the body language of suffering becomes for the martyr the language of combat between athletes. The Christian athlete must defeat the demon to receive the crown. The description of the gestures is spectacular in Perpetua's story. In her vision she was transformed into a man, given two assistants who anointed her in readiness for the combat, and directed by a trainer. The real combat is cast in arresting gladiatorial language. She fought the Egyptian (devil) to a finish:

"We drew close to one another and began to let our fists fly. My opponent tried to get hold of my feet, but I kept striking him in the face with the heels of my feet. Then I was raised up into the air and I began to pummel him without as it were touching the ground. Then when I noticed there was a lull, I put my two hands together linking the fingers of one hand with those of the other and thus I got hold of his head. He fell flat on his face and I stepped on his head.

"The crowd began to shout and my assistants started to sing psalms. Then I walked up to the trainer and took the branch. He kissed me and said to me: 'Peace be with you, my daughter!' I began to walk in triumph towards the Gate of Life. Then I awoke."[257]

The combat was crucial in the time of persecution because only through it would the power of the devil be destroyed and the security of the Christians guaranteed. The blood of the martyrs became indeed the seed (Tertullian, Apol. 50)! For the Christians, faith in Christ was something worth dying for. This conviction made them attract adherents and created an environment of security (i.e, the Christian community) for members. The victory of the martyrs not only blunted the power of the evil powers to attack, but helped those who have been conquered by the sting of the devil to raise their heads and be freed from the evil that formerly oppressed and injured them. No wonder the demons, according to Origen, foreseeing their sure defeat, found it unprofitable to provoke further persecutions.[258] And when the Church gained its peace, it recognized the priestly-expiatory sacrificial role of the martyrs by permitting confessors, who were tortured but later liberated, to reconcile the *lapsi* who failed in the face of persecution. Furthermore, a confessor did not need any further commissioning (ordination) to become a presbyter.

We conclude with Rordorf that Origen and the Fathers before him saw the sacrifice of the martyrs as a reenactment of Christ's sacrifice on the cross. Both have expiatory value. The martyr's sacrifice, deriving from the universal unrepeatable sacrifice of Christ, does not diminish it. Rather, like the Eucharist, it is limited in time and space. But through both the Eucharist and the bloody sacrifice of the martyr, "God wishes to reenact the sacrifice of his Son in time and for a specific community."[259] The church of the martyrs was able to bear witness publicly (open bodily combat) to Christ. In this way the martyrs dramatized in the public arena of life in this world *(saeculum)* the memorial of the Christian founding story, which is normally celebrated in the Eucharist. This transition ritual of physical suffering is a *thusia* (i.e., the highest act of worship). Through it or in it Christians pass from this life into the heavenly liturgy. Martyrdom became a painful, personal appropriation of the Christian story by the confessing Christians. Thus this gesture, which is real-symbolism, (re-)created the Church.

The Eucharistic Memorial: The Vehicle of Realizing and Transmitting the Christian Foundation Story

In chapter two we noted that the house-churches gathered around a meal to keep the memory of Jesus. This meal included the noncultic meal of satiety *(agape)* and the cultic Eucharistic rite. The Eucharistic rite (the Lord's Supper or Breaking of Bread) became the crucial

Christian ritual. It was so vital to the community's interpretation of the critical passage of its founder that its institution was made the first chapter of the narrative of this passage. The narrative successfully interpreted the death of Jesus as self-gift. According to Luke, at the Eucharistic rite the recognition of the Lord as risen (life-giver) is realized (Luke 24:13-34); consequently, the church-community is brought into existence.

The Christian Eucharist, therefore, comes across as the one fundamental rite of the Christian assembly, a rite that in a true sense creates the assembly because its consuming intent is recalling the self-gift of Jesus, its Lord and almighty life giver. In this segment, we will show (1) the centrality of the Eucharistic celebration in a Church undergoing persecution — the indefectible food of the martyrs that also became the means of defending the value and reality of the created world against Gnostic speculations — and (2) the Eucharistic Prayer as a vehicle for keeping the memory of Jesus alive.

The Eucharist as Principal Ritual of a Persecuted Christian Community.

THE FUNDAMENTAL CHRISTIAN NOURISHMENT: CAUSE FOR THE SUSPICION OF THE NON-CHRISTIAN NEIGHBORS. Meals not only give nourishment but are social boundary markers, as discussed in chapter two. In the pre-Nicene Church, participation in the Christian Eucharist was a matter of secrecy. This secrecy led to suspicion and accusations. Minucius Felix in his *Octavius* (third century C.E.) painted a lurid picture of the supposed Christian *flagitia* (crimes): the core ritual of the gathering is said to be the sacrificial murder of a child whose body and blood the murderous sect ate and drank; on an appointed day they gathered for feasting and drinking and indulged in incestuous practices.[260] Unfortunately, some Christian groups (referred to as libertine gnostics) may have turned their *agape* ('love-feast') into occasions for sexual licence.[261] Benko has argued that genuine features of the Christian doctrine and practice are discernible in the aberrant Eucharists of Phibionite gnostics described by Epiphanius. These include realities like the intimate bonding/fellowship *(koinonia)* that the Eucharist symbolized, expressed in the *agape* and the kiss of peace; the divine presence in those who know God expressed in 1 John 3:9 as God's seed *(sperma)* abiding in Christians, etc.[262] These errors must have done a lot of damage to the evolving "Great Church" because outsiders were not in a position to make the nice distinctions between orthodox and marginal Christian groups. Pliny the Younger, however, testified that the Christian food was "ordinary and harmless."[263]

For the Christians the Eucharistic meal was indispensable. Pliny was not given the whole picture by the *ministrae* (deaconesses) whom he interrogated under torture. His assertion that "they had ceased this practice after my edict in which, in accordance with your orders, I had forbidden secret societies,"[264] may apply to the evening *agape* but not to the morning Eucharistic rite. In the thick of the persecutions the Eucharist was celebrated right inside the imperial prisons. From his place of hiding, Cyprian of Carthage, who kept contact with his flock through his letters, counseled prudence about visiting the confessors. But he took it for granted that the Eucharist was celebrated for them:

"And so take counsel and care that moderation makes visiting safer; in particular the presbyters who celebrate the offering there before the confessors should take it in turns to go individually, accompanied each by a different deacon, because the risk of resentment is diminished if the people who visit and meet together change and vary."[265]

The reason for such risks was clear to the Church: the Eucharist empowers the confessors and martyrs to bear witness to the Lord. It is the greatest safeguard against the enemy. In the acts of martyrdom of Montanus and Lucius, the imprisoned confessors who were denied earthly food were nourished not only with the vision of the drink of eternal life (symbolized in the milk), but were also fed with the *alimentum indeficiens* (food that does not fail, cf. Luke 12:33). According to the narrator, the Eucharist was the way the Lord offered "us refreshment in our suffering" *(ita laboris nostris refrigerium dominus . . . praebuit).* It was a happy surprise to the prisoners that the "most stubborn obstacle of our imprisonment" was pierced and the subdeacon Herenianus and the catechumen Januarius "ministered to all of us that food that does not fail." The effect of this ministry was predictable: "This assistance gave us great light in our illness and our suffering. Indeed, it restored to health those who had already fallen ill because of those privations, especially the disagreeable rations and cold water. For his glorious works we all give thanks to God."[266]

The presbyter Lucian of Antioch was said to have celebrated in the dark of the prison with other inmates. Since Lucian was bound hands and feet, the bread was deposited on his chest when they celebrated and broke bread together. All forty-seven of the martyrs of Abitinia in North Africa were rounded up during their Eucharistic assembly on the Lord's day. Their bishop had turned traitor *(traditor)* and handed over the books to their persecutors, as many ecclesiastics did. Having been deprived of the Eucharist for too long a time, they found another presbyter to preside. At their trial the proconsul interrogated Emeritus, in whose house the celebration took place. Emeritus told the tribunal that he could not stop his brothers from gathering in his house because "it is impossible for us to live without celebrating the Lord's Supper." They were condemned. In prison, they held a council denouncing and excommunicating the *traditor* clergy who submitted the Christian books, stating that these traitors would not share with them the promised paradise.[267]

Anywhere the Christians found themselves became a place of assembly to pray and celebrate the rite that recalled the sacrifice of the Lord. Whether in the "field, the desert, ship, inn, or prison," they never failed to celebrate. They believed that "the most brilliant festival of all was kept by the fulfilled martyrs, who were feasted in heaven."[268]

The need to be strengthened by the body and blood of Christ in order to pour out their blood along with him made them risk their lives in order to celebrate. This conviction that the Eucharist was both a safeguard and energizer led Cyprian to decree that those who had fallen *(lapsi)* and were doing penance should be reconciled and given communion. The Council of Carthage (April 251, after the Decian persecution) agreed to reconcile only those who bought certificates *(libelli)* of sacrifice, but all those who sacrificed, poured libations, or offered incense could be reconciled at their death bed. However, the threat of a new persecution was looming large, and Cyprian was persuaded that the conciliar decisions should apply only in time of peace. Thus, fallen Christians who were healthy, who repented, and who were doing penance were to be reconciled and brought to communion in order to be strengthened to face the impending martyrdom. For, "a man cannot be fit for martyrdom if he is not armed for battle by the Church; his heart fails if it is not fired and fortified by receiving the Eucharist."[269]

All the above go to show the central place of the Eucharist in the life of the community. One may then appreciate the Eucharistic (thanksgiving) and sacrificial description of the martyr's passage, as is presented in the writings of Ignatius of Antioch and the martyrdom of Polycarp. The Eucharist is a recalling of the events of the Christian story; a representation of these events; a feast that binds the martyrs to the Lord and to one another; a food that strengthens the martyr to follow the road of martyrdom traced by the Lord — becoming one with the Lord in an eminent way, merging the martyr's blood with the blood of the Lamb, and giving it the same expiatory value as the blood of Christ.

When one talks of the Christian rite *(de ritu christiano)*, one is talking about the Eucharist. In the epitaph of Abercius (the oldest stone monument that mentioned the Eucharist, second century C.E.), this food of Christians is referred to as "the fish from the spring" given "to friends to eat, always having sweet wine and giving mixed cup with bread." Only the initiates will appreciate the mystical meaning and nourishment provided by *ichthus* (fish/Christ/food). The gathering together to eat creates the environment for telling the story of Christ. The narrative makes Christ present in the gathering as the one who nourishes and strengthens through the food that is as sweet as honey. In peacetime and under persecution the early Christians took the Eucharist as nourishment and as the most telling symbol of the Christian story. The inscription of Pectorius of Autun (whose language resembles that of Abercius, though it is dated to the second half of the fourth century) possibly quotes an ancient poem that sums up for us how Christians savor the Eucharist:

"[Thou] the divine child of the heavenly Fish,
Keep pure thy soul among mortals.
Because thou receivest the immortal
Fountain of divine water
Refresh thy soul, friend, with the
Ever flowing water of wealth-giving wisdom.
Take from the Redeemer of the saints
The food as sweet as honey:
Eat with joy and desire, holding the Fish
In thy hands.
I pray, give as food the Fish, Lord and Savior.

May she rest peacefully, my mother,
So I pray to thee, [thou] light of the dead.
Aschandius, father, my heart's beloved,
With my sweet mother and my brothers
In the peace of the Fish remember thy Pectorius."[270]

BOUNDARY BETWEEN HERESY AND ORTHODOXY DETERMINED BY THE EUCHARISTIC SACRIFICE: IRENAEUS OF LYONS AND GNOSTICISM. The "libertine" gnostic group (the Phibionites) caused damage to the Christian cause during the persecutions. Their materialist transformation of Christian symbols — *sperma* into ritual use of semen, "love-feast" into sexual promiscuity, communion in the "body and blood" of the Lord into ritual murder and anthropophagy — was reprehensible to the "Great Church." It was a destruction of sacramentality. According to Eusebius the historian, they were proscribed by the Church.[271]

The Valentinian Gnostics presented a more devastating problem because of their radical dualism. This dualism claimed that the created world was not the work of the propator (*Bythus,* the Highest God, Father of all). It was rather the work of an inferior and ignorant angel (demiurge), who had no knowledge of the propator but was fashioned in imitation of him. The production of the demiurge was the handiwork of Achamoth (or Enthymese or inferior Sophia), the offspring of the disordered desire of the true Sophia to contemplate the Highest God. This aeon (i.e., Achamoth) was chased out of the pleroma (made up of thirty aeons), and the true Sophia was retained within the pleroma. Achamoth in dark distress produced matter and a psychic substance. From the psychic substance he formed the demiurge. On his own part the demiurge created heaven and earth, then formed humans from fluid, fusible, and material substance merged with the psychic substance. But unknown to the demiurge (the creator, god of the Old Testament), Achamoth added the spiritual element *(pneuma)* into some humans. Thus there emerged three human types: the material, the psychical, and the spiritual.

The problem this gnostic plastic cosmogony posed to the Christian Church is seen in its treatment of matter and its understanding of Jesus the Christ. According to the Valentinians, Jesus the Savior, also called Christ, was the joyous product of the aeons' symphony of praise of the Father (Bythus). This aeon (Jesus the Savior) entered the world to save humans, but he was contaminated with no material substance. Matter is evil, a product of darkness and disorder. Jesus borrowed the immateriality of Achamoth and only looked like a man. Among humans only the psychical and spiritual types are redeemable — the first with great difficulty and the second with relative ease. The material type is doomed to perdition.[272]

The procedure of the Christian apologists (especially Irenaeus and Tertullian) was to highlight the value of the material world and to stress the fusion of the spiritual and the material dimensions as realized in the incarnation. For Irenaeus, the Eucharistic rite, celebrated by both orthodox Christians and the heretical groups, was a powerful tool to save the Christian way. More than any other apologist, Irenaeus reduced the tendency to excessively allegorize the materiality of cultic offerings. And he successfully combined in one synthesis the pure or spiritual sacrifice and the material oblation, which gives the inner act of the sacrifice its visible form. His theology of sacrifice (precisely of Eucharistic sacrifice) is more realist than that of Clement of Alexandria, Origen, and even Tertullian.[273] His Eucharistic arguments are best exposed in *Adversus Haereses (Against the Heresies)* IV and V. He espoused the common philosophical and rabbinic opinion that God had no need for sacrifices, but that they were beneficial to those who presented them (4.17.1).[274] Sacrifices do not make one holy, rather it is the disposition of the heart (a pure conscience) that makes the sacrifice holy (4.18.3). However, against the Gnostic claim that matter is evil, Irenaeus stressed the material reality of the bread and wine (offering of first fruits) of the Eucharist. Jesus offered and commanded his disciples to offer these products of God's creation in thankfulness as his body and blood (4.17.5). This is the pure sacrifice prophesied by Malachi. The Christ offered is an actual fleshly man and not simply a spiritual invisible man (5.2.3).

For Irenaeus, sacrifice is real. Despite his dislike for the Jews (whose hands are tainted with blood, 4.18.4), he stressed both the reality and value of the Old Testament sacrifices (4.18.1–3). All these sacrifices are recapitulated in that of Christ, which the Church alone offers. The heretical groups do not offer this same sacrifice because they claim that the world was created in ignorance, weakness, and passion. If their opinion is to be followed they actually sin against "their father" by their offering instead of giving him thanks. If they refuse to recognize the Lord as son of the Creator, Irenaeus asked, how can they justify their acceptance of the bread and cup, over which thanks have been given, as his body and blood? (4.18.4). Thus either the Gnostics change their viewpoint or they stop celebrating the Eucharist. Irenaeus wrapped up his argument by declaring that his opinion is proven by the Eucharistic practice of the Christian assembly — the rule of prayer confirming the rule of faith *(lex orandi, lex credendi).*

"Let them, therefore, either alter their opinion, or cease from offering the things just mentioned. But our opinion is in accordance with the Eucharist, and the Eucharist in turn establishes our opinion. For we offer to Him His own, announcing consistently the fellowship and union of the flesh and Spirit. For as the bread, which is produced from the earth, when it receives the invocation of God, is no longer common bread, but the Eucharist, consisting of two realities, earthly and heavenly; so also our bodies, when they receive the Eucharist, are no longer corruptible, having the hope of the resurrection to eternity" (4.18.5).

This teaching of Irenaeus — that the Christian assembly offers to God what is "his own" — became entrenched in the Christian Eucharistic tradition. In the Byzantine anaphoras of Basil and Chrysostom, and the Egyptian anaphora of St. Mark, the phrase *ta sa ek tôn sôn prospherontes* or *soi ek tôn sôn dôrôn,* which corresponds to the *de tuis donis ac datis* of the Roman Canon, emphasizes the materiality of the gifts offered in thanksgiving (as sacrifice of praise) that are transformed into the body and blood of the Lord.[275] The faithful were encouraged to bring their offerings to the celebration. These offerings were referred to in sacrificial terms, especially in North Africa. Cyprian saw the bishop as *sacerdos* (priest) who offered the Lord's sacrifice of bread and wine. These pre-Nicene references to the material offering are not all anti-Gnostic. Rather they are a development of the Christian tradition in a more measured pattern than the excessive speculations of the Gnostics. Credit goes to Irenaeus for the theological systematization of the intrinsic value of material (earthly) reality and human history (from Adam to Christ). Jesus Christ summed up or recapitulated *(anakephalaiosis)* all this reality into himself (3.21.10–22.4). For Irenaeus the clearest way the Christian tradition daily or frequently expresses this intrinsic value of earthly reality is linked (as symbol, *symbolon*) to the Christian story of redemption:

the products of the earth are offered by the Church in thanksgiving as the body and blood of the Lord; this product of the earth over which the blessing is pronounced nourishes the body of believers, planting into them the seed of the resurrection. Therefore, the Eucharistic practice of Christians *(lex orandi)* proves the theological position of Irenaeus *(lex credendi)*.

The Eucharistic Prayer (Verbal Ritual) Sums Up and Communicates the Christian Story. When Pliny remarked that Christians sang their praise to Christ as to their god (*carmenque christo quasi deo dicere)*, he was indicating how the Christian belief became expressed in hymnic prayer. Pliny was not given text of such a hymn, but from the second half of the first century, doxologies addressed to God were also addressed to Christ. We have already noted such a practice within the assembly of the Church of the Apocalypse (cf. Rev 1:5-6; 5:13). The New Testament has hymns of the sapiential type that were developed in contact with Wisdom speculations emphasizing Jesus' nature as preexistent incarnate wisdom, humbled and yet exalted (cf. John's Prologue; Phil 2:6-11; Heb 1:3-4; Col 1:15-20).[276] It is interesting that a non-Christian Roman official was able to put his finger on Christocentric prayers (hymns, doxologies, within or outside the Eucharistic celebration) as differentiating the Christian way from other associations.[277]

The remark by Pliny leads us to consider the content and function of Christian prayer at the meal gatherings. This investigation is not idle because other contemporaneous associations whose origins predated the Christian movement have similar practices of ritual meals. As we shall see in the next chapter, their rituals were too close to the Christian rite to arouse a Christian defense. Justin, Tertullian, and other apologists saw the parallels as the work of wicked demons. Recent studies of the mystery cults, like the cult of Mithra, have tried to show the absence of a causal link between the cults and the Christian rituals. Whatever the parallels, the Christian Eucharistic Prayer, which recalls or proclaims the founding story of Christianity, makes the difference clear.[278]

The meal is a powerful symbol, as we have often remarked. Cultic meals symbolize a sharing of life. They establish a bond with the divinity and a fellowship among members of the group. But the nonverbal ritual gesture of eating and drinking is not demarcated from one religious association to another except by the verbal ritual complement. The prayer or incantation in the context of the ritual meal-gathering demarcates the first as Mithraic and the other as Christian. Therefore, the Christian meal (Eucharistic) prayers spell out the shared awareness of the group to distinguish it from other groups.

THE EUCHARISTIC PRAYER NARRATES THE CHRISTIAN STORY. The realist Eucharistic theology of Irenaeus in *Adversus Haereses* states that the acceptable sacrifice, the offering of the first fruits, accomplished only by the Church, is an offering to the Creator, "with giving of thanks," of the things taken from his creation.[279] The giving of thanks *(eucharistia)* makes the bread, which receives the "invocation" of God *(epiclesis)*, no longer common bread, but the Eucharist.[280] Both the prayer and the offering are called *eucharistia.*

Irenaeus' use of *eucharistia* confirms an earlier practice very clearly attested in Justin's more detailed description of the Christian Eucharistic meal and prayers. In his description of Christian initiation, which is sealed by the Eucharistic liturgy,[281] bread and a cup of wine mixed with water are brought. The president of the assembly takes these elements and "gives praise and glory to the Father of the universe, through the name of the Son and of the Holy Ghost, and offers thanks at considerable length for our being counted worthy to receive these things at His Hands." The assembly responds to the president's prayers and thanksgiving by saying "Amen."[282] The food over which thanks has been given ("eucharistified" food) is distributed and called *eucharistia:* the "flesh and blood of that Jesus who was made flesh." It is blessed by the prayer of his Word.[283] The same procedure is used for the Sunday Eucharist.[284]

Though Justin did not give a sample of a Eucharistic Prayer, he gave sufficient indications of the motifs of the prayer that demarcate the meal assembly as Christian. It appears to be close to the pattern of the Jewish Grace *(birkat ha-mazon)*, since it opens with the praise and glory of God as Father of the universe. It narrates God's creative action in the universe, but it has become a praise in the name of Christ and the Holy Spirit. Thus the key symbols that shape the awareness of the Christian assembly are prominent. Finally, it is a praise and thanksgiving which, naturally, dwells on recounting the salvation God accomplished in Christ (the heart of the Christian mystery, the paschal mystery). As Justin states in his *Dialogues with*

Trypho, the Eucharistic bread is offered "in remembrance of the passion he endured for all those souls who are cleansed from sin." That is why Christians "thank God for having created the world, and everything in it, for the sake of mankind, for having saved us from the sin in which we were born, and for the total destruction of the powers and principalities of evil through him who suffered in accordance with his will."[285] The prayer thus highlights a positive Christian attitude toward creation and the gifts derived therefrom (as in the Jewish Grace); then it develops the specific Christian story — the salvation of all humans through the death-resurrection of Jesus.

The thanksgiving prayer of the Didache is still closer to the Jewish Grace than Justin. Opinions are divided as to whether it is really a Eucharistic Prayer or a prayer for the *agape.*[286] The absence of an institution narrative in the prayer makes some think that it is not a Eucharistic Prayer. Whether it is a Eucharistic Prayer or not, its thanksgiving for the banquet of wisdom turns around the mediation of this gift of the Father through his child Jesus. The thanksgiving prayer of the Didache appears to be a deliberate spiritualization of the thanksgiving for food in the Jewish Grace. For example:

"We give thanks to you, holy Father, for your holy Name which you have enshrined in our hearts, and for the knowledge and faith and immortality which you made known to us through your child Jesus; glory to you for evermore.

"You, almighty Master, created all things for the sake of your Name, and gave food and drink to mankind for their enjoyment, that they might give you thanks; but to us you have granted spiritual food and drink and eternal life through your child Jesus. Above all we give you thanks because you are mighty; glory to you for evermore. Amen."[287]

The Christian Eucharistic Prayer, as thanksgiving praise of God, displays in narrative form God's redemptive achievement in Jesus Christ. It is rooted in the mode of the Jewish *berakah* (blessing). The Christian specificity emerges in the overriding position of the memorial-recollection of Jesus Christ. In the prayer of Hippolytus, a very influential model of the Christian Eucharistic Prayer,[288] the recollection of the Jesus event in narrative-memorial is very sharply brought out. We use it as our chief example of the early Christian Eucharistic Prayer.

THE APOSTOLIC TRADITION OF HIPPOLYTUS. In the *Apostolic Tradition* (ca. 215 C.E.) we find what may be the most primitive and undisputed record of a Christian Eucharistic Prayer. Indeed Hippolytus' work contains texts of primitive Christian rites and practices (baptism, Eucharist, ordination, ecclesiastical discipline, etc.).[289] The content and structure of the Eucharistic Prayer of the *Apostolic Tradition* displays a nucleus that has more or less been maintained and expanded by the various liturgical traditions of the Eastern and Western Church. Though Hippolytus' text is not supposed to be obligatory, as he himself testified,[290] the various components of the prayer — introductory dialogue, thanksgiving for (creation and) redemption, institution narrative, *anamnesis*, epiclesis, and doxology — are found in the texts that became standard in the fourth century. The original Greek text of Hippolytus' prayer is lost. But the popularity of the *Apostolic Tradition* ensured its survival in the Latin, Coptic, Arabic, and Ethiopic versions.[291] The Hellenistic pattern of the prayer is suggested by its unbroken thought flow: one single prayer addressed to the father through Christ the child. This primitive (traditional) pattern of addressing all prayers to the father through the son has been maintained by the Eucharistic Prayer tradition despite the fact that hymns and prayers are addressed to Christ from New Testament times. Origen argued that this is the only Christian way to pray. In North Africa where we have the first clear evidence of fixed, as opposed to improvised, liturgical texts, the Eucharistic Prayer addressed the father through the son:

"In prayers let no one name [address] the Father instead of the Son, or the Son instead of the Father. And when one stands at the altar let prayer always be directed to the Father. If anyone copies out prayers for himself from elsewhere, these should not be used unless he has first discussed them with more learned brethren."[292]

The thanksgiving and other component parts of the Eucharistic Prayer of the *Apostolic Tradition* (as well as those of other Eucharistic Prayers) keep alive in the Christian assembly the memorial of the central events of the Christian story addressed to the father through Christ. In the Christian celebration of the Lord's Supper, the prayer exalts and thanks God by recounting the redemptive work achieved in Christ. This Eucharistic memorial makes the assembly relive these central events. The full text of the prayer of the *Apostolic Tradition* brings this out clearly. After the introductory dialogue, the thanksgiving continues as follows:

"We render thanks to you, O God, through your beloved child Jesus Christ, whom in the last times you sent to us as a savior and redeemer and angel of your will; who is your inseparable Word, through whom you made all things, and in whom you were well pleased. You sent him from heaven into a virgin's womb; and conceived in the womb, he was made flesh and was manifested as your Son, being born of the Holy Spirit and the Virgin. Fulfilling your will and gaining for you a holy people, he stretched out his hands when he should suffer, that he might release from suffering those who have believed in you.

"And when he was betrayed to voluntary suffering that he might destroy death, and break the bonds of the devil, and tread down hell, and shine upon the righteous, and fix a term, and manifest the resurrection, he took bread and gave thanks to you, saying, 'Take, eat; this is my body, which shall be broken for you.' Likewise also the cup, saying, 'This is my blood, which is shed for you; when you do this, you make my remembrance.'

"Remembering therefore his death and resurrection, we offer to you the bread and the cup, giving you thanks because you have held us worthy to stand before you and minister to you.

"And we ask that you would send your Holy Spirit upon the offering of your holy Church; that, gathering her into one, you would grant to all who receive the holy things [to receive] for the fullness of the Holy Spirit for the strengthening of faith in truth; that we may praise and glorify you through your child Jesus Christ; through whom be glory and honour to you, to the Father and the Son, with the Holy Spirit, in your holy Church, both now and to the ages of ages. Amen."[293]

Concluding Remarks: The Uniqueness of the Christian Story

The striking difference between our handling of the Christian story (myth-symbol) and the Nri, Mesopotamian, or even the Jewish foundation narratives, is that our commentary is less detached. This is because I am a Christian. However, we did not shy away from using sources that are critical of the Christian practice. These sources help us sharpen the difference between Greco-Roman religious practice and Christianity. The position of the Christian foundation story as living myth is demonstrated in the life and worship of early Christians. In other words, the narrative of the way Jesus lived, died, and became recognized as life-giver (as risen), is ever present and reactualized in Christian life and worship.

In the first place, the life of Christians is understood as worship. This is because Christian living ideally displays, or becomes a narration of, the way Jesus lived and died (the foundation story). Consequently, martyrdom becomes a representation or a reenactment of the Christian story. It is indeed the highest form of Christian prayer because, as a sacrifice unto death that is absorbed into the sacrifice of Christ, it shares in the supreme worship of the father by Christ and his members.

Second, the most powerful ritual-symbol that carries and communicates the Christian story is the Eucharistic memorial. The synoptic gospels give it a prominent position as cultic (ritual) narrative. Its institution introduces the narrative of the passion, death, and resurrection of the Lord. In this way the Eucharist is endowed with the power of being both the vehicle and interpreter of the paschal mystery. Through it the assembly relives the Christian foundation story; in it the mystery of Christ is fully manifest.

The power of the Eucharist as controlling Christian ritual-symbol is evident in the church of the martyrs. Then, there was the imperious necessity to assemble in private houses or imperial dungeons to celebrate. This proves that the Eucharist is the crucial means through which they recognize themselves as Christian, because in it they live and narrate their foundation story. The records of the *Acts of the Christian Martyrs* lead us to affirm that without the Eucharist there will be no Christian assembly. Like the passion of the Lord, the Eucharistic memorial serves as an introduction into and an interpretation of the passion of the Christian martyr.

The uniqueness of the Christian story does not lie in the pattern of recalling the past in the present or in the historical truth of the death-resurrection of Jesus as opposed to, for example, the Nri myth or the *Enuma Elish.* The uniqueness, for Christians, lies in the power of our Christian foundation story to move and sustain us in assembly and life. The verification of the truth of our story lies in participating in the Eucharistic celebration (and in other Christian rituals) and in living the imitation of Christ as narrated in the foundation story.

NOTES

1. See W. T. Stevenson, "Myth and the Crisis of Historical Consciousness," *Myth and Crisis of Historical Consciousness*, ed. L. W. Gibbs and W. T. Stevenson (Missoula, Mont.: Scholars Press, 1975) esp. 6–9.

2. As an example one may consult two studies, one from a classicist and the other from a literary critic, that review the various definitions of myth and other kinds of story: G. S. Kirk, *Myth: Its Meaning and Function in Ancient and Other Cultures* (Cambridge: Cambridge University Press, 1970); I. Okpewho, *Myth in Africa: A Study of Its Aesthetic and Cultural Relevance* (Cambridge: Cambridge University Press, 1983).

3. Okpewho, *Myth in Africa,* 69.

4. Kirk, *Myth,* 282–4.

5. A comprehensive list of the theories is provided by G. S. Kirk in his "On Defining Myths," *Sacred Narrative: Readings in the Theory of Myth,* ed. A. Dundes (Berkeley: University of California Press, 1984) 54–55.

6. See V. Y. Mudimbe, *The Invention of Africa: Gnosis, Philosophy, and the Order of Knowledge* (Bloomington and Indianapolis: Indiana University Press, 1988).

7. Jung and Kerenyi, *Introduction to a Science of Mythology* (London: Routledge & Kegan Paul, 1970) 100–1. For a critique of Jung's position see Kirk, *Myth,* 275–80; Okpewho, *Myth in Africa,* 10–15; W. Soyinka, *Myth, Literature and the African World* (Cambridge: Cambridge University Press, 1990) 33–36. A recent study of archetypes in Jung and others is contained in D. R. Griffin, ed., *Archetypal Process: Self and Divine in Whitehead, Jung, and Hillman* (Evanston, Ill.: Northwestern University Press, 1989).

8. E. Cassirer follows Freud and Schelling to define myth as tautegorical in his *The Philosophy of Symbolic Forms: Mythical Thoughts* (New Haven, Conn.: Yale University Press, 1955) 5. For a critique of Cassirer see Kirk, *Myth,* 261–8; Okpewho, *Myth in Africa,* 27–30.

9. Each of the contributors in Dundes' *Sacred Narrative* presents a distinctive viewpoint on the issue. See J. Campbell's outline that we follow in his *The Masks of God: Creative Mythology* (New York: Penguin, 1976) 4–8, 608–24.

10. Cf. J. Vidal, "Aspects d'une Mythique," *Le Mythe: Son Langage et son Message,* Actes du colloque de Liège et Louvain-la-Neuve, ed. H. Limet and J. Ries (Louvain-la-Neuve: Centre d'Histoire des Religions, 1983) esp. 36–43; M. Eliade, "Cosmogonic Myth and 'Sacred History,'" *Sacred Narrative,* 140–1; Kirk, *Myth,* 283–4.

11. M. Eliade, *Myths, Dreams and Mysteries* (London: Collins, 1960); L. Honko, "The Problem of Defining Myth," *Sacred Narrative,* 50.

12. Campbell, *The Masks of God,* 611.

13. Eliade, "Cosmogonic Myth and 'Sacred History,'" 141; idem, *Myths, Dreams and Mysteries,* 16.

14. Campbell, *The Masks of God*, 4–5.

15. Cited by Cassirer, *The Philosophy of Symbolic Forms*, 5.

16. Campbell, *The Masks of God*, 6.

17. C. Jung, *Memories, Dramas, Reflections* (New York: Random House, 1963); cited by G. H. Slusser, "Jung and Whitehead on Self and Divine: The Necessity for Symbol and Myth," *Archetypal Process*, 87.

18. This is Polanyi's idea of the metaphor and symbol. See A. F. Sanders, "Religion and Science as Cultural Systems: Polanyi's View on the Problem of Meaning," *Nueu Zeitschrift für Systematische Theologie und Religionsphilosophie* 27/2:1985, 92.

19. See Slusser, "Jung and Whitehead," 86.

20. M. Polanyi and H. Prosch, *Meaning* (Chicago: University of Chicago Press, 1975) 132; cited by Sanders, "Religion and Science," 93.

21. Campbell's book develops this aspect of creativity in mythology. See also his *Myths to Live By* (New York: Bantam Books, 1972). Of interest for the study of the kind of creativity described above is S. Langer's *Philosophy in a New Key: A Study in the Symbolism of Reason, Rite, and Art*, 3rd ed. (Cambridge and London: Harvard University Press, 1957).

22. Kirk, *Myth*, 23ff.; Okpewho, *Myth in Africa*, 45ff.

23. See Jousse, *Anthropologie du Geste* (Paris: Resma, 1969); A de Waal Malefijt, *Religion and Culture: An Introduction to the Anthropology of Religion* (New York: Macmillan Co., 1968) ch. 7; I. Babour, *Myth, Models and Paradigms* (San Francisco: Harper & Row, 1976) 25.

24. See the recent study of J. N. Oriji, *Traditions of Igbo Origin: A Study of Pre-colonial Population Movements in Africa* (New York: Peter Lang, 1990) 4, 15–16. Oriji cites as his sources papers presented at the Workshop on the Foundations of Igbo Civilization, Institute of African Studies, University of Nigeria Nsukka, in 1980, especially the papers of D. D. Hartle ("The Frame Work of Pre-History in Igboland") and F. N. Anozie ("The Old Stone Age in Igboland").

25. See A. E. Afigbo, "Prolegomena to the Study of the Culture History of the Igbo-Speaking Peoples of Nigeria," *Igbo Language and Culture*, ed. F. C. Ogbalu and E. N. Emenajo (Ibadan: Oxford University Press, 1975) 36; E. Isichei, *A History of the Igbo People* (London: Macmillan Co., 1976) 3–4.

26. T. Shaw, *Igbo-Ukwu: An Account of Archaeological Discoveries in Eastern Nigeria*, 2 vols. (London: Faber and Faber, 1970). Most of this historical introduction condenses what I already presented in "Igbo World and Ultimate Reality and Meaning," esp. 188–94.

27. See J. Greenberg, *The Languages of Africa* (Bloomington: Indiana University Press, 1966) 8. R. Armstrong suggests that the split in the parent stock of the Kwa linguistic group may have occurred five to six thousand years ago. See his "Glottochronology and West African Linguistics," *Journal*

of African History 3:1962, 284; and his *The Study of West African Languages* (Ibadan: Ibadan University Press, 1964) 22–23.

28. Oriji, *Traditions of Igbo Origin,* especially ch. 2.

29. See the authoritative work of M. A. Onwuejeogwu, *An Igbo Civilization: Nri Kingdom and Hegemony* (London: Ethnographica and Ethiope, 1981).

30. A. G. Leonard, *The Lower Niger and Its Tribes* (London: Frank Cass, 1906) 37.

31. Afigbo, "Prolegomena," 38–41.

32. The narrative is published in E. Isichei, *Igbo Worlds: An Anthology of Oral Histories and Historical Descriptions* (Philadelphia: Institute for the Study of Human Issues, 1978) 21–24. Nwaokoye Odenigbo was then 83 years old. His narrative was carefully cross-checked by Onwuejeogwu and compared with records by Thomas and Jeffreys (see below).

33. This commentary draws from my "Nri Myth of Origin and Its Ritualization: An Essay in Interpretation," *Religion and African Culture: I: Inculturation: A Nigerian Perspective,* ed. E. E. Uzukwu (Enugu: Spiritan Publications, 1988) 92–101.

34. N. W. Thomas, *Anthropological Report on the Ibo-Speaking Peoples of Nigeria* (London: Harrison, 1913–14) 50. *Cuku = Chukwu.*

35. P. Ricoeur, *The Symbolism of Evil* (Boston: Beacon Press, 1967) 162–3.

36. D. I. Nwoga, *The Supreme Being as Stranger in Igbo Religious Thought* (Ekwerazu, Mbaise: Hawk Press, 1984) 41–48.

37. See T. M. Olshewsky, "Between Science and Religion," *Journal of Religion* 62/3:1982, 253.

38. Nwoga rests his thesis on evidence drawn from colonial and missionary writers and then from literary critics. On the other hand, the indigenous origin of *Chukwu* is stoutly defended. During a recent symposium on *Healing and Exorcism: The Nigerian Experience,* held at the Spiritan International School of Theology, Enugu, 1989, theologians of Christian and indigenous religions like E. I. Metuh and C. U. Manus opposed Nwoga, amassing their own evidence in support of the originary position of *Chukwu* in Igbo cosmology. The issue is not resolved, but the debate cautions against making categorical statements on cult symbols employed by a people like the Igbo with many culture centers.

39. Onwuejeogwu, *An Igbo Civilization,* 25.

40. See the following authors: Onwuejeogwu, *An Igbo Civilization,* ch. 5; Thomas, *Anthropological Report,* 48–56; M.D.W. Jeffreys, "The Divine Umundri King," *Africa* VIII:1935, 346–54; idem, "Additional Steps in Umundri Coronation Ceremony," *Africa* IX:1936, 403–6; C. K. Meek, *Law and Authority in a Nigerian Tribe* (London: Oxford University Press, 1937) 153–5, 162–3; R. N. Henderson, *The King in Every Man: Evolutionary Trends in Onitsha Ibo*

Society and Culture (New Haven, Conn.: Yale University Press, 1972) 252–62, 270–9, 368–77, 514–23.

41. Jeffreys, "The Divine Umundri King," 347.

42. On the *Ofo* see C. I. Ejizu, *OFO: Igbo Ritual Symbol* (Enugu: Fourth Dimension Publishers, 1986). Among studies on the kola-nut see V. C. Uchendu, "'Kola Hospitality' and Igbo Lineage Structure," *Man* LXIV:1964, 47–50; Henderson, *The King in Everyman*, 371–81; C.C.A. Nwokocha, "The Kola — Igbo Symbol of Love and Unity — A Valuable Starting Point for the Study of the Eucharist" (Th.D. dissertation, Universitas Urbaniana Rome, 1969).

43. M.J.C. Echeruo, *A Matter of Identity*, 1979 Ahiajioku Lecture (Owerri: Ministry of Information, Culture, Youth and Sports, 1979) 18; cited by Nwoga, *The Supreme Being*, 28.

44. For details see, among others, G. I. Jones, "Ibo Land Tenure," *Africa* XIX:1949, esp. 316–21; W.R.G. Horton, "God, Man, and the Land in a Northern Ibo Village-group," *Africa* XXVI:1956, 23; Thomas, *Anthropological Report*, 29, 56, 59; Afigbo, "Prolegomena," 42–43; Nwoga, *The Supreme Being*, 66. See also my Th.D. dissertation, *Blessing and Thanksgiving among the Igbo*, 240–53.

45. This custom is dramatically painted by C. Achebe in the person of Okonkwo, the hero of his novel *Things Fall Apart* (London: Heineman, 1958). Okonkwo had accidentally killed a youth. Achebe narrates, "The only course open to Okonkwo was to flee from the clan. It was a crime against the earth goddess to kill a clans-man, and a man who committed it must flee from the land. The crime was of two kinds, male and female. Okonkwo had committed the female, because it had been inadvertent. He could return to the clan after seven years" (113). When the same Okonkwo committed murder, later on in the story, he had no option but to commit suicide (183–7).

46. Meek, *Law and Authority*, 209. In addition the family of the murderer provided a cow, a goat, a fowl, two yards of cloth, and a keg of gun powder for the funeral rites of the victim.

47. See Onwuejeogwu, *An Igbo Civilization*, 28. For the testimony of Nri neighbors about slavery see Isichei, *Igbo Worlds*, 30–34.

48. See J. Hick, "The Non-Absoluteness of Christianity," *The Myth of Christian Uniqueness*, ed. J. Hick and P. F. Knitter (Maryknoll, N.Y.: Orbis Books, 1987) esp. 24–34.

49. E. Isichei, *A History of the Igbo People*, 47. However, this ideal is contradicted by the evidence that the dead ruler (priest-king?) of the Igboukwu excavations (Nri culture) was buried with slaves.

50. See Onwuejeogwu's second interview with Nwaokoye Odenigbo in Isichei, *Igbo Worlds*, 27–28. Okoli Ijeoma, who was a native of Ikelionwu near Awka, used Abam mercenaries (Ada people) to wage war in order to capture slaves (104–7).

51. Cited by Cassirer, *The Philosophy of Symbolic Forms*, 6.

52. The two quotes are recorded (respectively) by P. A. Talbot in his *The Peoples of Southern Nigeria*, vol. 2 (London: Cass, 1926) 44; and his *Some Nigerian Fertility Cults* (London: Oxford University Press, 1927) 60. See also his *Tribes of the Niger Delta* (London: Cass, 1967) 25.

53. See J. Alexander and D. G. Coursey, "The Origins of Yam Cultivation," *The Domestication and Exploitation of Plants and Animals*, ed. P. J. Ucko and G. W. Dimbley (London: Gerald Duckworth and Co., 1969) 405–25; D. G. Coursey, "The Origins and Domestication of Yams in Africa," *Origins of African Plant Domestication*, ed. J. Harlan et al. (Hague: Mouton Publishers, 1976) 383–408.

54. D. G. Coursey, *Yams* (London: Longmans, 1967) 198; cited by Oriji, *Traditions of Igbo Origin*, 4.

55. See F. A. Arinze, *Sacrifice in Ibo Religion* (Ibadan: Ibadan University Press, 1970) 86.

56. Meek, *Law and Authority*, 35.

57. Henderson, *The King of Everyman*, 396, 392–400. See also Uchendu, *The Igbo of Southeast Nigeria*, 99; Uzukwu, *Blessing and Thanksgiving*, 257–63.

58. A sample of such *Ahiajoku Lectures* may be seen in the following titles: M.J.C. Echeruo, *A Matter of Identity: Aham Efula* (1979); B. O. Nwabueze, *The Igbo in the Context of Modern Government and Politics in Nigeria: A Call for Self-Examination and Self-Correction* (1985); P.N.C. Okigbo, *Towards a Reconstruction of the Political Economy of Igbo Civilization* (1986), and so on. All these are published in Owerri, Imo State by the Ministry of Information, Culture, Youth and Sports.

59. Nwoga, *The Supreme Being*, 46.

60. Olaudah Equiano, *Equiano's Travels: His Autobiography. The Interesting Narrative Life of Olaudah Equiano or Gustavus Vassa the African*, abridged and ed. P. Edwards (London: Heinemann, 1969, first published in 1789).

61. C. I. Ejizu, "Ritual Enactment of Achievement: *Ikenga* Symbol in Igboland," *Paideuma* 37:1991, 233–51.

62. Isichei, *Igbo Worlds*, 25.

63. Horton, "God, Man and the Land," 18–23; Talbot, *Tribes of the Niger Delta*, 27.

64. Uzukwu, "Igbo World and Ultimate Reality and Meaning," 196–7; see also Henderson, *The King of Everyman*, 110.

65. Uchendu, *The Igbo of Southeast Nigeria*, 95, 101.

66. Horton, "Judaeo-Christian Spectacles: Boon or Bane to the Study of African Religions," 412; C. R. Gaba, *Scriptures of an African People* (New York: 1973) 3–4.

67. Citations are taken from the critical edition of L. W. King, *The Enuma Elish: The Seven Tablets of Creation*, vol. 1 (New York: AMS Press, 1902, 1976

reprint). Since King's edition does not contain additions to Tablets V–VII, quotes from these tablets will be taken from *Ancient Near Eastern Texts (ANET)*, 3rd ed., ed. J. B. Prichard (Princeton, N.J.: Princeton University Press, 1969). All quotes from Prichard are indicated *ANET*.

68. W. G. Lambert, "Studies in Marduk," *Bulletin of the School of Oriental and African Studies* 47:1964, 4; J. Bottero, "Les Noms de Marduk, l'Ecriture et la 'Logique' en Mesopotamie," *Essays in the Ancient Near East in Memory of Jacob J. Finkelstein*, ed. M. de Jong Ellis (Hamden, Conn.: Archon Books, 1977) 5–28; P. Michalowski, "Presence at Creation," *Lingering Over Words: Studies in Ancient Near Eastern Literature in Honor of William L. Moran*, ed. T. Abusch et al. (Atlanta: Scholars Press, 1990) 394.

69. See the following works: P. W. Hollenbach, "The Constitution of Human Community in Two Ancient Civilizations," *Biblical Literature: 1974 Proceedings*, comp. F. O. Francis (Florida: American Academy of Religion, 1974) 15–16; R. J. Clifford, "The Hebrew Scriptures and Theology of Creation," *Theological Studies* 46:1985, 509; J. Groenbaek, "Baal's Battle with Yam: A Canaanite Creation Fight," *Journal for the Study of the Old Testament* 33:1985, 29.

70. W. G. Lambert, "A New Look at the Babylonian Background of Genesis," *Journal of Theological Studies* 16:1965, 291.

71. See his review of W. Sommerfeld's thesis *Der Aufstieg Marduks* (Kevelaer: Butzon und Bercker, 1982), in his "Studies in Marduk," 1–9. See also A. Kragerud, "The Concept of Creation in Enuma Elish," *Ex Orbe Religionum: Studia Geo Widengren* (Lugduni Batavorum: Brill, 1972) 39–49.

72. This is the view of Sommerfeld. See Lambert's review of Sommerfeld's book in "Studies in Marduk," esp. 1–3.

73. See *Code of Hammurabi, ANET*, 164–5 (prologue, i:1–40; v:11–22); see also H. H. Schmid, "Creation, Righteousness, and Salvation: 'Creation Theology' as the Broad Horizon of Biblical Theology," *Creation in the Old Testament*, ed. B. W. Anderson (Philadelphia: Fortress Press, 1984) 104. W. G. Lambert states his position on the historical rise of Marduk in his "The Reign of Nebuchadnezzar I: A Turning Point in the History of Ancient Mesopotamian Religion," *The Seed of Wisdom: Essays in Honour of T. J. Meek*, ed. W. S. McCullough (Toronto: University of Toronto Press, 1964) 3–13; see also J. A. Black, "The New Year Ceremonies in Ancient Babylon: 'Taking Bel by the Hand' and a Cultic Picnic," *Religion* 11:1981, 39–59, esp. 39–40.

74. Cited by H.S.F. Saggs, *The Encounter with the Divine in Mesopotamia and Israel* (London: Athlone Press, 1978) 48–49.

75. Lambert, "Studies in Marduk," 4. See also S.G.F. Brandon, "The Propaganda Factor in Some Ancient Near Eastern Cosmogonies," *Promise and Fulfillment: Essays Presented to Professor S. H. Hooke*, ed. F. F. Bruce (Edinburgh: T. and T. Clark, 1963) 20–35, esp. 28–30.

76. F. M. Conford, *The Unwritten Philosophy and Other Essays* (Cambridge, Mass.: Cambridge University Press, 1967) 110; cited by Michalowski, "Presence at Creation," 384.

77. Cf. Kragerud, "The Concept of Creation in Enuma Elish," 40.

78. Ibid., 41.

79. Ibid., 42.

80. See King, *Enuma Elish,* 3, n. 14.

81. King, depending on Berossus, translates "My blood will I take and bone will I [fashion], I will make man" (VI:5–6). Thus Marduk formed humankind from his own blood mixed with earth (King, *Enuma Elish,* 88–89).

82. In addition to other works of Lambert already cited, see also his "Ninurta Mythology in Babylonian Epic of Creation," *Keilschrifliche Literaturen,* ed. K. Hecker and W. Sommerfeld (Berlin: Dietrich Reimer Verlag, 1986) 55–60.

83. See M. Eliade, *The Myth of the Eternal Return; or Cosmos and History,* trans. W. R. Trask (New York: Pantheon Books, 1954).

84. King, *Enuma Elish,* 86–87.

85. Here I draw from Michalowski's "Presence at Creation," 388ff. The text of *Atra-hasis* is found in *ANET,* 104–6, 512–4.

86. Michalowski, "Presence at Creation," 388.

87. Hollenbach, "The Constitution of Human Community," 17.

88. See Hefner, "God and Chaos: The Demiurge versus the Ungrund," *Zygon* 19/4:1984, 479.

89. *Gilgamesh,* XI:156–61; *ANET,* 95; *Atra-hasis* IV:34–35. See also Michalowski, "Presence at Creation," 387–9.

90. Michalowski, "Presence at Creation," 389.

91. F. Thureau-Dangin, *Rituels accadiens* (Paris: E. Leroux, 1921). This contains three rituals; the *akitu* ritual starts on 127.

92. What follows is taken from J. A. Black, "The New Year Ceremonies in Ancient Babylon." See also J. Z. Smith, "A Pearl of Great Price and a Cargo of Yams: A Study in Situational Incongruity," *History of Religions* 16/1:1976, 1–19.

93. Black, "The New Year Ceremonies," 49–50.

94. I follow the translation of *ANET;* where necessary I translate from the French version of Thureau-Dangin.

95. Smith, "A Pearl of Great Price," 4–7.

96. Black, "The New Year Ceremonies," 46, 56.

97. Chief among the commentators are Smith, Black, Michalowski, and Hollenbach. See their articles already cited.

98. Black, "The New Year Ceremonies," 54.

99. See Smith, "A Pearl of Great Price," 6.

100. See A. R. George, "Sennacherib and the Tablet of Destinies," *Iraq* 48:1986, 133–46, esp. 138–9.

101. Black, "The New Year Ceremonies," 45–46.

102. Ibid., 46–48.

103. Lambert, "The Reign of Nebuchadnezzar I," 11.

104. See Lambert, "Ninurta Mythology," 59–60.

105. W. G. Lambert, "The God Assur," *Iraq* 45:1983, 82–86.

106. Michalowski, "Presence at Creation," 389–90, and n. 32.

107. Cited by Saggs, *The Encounter with the Divine*, 81.

108. P. Machinist, "Literature as Politics: The Tukulti-Ninurta Epic and the Bible," *Catholic Biblical Quarterly* 38:1976, 455–82.

109. Text cited from ibid., 463.

110. Ibid., 470–4.

111. Michalowski, "Presence at Creation," 389–94.

112. Citation from George, "Sennacherib and the Tablet of Destinies," 134.

113. Hollenbach ("The Constitution of Human Community") contrasts sharply the difference between Mesopotamian myths and myth in Israel — the first emphasizing determinism, and the second highlighting freedom. Our position against this is clarified below.

114. See N. K. Gottwald, *The Tribes of Yahweh: A Sociology of the Religion of Liberated Israel 1250–1050 B.C.E.* (Maryknoll, N.Y.: Orbis Books, 1979, 1985 reprint) 28–31. See also Saggs, *The Encounter with the Divine*, ch. 3, "The Divine in History"; B. Albrektson, *History and the Gods* (Lund: CWK Gleerup, 1967).

115. See J. H. Hayes and J. M. Miller, eds., *Israelite and Judaean History* (Philadelphia: Westminster Press, 1977) 149–66. See also the brief summary by R. Burns, "The Book of Exodus," *Concilium* 189/1:1987, 11–21.

116. Hayes and Miller, *Israelite and Judaean History*, 266; the basic elements of the various hypotheses are found in ch. 4.

117. In addition to Gottwald's *Tribes of Yahweh*, see also the reviews of his book, published as "Theological Issues in *The Tribes of Yahweh* by N. K. Gottwald: Four Critical Reviews," and his response, "The Theological Task after *The Tribes of Yahweh*," all published in *The Bible and Liberation: Political and Social Hermeneutics*, ed. N. K. Gottwald (Maryknoll, N.Y.: Orbis Books, 1983) chs. 11 and 12 respectively. See also H. Shank's interview of Gottwald, where he prefers "social revolution" to "peasant revolt," in "Israel's Emergence in Canaan: *BR* Interviews Norman Gottwald," *Bible Review* 5/5: Oct. 1989, 26–34.

118. See Hayes and Miller, *Israelite and Judaean History*, 267ff.

119. Ibid., 304.

120. Gottwald, *The Tribes of Yahweh*, 345–86. On the possibility that the presence of the ark defined which sanctuary would become the national sanctuary see F. M. Cross, *Canaanite Myth and Hebrew Epic* (Cambridge, Mass.: Harvard University Press, 1973) 89, n. 23.

121. Mendenhall, who sees the Exodus as a peasant revolt, accepts this position. See Hayes and Miller, *Israelite and Judaean History,* 277.

122. See "Theological Issues in *The Tribes of Yahweh."*

123. Gottwald, *The Tribes of Yahweh,* 72–73.

124. Ibid., 77.

125. Details of these views are contained in part 3 of Gottwald's *The Tribes of Yahweh.*

126. Gottwald's clear statement of his sociological approach as opposed to classical biblical theology is argued in his *The Tribes of Yahweh,* parts 8–11.

127. Ibid., 88. Gottwald gives a list of those who reject von Rad's thesis on 723–4, nn. 72–73.

128. See the following works: R. de Vaux, *Ancient Israel: Its Life and Institutions* (London: Darton, Longman and Todd, 1961) 493–5; H. J. Kraus, *Worship in Israel: A Cultic History of the Old Testament* (Oxford: Basil Blackwell, 1966) 55–61; R. Martin-Achard, *Essai biblique sur les Fêtes d'Israel* (Genève: Labor et Fides, 1974) 52–74; M. Delcor, "Commémorer a Qumran: l'Historicisation des Fêtes," *La Commémoration,* Colloque du Centenaire de la Section des Sciences Religieuses de l'Ecole pratique des Hautes Etudes, ed. P. Gignoux (Louvain-Paris: Peeters, 1988) 155–62.

129. Kraus, *Worship in Israel,* 58.

130. Philo, *De Spec. Leg.* 2.179–81; cited by J. Danielou in his *The Bible and the Liturgy* (Notre Dame: University of Notre Dame Press, 1966) 321–2. See Gottwald, *The Tribes of Yahweh,* 667–99, for a discussion on the distinctive character of Israel's God; see also the classic work of Cross, *Canaanite Myth and Hebrew Epic.* In chapter 3 Cross shows how Yahweh assumed the features of ᵓEl, the Ancient One of Canaanite religion.

131. See A. Murtonen, "The Use and Meaning of the Words Lebarek and Berakah in the Old Testament," *Vetus Testamentum* IX:1959, 158–77.

132. *The Book of Jubilees or the Little Genesis*, trans. from the Ethiopic text by R. H. Charles, with an intro. by C. H. Box (London: SPCK, 1917); for the dating of the Book see vii. See also Martin-Achard, *Essai biblique,* 58ff.

133. Martin-Achard, *Essai biblique,* 63–65.

134. J. B. Segal, *The Hebrew Passover: From the Earliest Times to A.D. 70* (London: Oxford University Press, 1963) 115–7; Cross, *Canaanite Myth and Hebrew Epic,* 84, n. 15.

135. Mishnah *Taanit* 4.8F–H; cf. de Vaux, *Ancient Israel,* 496.

136. Mishnah *Sukkah* 5.1.

137. Mishnah *Sukkah* 4.9B and 5.4H.

138. Mishnah *Sukkah* 5.4A–B.

139. See K. Hruby, "La Fete des Tabernacles au Temple, à la Synagogue et dans le nouveau Testament," *L'Orient Syrien* 7:1962, 163–74, esp. 168–9; Martin-Achard, *Essai biblique,* 86–87.

140. Cross insists that if Jeroboam established a non-Jahwistic cult he would have lost out in the campaign to woo his people away from the shrine of the ark in Jerusalem. Jeroboam's real sin was in setting up a sanctuary to rival Jerusalem. See Cross, *Canaanite Myth and Hebrew Epic,* 73–74.

141. See Martin-Achard, *Essai biblique,* 78–79, 85–86; de Vaux, *Ancient Israel,* 496–7.

142. Martin-Achard, *Essai biblique,* 85–86.

143. Segal, *The Hebrew Passover,* 75.

144. See de Vaux, *Ancient Israel,* 490–1.

145. See Segal, *The Hebrew Passover,* ch. 4.

146. Ibid., 175.

147. This view is favored by de Vaux, Kraus, and Martin-Achard.

148. See de Vaux, *Ancient Israel,* 489; Segal, *The Hebrew Passover,* 163.

149. De Vaux, *Ancient Israel*; Segal, *The Hebrew Passover,* 168–70; Martin-Achard, *Essai biblique,* 31–32.

150. See Segal, *The Hebrew Passover,* 216–9.

151. See B. S. Childs, "A Traditio-Historical Study of the Reed Sea Tradition," *Vetus Testamentum* 20:1970, 406–18, esp. 411, 415. Cross replies to Childs in his *Canaanite Myth and Hebrew Epic,* 103–5.

152. See H. J. Farby, "Gedenken und Gedächtnis im alten Testament," *La Commémoration,* 147.

153. See B. S. Childs, *Memory and Tradition in Israel* (London: SCM, 1962) 68; E. E. Uzukwu, *Anamnesis in Africa: The Jewish-Christian Concept of Memorial and the Igbo of Southern Nigeria* (Toronto: [unpublished M.Th. thesis] St. Michael's College, 1976) 22.

154. See J. Loza, "Les Catéchèses Etiologiques dans l'ancien Testament," *Revue Biblique* 78:1971, 481–500, esp. 496–9.

155. Farby, "Gedenken und Gedächtnis," 151; see also Martin-Achard, *Essai biblique,* 38–39.

156. See *The Passover Haggadah,* ed. N. N. Glatzer (New York: Shocken Books, 1969) 49. Based on the Haggadah Studies of E. D. Goldschmidt.

157. Mishnah *Pesahim* 10.4J.

158. Y. Yerushalmi, *Zakhor* (Seattle and London: University of Washington Press, 1982) 44. In some older prayer books (like the *Rav Amram Gaon* and the later *Saadia Gaon*) the liberation from Egypt does not appear in the grace. It probably made its first appearance in the *Machzor Vitry* of Rabbi Semchah ben Samuel (1100 C.E.).

159. Hedegard, *Seder Rav Amram Gaon,* 152.

160. See P. Tihon, "Theology of the Eucharistic Prayer," *The New Liturgy,* ed. L. Sheppard (London: Darton, Longman and Todd, 1970) 179–80; Uzukwu, *Anamnesis in Africa,* 36–38.

161. *Passover Haggadah,* 21 and 85 respectively.

162. H. Gunkel, *The Psalms: A Form-Critical Introduction* (Philadelphia: Fortress Press, 1967) 32.

163. C. Westermann, *Praise and Lament in the Psalms* (Atlanta: John Knox Press, 1981) 52, 170, 174.

164. Ibid., 215.

165. Ibid., 215ff.

166. Cross, *Canaanite Myth and Hebrew Epic*, 87–88, 107–8; Westermann, *Praise and Lament*, 56; R. J. Clifford, *Fair Spoken and Persuading: An Interpretation of Second Isaiah* (New York: Paulist Press, 1984) 21–23, 165–81.

167. Westermann, *Praise and Lament*, 220; cf. Childs, *Memory and Tradition in Israel*, 31; Gunkel, *The Psalms*, 25; Clifford, "Hebrew Scriptures and the Theology of Creation," 512.

168. In addition to Gunkel and Westermann, see also S. Mowinckel, *The Psalms in Israel's Worship*, trans. D. R. ApThomas, 2 vols. (Oxford: Basil Blackwell, 1962); A. Weiser, *The Psalms* (London: SCM, 1962).

169. Westermann, *Praise and Lament*, 221.

170. Weiser, *The Psalms*, 68, 80.

171. Gunkel, *The Psalms*, 15; Westermann, *Praise and Lament*, 61ff.; Clifford, *Fair Spoken and Persuading*, 169–70.

172. Childs, *Memory and Tradition in Israel*, 39; Gunkel, *The Psalms*, 34. G. von Rad believes that the prophetic message is rooted in the saving history, yet the prophetic conviction places them outside the saving history as understood up to then by Israel. See his *Old Testament Theology*, vol. 1 (New York: Harper & Row, 1962) 128; *Old Testament Theology*, vol. 2 (London: Oliver and Boyd, 1965) 303; see also D. G. Spriggs, *Two Old Testament Theologies* (London: SCM, 1974) 57.

173. Farby, "Gedenken und Gedächtnis," 143.

174. Gottwald, *Tribes of Yahweh*, 144.

175. Von Rad, *Old Testament Theology*, vol. 1, 220–30; idem, *The Problem of the Hexateuch* (Edinburgh: Oliver and Boyd, 1966) 90; P. R. Ackroyd, *Exile and Restoration* (Philadelphia: Westminster Press, 1968) 81.

176. Gottwald, *Tribes of Yahweh*, 145.

177. In addition to Farby and Childs, see also E. P. Blair, "An Appeal to Remembrance: The Memory Motif in Deuteronomy," *Interpretation* 15:1961, 41–47; and my *Anamnesis in Africa*, 13–15.

178. Farby, "Gedenken und Gedächtnis," 144; Childs, *Memory and Tradition in Israel*, 53; Blair, "An Appeal to Remembrance," 45; von Rad, *Theology of the Old Testament*, vol. 1, 85, 226; Yerushalmi, *Zakhor*, 44.

179. Farby, "Gedenken und Gedächtnis," 146.

180. See L. R. Fisher, "Creation at Ugarit and in the Old Testament," *Vetus Testamentum* 15:1965, 313–24; A. S. Kapelrud, "Creation in the Ras Shamra Texts," *Studia Theologica* 34:1980, 1–11; Clifford, "Hebrew Scriptures and the Theology of Creation"; Cross, *Canaanite Myth and Hebrew Epic*, chs. 6 and 7.

181. Cross, *Canaanite Myth and Hebrew Epic,* 107–8; D. J. McCarthy, "Creation Motifs in Ancient Hebrew Poetry," *Creation in the Old Testament,* 74–89.

182. See the collection of essays on the theology of creation in Anderson's *Creation in the Old Testament;* see W. H. Bellinger for a good summary of opinions on the issue in his "Maker of Heaven and Earth: The Old Testament and Creation Theology," *Southwestern Journal of Theology* 32:1990, 27–35.

183. In addition to the views of Fisher, Kapelrud, and Clifford, see also J. W. Bowker, "Cosmology, Religion, and Society," 25/1:1990, 723, esp. 9–10; Groenbaek, "Baal's Battle with Yam"; H. Ringgren, "Bara," *Theological Dictionary of the Old Testament,* vol. 2, ed. G. J. Botterwech and H. Ringgren (Grand Rapids, Mich.: Eerdmans, 1974–75) 246–7.

184. Kapelrud, "Creation in the Ras Shamra Texts," 3.

185. Clifford, *Fair Spoken and Persuading,* 59–67; idem, "The Hebrew Scriptures and the Theology of Creation," 509.

186. Fisher, "Creation at Ugarit," 320–1; Cross, *Canaanite Myth and Hebrew Epic,* 43, 120.

187. H. H. Schmid, "Creation, Righteousness, and Salvation: 'Creation Theology' as the Broad Horizon of Biblical Theology," *Creation in the Old Testament,* 104.

188. Cross, *Canaanite Myth and Hebrew Epic,* 190–4.

189. Clifford, "The Hebrew Scriptures and the Theology of Creation," 518; for a detailed overview see his *Fair Spoken and Persuading,* ch. 1, esp. 9–14.

190. Clifford, *Fair Spoken and Persuading,* 5, 9–27.

191. Von Rad, *Old Testament Theology,* vol. 2, 118; Cross, *Canaanite Myth and Hebrew Ethic,* 135–6, 343–6.

192. C. Westermann, *Genesis 1–11: A Commentary,* trans. by J. J. Sullivan (Minneapolis: Augsburg Publishing House, 1984) 142–58, esp. 157–8. Some of P's material used in the creation narrative is drawn from Babylonian stories like *Enuma Elish, Atrahasis,* and the epic of *Gilgamesh;* cf. Gen 1:1–2:4; or simply Genesis 1–11. See also Clifford, *Fair Spoken and Persuading,* 51–55; Childs, *Memory and Tradition in Israel,* 58.

193. See C. R. North, "The 'Former Things' and the 'New Things' in Deutero-Isaiah," *Studies in Old Testament Prophecy,* ed. H. H. Rowley (New York: Scribner, 1950; Edinburgh: Clark, 1957) 111–26; A. Bentzen, "On the Ideas of 'the Old' and 'the New' in Deutero-Isaiah," *Studia Theologica* 1:1948, 183–7; Ackroyd, *Exile and Restoration,* 130ff.; Childs, *Memory and Tradition in Israel,* 58–59.

194. Clifford, "The Hebrew Scriptures," 519; von Rad, *Old Testament Theology,* vol. 2, 246–47.

195. Cross, *Canaanite Myth and Hebrew Ethic,* 345.

196. Childs, *Memory and Tradition,* 59.

197. Bernhadt, "Bara," *Theological Dictionary of the Old Testament*, vol. 2, 245.

198. Westermann, *Genesis 1–11*, 98–100.

199. See de Vaux, *Ancient Israel*, 418ff.; J. Milgrom, *Studies in Cultic Theology and Terminology* (Leiden: Brill, 1983) esp. chs. 1, 4, and 5.

200. De Vaux, *Ancient Israel*, 418; Milgrom, *Studies in Cultic Theology*, chs. 3–4.

201. Clifford, "Hebrew Scriptures and Creation," 520–3.

202. Ricoeur, *The Symbolism of Evil*, 241.

203. Milgrom, *Studies in Cultic Theology*, 59–60.

204. For the *zebah* see de Vaux, *Ancient Israel*, 417–8, 426–9; S. Daniel, *Recherches sur le Vocabulaire du Culte* (Paris: Librairie C. Klincksieck, 1966); W. B. Stevenson, "Hebrew ʿOlah and Zebah Sacrifices," *Festschrift Albert Bertholet*, ed. V. Baungartner et al. (Tübingen: J.C.B. Mohr, 1950) 488–97.

205. Stevenson, "Hebrew ʿOlah and Zebah Sacrifices," 492.

206. See Mishnah *Berakot* 2.2. The *Shema'*, literally "Hear [O Israel]," is the first word of a group of passages from Scripture (Deut 6:4-9; 11:13-21; Num 15:37-41). It must be recited daily in the morning and evening prayer.

207. See S. Zeitlein, "The Morning Benedictions and the Readings in the Temple," *Jewish Quarterly Review* XLIV:1953–54, 330–3; M. Liber, "La Récitation du Schema et des Bénédictions," *Révue d'Etudes Juives* LVII:1909, 161–93.

208. Mishnah *Yoma* deals with atonement. L. Finkelstein strongly favors the benedictions for the Law, Temple service, and thanksgiving. See his "The Development of the Amidah," *Jewish Quarterly Review* N.S. XVI:1925–26, 40. However, M. Liber is not too sure; see his "Structure and History of the Teffilah," *Jewish Quarterly Review* N.S. XL:1949–50, esp. 343–4.

209. Westermann, *Genesis 1–11*, 140; Murtonen, "The Use and Meaning of the Words Lebarek and Berakah in the Old Testament," esp. 176–7; Uzukwu, *Blessing and Thanksgiving*, 15–23.

210. For the literature on the blessing see my *Blessing and Thanksgiving*. For a representative viewpoint see, in addition to Murtonen, J. Scharbert, "Brk, Berakah," *Theological Dictionary of the Old Testament*, vol. 2, 279–300; J. Guillet, "Le Langage spontané de la Bénédiction dans l'ancien Testament," *Recherches des Sciences Religieuses* LVII:1969, 163–204.

211. R. J. Ledogar, *Acknowledgment: Praise Verbs in the Early Greek Anaphoras* (Rome: Herder, 1968) 122.

212. K. Hruby traces the origin of the synagogue from the meeting in the various provinces. See his "Les Heures de Prière dans le Judaïsme à l'Epoque de Jésus," *La Prière des Heures*, ed. J. Cassien and B. Botte (Paris: Cerf, 1963) 59–84; see also A. Z. Idelsohn, *Jewish Worship and Its Developments* (New York: Schocken Books, 1972) esp. ch. 3.

213. We have shown in this study that Israel's uniqueness does not lie in its grasp of history. See again the following authors: Albrektson, *History and*

the Gods; Saggs, *The Encounter with the Divine in Mesopotamia and Israel,* esp. ch. 3, "The Divine in History"; Gottwald, *The Tribes of Yahweh,* esp. 667–91; M. Smith, "On the Difference Between the Culture of Israel and the Major Cultures of the Ancient Near East," *Journal of Ancient Near Eastern Society* 5:1973, 389–95; idem, "The Common Theology of the Ancient Near East," *Journal of Biblical Literature* 71:1952, 135–47; G. W. Trompf, *The Idea of Historical Recurrence in Western Thought: From Antiquity to the Reformation* (Berkeley: University of California Press, 1979).

214. Cross, *Canaanite Myth and Hebrew Epic,* 65–71.

215. See F. J. van Beeck, *God Encountered: A Contemporary Catholic Systematic Theology,* vol. 1, "Understanding the Christian Faith" (New York: Harper & Row, 1989) 195–8.

216. E. Ferguson, "Spiritual Sacrifice in Early Christianity and Its Environment," *Aufstieg und Niedergang der Römischen Welt,* II.23.2, ed. H. Temporini and W. Haase, (Berlin: Walter der Gruyter, 1980) 1151–89, esp. 1165.

217. See, for example, C. Mohrmann, *Etudes sur le Latin des Chrétiens* (Rome: Edizioni di Storia e Litteratura, 1961), especially her study of "Rationabilis-Logikos," 179–87; see also my *Blessing and Thanksgiving,* 129–30, 146–7, 178–80.

218. Ignatius of Antioch, *Epistle to the Romans,* nn. 2 and 4 in *Early Christian Writing: The Apostolic Fathers,* trans. M. Stanforth (Middlesex: Penguin, 1968, 1975 reprint).

219. See "Martus, Marturéô, marturia, marturion," *Theological Dictionary of the New Testament,"* vol. 4, ed. G. Kittel (Grand Rapids, Mich.: Eerdmans, 1967) 474–508.

220. W.H.C. Frend, *Martyrdom and Persecution in the Early Church: A Study of a Conflict from the Maccabees to Donatus* (Oxford: Basil Blackwell, 1965) esp. 19–22. See also Z. Stewart, "Greek Crowns and Christian Martyrs," *Antiquité Païenne et Chrétienne: Mémorial André-Jean Festugière,* ed. E. Lucchesi and H. D. Saffery (Genève: Patrick Cramer, 1984) 119–24, esp. 120.

221. *Acts of the Scillitan Martyrs,* no. 14 in *The Acts of the Christian Martyrs: Introduction, Texts and Translations by Herbert Musurillo,* comp. H. Musurillo et al. (Oxford: Clarendon Press, 1972).

222. See R. L. Wilken, *The Christians as the Romans Saw Them* (New Haven, Conn.: Yale University Press, 1984) 25–26.

223. *Epp.* 10.96.5, written ca. 112 C.E. See *Documents of the Christian Church,* 2nd ed., sel. and ed. H. Battenson (London: Oxford University Press, 1963) 4.

224. Before the legalization of Christianity and after the peace of Constantine, edict of Milan (313 C.E.), the core Christian ritual (the Eucharist) was a secret cult. The Christian worship could not be called public worship in the way it was known when it became a legal religion in the fourth century. See G. Dix, *The Shape of the Liturgy* (London: Dacre, 1975) ch. 11.

225. Wilken, *The Christians as the Romans Saw Them,* 53–54. The following summary of Roman religious sensibility is dependent principally on Wilken's work; see especially 48–67.

226. Ibid., 56.

227. Cicero, *Nat. D.* 1.3–4, cited by Wilken, *The Christians as the Romans Saw Them,* 58–59.

228. Augustine, *City of God* 3.4.

229. *Acts of the Scillitan Martyrs,* nos. 1–6 in *The Acts of the Christian Martyrs.*

230. See Wilken, *The Christians as the Romans Saw Them,* 60–61. The text being cited is *On Superstition,* attributed to Plutarch.

231. E. R. Dodds, *Pagan and Christian in an Age of Anxiety* (Cambridge, Mass.: Cambridge University Press, 1965) 120–1.

232. Tertullian, *Apology* 40. For proof that the Christian sect was seen as a state within a state see Origen, *Contra Celsum* 3.55; 8.35, 68–75; Dodds, *Pagan and Christian,* 105, 114.

233. See J. G. Gager, *Kingdom and Community: The Social World of Early Christianity* (Englewood Cliffs, N.J.: Prentice-Hall, 1975) 97–99.

234. Cited by ibid., 102.

235. See M. Meslin, *Le Christianisme dans l'Empire Romain* (Paris: Presses Universitaires de France, 1970) esp. 75–76.

236. See P. Garnsay, "Religious Toleration in Classical Antiquity," *Persecution and Toleration: Papers Read at the Twenty-second Summer Meeting and the Twenty-third Winter Meeting of the Ecclesiastical History Society,* ed. W. J. Sheils (Great Britain: Basil Blackwell, for the Ecclesiastical History Society, 1984) 6–9.

237. Dodds, *Pagan and Christian,* 134–5.

238. *The Martyrdom of Saints Perpetua and Felicitas,* nos. 3 and 5 in *The Acts of the Christian Martyrs,* 109, 113. See also Origen, *Contra Celsum* 3.55.

239. See A. D. Nock, *Conversion* (Oxford: Oxford University Press, 1933, 1963 reprint); Dodds, *Pagan and Christian,* 27–35; M. A. Rossi, "The Passion of Perpetua, Every Woman of Late Antiquity," *Pagan and Christian Anxiety: A Response to E. R. Dodds,* ed. R. C. Smith and J. Lounibos (London: University Press of America, 1984) 53–86, esp. 62.

240. Justin, *Apology* 2.4; *The Martyrdom of Polycarp,* esp. nos. 4 and 5 in *The Acts of the Christian Martyrs,* 5–6; see also E. Pagels, "Christian Apologists and the 'Fall of the Angels': An Attack on Roman Imperial Power," *Harvard Theological Review* 78/34:1985, 301–25, esp. 308.

241. See the study of A. Hamman, "La Confession de la Foi dans les Premiers Actes des Martyrs," *Epektasis: Mélanges Patristiques offerts au Cardinal Jean Daniélou,* ed. J. Fontaine and C. Kannengiesser (Paris: Beauchesne, 1972) 99–105, esp. 101.

242. Musurillo, *The Acts of the Christian Martyrs,* lvii (citing Harnach).

243. *Martyrdom of Polycarp,* no. 15 in *The Acts of the Christian Martyrs,* 15.

244. *Passio Maculi* in *Patrologia Latina* 8.760–6; *Passio Maximiani, PL* 8.767–74, all cited by M. Meslin, "Vases Sacré, et Boissons d'Eternité dans les Visions des Martyrs africains," *Epektasis,* 139–53, esp. 140–2.

245. See Frend, *Martyrdom and Persecution in the Early Church,* 268–94.

246. *Martyrdom of Polycarp,* no. 18 in *The Acts of the Christian Martyrs,* 17.

247. *Martyrdom of Polycarp,* no. 14 in *The Acts of the Christian Martyrs,* 13–14.

248. Cited by Eusebius, *Ecclesiastical History* 7.22.4.

249. *Martyrdom of Polycarp,* nos. 5 and 8 in *The Acts of the Christian Martyrs.*

250. *Martyrdom of Saints Perpetua and Felicitas,* no. 7 in *The Acts of the Christian Martyrs,* 115.

251. Rossi, "The Passion of Perpetua, Every Woman of Late Antiquity," 59, cites Homer's *Odyssey* XI and Virgil's *Aenied* VI as examples of ancient literature where the suffering of the dead is narrated. See also Meslin, "Vases Sacrés et Boissons d'Eternité," 145–7.

252. *The Martyrdom of Saints Perpetua and Felicitas,* no. 8 in *The Acts of the Christian Martyrs.*

253 Origen, *Exhortation to Martyrdom* nn. 11 and 30, in his *Prayer: Exhortation to Martyrdom,* trans. and annotated by J. J. O'Meara (Westminster, Md.: Newman Press, 1954). See also W. Rordorf, "La 'Diaconie' des Martyrs selon Origène," *Epektasis,* 395–402.

254. Origen, *Exhortation to Martyrdom* n. 30.

255. Origen, *Homilies on the Book of Numbers* 18.1; cited by Rordorf, "La 'Diaconie' des Martyrs," 397–8. See also Tertullian, *Scorpiace* n. 6; Frend, *Martyrdom and Persecution,* 358.

256. Justin, *Apology* 5; Tertullian, *Apology* 2. See also Pagels, "Christian Apologists."

257. *The Martyrdom of Saints Perpetua and Felicitas,* no. 10 in *The Acts of the Christian Martyrs.*

258. Origen, *Commentary on John* 6.36, in *The Ante-Nicene Fathers,* vol. 9, ed. A. Menzies (New York: Charles Scribner's Sons, 1906) 377–8; idem, *Contra Celsum* 6.44; Rordorf, "La 'Diaconie' des Martyrs," 399–400. The *Martyrdom of Polycarp* "put a stop to the persecution . . . as though he were putting a seal upon it" (no. 1).

259. Rordorf, "La 'Diaconie' des Martyrs," 400.

260. Minucius Felix, *Octavius* 9.5–6; Wilken, *The Christians as the Romans Saw Them,* 17–20.

261. Wilken, *The Christians as the Romans Saw Them,* 20–22; S. Benko, "The Libertine Gnostic Sect of the Phibionites According to Epiphanius," *Vigiliae Christianae* 21:1967, 103–19. A. Henrichs compares information from Justin, Tertullian, Minucius Felix, Clement of Alexandria, Eusebius, and the Cologne Gnostic Document on crimes attributed to Christians in his "Pagan Rituals

and the Alleged Crimes of the Early Christians: A Reconstruction," *Kyriakon: Festschrift Johannes Quasten,* vol. 1, ed. P. Granfield and J. A. Jungmann (Munster: Verlag Aschendorff, 1970) 18–35.

262. S. Benko, "Pagan Criticism of Christianity During the First Two Centuries A.D.," *Aufstieg und Niedergang der Römischen Welt,* II.23.2, ed. H. Temporini and W. Haase (Berlin: Walter der Gruyter, 1980) 1055–118, esp. 1084–9.

263. Pliny, *Ep.* 10.96.7.

264. Pliny, *Letters,* English translation by W. Melmoth, Book X, Letter 96, "To the Emperor Trajan," and Letter 97, "Trajan to Pliny" (Cambridge, Mass.: Harvard University Press; London: Heinemann, 1958).

265. Cyprian, *Letter* 5.2.1. *The Letters of Cyprian of Carthage,* vol. 1, "Letters 1–27," trans. and annotated by G. W. Clarke, Ancient Christian Writers no. 43 (New York: Newman Press, 1984).

266. *The Martyrdom of Saints Montanus and Lucius,* no. 9 in *The Acts of the Christian Martyrs,* 220–3. See also Meslin, "Vases Sacrés et Boissons d'Eternité," 148–9.

267. *Acta Saturnini,* nn. 9 and 11; *PL* 689ff. See A. Hamman, "La Prière chrétienne et la Prière païenne, Formes et Différences," *Aufstieg und Niedergang der Römischen Welt,* II.23.2, ed. H. Temporini and W. Haase (Berlin: Walter der Gruyter, 1980) 1190–247, esp. 1207–8.

268. Eusebius, *The History of the Church from Christ to Constantine* 7.22.4, trans. with an introduction by G. A. Williamson (New York: New York University Press, 1966).

269. Cyprian, *Letter* 57.4.2, 57.2.2, and 57.3.2. *The Letters of Cyprian of Carthage,* vol. 3, "Letters 55–66," trans. and annotated by G. W. Clarke, *Ancient Christian Writers,* no. 46 (New York: Newman Press, 1986). The decisions of the Council of Carthage are explained by Cyprian in *De Lapsi* 7.15.

270. See the *Inscription of Abercius and Pectorius* in J. Quasten, *Patrology,* vol. 1 (Westminster: Newman Press, 1950) 171–3, and 173–5 respectively.

271. Eusebius, *The History of the Church* 4.7.11.

272. Most of our information about Valentinian Gnosticism comes from Irenaeus' *Against the Heresies,* esp. 1.1–8. The Nag Hammadi Papyrus contains the Valentinian "Gospel of Truth." Tertullian and Hippolytus also discuss the gnostics and their system. Tertullian in *De Prescriptionis* draws from the writings of Irenaeus.

273. R. Rodopoulos, "Irenaeus on the Consecration of the Eucharistic Gifts," *Kyriakon: Festschrift Johannes Quasten,* vol. 2, ed. P. Granfield and J. A. Jungmann (Munster: Verlag Aschendorff, 1970) 845. See also G. Quispel, "The Origin of the Gnostic Demiurge," *Kyriakon,* vol. 1, 271–6; J.N.D. Kelly, *Early Christian Doctrines* (New York: Harper & Row, 1978) 22–28.

274. See the historical exposition of this teaching from pre-Christian times by E. Ferguson, "Spiritual Sacrifice in Early Christianity and Its Environment," 1151–89.

275. For the location of the phrase in the relevant Eucharistic Prayers see Hanggi and Pahl, *Prex Eucharistica,* 114 (St. Mark), 227 (John Chrysostom), 237 (Byzantine Basil), 434 (Roman Canon).

276. See E. Schillebeeckx, *Christ: The Experience of Jesus as Lord* (New York: Seabury Press, 1980) 168ff., 184ff., 351ff.

277. Meeks suggests that Pliny's remarks may be referring to Christian baptismal hymns similar to New Testament hymns having baptism as their *Sitz im Leben*. See his *The First Urban Christians: The Social World of the Apostle Paul* (New Haven, Conn., and London: Yale University Press, 1983) 152. See also van Beeck's interesting discussion of Pliny's remark in his *God Encountered,* 145–51.

278. See, for example, G. Lease, "Mithraism and Christianity," *ANRW* II:23.2 (1980) 1306–32, esp. 1323ff.; see also Gager, *Kingdom and Community,* 132–4.

279. *Adversus Haereses* 4.18.4.

280. Ibid., 4.18.5.

281. Justin, *Apology* 1.65–66.

282. Ibid., 1.65.

283. Ibid., 1.66.

284. Ibid., 1.67.

285. Justin, *Dialogues with Trypho* 41.1–3.

286. See J. P. Audet's critical edition of the Didache, *La Didaché: Instruction des Apôtres* (Paris: Librairie Lecoffre, 1958). Audet gives a rich bibliography on x–xvi.

287. Didache 10. Text from *Prayers of the Eucharist: Early and Reformed,* 3rd ed., trans. and ed. with commentary by R.C.D. Jasper and G. J. Cuming (New York: Pueblo, 1987) 23–24.

288. An expanded version of this Eucharistic Prayer is in use in the Ethiopian liturgy *(The Anaphora of the Apostles).* In the recent reforms of the liturgy in the West, it has been adopted by the Roman liturgy (Eucharistic Prayer 2), the Church of England (Prayer 3), and the American Lutherans (Prayer 4). See Jasper and Cuming, *Prayers of the Eucharist,* 34.

289. See G. Dix, *The Treatise on the Apostolic Tradition of St. Hippolytus of Rome* (London: SPCK, 1937); B. Botte, *La Tradition Apostolique de Saint Hippolyte* (Munster: Aschendorffsche Verlagsbuchhandlung, 1963).

290. "It is not altogether necessary for him [the bishop] to recite the very same words which we gave before as though studying to say them by heart in his thanksgiving to God; but let each one pray according to his own abil-

ity. . . . Only let his prayer be correct and right [in doctrine]" (*Apostolic Tradition* 10.4–5, as in Dix, *The Treatise,* 19).

291. The *Apostolic Tradition* has more influence in Alexandria and Syria than in Rome, leading some to doubt that it represents Roman practice. For example, it influenced *The Egyptian Church Order,* the *Testamentum Domini,* and the anaphora of the eighth book of the *Apostolic Constitutions* (the Clementine Liturgy). For these liturgical books see R. H. Connolly, *The So-Called Egyptian Church Order and Derived Documents* (Cambridge: 1916); I. E. Rahmani, *Testamentum Domini Nostri Jesu Christi* (Hildesheim: 1968, 1st published, 1899); Hanggi and Pahl, *Prex Eucharistica,* 82–95 (for text of the anaphora of the eighth book of the *Apostolic Constitutions*). A. Faivre gives a summary of the difficulties surrounding the authenticity of the *Apostolic Tradition* in his "La Documentation canonico-liturgique de l'Eglise ancienne. II. Les 'Unités littéraires' et leurs Relectures," *Revue des Sciences Religieuses* CCVI/4:1980, 273–97, esp. 279–86.

292. Third Council of Carthage 397, cn. 23 — *Acta Conciliorum et Epistolae Decretales ac Constitutiones Summorum Pontificum,* vol. 1 (Paris: 1715) 963. The translation is from A. Bouley, *From Freedom to Formula: The Evolution of the Eucharistic Prayer from Oral Improvisation to Written Texts* (Washington, D.C.: The Catholic University of America Press, 1981) 162. For Origen's view on the correct manner of prayer see ch. 15 in his *Prayer: Exhortation to Martyrdom,* trans. and annotated by J. J. O'Meara, Ancient Christian Writers no. 19 (New York: Newman Press, 1954); see also Bouley, *From Freedom to Formula,* 138–42.

293. Translation of Jasper and Cuming, *Prayers of the Eucharist,* 35.

Chapter Four

Passage Through Life and Its Ritual Hallowing: Toward a Contextual Celebration of the Christian Sacraments

The narration of the foundational story of a group projects the group's awareness of its world and helps individuals adjust to the great world, to their fellow humans, and be at peace with themselves. In the myth-narrative life is revealed in its depth. The impact is more striking when the narrative is executed in a ritual context. Participants experience the renewal of their very lives. This was explored in the previous chapters.

This chapter focuses on the process of the natural (or biological) development of humans, their passage through time (from birth to death), and the social creation or re-creation of their identity by passing through society's ideal or ritual time. We focus on the social or religious functions that fall on individuals or groups and the intervention of ritual in the socialization of these passages. Rites of passage are those rituals devised through the experience of sociocultural groups to lead "ritual passengers" through life cycles or crises in a universe where a happy interaction prevails between spirits and humans. Primarily, the rites integrate "human and cultural experiences with biological destiny: birth, reproduction, and death."[1] Through these rites the group projects its vision of humans as they journey through time.

Passages imply change, time, and space. The change that is our concern here deeply impacts the individual not only on the physical (biological) level, but also on the psychological and spiritual dimensions. The social group sets aside ritual time and space, where it draws individuals into ritual experiences that help them establish a time frame re-created through depth contact with society's ritual time. The "passengers," in the words of Cicero, have learned the very basis of life. In their passage they "have gained the power not only to live happily, but also to die with better hope" *(ita re vera principia vitae cognovimus; neque solum cum laetitia vivendi rationem accepimus, sed etiam cum spe meliore moriendi).*[2] The shock of passing through puberty or entering into marriage is sublimated or sanctified thanks to a ritual ordeal (especially at the *liminal* or *transition* stage) established by the social group. The assumption of kingship or priesthood; the entrance into age sets or secret societies; the consecration as virgins, monks, or sacred prostitutes; etc., involve a passage whereby the ideal of the group is embraced by the individual. The time of the individual is transformed by contact with the ideal (group's) ritual time. The passage therefore involves not only a movement from one physical, psychological, or social stage to another, but it also alters the person's religious or spiritual perception of himself or herself.[3]

Passage rites may be rites of initiation or life-crises rituals. A threefold structure is followed in whichever rite so as to insert the individual into the group's ideal (ritual) time. The threefold structure, as identified by van Gennep and developed by Turner, are the rites of separation, transition, and incorporation.[4] This threefold structure will help us assess the impact of traditional African initiation rites on Christian initiation. But we will first examine the nature of the ritual time into which ritual "passengers" are inserted and what distinguishes it from the ordinary/normal time. This serves as a contextual introduction to the concerns of this chapter. In Africa the normal everyday ("profane," Durkheim) activity is withdrawn with ease into ritual time, thereby heightening the interplay between religious ritual and profane activity, two *different* dimensions of life that are nevertheless interlocked. This is what Zeusse calls the "transcendental significance of everyday life," and, consequently, its sanctification.[5] Next we will center our exploration on initiatory passage rites.

Our option to concentrate on initiatory passage rites not only limits the scope of this chapter, but also helps bring into prominence those rituals that may aid us in sharpening the African Christian appreciation for Christian initiation rites. We make no apologies for this. As African Christians we exercise our right to live and interpret the received Christian tradition in terms of the sets of assumptions of the African practice and discourse. During the time of the Fathers of the Church, as we will see, the mysteries of the Greco-Roman world made a considerable impact on the Christian practice and discourse of the sacraments, in general, and of initiation, in particular. Therefore, those rituals in which boys and girls are initiated into manhood and womanhood (also known as puberty rites), or the rituals for entering into age sets, secret societies, kingship or priesthood, etc., will attract the attention of this study more than other types of passage rites. This will lead us to argue not only for renewal in the practice of Christian initiation, but also for the need to create new passage rites.

The combined effects of secularization, modernity, and the world religions (especially Christianity and Islam) have no doubt eroded the impact of traditional African initiation and life-crises rituals. These have created both psychological and social problems. As we noted in chapter one, modernity, along with the postcolonial deception, has introduced a whole range of questions and anxieties impacting on religious and other sociocultural practices. To answer the questions and resolve the anxieties contemporary African behavior is innovative, syncretistic, and puzzled. In the search for patterns of wholeness, individuals and groups have recourse to traditional religious rituals or to the rituals of the mainline Christian Churches (especially healing sessions of reputed Roman Catholic or Protestant priest-healers), independent or Zionist Churches, new religious movements, and occult groups. These employ one passage rite or another to minister to their clients. We shall refer to their practices insofar as they help to project the need for the renewal of our current practice of initiation and the development of adequate and new passage rites.

THE NATURE OF RITUAL TIME

All religious and social groups create ritual space and time to celebrate, initiate neophytes, or minister to the various needs of adherents or members. In traditional African societies the arrival of a newborn is cause for joy. It calls for the first passage rite experienced by the new entrant into the social world. The neonate has to be given a name (social birth) in order to be recognized as a person. The naming ceremony becomes the first experience by the child of the ideal time of the society — the beginning of the journey in time (from birth to death) marked with significant rituals. While not reducing individuality the rites contribute immensely in forming the individual's personal identity through sharing in the society's vision of life.

Each human has his or her own destiny, his or her own time frame. Thus no two individuals are really the same or experience the same ritual in exactly the same way. As Elliott Jaques asserts:

"No two men living at the same time live in the same time. Each one, living at the same moment, has his own personal time perspective, his own living linkage with past and future, the content of which, and the scale of which, are as different between one person and another as are their appearances, their fingerprints, their characters, their desires, their very being. . . . But that different people live in different time scales, or in different temporal domains as I shall refer to them, may not be so self-evident. Yet it has profound and far-reaching consequences for everyone. It is through the recognition of these different time scales within which people live that many of the mysteries of time can be resolved, and time itself may be understood."[6]

Put in the myth-narrative of the Igbo or Yoruba of Nigeria, each human is led through time by his or her *chi* or *ori* in a unique way. The social group establishes, according to its experience, rituals to follow the physical or social development of each person in time. High points of this passage are established not only to demarcate the passage, but also to deepen the spiritual life of each passenger. The structure of time into which the ritual passengers are introduced is different from, though happening within, the normal (profane) passage of days, weeks, months, seasons, and years.

The Difference Between Ritual Time and Ordinary Time

Each sociocultural group has a way of marking out periods of the day, days in the week, weeks in the month, and months in the year. These demarcations have reference to economic (productive) activity and the motion of the heavenly bodies. For example, while the Igbo have a four-day week controlled by the movement from one marketplace to another, the Romans have a seven-day week tied to the motion of the heavenly bodies. In addition, each social group has an idea of the three major dimensions of time: past, present, and future. It is within the chronological sequence of days, weeks, months, and seasons of the year that an annual calendar is planned. The organization of the calendar, which falls into the hands of priests or rulers, plots out the time (duration) for ritual and ordinary activities. Ritual may accompany ordinary economic activities (like planting and harvesting). Even the evident happy result of economic activity, manifest in an accumulation of goods, is given ritual recognition in many communities through membership in certain societies or through the reception of chieftaincy titles. But ritual time, as a category of time different from durational (ordinary) time, exerts its force most strongly among individuals through passage rites. In rites of passage the individual (ritual passenger) is drawn into the socially established sacred time, encounters the divinity or divinities of the group, and is drawn into divine time (or timelessness); the individual undergoes the shaping or reshaping of his or her personal time frame.

The ritual time into which ritual passengers are drawn is a symbolic myth-narrative time. It creates the occasion to recite (in metrical or rhythmic form followed by adequate gestures) the story of the establishment, by the ancestors, of a particular cult into which descendants or neophytes are being initiated (like the Bagre ritual among the LoDagaa of Northern Ghana).[7] It is a time in which "initiands" not only become contemporaneous with the events narrated, but also assume the characteristics of the originary narrative (as happens in the Lyangombe cult in parts of Zaire, Rwanda, and Uganda, and in rites of the enthronement of kings or ordination of priests).[8] It is a time in which the key cultural values of the group are projected and learned (e.g., the concentration on learning the collections of proverbs during the different stages of the Bwami initiation rite among the Lega of Eastern Zaire, or learning different crafts and medicines in the Poro secret society very popular in Sierra Leone, Guinea, and Liberia).[9] The intent of the ritual process is to effect a change in the person of the ritual passenger — a transformation realized through the psychosocial effects of living in ritual time. As Zeusse describes it, "the ego and the body are opened to a transcendental order whose power irresistibly shapes the self through the mysteries of time."[10]

This kind of time into which ritual passengers are introduced, when set apart in a ritual space (initiation camp), is different from the ordinary durational time that passes on as candidates or celebrants are immersed in ritual time. Some have described this time as static or cyclic. This description, needless to say, is justified because the narrative time is interlocked with the primordial time of the ancestors; sometimes, the "initiands" (e.g., the boys and girls being initiated into manhood and womanhood) are inducted at a certain age cycle. The cyclical time, of course, is best illustrated in the new year cycle of ritual renewal (which has been described with some exaggerations by Eliade).[11]

The static conception of ritual time is prompted by the repetitive logic of ritual behavior described in chapter two. The ritual pattern of communication is formalized. Thus in initiation rites and other passage rites one is immersed into what Bloch calls "a total bonded experience" going back to primordial (ancestral) times. But as was pointed out in chapter two, the narrative time is not numerically identical to the primordial actions posited in time by the ancestors. It is rather a symbolic time that creates the environment whereby ancestral time, while not replacing the present time, influences (transforms) the actors in the present. For no matter how we try to objectify time, it is the subjective *distentio animi* (extension, tension, or deployment of the soul; Augustine) that imposes itself in ritual time, and to a certain extent in durational time. As Augustine reflects in his Confessions:

"What is now plain and clear is that neither future nor past things are in existence, and that it is not correct to say there are three periods of time: past, present and future. Perhaps it would be proper to say there are three periods of time: the present of things past, the present of things present, the present of things future. For, these three are in the soul and I do not see them elsewhere: the present of things past is memory; the present of things present is immediate vision; the present of future things is expectation. If we are permitted to say this, I see three periods of time and I admit there are three. . . . But, how is the future, which does not yet exist, decreased or eaten up, or how does the past, which is no longer existing, increase, unless because of the fact that three functions occur in the mind which is doing this? It looks ahead, it attends, and it remembers — in such a way that what it looks forward to passes through what it is attending to into what it is remembering."[12]

Memory, therefore, plays a key function in ritual time, but the remembering is active, making present.

Some Christian biblical historians and students of African religion claim that the cyclic or static (and consequently ahistorical) conception of time, as opposed to the linear (historical) pattern, characterizes

Africa. On the other hand, the Jewish-Christian and Western tradition is characteristically linear and historical. This claim is hardly sustainable. We have already shown that the experience of the day, week, month, season, and year is a universal human experience tied to the movement of the heavenly bodies and to economic activity. Like humans in other parts of the world, Africans engage in economic activity, and the desire not only to satisfy immediate needs but also to ensure upward social mobility (e.g., the numerous grades of titles available in Igbo society) imposes long term planning.

Chapter three also shows that various sociocultural groups have diversified myth-narratives to which they "return" by ritual memorial at demarcated periods in the life of each group. The return to such narratives is not typically African. It is rather another universal human religious phenomenon. However, the content of the ritual time may be as varied as people. Nevertheless, there is a difference in the way the cycle of seasons, of birth and death, of initiation rites with their recourse to ancestral models, impacts on many African communities. These project the ancestors (the living dead) into the living present. The world of spirits, though different from the world of the living, overlaps with the latter. Ritual time overlaps with durational time. As a result, many African peoples are drawn very close to the ancestral pool (ritual time), and the ancestral gestures become "normally" part of durational time. Therefore, the more one makes the round of this spiritual pool the closer one is to fruitful life and to the knowledge of the world. "The dance around the masquerade is in circles" (*eleghede ka ana agba mmanwu,* Igbo). Even the spectators do not stand on one spot to watch the masquerade *(anaghi akwu otu ebe ekiri mmanwu)*, rather they move around; for, the walk of the snake is in circles *(okirikiri bu ije agwo)*, and if one wants to sell the tortoise, one has to carry it around *(mbughali ka eji ele mbe)*. This circular or cyclic motion of "life-ing" (interacting humans in the universe) is captured by the Yoruba in the mythical depiction of the universe as a calabash or life in the universe as the snake spawn tail in the mouth. At each point of the circle (social or ritual event, stage of biological development) life is lived (played out) in full. At the core of the circle is the ancestral pool that is not simply a frozen, unalterable, static time, but rather a living, dynamic reality relevant in the present, adaptable to the present to ensure creativity in human life. Ritual time and durational time, as we have stressed, are not polar opposites (antagonists), they are different but related. As Smith clarifies: "Ritual is a relationship between 'nows' — the now of everyday life and the now of ritual place; the simultaneity, but not the coexistence of 'here' and 'there.'"[13] The religious and the ordinary interact with ease, though they are not confused. The African becomes, understandably, incurably religious.

I therefore partially agree with Mbiti that the orientation of life in Africa is toward ancestral time.[14] This applies strictly to ritual time made present through ritual memorial. But his thesis that, as a general rule, "To Akamba and other African peoples, history moves 'backwards,' and cannot therefore head towards a goal, a climax or termination,"[15] is hard to sustain. Even though time is hardly conceived in Africa as devoid of content,[16] it is evident that people plan ahead for years on the socioeconomic and ritual levels. In a highly competitive society like the Igbo, the need to accumulate wealth to "move up" is a preoccupation through time. Chinua Achebe paints an arresting picture of this in the principal character of his novel *Things Fall Apart,* Okonkwo. Okonkwo's father Unoka lacked ambition and did not take any titles. Therefore, in order to avoid the shame of being like his father, Okonkwo had to work hard to take many titles (involving years of planning and accumulation of wealth). He was, however, distressed that his son Nwoye was not interested in looking into the future and embracing it "like a man," as Okonkwo himself did. This passion for upward mobility (to "get up" according to Uchendu) is a preoccupation not only of individuals, but also of whole village-groups.[17] As further illustration, one could cite the Niomoun (Diola) of Senegal, whose *bukut* rite of initiation is held every twenty to twenty-five years. This involves long term planning by ritual experts and long term expectation by prospective initiates. Those initiated vary from age brackets nine to ten years, fifteen to sixteen years, and over sixteen years.[18] Mbiti's claim that future time does not go "beyond a few years at most" is inaccurate.[19]

Mbiti's thesis, with the intent of demonstrating the absence of linear time among Akamba and Africans in order to rest his arguments for a unique Christian eschatology, is dependent on the theory of time and history developed in the nineteenth century by the Religion History School. According to Smith's assessment of the evidence, this school pictures other people's perception of time as cyclic and nonhistorical (specifically the Babylonians and Canaanites), while the chosen people of Yahweh (Jews and Christians) have the unique privilege of living in a historical (linear) time perspective. Christians (and Jews) celebrate the "irruption" of the sacred (divine revelation) into durational time (history; Otto, Eliade), while the primitives abolish and annul time and history.[20] The issue of divine intervention in history in the ancient Near East and in Israel was treated in the previous chapter. We do not intend to rehash arguments in favor of or against Mbiti's thesis here.[21] We rather reaffirm that while the heavenly bodies (especially the sun and the moon) help each people count the sequence of events (or the passage of time), there are a number of ways in which each group images its ideal ritual time, which Costariadis calls "imaginary time." The claim of uniqueness by each religious group is based on prior commitment as shown in the myth-narrative. There is nothing in the nature of the universe that necessarily declares a particular claim as the unique revelation. As Costariadis says:

"In relation to imaginary time, as well as to the whole edifice of imaginary significations erected by each society, we ask: how must the world be, in itself, in order that this amazing and unlimited variety of imaginary edifices can be erected. The only possible answer is: the world must be tolerant and indifferent as between all these creations. It must make room for them, and for all of them, and not prevent, favor, or impose any among them over and against the others. In short: the world must be void of meaning. It is only because there is no signification intrinsic to the world that humans had, and were able, to endow it with this extraordinary variety of strongly heterogeneous meanings. It is because there is no voice thundering from behind the clouds, and no language of Being, that history has been possible."[22]

The unique contribution of Africans to religious practice is the experience of the transcendent in the ordinary, of ancestral time in durational time, the one not destroying but revealing the other. Passage rites in their everyday use for symbolic purposes, in changing forest/bush into initiation groves, testify to this contribution. We now examine the rites of initiation in detail.

THE INCULTURATION OF SACRAMENTAL CELEBRATION OF CHRISTIAN INITIATION

The Social Setting of Christian Initiation in Africa

In traditional Africa initiatory passage rites formed the bedrock for socialization, entrenching personal identity in a world of interrelationship, and, consequently, determining the assumption of social and religious roles. In most of sub-Saharan Africa, these rites no longer constitute the controlling variables for the social definition of person. They may still be found among traditionalist ethnic groups like the Edo (Nigeria), in countries where traditional religion still plays a dominant role, as in Togo and Benin Republic, and in resistant culture areas of given ethnic groups like the Afikpo and Abakaliki areas of Igboland (Nigeria). Even in places where the practice is popular, secularization, modernity, and the world religions (Christianity and Islam) restrict the influence the rites may have on initiates and on the wider society.

In Christianity the rite of initiation also plays the function of the fundamental definition of the Christian person (sons and daughters of God). The rite, which includes the sacraments of baptism, confirmation, and Eucharist, is best described in Pauline terms as a dying and rising with Christ — a good linguistic imagery of the ordeal that ritual passengers in Africa (and elsewhere in the world) undergo during initiation. According to the general introduction to the new Rite of Christian Initiation of Adults:

"Through the sacraments of initiation men and women are freed from the power of darkness. With Christ they die, are buried and rise again. They receive the Spirit of adoption which makes them God's sons and daughters and, with the entire people of God, they celebrate the memorial of the Lord's death and resurrection" (no. 1).[23]

Despite the transforming intent of the sacraments of initiation, their impact on recipients, on the church-community, and on the wider society remains very limited. There are many reasons for this. Infants, children, and adults are all initiated. The infants and children receive a name (naming ceremony) and undergo a ritual whose effectiveness is dependent on the faith of parents/sponsors/community. In their case Augustine's authoritative teaching is upheld: *sacramentum fidei fides est* (the sacrament of faith is faith).[24] The absence of other initiatory rites to cope with biosocial development (life cycle) and the predictable or unpredictable life crises affects the integral maturity of those initiated as infants or children, and consequently affects the quality of life of the social group and Church.[25] Adult candidates have the opportunity to make a choice between one religion and another, between one way and another (conversion). But the insistence on cerebral knowledge (learning the catechism), as opposed to knowledge through action (the method of traditional initiation), sets limits on the impact of adult initiation.

All over Africa secularization and modernity, communicated through Western education and the colonial and postcolonial political arrangement, have contributed most in weakening any impact that Christian initiation may have on initiates and the community at large. Through secularization, religious institutions (no matter how powerful they may be) are no longer in control of society. Second, secularization makes the religious person, according to Peter Berger, be "confronted with a wide variety of religious and other reality-defining agencies that compete for his allegiance, or at least attention, and none of which is in a position to coerce him into allegiance."[26] In Nigeria, where Moslem and Christian fundamentalists are frequently locked in bloody conflicts, the frequent call by Christian leaders on government to guarantee the secularity of the state shows the desire for a clear separation between the political regime and religious groups.[27]

Modern education has brought into Africa the notion of human consciousness that predominated in the West since the Enlightenment. The "heroic ego," according to Jungian analysts, is characteristic of this modern consciousness. The emphasis on the "isolated individual psyche and the values of autonomy" have made positive contributions to the humanization process. However, as Moore argues:

"The heroic ego of modernity has proven to have a fatal flaw — a flaw grounded in its fantasy of mastery, control, unfalsified perception and moral superiority. Given this view of an ego which is free of its biosocial matrix and which, once formed, is not in need of metamorphosis — and therefore has no need of ritual means of transformation — change is believed to occur primarily through education and realpolitik."[28]

Since Christianity was the principal tool for the communication of this consciousness, through the predominant Christian role in education in Africa, it is not surprising that the mainline Christian Churches concentrate attention, during the preparatory stage of initiation, on learning by rote Scripture passages or portions of the catechism. This necessarily reduces the impact of the sacraments of initiation on the individual and the society.

Some Christians and non-Christians in Africa fear that the new kind of person that emerges through Christian initiation may entrench the erosion of morality in society if the Christian ritual is not in some way backed up by adaptations of traditional rites of initiation. This can be illustrated by the conflict raging among Christians in Ezza (Abakaliki diocese, Nigeria) over whether or not to adapt ritual circumcision into Christianity. In the traditional practice the high point of the ritual involves a dedication of the initiand to Ani (Ala, the Earth Deity, guardian of morality and provider of fertility) and the erection of the cult of the personal *chi (ochi* or *uwa).* The initiation thus establishes a network of relationship between humans and spirits. At the completion of the ritual process one becomes man or woman with socioreligious rights and duties.[29]

The conflict in Ezza split the Christian community into those who totally reject the traditional ritual and those who want to adapt it for the use of Christians. Those in favor of adaptation are again split into moderates and radicals. The bone of contention is about the dedication to the Earth Spirit (Ani) after the ritual bath in female ritual circumcision. The moderates state the traditional practice as follows:

"The second stage of circumcision . . . lasts for four days. On the last day, the initiate would take [a] bath in the yam barn where thereafter she collects some soil from the barn which she deposits under the drinking pot of her mother-in-law. This formally hands over the activities of the initiate, now a complete woman, to the god of land — *Ani."*

Then they propose: "At the end of the second circumcision, the dedication to the god of land — *Ani* — by allowing the initiate to carry the soil from the barn should be replaced with dedication to Christ the Lord [prayers]."[30]

On the contrary, the radicals insist that the crucial dedication to the Earth Spirit should be retained:

"We have also examined the modifications made by the committee for easy adoption by Christians. We noted that they went to some extremes to protect the interest of Christians. We accept these modifications with the exception of the following: The picking of soil by a female initiate from the barn to the house (under the drinking pot of her mother-in-law) only hands her over to the god of land — *Ani* — for good moral behaviours. For moral reasons this section should be retained. There is good reason to believe that if women are let loose morally after circumcision, the society shall be filled with illegal children with strange behaviours."[31]

The leadership of the Catholic Church in the Abakaliki diocese considers any concession in the form of adaptation of traditional practice as paganism or sacrilege.[32]

The conflict in Ezza is only an example of the new social situation that prevails in Africa because of the erosion of traditional values by secularization and modernity. On the individual personal level the disorientation is very profound. It has driven Africans toward what Ndiokwere characterizes as the search for security.[33] Ritual leaders or charismatics who present substitutes to what appears lacking in the person and society ("compensators"; Bainbridge and Stark)[34] are very much sought after. Healing becomes the organizing motif. A similar situation prevails among Africans of the Diaspora. An initiate into Haitian voodoo declares:

"I saw that healing is the goal of all Vodou ritualizing. People bring the pains, problems, crises and sore points of their lives to this system. . . . Almost without exception, it is a life crisis that spurs a person to undergo initiation in the Haitian Vodou. Problems of health, love, work, or family life are diagnosed within Vodou as due to disruptions in the web of relationships that define a person."[35]

In Africa, miracle healers of all shades and forms present their solution to crises in social life (witchcraft, job opportunities, etc.) or crises imposed by one's life cycle (securing a husband or wife). A pamphlet published recently by a Catholic priest sums up the ailments healed through prayer. The title of the pamphlet itself is suggestive as regards the cause of ailments and their cure: *Welcome Jesus, Bye Bye Satan: Spiritual Pills to Overcome Your Problems.*[36] The list of ailments includes resolution of conflicts in the family, among friends, and between business partners; infertility and/or frequent miscarriages; protection against enemies; success in examination/interview; victory in a court case; finding a suitable spouse; victory in a land dispute; progress in business; job security/promotion; demonic possession (evil spirits, *ogbanje,* mermaid, bad dreams, witches, etc.); unemployment; sickness, etc.[37] Most pastors are presented with similar problems, and they devise rites (prayers, fasting, imposition of hands, anointings, etc.) to help their clients pass through these crises. The situation has become so widespread that a Cameroonian priest-theologian groaned, "priests have turned into traders and healers."[38]

In addition to the above, Africans seek initiation into esoteric non-Christian groups originating from America or the Far East. The reasons for entering into such groups may range from the psychopathological to the economic and the sociocultural.[39] Thus in cities like Kinshasa, Brazzaville, Abidjan, Lagos, Freetown, and Monrovia one finds an increasing number of Africans joining the Mahikari, Moonists, Rosicrucians, Eckankar, or the Grail Movement. Occult groups like the Freemasons and the local Ogboni get steady members into their secret societies. In Nigerian Universities initiation into cult groups like the Buccaneers or Pyrates is a common phenomenon. The activities of these groups have led to loss of life and the breakdown of law and order. Due to the rituals and activities of these cult groups, government has been frequently obliged to close down these institutions.

We stress then that the African social setting in which one will explore the inculturation of the sacraments of Christian initiation is beset by a multiplicity of problems and equally multiple problem-solving techniques. It is a setting where the traditional African pattern has been eroded or rendered very weak, but new forms of these traditional patterns are found among occult groups and new religious movements. The African person reveals himself or herself as one who wants rites to re-create or reactivate webs of interrelationships between spirits and humans. The social African setting calls for Christian initiatory and passage rites that will adequately cater to biological cycles and social crises.

The situation in Africa is comparable to the human drama in the Greco-Roman world at the time when Christianity was emerging from its Jewish moorings. That period has been described by Dodds as "an age of anxiety."[40] It was a time when Christianity was competing with the mystery cults. An exploration of the interaction between Christianity and these cults, a situation of rejection and acceptance, which led to the development of Christian initiation rites adapted to the ambient culture, may help us evolve principles for the inculturation of the rites of Christian initiation in our African context.

Christianity and Greco-Roman Mysteries

The Christian way and the Hellenistic mysteries constituted a threat to one another. The reasons are not far to seek. They are all Asian religions that sought adherents from the same groups of people living in the Mediterranean basin and undergoing the same sociocultural upheaval. We will first summarize the social context that fertilized both Christianity and the mysteries; then we will draw out the ambivalent attitude of Christianity to the mystery cults.

The Social Setting that Awaited Christianity and the Mysteries

The Greco-Roman world that welcomed the Hellenistic mysteries and Christianity was a world in turmoil. The turmoil started with the bringing together of peoples of different societies and cultures under Greek rule (the Hellenistic revolution). Then, Roman rule ensured facility for communication. Furthermore, the imperial period (starting from Augustus) saw a reorganization of the Roman social world leading to greater presence of the provincial elite along with their behavior patterns in Rome and an increase in anxiety and the search for security.[41]

The most fertile center for the experience of the Greco-Roman "melting pot" is the city. In urban centers, where ethnic boundaries break down, there is a weak affiliation to local customs, an openness or receptivity to new ideas (like those propagated by philosophers, mystery religions, and Christianity), and a tendency toward individual search for salvation rather than the maintenance of religious bonds of kin groups. Only pariah groups like the Jews, whose sociocultural and religious practices are characterized by "resentment" (Weber), may manage to insulate themselves from the effects of the melting pot.[42]

Hellenistic cults, like the Eleusinian mysteries, satisfied individual spiritual (religious) quests. These cults developed rituals that assured initiates or adherents that they were a changed people and that their life-crises were resolved. For, the mysteries are cultic rites in which the destiny of a god is portrayed by sacred actions before a circle of devotees in such a way as to give them a part in the fate of the god. Elements common to the mysteries include an initiation act that emphasizes the experience of salvation in the present and in the future as the goal of human existence on earth, and an identification with the fate of the transcendent divinity that passed through death to achieve immortality. Through this identification, salvation is achieved.[43]

Those attracted to these cults in Greco-Roman cities include plebeians, women (for some cults), freedmen, and slaves. They were either socially or economically disprivileged. The privileged aristocracy (more from the provinces than in Rome) were also initiated into the mysteries. Indeed, Roman emperors also became initiates. In this way they showed that the mysteries, which have been adapted to the Roman ideas of religion and social order (an adaptation that Christianity initially rejected), fulfilled cultural and political functions. An emperor like Hadrian frequented the mysteries, and Claudius attempted to transfer the festival center from Athens to Rome. The Greeks themselves who propagated the mysteries also saw in the practice an achievement of their political and cultural agenda. According to J. H. Oliver:

"The Greek aim, as it seems to me, was to put an end to ancient Hellenic rivalries and to unite all Hellenes and men of Hellenic education, to unify the world of city states against the encroachment of barbarism within the empire, and to promote loyalty of the cities to the old Hellenic cults and to the vicar of Zeus on earth, the Roman Emperor."[44]

Emperors may have their hidden (sociopolitical) agenda for participating in the mysteries, though genuine spiritual and religious needs may not be excluded. But the receptivity of the aristocracy (senators and equestrians) to the mystery religions shows the extent to which upper-class Romans were reformed by the internal crises experienced during the imperial period. The aristocracy, according to Weber's thesis, are generally conservative (past-oriented) in religious practice. They seek from religion chiefly the psychological assurance of their legitimacy. They are thus not carriers of a rational religious ethic.[45] However, the destabilization of the traditional Roman aristocracy through bloody purges during the regime of the Julio-Claudians

(Tiberius, Caligula, Claudius, and Nero) led to the promotion of *novi homines* (Tacitus), from the provinces, to fill senatorial posts. These "self-made men" of non-Roman and non-Italian origin brought new attitudes and new religious practices.[46] In this way the traditional conservative attitude of the Roman aristocracy became weakened. The Roman aristocracy, while holding onto the established social order of Rome, could associate itself with the more respectable Oriental cults (this hardly includes Christianity, which was both novel and lacking in antiquity).

The above summary is the social situation that prevailed in the cities prompting city-dwellers to search for security among philosophical groups, the mysteries, and Christianity. In the countryside *(pagus)*, a vigorous mass of Italian people followed traditional Roman rites with devotion.[47]

Conflict Between Christianity and the Mysteries: The Christian Offensive

The mysteries must have constituted a sufficient threat to Christianity to prompt the attack of Christian apologists. Christianity, as a new religious movement coming from Asia, was itself looked upon as a mystery cult. The satirist Lucian of Samosata (ca. 115–200 C.E.) described Christianity as a new mystery *(kainê teletê)*.[48] Because of the secrecy or reserve Christians maintained with regard to their practices (rites), Tertullian could concede that Christianity is a mystery. "If we always keep our secrets, when were our proceedings made known to the world? . . . Not, surely, by the guilty parties themselves [i.e., Christians]; even from the very idea of the thing, the fealty of silence being ever due to the mysteries. The Samothracian and Eleusinian make no disclosures."[49]

Christianity, like its parent Judaism, is an exclusivist religion. But as we saw above, Christians were living in Greco-Roman cities where the mysteries were a living religion; a religion responding to the quests of the times inasmuch a creative way as the new arrival to the religious marketplace (Christianity). Christians discovered to their dismay that strong resemblances existed between their rites (especially baptism and Eucharist) and the rituals of the mysteries. Christian apologists went on the offensive, not only to explain the difference between what is done in the mystery building *(telesterion)* and in the Christian place of gathering *(ekklesia* or *epi tô autô)*, but also to make the mysteries an object of caricature.[50]

In the Eleusinian or Samothracian process of initiation, ritual gestures are characterized by what is done *(dromena)*, what is said *(legomena)*, and what is seen (i.e., sacred objects shown to initiates, *deiknymena*).[51] The Christian offensive was directed principally against what is done. Of all the cults, the Mithraic cult of Persian origin was targeted. The divinity, Mithra, which accumulated astrological and eschatological elements in its passage through Chaldea and Mesopotamia, was particularly attractive to the Roman military (guardian of the legions). It had over one hundred meeting places in Rome alone. And under Diocletian, its cult was promoted to state religion (guardian of the empire), and the celebration of the solar deity (*sol invictus*, 25 December) was identified with Mithra.[52]

The Christian apologists generally claimed that the parallels between Christian and Mithraic rituals or the rituals of other cults were the result of demonic instigation. This view was shared by Justin Martyr, Tertullian, Clement of Alexandria, Origen, Firmicus Maternus, Jerome, and other apologists in their attack on the mysteries. It is also one of the popular attitudes of Christian writers toward Greco-Roman religions. Tertullian, who saw both heresy and idolatry as originating from the same evil demon, accused the demon of perverting the truth and "by mystic rites of his idols [he] vies even with the essential portions of the sacraments of God."[53]

"He, too, baptizes some — that is, his own believers and faithful followers; he promises the putting away of sins by a laver [of his own]; and if my memory still serves me, Mithra there, [in the kingdom of Satan,] sets his marks on the foreheads of his soldiers; celebrates also the oblation of bread, and introduces an image of a resurrection, and before a sword wreathes a crown."[54]

The apologists were not content with blaming the demons for these rituals; they also stressed the impotence of the mystery rites. The nations, according to Tertullian, deceive themselves by believing that their waters of ritual washing are hallowed like the Christian baptismal waters sanctified through the word of invocation, while in reality the washings in the Isis or Mithraic initiations are "with waters which are widowed."[55] And, writing about the *taurobolium* (a type of baptism of blood in the cult of Cybele), Prudentius' hymn is highly suggestive of the caricature in which Christian polemicists held the "pagan" rites:

"This man [the initiate] defiled by such impurity and filth,
Bespattered with the gore of recent sacrifice
The crowd with reverential awe salutes and glorifies,
Because they think a dead ox's blood has hallowed him,
As he was crouching in that dreadful cave below."[56]

Christian antagonism did not stop at verbal conflict. Violence was directed against the shrines or cult centers of Mithra and other deities. In some places their temples were turned into churches: "Already the Egyptian Serapis has been made a Christian."[57] When Christians took control of Roman society in the fourth century, they set out to violently and irrevocably destroy the last vestiges of Mithraism. Jerome painted an arresting picture of such a destruction in his letter to Laeta:

"Did not your own kinsman Gracchus whose name betokens his patrician origin, when a few years back he held the prefecture of the City, overthrow, break in pieces, and shake to pieces the grotto of Mithras and all the dreadful images therein? Those I mean by which the worshippers were initiated as Raven, Bridegroom, Soldier, Lion, Perseus, Sun, Crab and Father? Did he not, I repeat, destroy these and then, sending them before him as hostages, obtain for himself Christian baptism?"[58]

Finally, Christians took the ultimate step of killing members of the Mithraic cult and burying them under the rubble of their places of worship to desecrate such sites. The antagonism, and the Christian fear of these mysteries, must have been great.[59] The religious liberty *(libertatem religionis)* claimed by Tertullian when Christianity was sociopolitically weak was ignored by Christians when they came into power. This "taking away of religious liberty" and forbidding "free choice of deity" created the situation whereby people no longer worshiped according to their inclination, rather they were "compelled to worship against it."[60]

When the social order came under the control of Christians, the time was ripe to absorb the language and the patterns of the mysteries to reinterpret participation in the Christian sacraments. Christian initiation then introduced neophytes inside the mysteries. Cyril of Jerusalem enunciated with ease this principle of mystagogy by declaring, "seeing is far more persuasive than hearing."[61] We now turn to the Christian appropriation of mystery concepts and practices into their sacraments.

Christian Initiation as an Induction into the Christian Mysteries

Before the Christian domination of the religio-social order in the Roman empire, it was difficult for the apologists to employ mystery language to explain the Christian rites or to refer to Christianity as a mystery religion. Tertullian, who grudgingly made such a concession, was also virulent in his attack of the mysteries. However, as he attacked the cults, especially of Mithra, he was ready to point to some of their practices for Christian emulation. For example, one of the high points in the Mithraic initiation process is the rejection of any crown offered the initiate after being branded — Mithra is his only crown. Such a show of faithfulness by the devotees of the devil, says Tertullian, was intended to put to shame those Christians who accept earthly crowns (military laurels); they fail to realize that Christ is their leader and crown, that they are soldiers of Christ.[62]

Clement of Alexandria, who sojourned in a city alive with the mysteries, derided many of the cults for their impiety and absurdity.[63] Yet he was the first of the Fathers to have courageously adopted mystery concepts to explain the Christian practices. Concluding his *Exhortation to the Heathen,*[64] he invited his non-Christian audience to approach the Church, which is the "haven of heaven." There they shall see God and "be initiated into the sacred mysteries." The light of the Christian mysteries, Christ himself, is brighter than the sun; a light that banishes fear and darkness. Clement's description of the illumination of the Christian mysteries calls to mind Plutarch's account of the ritual process initiates undergo:

"At first abortive and wearisome wandering about, various unsuccessful and perilous passages in the darkness. Then, just before the rite itself, all manner of terrors, shuddering and trembling, silence and anxious wonder. After this, a wonderful light breaks in on everything, friendly landscapes and meadows receive us and we become aware of voices and dances and of the splendor of sacred songs."[65]

On his own part, Clement of Alexandria was intent on outbidding the mysteries to underscore the preeminence of the Christian rites:

"O truly sacred mysteries! O stainless light! My way is lighted with torches, and I survey the heavens and God; I become holy whilst I am initiated. The Lord is the hierophant, and seals while illuminating him who is initiated, and presents to the Father him who believes, to be kept safe for ever. Such are the reveries of my mysteries. If it is thy wish, be thou also initiated."[66]

If Clement took the initial (and bold) step of making the Christian rites meaningful to Alexandrians in terms of mystery concepts, this necessary task of inculturation was undertaken with deliberate vigor after the peace of Constantine. By then the Oriental mysteries have been defeated. Their defeat was not only caused by the withdrawal of official support for the cults (as is the case with the Mithraism), nor by the Christian persecution and intolerance of other cults. Rather they lacked the one overriding principle that ensured the Christian success: a radical sense of community. If Mithraism had a radical experience of community — "open to all, insistent on absolute and exclusive loyalty, and concerned for every aspect of the believer's life"[67] — the withdrawal of official support may not have resulted in such a rapid demise. Gager has argued that this radical sense of community and the power of the Christian commonwealth (cf. Tertullian),[68] which Christians inherited from the Jewish synagogue, are the most plausible reasons for the Christian success.[69]

Assured of the demise of the mysteries, the Fathers developed a teaching on the sacraments that employed mystery terminology. They incorporated patterns or gestures linked with the mysteries into the Christian rites. Terms like initiates *(memnemenoi)*, teachers of the mysteries *(mystagogoi)*, mystery teachings *(mystagogia)*, became current in Christian initiation. Baptism was called *photismos* (illumination) or *sphragis* (seal) or simply *mysterion* (mystery, used also for the Eucharist). The presiding bishop did not shy away from being called *protomystes* (first initiate), and the clerical tonsure was adopted from the practice of Isian priests with relative ease.[70]

The Oriental mysteries had other far-reaching impacts on the Christian practice. Baptism did not follow conversion *(metanoia)* as in the New Testament. Rather, a preparatory period of between three to five years was developed. There was a boundary between the baptized (initiates) and the nonbaptized catechumens and inquirers (noninitiates). The discipline of silence *(disciplina arcani)* was imposed with rigor. The initiates were to say nothing to the catechumens if these inquired about the mysteries. In homilies, which were often open to noninitiates, veiled language was often employed by Cyril of Jerusalem, John Chrysostom, Theodore of Mopsuestia, and Augustine (all great preachers) in order to guard the secret of the mysteries.

"I wish to remind you who are initiated of the response, which on that evening those who introduce you to the mysteries bid you make; . . . I desire indeed expressly to utter it, but I dare not on account of the uninitiated; for these add a difficulty to our exposition, compelling us either not to speak clearly or to declare unto them the ineffable mysteries. Nevertheless . . . I will speak as through a veil."[71]

Catechumens were naturally excluded from the Liturgy of the Eucharist (participating only in the Liturgy of the Word). Holy things were spoken before the holy and dispensed to them.[72] One can compare the Christian practice with the action of Emperor Augustus, who dismissed his cabinet *(consilium)* and audience (all noninitiates) when priests of the mysteries came to discuss secret matters of cult. And, generally, those who were not pure and upright (*katharoi tas cheiras,* primarily murderers) were excluded from the Oriental mysteries.[73]

Christian conversion in the post-Constantinian Church was in itself a ritual process. Candidates enrolled together were called competents *(competentes)* because they were seeking baptism together *(petentes simul)*. Their long period of catechumenate (three to five years) constituted a test. As catechumens they echo in their conduct what they heard in the Church.[74] Their liminal or threshold experience at the end of the catechumenate recalls the experience in the mysteries and in initiation rites in contemporary Africa. Finn's study of the ritual process in North Africa highlights, from the writings of Augustine and Quodvultdeus, the core process enacted throughout the period of Lent reaching its peak during Holy Week, especially Holy Saturday. For the competents (assembled for forty days in one place; e.g., Hippo) the Lenten observance was very strict (no wine, no meat, no baths, no public entertainment, and no use of marriage). Then the scrutinies (examination of candidates) along with exorcisms and the renunciation of the devil and his pomps were a real ordeal. Light comes after the confession of the Trinity; one is introduced inside the Christian mysteries. The feeling of passing through darkness, as part of the ordeal of liminality, is best brought out in the ritual drama (exorcism and renunciation of the devil) endured by the competents on

Holy Saturday night. Candidates emerge from the dark barefoot; they are tired from fasting and keeping vigil; unwashed, heads bowed, the exorcist breathes down each one of them hurling insults and curses at the mysterious (demonic) occupant of their being; then they renounce the world. Quodvultdeus sums it up in his homily:

"From a secret place you were each presented before the entire church, and then with your head bowed, which was proudly upright before, and standing barefoot on goat skin, the scrutiny was performed on you, and while the humble and most noble Christ was invoked, the proud devil was rooted out of you. All of you were humble of demeanor and humbly you pleaded by praying, chanting, and saying: 'Probe me, Lord, and know my heart' (Ps. 138:3). He has probed, he has weighed, he has touched the hearts of his servants with his fear; by his power he has caused the devil to flee, and he has freed his household from the devil's way."[75]

The emergence of the ritual passengers from this ordeal is their enlightenment *(photismos)* — profession of faith, baptism, and Eucharist. But in this threshold experience dread plays a significant role — fear of the devil and the world. The danger of the world symbolized in the internal desire (*libido,* Augustine) to sin or in the external entertainment industry (Quodvultdeus) persists even after baptism. The fear of falling back into sin and the ordeal of penance *(exomologesis)* made some to postpone baptism until the deathbed. It is in reaction to this that Chrysostom chided: "If the mysteries be excellent and desirable, let none receive baptism at his last gasp. For that is not the time for giving of mysteries but for making of wills; the time for mysteries is in health of mind and soundness of soul."[76] Therefore, Finn is right that the whole Christian assembly that participated in the initiation process of Holy Saturday night shared in the liminality of the competents. They have been taught that conversion is realized through fear and not through hope.[77]

This aspect of fear permeates the homiletic explanation of the mysteries (baptism and Eucharist). Especially in the Syrian tradition, Cyril of Jerusalem, Chrysostom, and Theodore of Mopsuestia adopted in their homilies the aspect of danger associated with the sacred. The Eucharist is described as "most dread-ful" (*phrikodestatos,* i.e., causing one's hair to stand on end); the Christian mysteries are frightful and terrifying *(phrikta kai phobera),* making people freeze with awe.[78] It is not surprising that with the dread surrounding the Eucharistic mystery the sanctuary veil, and later the iconostasis, would be introduced in the East to shield the holy of holies from the faithful.

We see from the above that the influence of the mysteries radically modified the liturgical structure and the meaning of Christian initiation. The sheer number of converts from the post-Constantinian era made a change in the ritual process necessary. The expectations of Greco-Romans and the practice of Oriental cults (of which Christianity formed a part) constituted ready-to-hand models for a Christian Church that had eliminated the threat of the cults.

The New Testament practice of conversion-initiation or Spirit-baptism and the Pauline baptismal theology (baptized into death with Christ, Rom 6:1-5; putting on Christ, Gal 3:27; anointed and sealed, 2 Cor 1:21-22; buried with him to be raised with him, Col 2:11-12) prepared the way for the transformation of Christian initiation under the influence of patterns of the mystery religions. Scholars today stoutly deny that neither Paul's use of *mysterion* (mystery) nor his description of baptism as a sacramental process is dependent on the Oriental mysteries.[79] But there is hardly any doubt that Hellenistic Christians wanted to understand becoming Christian in terms of initiation into mystery cults. The conflict at Colossae (Colossians 2) was not unconnected with the desire of Christians to be initiated into the cults in order to escape from fate and the forces.[80] Paul was opposed to such a syncretization of Christianity (Dibelius). He stood for both the exclusiveness and the superiority of Christianity.[81] However, the evidence from the patristic period shows a radical shift in the context and the appearance of questions and answers different from the concerns of Jewish Christianity. The context of the Greco-Roman world raised new questions because of its peculiar anxieties that drove people to search for security. The response of the patristic period involved a radical adaptation of the concerns, teachings, and practices of Jesus and the apostolic and post-apostolic Christianity. The man Jesus, who announced the kingdom and called for repentance in Galilean villages, and who was preached as the Christ by the apostolic Church, remained the same. But the implantation of his gospel in Greco-Roman soil called forth all the energies and genius of Christianity. Christianity presented a story of salvation accomplished through the life of a savior who was both human and divine. Individuals embrace this salvation by going through a ritual process where initiands pass (or are led) through the darkness of evil demons (inhabiting initiands and the world). Having passed through this ordeal (thanks to exorcisms and renunciation of the devil and the world), they profess their faith in the mystery of the Trinity, are baptized, and share in the Eucharistic mystery. In this way, Jewish Christianity (an Oriental religion) turned native in Greek, Roman, and Egyptian cities. It became modified (in its concerns and teachings) in the process of transforming the Greco-Roman world. Our next task is to explore how similar quests and anxieties in contemporary Africa may be directed by Christian initiatory (passage) rites.

Toward a New Practice of Christian Initiation in Africa

Our analysis of the social setting for the study of Christian initiation in Africa highlights the disquiet among African Christians about the effectiveness of the present practice of Christian initiation. Despite the diminishing importance of traditional religion, which props the native initiation rites, this religion and the rites retain their attraction. The pedagogy of native African initiations addresses the whole person: *body* (channel of knowing through doing, in adequate gestures; hardened and sharpened to live, in awareness, the depth of the world of relationship; readied to carry out wishes of the community whose secrets it embodies and guards), *memory* (assimilating stories and patterns of behavior communicated with adequate body rhythms), *soul* (establishing new relationship with spirits, and transformed to adopt new ways of being human through precisely the new relationships mediated by tradition). These positive qualities of native African initiations make concerned Christians wish for and propose a Christian initiation whose pedagogy is not "purely intellectual" but must include "emotional [affective] elements" that would give a greater human density to the truth being communicated.[82]

Most of sub-Saharan Africa received the message of Christianity only in the last century. This partly explains the ambivalent attitude of African Christians toward ancestral rituals. They are rejected officially (and by the majority of Christians) as pagan. Yet they are admired because of the kind of human type generated from the initiation groves. But, as noted above, traditional initiation rites have very limited impact today in African communities. The close kin groups and the village set up, which are the environment for experiencing and expressing the impact of the rites, have been considerably weakened by the emergence of the modern sociopolitical order. Furthermore, the massive impact of Christianity and Islam on Africans may indicate that the patterns of initiation of these world religions may prevail over the receding ways of African traditional religion. Nevertheless, traditional initiatory (passage) rites are not yet dead. They carry both cultural and religious messages. Consequently, they may continue to influence patterns of the rites of the world religions as they are influencing secret societies. Furthermore, the peculiar life-crises questions raised within each sociocultural group and the corresponding native ritual responses may retain the pertinency of patterns of African initiation rites. Cultural revival sometimes projects the externals of these rites without their spiritual depth. Ritual passengers may, thereby, be touched only in a superficial way. But the mainline Churches have felt their impact to the point of either stressing the need to shield their faithful from the effects of these rites or negotiating with the leaders of the tradition to limit Christian participation only to the sociocultural elements. Among Roman Catholics, who are the main focus of our study, few efforts have been made to provide alternative Christian rituals to replace the corresponding traditional rites. Some of these efforts will be examined in the next chapter.

In this segment we will examine (1) the dominant Christian attitudes to African traditional initiatory rites, an attitude that moved from condemnation to varied patterns of adaptation or accommodation, and (2) the patterns of creatively appropriating the structures of African initiation rites to enable Christians to enrich and expand Christian rites.

Christian Attitudes to Traditional African Rites of Initiation

Rejection. In an Isienu parish bulletin of 21 February 1993 a strongly worded announcement appeared about Christians being involved in title-taking, a ritual hallowing of achieved status among the Igbo.

"No Christian should participate in any paganish way of title taking. Examples of such title taking are as follows: 'Ikpo-Ama, Ichi-Onyeishi-uma-nna, Onyisi Umuada.' Others are 'Ichi-Igwe, Ozioko-oha, Asogwa-Oha, Ozo.' Christians are banned to neither attend nor offer any material or physical help to a pagan taking the title. This is because every glory for it goes direct to satan [ancestral spirit]. The scripture tells us that no one can serve two masters at a time. One cannot serve God and the devil at the same time."[83]

The language of such an announcement may appear surprising in these times of interreligious dialogue and inculturation. But it reflects the combative mood of many pastors (bishops and priests) in areas where traditional rites hold sway. Untitled persons in Nsukka and many parts of Igboland are deprived of certain rights in certain community gatherings. Among the Igbo, titles express wealth and ritually confer the exercise of power that wealth brings. They are open only to the free-born. Missionaries in Eastern Nigeria (especially from Shanahan to Heerey) shielded Catholics from these titles because of their discrimination against slaves and their "paganism."[84]

Generally the attitude of missionaries and their successors to African traditional religious rites was negative. The initiation and transition rites of Africa defined a person in his or her religious, social, political, and cultural dimensions. Christianity, as a new religion, looks for people to convert to Christianity. For, unlike traditional religion, "men are made, not born, Christians."[85] To make one a Christian implies a (re-)definition of the person through the Christian initiatory rites. That is why the key areas of confrontation between Christianity and African religion are the initiation passage rites.[86] Pastors and theologians (especially before Vatican II) argued that it was necessary to abolish traditional initiation rites in order to implant the Christian initiation. "One does not move from one signification [incorporation into a tribe] to a second which is radically different [incorporation into the Church of Christ] by way of the same external signs."[87] Sometimes the "perplexing analogies" (Sanon) between what is done *(dromena)* in traditional initiation and what is done in Christian initiation make Christian leaders even more determined not to compromise the traditional rites.[88] From the voodoo in Benin Republic and Haiti, to the *Nyau, M'Bona, Lyangombe, Polon,* or *hania* rites in Malawi, Burundi, and Guinea, the general reaction of rejection prevailed. To instill this violent break with the traditional rites in the minds of neophytes, the renunciation of the devil was expanded to include a renunciation of African cults (as among Haitian Catholics, and as suggested by Seumois).[89] The 1972 Rite of Christian Initiation of Adults includes the renunciation of false worship (i.e., worshiping spiritual powers, calling on the shades of the dead, or obtaining benefits from magical arts) in the renunciation of Satan (nn.

78, 80). But this may not be understood as a rejection of traditional initiation rites. The general introduction to the Rite of Christian Initiation of Adults leaves ample room for the adaptation of "initiation ceremonies in use among some peoples" (n. 31). This attitude of rejection, which is comparable to the rejection of the mysteries in patristic times, coexists with the recognition of the superior pedagogy of African initiation rites when compared with the poor school-type method of Christian catechetics.[90] The resistance of Christians (Catholics) to the radical rupture between their culture and their practice of Christianity necessitated compromises by Church authorities.

Accommodation and Adaptation. When the announcement about title-taking was made in Imilike-agu (an out-station of Isienu parish) there was an uproar. Right or wrong, the majority of older women and men who have been initiated (traditionally or "paganish-ly") as head of the kindred (Onye-isi-umu-nna) or head of the daughters (Onye-isi-umu-ada) do not consider such transition rites as offensive to their Christian faith. The bishop of the diocese of Nsukka has set up committees to study all patterns of initiations, passage rites, funeral ceremonies, etc., in view of the inculturation of Christianity in the diocese.[91]

The above reaction in 1993 is continuous with similar reactions of Christians not only in Igboland, but all over sub-Saharan Africa. In one chapter of their book *Enraciner l'Evangile,* Sanon and Luneau assembled testimonies of various patterns of such reactions and the effort made by Church authorities to accommodate traditional initiation rites within a genuine practice of Christian life.[92] In some cases individual missionaries swam against the current to repudiate the Christian denunciation of traditional initiations as devilish. Through such efforts some of them gained access to the initiation groves. Father Lassort used such an approach in 1944 to bring both catechists and nurses into the *polon* initiation camp. In this way it became possible to incorporate Christian instruction and medical care into the local ethnic (Guinean) ritual.[93] Father Zappa showed a similar resourcefulness and creativity with the West Niger Igbo in 1915. While the Ozo titles were being condemned east of the Niger in the first Catholic Congress presided over by Shanahan (1915), Zappa was signing an agreement with the elders on how to initiate Christians into the traditional title-taking.[94]

In some other cases the Christian population felt the need to keep the traditional initiation in addition to baptism. In 1980 in Marona, a city in north Cameroon, forty children undergoing instruction for baptism were secluded for a month and initiated. The Christian parents responsible for the action justified themselves by saying, "We cannot leave our children like that," i.e., uninitiated. Selected passages from the gospels and Christian prayers formed part of this traditional initiation.[95] In 1978, Father Kolie, a Guinean priest, was faced with the choice of either seeing Christian young women leave en masse to initiation groves for their initiation (called *hanin* among the Guerze), or devising an alternative ritual. Since he had no power over the matrons in charge of initiation, he decided to organize an initiation camp that would have Christian matrons as initiation directors. The seclusion lasted for thirty-seven days, and 125 women and girls were initiated. The young women were reaffirmed in the faith in their ancestors and in Christ.[96]

Apart from these efforts by individual priests or a group of Christians to accommodate or adapt native transition rites to the Christian life, dioceses or parish communities with the approval of the bishop have reached agreements with village-group elders or chiefs to remove elements of the initiation rites that hurt Christian feelings and beliefs so that Christian candidates may be admitted to traditional initiation. Such an agreement was reached in Chad (the Sara region). In 1966 Christian youth were able to follow the *yondo* initiation rites as Christian.[97] In Awka diocese of Nigeria, the authorities refused all adaptation of the young women transition rites into marriage *(Okuko-Onye-Uwa)*, which involved divination and the sacrifice of a hen to the young woman's personal *chi*.[98] But the diocese quickly arrived at an agreement with the elders in charge of the various title societies in different towns under its jurisdiction. The agreement signed with the Awka Titled Society on 6 July 1978 stated that: "The religious ceremonies traditionally connected with title-taking are hereby recognized as non-essential to the title itself. Therefore the titled man who takes the title without these ceremonies must be regarded as fully titled."[99]

The aim of the agreement is to allow Christians to share in the social benefits accruing from initiation into *ozo* and other titles. It is thus not a Christianization of the title system. As another agreement in the diocese signed on 23 April 1987 states: "These conditions do not aim at Christianizing the Ozo title or rather any other title. They merely aim at removing the pagan religious elements contrary to the Christian faith, so that Christians may take them as purely social titles."[100]

The above efforts to accommodate or adapt the native African initiation process to Christian life is a clear assertion that the cultural definition of the African person is not to be erased so that one would become a Christian. However, the reduction of the rites to the purely nonreligious dimension undermines the deep meaning of the initiation process itself. The "initiands" live such depth of meaning during the liminal or threshold or transition periods of the process. They live the sameness (*communitas;* Turner) of all humans; they receive and learn the will of the community; they learn how to recognize and listen to the spirits. They realize that humans must die in order to grow. These are religious ways of saying that the initiands are created anew, that they are changed to become new persons.[101] This religious experience undergirds the spirituality and ethics of native African initiations. During this period of seclusion, initiands are opened up bodily to be in tune with the universe, with one another, and with the depth of the self — an experience heightened by the unstructured setup of the transitional or liminal period.[102] The Igbo refer to a person emerging from such an experience in the following ways: *odalu muo* (he or she plunged or fell into spirit, thereby becoming spirit) or *odalu ogwu* (he or she plunged or fell into medicine, for those initiated as native doctors). It is on the basis of the spirituality of initiation that the ethical responsibility of status conferred by initiation is understood. Ultimately the social status given to initiates belongs to the community and is for the service of the community and not for selfish gains. That is why the presence of the community is very prominent from the rites of separation through the transition rites to the rites of incorporation. The community participation, and the excitement that is most palpable during the rite of incorporation, shows that the whole ritual is a reenactment (and therefore a reaffirmation) of the moral order to which the community is committed. Consequently, no neophyte will act only in terms of rights conferred by the new status; he or she may not selfishly follow his or her psychological urges. The good of the community remains primary.[103]

From the above points about the ethics and spirituality of traditional initiation rites, one may appreciate the negative results of reducing these rites to their sociocultural elements. The agreement binding Christians only to the social elements of the rites impoverished the initiation for boys among the *bobo* (Bourkina Faso) leading to varied reactions: lack of interest in the reformed rites or persistence in the full traditional process.[104] Among the Igbo the enthusiasm for the reestablished aristocratic *ozo* and other titles is maintained. However, the depth of spirituality and ethical responsibility that are part and parcel of the life of a person of title are often lacking. In addition, some neophytes find a way of having all the traditional rituals performed despite the fact that this is expressly ruled out in thc agreement.[105] If these rites are important for authentic human living in Africa, then Christian communities must courageously assume them and reflect on their deep meanings in order to convert them into Christian rites having socioreligious impact.

Creative Christian Appropriation of Patterns of Traditional African Initiation and Transition Rites

The opening created by Vatican Council II to the pluricultural reality of the Catholic Church moved the council fathers to recognize the values in certain elements of African practice. The understanding of adaptation, by the Church, is given its widest meaning in the question of Christian initiation. Not only are elements of initiation rites among various peoples "capable of being adapted to Christian ritual" admissible, there is a renewed insistence in the 1972 Rite of Christian Initiation of Adults for the creation of new rituals responding to local needs.[106] Therefore, the fundamental enterprise of Christian communities in Africa is to adapt creatively (inculturate) the rite of Christian initiation to genuine traditions of their village- or ethnic-group. This has been achieved with a measure of success in the diocese of Diebougou (Bourkina Faso) through the creation of the Moore ritual. This ritual, as will be shown in the next chapter, brings together elements in the process of various traditional rites (hospitality, boy's initiation, enthronement of chiefs, etc.) to create a sumptuous baptismal rite enacted during the paschal celebration.

In the application of the proposal for adaptation contained in *Sacrosanctum concilium,* no. 65 (as done in the Moore ritual) patterns of African initiation rites supplement or conflate whatever is considered the core of Christian initiation. This brings to prominence local signs and symbols through which the ordinary and everyday come to be carriers of a surplus of meaning (as becomes evident in the secret revelations of traditional initiation).[107] The emphasis on the ritual process and on the active participation by the community uplifts what was done in the limited village- or ethnic-group to serve the wider Christian community. The traditional or cultural becomes converted, as persons are converted, into Christianity.[108]

This creative reworking of Christian initiation (which centers on the baptismal rite) is one way of appropriating the wealth of the (rapidly disappearing) African rites of initiation. The structure and content of Christian initiation that has been received through the centuries are a process to be followed by adults. The fathers of the Vatican Council II were interested in initiating the adults of the mission lands into Christianity. But since the sixth century the majority of those initiated have been infants.

We quoted Tertullian earlier as saying that people are not born Christian, but rather are made so.[109] However, child baptism creates a situation where people are both made and born Christian. The induction of children into the Christian community through the petition of their parents parallels making infants members of a given village-group or ethnic body. Tertullian saw the difficulty. The initiation ritual into the Christian mystery is an adult passage rite. Therefore, he argued that children should be excluded from it:

"And so, according to the circumstances and disposition, and even age, of each individual, the delay of baptism is preferable; principally, however, in the case of little children. . . . The Lord does indeed say, 'forbid them not to come unto me.' Let them 'come,' then, while they are growing up; let them 'come' while they are learning, while they are learning whither to come; let them become Christians when they have become able to know Christ. Why does the innocent period of life hasten to the 'remission of sins?'"[110]

Predictably, the Church rejected Tertullian's opinion and continued initiating children with an adapted adult ritual.[111] This wisdom of the Church not only interprets Christian initiation as a conversion to the Christ (*metanoia* required of adults), but it also converts the initiation process into a biosocial experience. In other words, the life of Christ (or being Christian) may be experienced at various stages of human physical development. This begins with the imposition of a Christian identity on the newborn (enlightening them and opening them up for other Christian delights; Theodoret of Cyrus), and continues in the assumption of various roles within the community. In this way the seven Christian sacraments may be interpreted as passage or transition rites.[112]

The recognition of the positive values of the traditional initiation rites may thus not only project certain elements of these rites to be selected or a dynamic pedagogy to be emulated. Rather, it also creates the opportunity to confront the various steps of initiation into the living tradition of a village-group or ethnic body and initiation into Christianity. In this confrontation, the best of both traditions emerge in a renewed practice of Christian initiatory and passage rites. Entrance into each stage introduces candidates, through participation, into the mystery (as the fathers of the Christian Church understood it).[113] No stage exhausts the mysteries. Rather as one matures, in age and experience (going through predictable and unpredictable events of life), one learns, through receiving from the tradition, the depth of the mystery that life is to all of us (as is experienced in the African initiatory and passage rites).

This interaction between the patristic understanding of initiation as entrance into mystery and the various steps of the ritual process of initiation into the mystery (as practiced by various peoples) may have influenced the development of the catechumenate since Vatican II. Going through the stages of the catechumenate becomes a way of gradually being initiated into the mysteries.[114] The pattern of catechumenate by stages has been creatively utilized not only in Africa (e.g., the Franco-phone West African countries), but also in the rest of the Church (e.g., France) for the religious instruction of those who were baptized as children. In this way the seed of the mystery received by or planted in children is activated through a process experienced as one matures in age and social responsibility.[115]

The confrontation of the making of a human person in village or ethnic-group and the Christian Church sharpens the experience of community in both, a community that equips individuals to pass through life and that renews itself through the communal experience of such passage rites. No doubt the village- or ethnic-group cluster of kin relationship is very limited as compared to the Christian "commonwealth." But the emotions of belonging and the tight demands made on individuals are entrenched and renewed through initiation and other passage rites. In this way the kingroup, through the community consciousness experienced and renewed in the rites, touches intimately all aspects of an individual's life. Today, however, as we have often noted, there is no ethnic group in Africa where this ideal community consciousness (created by the *communitas* experienced in liminal or transitional periods) is found. The ubiquitous state, secularization, and the world religions make such a community impossible. But it is precisely the strength of this community consciousness that still attracts Africans. It is such consciousness that probably ensured the victory of Christianity over the mystery religions. It is such a sense of community that an inculturated African Christianity must try to develop.

The Christian attack on African traditional religion that centers principally on its doctrinal structure may be justified. But African traditional religion is more resourceful in equipping its members to pass through physical development, social maturity, and predictable and unpredictable events that may touch a person's life (life crises). Christianity, since its birth, by God's grace in the time of Caesar Augustus (Eusebius), has developed tested patterns of addressing the wider world. It is today called upon by Africans to combine these resources creatively with the multiplicity of African rituality in order to give African Christians dynamic communities in which to live and change their world.

African religions may not be too interested in the coherence of doctrines or in the systematic development of such doctrines. But they have tested patterns of forming humans to live in the world. No matter how changed such a world is, these basic patterns of forming humans to live creatively in the world are not to be overlooked.[116] It is instructive that membership of secret cults in Nigerian universities comes from children of the elite. These are supposed to be over indulged and then alienated from their culture. But the ordeal that candidates undergo during the initiation into these cults parallels what occurs in some initiation groves (like the Poro society popular in Guinea, Sierra Leone, and Gambia). According to the report of a vice-chancellor of one of the universities, "they subject them [the candidates] to gruesome bodily torture, to the extent that the weak ones, who cannot withstand the excruciating pains, may die in the process."[117] These deviant rites testify to the crying need of a Christian community that is strong enough to bind members together, to lead members through predictable and unpredictable events of life, and that renews itself specifically by celebrating such rites. The basis of such rites, and their matrix, is the initiation rite. An inventory of rites that can be adapted, assumed, or modeled according to Christian principles and traditional pedagogy must take into consideration the changed situation of the wider world as it affects Africa. One may possibly live and pass through the critical cycles of life — birth, puberty, marriage, and death — without going through a ritual process. But anthropological studies have yet to reveal evidence of societies without rituals at these crucial cycles. The evidence reveals either more or less elaborate rites.[118] Christian rites exist for marriage and death. Birth rites are limited to baptism (though among some African groups, e.g., the Yoruba of Nigeria, the traditional naming ceremony has been Christianized). However, the fairly long passages from childhood to puberty and from puberty to marriage, along with the increasing assumption of social responsibility, have hardly attracted Christian rites. This is a period of life that attracts many passage rites in traditional Africa. It is true that as a society becomes more complex, rites may become fewer. But as an impersonal state takes over the formation of its citizens (mainly through the school system), the spiritual (holistic) formation of humans falls on smaller groups (village-group, Churches, other religious movements). Therefore, there is no reason why entrance into and graduation from schools (primary, secondary, and tertiary levels) should not be marked by adequate passage rites. And the Churches may pay close attention to boys and girls going through the critical period of puberty providing them with adequate rites that would merge the best of the ancestral and Christian traditions.

Marriage is a critical passage replete with traditional and Christian rites. Efforts have been made to create one passage rite integrating the traditional African and the received Western Christian patterns (e.g., in Chad and Nigeria). But rituals have not been devised to cope with marriage in crisis, separation (divorce), and especially the pains of widowhood. In many parts of Igboland crisis in marriage is transited not only through counseling but also through the ceremony of *igba ndu* (a ritual covenant between husband and wife to eliminate suspicion and renew the promise of fidelity). Many Catholic priests adopt a Christianized pattern of *igba ndu* ritual as an answer to deep crises in interpersonal relationships (whether between individuals or groups). But the most traumatic crisis that women face in Africa —

widowhood — has generally been left unattended by the Churches in Africa. The legacy of the African tradition is most dehumanizing for the widows. Sometimes widows are treated as if they killed their husbands.[119] Rituals with emphasis on the liberation of widows are overdue. Mature widows may also be entrusted with ministry in the Church, as was practiced in the New Testament and the Syriac Churches,[120] to entrench the freedom initialed in Christian baptism.

Frequent references have been made to the *ozo* and other titles as a pattern of recognizing achievement for men in Igbo society. There are also the *lolo* and other titles for successful women. It is important that such rituals be given a place within the Christian community so that the deep spirituality and moral responsibility associated with success in the world of business (a success that is a gift of God) be not lost on the wealthy. The New Testament Church (house-churches) assembled in houses of members who were wealthy enough to provide room for such gatherings. Similarly, the progress toward achievement may also be ritually recognized. Apprentices in some parts of Igboland have formed the habit of soliciting the blessing of priests at the completion of their apprenticeship. Some bring their tools or endowment funds from their mentors to prayer centers. In this way a rite of passage (a blessing) may strengthen them to begin their own trade. One may still add unpredictable crises in life like prolonged illnesses, accidents, disorders of all sorts, the experience of the paranormal, as areas where transition rites may be needed. In many parts of Africa this has been catered for by charismatic prayer. The mainline Catholic and Protestant Churches, the independent or Zionist Churches, and the new religious movements are all involved in providing prayers or healing sessions and a welcoming community for such needy people.

The above inventory of rites that may be developed in the practice of Christianity in Africa are drawn from the resources of African ritology. They are necessarily local because ritual must emerge from ethnic experience. The power of the ritual, as was noted in chapter two, is in "doing": one believes what one does, one may become what one does. The influence of a particular rite lies in its power to respond to questions of life. Such influential rituals are adaptable from one group to another. Religion gives rituals a sacred anchor. Christianity should naturally offer a Christian anchor to the rites. The Christian interest may, therefore, not be limited to the social effects of initiation rites.

Some may suspect that such an array of rituals to cross over cycles and crises of life may ultimately be diversionary. They may draw people away from the social, political, and economic causes of their life problems. They may fix initiands or ritual passengers to a conservative (traditional) view of life in the world. This suspicion may be valid. At the same time one should not underestimate the creative power of ritual performance (see chapter two). In the context of celebration (e.g., of initiations) the "should" and "ought" of ritual is counterbalanced by the "make believe" or "let's pretend" of play. This ludic element of ritual celebration liberates what has been bound by social structure. In the initiation camps (characterized by antistructure; Turner), initiands live in camaraderie, communion, oneness, or *communitas*. They are "betwixt and between." Therefore, the liminal context, despite its danger (strict prohibitions or taboos), may also come across as a source of renewal, innovation, and creativity. The boy's initiation among the *bobo* (Bourkina Faso) includes such activities as running, dancing, learning arts, stories, and songs, and climaxes with an acrobatic jump *(somazolo)* from the tree of initiation that must synchronize with the termination of a ritual song. Consequently, efficiency, cleverness, and creativity are instilled into the initiands. In such a sacred grove where one is shed of one's past status while not yet incorporated into another status, one may be led to develop a freer and deeper understanding of society and self. This constitutes the basis of the freedom to create.[121] Initiation and passage rites constitute an environment for this creativity. The integration of such rites into the Christian practice, along with their affective pedagogic method, may prove a healthy contribution by Christians to the rapidly changing patterns of life in Africa.

NOTES

1. B. Myerhoff, "Rites of Passage: Process and Paradox," *Celebration: Studies in Festivity and Ritual*, ed. V. Turner (Washington, D.C.: Smithsonian Institution Press, 1982) 109.

2. Cicero, *De Legibus* 2.36, cited by K. Clinton, "The Eleusinian Mysteries: Roman Initiates and Benefactors, Second Century B.C. to A.D. 267," *Aufstieg und Niedergang der Römischen Welt (ANRW)*, II.18.2, ed. H. Temporini and W. Haase (Berlin and New York: Walter de Gruyter, 1989) 1500.

3. See M. Eliade, *Rites and Symbols of Initiation* (New York: Harper & Row, 1958) x; see also Cazeneuve, *La Sociologie du Rite,* 125, and ch. 4; Grainger, *The Language of the Rite* (London: Darton, Longman and Todd, 1974) 20–22; J. S. La Fontaine, *Initiation: Ritual Drama and Secret Knowledge Across the World* (Middlesex: Penguin, 1985) 181–8.

4. A. van Gennep, *The Rites of Passage* (London: Routledge and Kegan Paul, 1960) 10–11; V. Turner, *The Ritual Process: Structure and Anti-Structure* (Chicago: Aldine, 1973).

5. E. M. Zeusse, *Ritual Cosmos: The Sanctification of Life in African Religions* (Athens: Ohio University Press, 1979) 3.

6. E. Jaques, *The Form of Time* (London: Heinemann, 1982) 3.

7. See J. Goody, "The Time of Telling and the Telling of Time in Written and Oral Cultures," *Chronotypes: The Construction of Time,* ed. J. Bender and D. E. Wellbery (Stanford, Calif.: Stanford University Press, 1991) 77–96, esp. 84ff.

8. See P. P. Gossiaux, "Mythe et Pouvoir — Le Culte de Ryangombe — Kiranga (Afrique équatoriale de l'Est)," *Le Mythe — Son Langage et son Message,* Actes du colloque de Liège et Louvain-la-Neuve 1981, ed. H. Limet and J. Ries (Louvain-la-Neuve: Centre d'Historie des Religions, 1983) 337–72.

9. See Zeusse, *Ritual Cosmos,* 5–11; V. R. Dorjahn, "The Initiation and Training of Temne *Poro* Members," *African Religious Groups and Beliefs: Papers in Honor of William R. Bascom,* ed. S. Ottenberg (Meerut, India: Archana Publications, for Folklore Institute, 1982) 35–62.

10. Zeusse, *Ritual Cosmos,* 108.

11. M. Eliade, *Cosmos and History: The Myth of Eternal Return* (New York: Harper & Row, 1959).

12. Augustine, *Confessions* chs. 20, 28. Translated by V. J. Bourke, *The Fathers of the Church: A New Translation,* vol. 21 (New York: Fathers of the Church, Inc., 1953).

13. J. Z. Smith, *To Take Place: Toward Theory in Ritual* (Chicago: University of Chicago Press, 1987); cited in his "A Slip in Time Saves Nine: Prestigious Origins Again," *Chronotypes: The Construction of Time,* ed. J. Bender and D. E. Wellbery (Stanford, Calif.: Stanford University Press, 1991) 75.

14. J. S. Mbiti, *New Testament Eschatology in an African Background* (London: Oxford University Press, 1971) esp. 24–32; see also his *African Religions and Philosophy* (London: Heinemann, 1969) ch. 3.

15. Mbiti, *New Testament Eschatology,* 31.

16. See the interesting comments of O. U. Kalu in his "Precarious Vision: The African's Perception of His World," *Readings in African Humanities: African Cultural Development,* ed. O. U. Kalu (Enugu: Fourth Dimension, 1980) 37–44, esp. 39–40.

17. This is a controlling theme of V. C. Uchendu's book *The Igbo of Southeast Nigeria* (New York: Rinehart and Winston, 1965); see also S.

Ottenberg, "Improvement Associations among the Afikpo Ibo," *Africa* 25:1955, 1–27.

18. See L. V. Thomas, "Mort symbolique et Naissance initiatique," *Cahiers des Religions Africaines* 7:1970, 41–73.

19. Mbiti, *New Testament Eschatology,* 30.

20. See Smith, "A Slip in Time Saves Nine."

21. See Zeusse, *Ritual Cosmos,* 110–12; N. S. Booth, "Time and Change in African Traditional Thought," *Journal of Religion in Africa* VII:1975, 81–91; D. C. Okeke, "African Concept of Time," *Cahiers des Religions Africaines* 7/14:1973 207–301.

22. C. Castoriadis, "Time and Creation," *Chronotypes: The Construction of Time,* ed. J. Bender and D. E. Wellbery (Stanford, Calif.: Stanford University Press, 1991) 52.

23. For the text of the new Rite of Christian Initiation of Adults see *The Rites of the Catholic Church as Revised by the Second Vatican Ecumenical Council* (New York: Pueblo, 1976).

24. Augustine, *Letter* 98.9–10, to Bishop Boniface. See *Saint Augustine: Letters,* vol. 2 (83–130), *The Fathers of the Church* (New York: Fathers of the Church, Inc. 1953) vol. 18.

25. In French-speaking West Africa there are experimentations to ensure ongoing formation and initiation of this category of Christians.

26. P. L. Berger, *The Sacred Canopy* (Garden City, N.Y.: Doubleday, 1967) 107, 126; see also J. K. Hadden, "Religion and the Construction of Social Problems," *Religion and Religiosity in America,* ed. J. K. Hadden and T. E. Long (New York: Crossroad, 1983) 17–30, esp. 17–20.

27. The study of this phenomenon has preoccupied the meetings of the Ecumenical Association of Nigerian Theologians and results have been published in their organ *Bulletin of Ecumenical Theology* vols. 2/1, 1989; 2/2–3/1, 1989–1990. See, for example, the contribution of J. Onaiyekan, "State Secularity and the Nigerian Church," vol. 2/1, 75–83.

28. R. L. Moore, "Ritual Process, Initiation and Contemporary Religion," *Jung's Challenge to Contemporary Religion,* ed. M. Stein and R. L. Moore (Wilmette, Ill.: Chiron Publications, 1987) 152–3.

29. See J. Odey, *Ritual Circumcision in Ezza and the Christian Faith* (Ibadan: Claverianum Press, 1986). For similar problems in the relationship between Christian initiation and traditional initiations see A. T. Sanon and R. Luneau, *Enraciner l'Evangile: Initiations Africaines et Pédagogie de la Foi* (Paris: Cerf, 1982).

30. Their letter cited by Odey, *Ritual Circumcision,* 19–20.

31. Ibid., 21–22.

32. Odey's booklet, which incorporates the official diocesan stand in the issue, makes this clear.

33. N. I. Ndiokwere, *Search for Security* (Benin City, Nigeria: AMBIK Press 1990).

34. See W. S. Bainbridge and R. Stark, "Cult Formation: Three Compatible Models," *Religion and Religiosity in America,* ed. J. K. Hadden and T. E. Long (New York: Crossroad, 1983) 35–53.

35. K. McCarthy Brown, "'Plenty of Confidence in Myself': The Initiation of a White Woman Scholar into Haitian Vodou," *Journal of Feminist Studies in Religion* 3/1:1987, 67–76, esp. 68–69.

36. By J. C. Atado, Sokoto, 1990.

37. Ibid., 40.

38. E. Messi Metogo, preface to F. Eboussi-Boulaga's *A Contretemps: L'Enjeu de Dieu en Afrique* (Paris: Karthala, 1991) 7.

39. See Bainbridge and Stark's suggestive study, "Cult Formation: Three Compatible Models."

40. E. R. Dodds, Pagan and Christian in an Age of Anxiety (Cambridge: Cambridge University Press, 1965).

41. See ibid., 3–4; Gager, *Kingdom and Community: The Social World of Early Christianity* (Englewood Cliffs, N.J.: Prentice-Hall, 1975) ch. 4; Nock, *Conversion* (Oxford: Oxford University Press, 1963) chs. 5–7; G. Lease, "Mithraism and Christianity: Borrowings and Transformations," *Aufstieg und Niedergang der Römischen Welt,* II.23.2, ed. H. Temporini and W. Haase (Berlin: W. Gruyter, 1980) 1306–32, esp. 1308–9.

42. See M. Weber, *The Sociology of Religion* (Boston: Beacon Press, 1963) 108–17.

43. Lease, "Mithraism and Christianity," 1309; see also D. H. Wiens, "Mystery Concepts in Primitive Christianity and in Its Environment," *Aufstieg und Niedergang der Römischen Welt,* II.23.2, ed. H. Temporini and W. Haase (Berlin: W. Gruyter, 1980) 1250–1.

44. J. H. Oliver, *Marcus Aurelius: Aspects of Civic and Cultural Policy in the East,* Hesperia, supplement 13 (Princeton, N.J.: American School of Classical Studies at Athens, 1970) 133–4, cited by Clinton, "The Eleusinian Mysteries," 1521. For the role of Hadrian in the mysteries see Clinton, "The Eleusinian Mysteries," 1516–25.

45. Weber, *The Sociology of Religion,* esp. chs. 6–8; see also Gager's *Kingdom and Community,* 97–101.

46. Tacitus, *Annals* 3.55; Gager, *Kingdom and Community,* 97–99.

47. See H. Weiss, "The Pagani Among the Contemporaries of the First Christians," *Journal of Biblical Literature* 86:1967, 42; cited by Wiens, "Mystery Concepts," 1266.

48. See Benko, "Pagan Criticism of Christianity," 1093–7.

49. Tertullian, *Apology* 7; cited in *The Ante-Nicene Fathers,* vol. 3, ed. A. Roberts and J. Donaldson (Edinburgh: T. and T. Clark, 1989).

50. For a study of Christian attitude to the mysteries see, for example, R.P.C. Hanson, "The Christian Attitude to Pagan Religions up to the Time of Constantine the Great," *Aufstieg und Niedergang der Römischen Welt,* II.23.2, ed. H. Temporini and W. Haase (Berlin: W. Gruyter, 1980) esp. 925–30; Lease, "Mithraism and Christianity"; Wiens, "Mystery Concepts."

51. See C. Gallant, "A Jungian Interpretation of the Eleusinian Myths and Mysteries," ANRW, II.18.2, 1989, 1540–63, esp. 1555; S. G. Cole, "The Mysteries of Samothrace during the Roman Period," ANRW, II.18.2, 1989, 1565–98, esp. 1576–79; L. J. Alderink, "The Eleusinian Mysteries in Roman Imperial Times," ANRW, II.18.2, 1989, 1457–97.

52. Lease, "Mithraism and Christianity," 1310–1.

53. Tertullian, *On Prescription Against Heretics* 40.

54. Ibid.; see also Justin, *Apology* 1.66.

55. Tertullian, *On Baptism* 5.

56. Prudentius, *Peristephanon,* lines 1046–50 of hymn 10, in *The Fathers of the Church,* vol. 62 (Washington, D.C.: Catholic University Press, 1962) 235; cited by Wiens, "Mystery Concepts," 1266. For the possible influence of Christian baptism on the development of the *taurobolium* into a total washing in blood, see Wiens, "Mystery Concepts," 1266–7.

57. Jerome, Letter 107.2, cited in *Nicene and Post-Nicene Fathers of the Christian Church,* 2nd series, vol. 6, ed. P. Schaff and H. Wace (Grand Rapids, Mich.: Eerdmans, 1983) 190.

58. Ibid.

59. See Lease, "Mithraism and Christianity," 1307ff., and n. 7.

60. Tertullian, *Apology* 26.

61. Cyril of Jerusalem, "Five Catechetical Lectures — Catechetical Lectures, XIX:1," *Nicene and Post-Nicene Fathers of the Christian Church,* 2nd series, vol. VII, ed. P. Schaff and H. Wace, (Grand Rapids, Mich.: Eerdmans, 1983) 144.

62. Tertullian, *The Chaplet* or *De Corona,* esp. no. 15.

63. See his *Exhortation to the Heathens,* esp. ch. 2, in *The Ante-Nicene Fathers,* vol. 2, trans. A. Roberts and J. Donaldson (Edinburgh: T. & T. Clark; Grand Rapids, Mich.: Eerdmans, 1989).

64. Ibid., ch. 12.

65. Cited by C. A. Kucharek, *The Sacramental Mysteries: A Byzantine Approach* (Combermere, Ont.: Alleluia Press, 1976) 34.

66. Ibid.

67. See Gager, *Kingdom and Community,* 140.

68. In *Apology* 38, Tertullian asserts, "We acknowledge one all-embracing commonwealth — the world."

69. Ibid., 132–42.

70. See Kucharek, *The Sacramental Mysteries,* 56ff.; Hanson, "Christian Attitude to Pagan Religions," 930; Wiens, "Mystery Concepts," 1268–9.

71. Chrysostom, *Homily 1 Cor 40:2,* cited in *Nicene and Post-Nicene Fathers of the Christian Church,* 2nd series, vol. 12.

72. See *Apostolic Constitutions* and other Eucharistic Prayer traditions. For a discussion of this declaration of exclusion in the Syrian tradition starting from the Didache and Book VIII of the Apostolic Constitutions, see C. Kucharek, *The Byzantine-Slav Liturgy of St. John Chrysostom* (Combermere, Ont.: Alleluia Press, 1971) 662–6.

73. See Clinton, "Eleusinian Mysteries," 1509, 1514.

74. See T. M. Finn, "It Happened One Saturday Night: Ritual and Conversion in Augustine's North Africa," *Journal of the American Academy of Religion* LVIII/4:1990, 591.

75. Sermones de Symbolo 1.1.4–7. Cited by Finn, "It Happened One Saturday Night," 596–7.

76. Chrysostom, *Homily in Acts of the Apostles* 1, as cited in *Nicene and Post-Nicene Fathers of the Christian Church,* 1st series, vol. XI.

77. Finn, "It Happened One Saturday Night," 610–1.

78. Citations from Kucharek, *The Sacramental Mysteries,* 60.

79. See G. Bornkamm, "Mysterion," *Theological Dictionary of the New Testament,* vol. 4, ed. G. Kittel (Grand Rapids, Mich.: Eerdmans, 1967) 802–27; R. Brown, "The Semitic Background to the New Testament Mysterion," *Biblica* 39:1958, 426–48; 40:1959, 70–87; Wiens, "Mystery Concepts," 1268–79.

80. See *Conflict at Colossae: A Problem in the Interpretation of Early Christianity Illustrated by Selected Modern Studies,* Sources for Biblical Studies 4, ed. and trans. with introduction and epilogue by F. O. Francis and W. A. Meeks (Missoula, Mont.: Society of Biblical Literature, 1973).

81. M. Dibelius, "The Isis Initiation in Apuleius and Related Initiatory Rites," *Conflict at Colossae,* 61–121, esp. 88–101.

82. A. Sarr, "Une Initiation Africaine, l'initiation sereer," Recherche et Conseil presbyterial de Dakar, 1971, 14; cited by Sanon and Luneau, *Enraciner l'Evangile,* 30.

83. St. Anthony's Isienu Parish Announcements, subsection C: *Title Taking.* To be involved in rituals considered pagan or to participate or support such initiations into traditional title taking attracts fines of between N50.00 to N100.00 (U.S. $3 to $6).

84. See *A Hundred Years of the Catholic Church in Eastern Nigeria 1885–1985,* ed. C. A. Obi (Onitsha: Africana-Fep, 1985) 147, 383–7.

85. Tertullian, *Apology* ch. 18.

86. See I. Linden, "Chewa Initiation Rites and *Nyau* Societies: The Use of Religious Institutions in Local Politics at Mua," *Themes in the Christian History of Central Africa,* ed. T. O. Ranger and J. Weller (London: Heinemann, 1975) 30–44.

87. R. Bureau, "Les Missions en Question," *Christus* 34:1962, 255–6; cited by Sanon and Luneau, *Enraciner l'Evangile,* 24.

88. In *Enraciner l'Evangile* Sanon and Luneau outline some of these glaring analogies in *bobo* and Christian initiations: the tree of the cross and the tree of initiation, procession into a large courtyard and procession into the house of God, giving a name that makes initiates live in communion of ancestors or saints, rhythm of formation in stages to acquire new knowledge and adult wisdom, putting on new clothes and being dressed in white (132–3).

89. See L. Hurbon, *Dieu dans le Vaudou Haïtien* (Paris: Payot, 1972) 21–27, esp. 25; Sanon and Luneau, *Enraciner l'Evangile,* 25–26.

90. Sanon and Luneau, *Enraciner l Evangile;* see also Moore, "Ritual Process," 152–3.

91. The program of the commission on inculturation is comprehensive as the minutes of the first meeting held on 2 January 1993 testify. Topics to be studied include title-taking, marriage ceremonies, burial/funerals, masquerading, initiations, ascriptive/traditional hereditary posts like Onyeisi, etc. From *Minutes of Meeting of the Inculturation* Commission of the Catholic Diocese of Nsukka held on 2 January 1993 at St. Theresa's Cathedral, Nsukka.

92. Ch. 4, "Evangeliser l'Initiation?"

93. Sanon and Luneau, *Enraciner l'Evangile,* 31–33.

94. What Fr. Zappa started in 1915, Fr. Duff completed in 1917. See A. O. Gbuji, *Pastoral on Title-Taking and Traditional Funeral Ceremonies,* diocese of Issele-uku (Nigeria), 1984, no. 20, 11.

95. Sanon and Luneau, *Enraciner l'Evangile,* 56.

96. Ibid., 41–42.

97. Ibid., 36–38.

98. A. K. Obiefuna, *The Church and Culture* (A Case Study in Awka), Awka, Nigeria: 1990, esp. 12–34, 60–66.

99. Agreement between the local Catholic community of Awka and the titled society of Awka, general principles, no. 2. This agreement is based on those signed in Onitsha Archdiocese in the 1960s.

100. Agreement between the local Catholic community of Abagana and the titled society of Abagana, preamble.

101. See Gennep, *The Rites of Passage,* 10–11, 21; V. Turner, *The Forest of Symbols: Aspects of Ndembu Ritual* (Ithaca, N.Y.: Cornell University Press, 1967) 96ff.; Turner, *The Ritual Process,* 94ff.; Grainger, *The Language of the Rite,* 21; R. Grainger, "The Sacraments as Passage Rites," *Worship* 58:1984, 215–6; La Fontaine, *Initiation,* 181–8.

102. This has been studied in great detail by Turner, as the full title of his book indicates: *The Ritual Process: Structure and Anti-Structure.*

103. See Turner, *The Ritual Process,* chs. 3–5, esp. pp. 105–8; La Fontaine, *Initiation,* 125. Sanon and Luneau stress the importance of the community

throughout their work, *Enraciner l'Evangile.* See, for example, the section titled, "Propos Humanistes sur l'Initiation," 104–29.

104. Sanon and Luneau, *Enraciner l'Evangile,* 34–36.

105. See Agreement between the local Catholic community of Awka and the titled society of Awka, general principles, esp. nos. 4 and 5. See also Gbuji, *Pastoral on Title-Taking,* no. 20.

106. *Sacrosanctum concilium,* no. 63b; General Introduction to the New Rite of Christian Initiation, nn. 30–31.

107. Children being initiated come to realize that the person behind the mask is the man they see every day, but they learn to call the mask spirit.

108. This is the way Sanon and Luneau reflect on the creative appropriation of native African initiation rites into Christianity. See *Enraciner l'Evangile,* esp. 149–62.

109. Tertullian, *Apology* 18.

110. Tertullian, *On Baptism* 18.

111. See P. de Clerck, "Un seul Baptême des Adultes et celui des petits Enfants," *La Maison Dieu,* 185:1991, 7–33.

112. See Gerard Fourrez, *Sacraments and Passages: Celebrating the Tensions of Modern Life* (Notre Dame, Ind.: Ave Maria Press, 1983).

113. See P.-M. Gy, *La Liturgie dans l'Histoire* (Paris: Cerf, 1990) esp. ch 1, "La Notion chrétienne d'Initiation," 17–39.

114. See Sanon and Luneau, *Enraciner l'Evangile,* 186–8.

115. For the use of the method of catechumenate by stages for the instruction of those baptized as children in French-speaking West Africa see the numerous reports on catechetics in *Le Calao.* For example, 57/1:1982; 77/1:1986; 93/2:1993.

116. See the resilience of the M'Bona cult before the changed political and religious situation in central Africa in M. Schoffeleers, "The Interaction of the M'Bona Cult and Christianity, 1859–1963," *Themes in the Christian History of Africa,* ed. T. O. Ranger and John Weller (Berkeley: University of California Press, 1975) 14–29.

117. See A. Usen and others, "Reign of Terror," *Newswatch,* March 12, 1990, 14–19, esp. 18.

118. See Myerhoff, "Rites of Passage: Process and Paradox," 127–8.

119. The unhappy situation of widows in Nigeria was recently explored by a woman lawyer, F. Ofodile, in her symposium paper: "The Right of Women in Nigeria (State and Church)," *Human Rights in Nigerian Society and Church,* the Second SIST Missiology Symposium, 29 Nov.–1 Dec. 1990. In some places, like Aboh (West Niger Igbo), widows may be required to sleep alongside their dead husbands. See C. Obi, "Town Where Widows Sleep with Their Dead Husbands," *Vintage People,* Lagos: 19–25 Feb. 1993, 7.

120. The widows have an important ministry in the Church of *Testamentum Domini.* See M. Arranz, "Les Rôles dans l'Assemblée chrétienne d'après le 'Testamentum Domini,'" *L'Assemblé Liturgique et les Différents Rôles dans l'Assemblée,* Conférences Saint-Serge, XXIIIe Semaine d'Etudes Liturgiques, Paris, 28 June–1 July 1976 (Roma: Edizioni Liturgiche, 1977) 43–77, esp. 62–66.

121. See Sanon and Luneau, *Enraciner l'Evangile,* 72–79; Myerhoff, "Rites of Passage," 116–7; Turner, introduction to *Celebration: Studies in Festivity and Ritual* (Washington, D.C.: Smithsonian Institution Press, 1982) 28–29. See also Turner's *The Ritual Process* and his *Dramas, Fields and Metaphors: Symbolic Action in Human Society* (Ithaca, N.Y.: Cornell University Press, 1974).

Chapter Five

Emergent Creative Liturgies in Africa

The discussion in the previous chapters prepares us to examine or display the emerging creative Christian liturgies in Africa. The gesture, the ritual-symbol, the myth-narrative, and the transition rituals that enable passengers to move with confidence through the various stages and crises of life in this world are all rooted in ethnic experience. Christian liturgy insofar as it is ritual-gesture, insofar as it is symbol, creating an environment for the encounter between God/Christ and the assembly, must be particular. This principle of particularity is evident in the diversity of Churches the apostles left behind. It was acknowledged from Irenaeus of Lyon to Gregory the Great. During the first wave of the unification of the liturgy in the West (eighth through ninth centuries, under Charlemagne and Alcuin), uniformity was preferred to difference. Stricter uniform rules were applied during the reform of Gregory VII (eleventh century, the second wave of liturgical unification in the West). This pontiff identified the uniform practice of the Roman liturgy as the only genuine expression of the Christian faith. However, the Eastern Churches always jealously guarded the principle of difference. The wind of change caught the West from Pius XII and climaxed in the Vatican Council II. It was a reaffirmation that particular practices do not introduce confusion, rather they display the vest of many colors that make up the unity of the body of Christ.[1]

We introduce this chapter with a brief account of the diversity of ways in which a united Church of Christ expressed the following of the master. This led to the emergence of the various groups or families of Christians within given sociocultural areas practicing different rites. Then we will describe and critically assess the emerging liturgical practices in various parts of sub-Saharan Africa as a continuation of the same process of diversification. The tensions that today accompany such divergent practices are only the normal birth-pangs of emergent rites. Our description will focus on English- and French-speaking West Africa, Central Africa, and East Africa.[2]

THE EMERGENCE OF MULTIPLE RITES IN THE ONE CHURCH OF CHRIST

The story of the Easter controversy gives us clear evidence of the negotiations in the post-apostolic Church to contain divergent practices. The churches of Asia Minor followed the ancient Jewish Passover practice by celebrating Easter (breaking their fast) on 14 Nisan, while Rome and the West moved the feast to the Sunday of Easter. The bishop of Rome (Pope Victor) was intent on imposing Roman practice on the churches of Asia. He threatened to break communion with Asia Minor. But Irenaeus of Lyon, called peacemaker by Eusebius, exhorted Victor to be tolerant. Irenaeus was negotiating "in behalf of the peace of the churches." He reminded Victor that his predecessors welcomed the divergent practice. He concluded, "the disagreement in regard to the fast confirms the agreement in the faith."[3] Even though the Great Church decreed a uniform calendar during the Council of Nicaea (325 C.E.), the point made by Irenaeus continued to be the prevailing principle.

The pattern of differing practices is not limited to establishing the liturgical calendar. The Latin Church in North Africa was frequently dogged with problems related to church membership. There were, for example, problems related to Novatian baptisms, Donatism, and the attitudes to adopt toward the *lapsi* (those who denied the faith during the persecutions). During the time of Cyprian, North Africa openly differed from Rome on both ecclesiology and church discipline. The North African Church refused to recognize heretical (Novatian) baptism, while Rome, under Pope Stephen, held the opposite view. Consequently, Stephen refused to receive a delegation from North Africa. Cyprian's response was to insist that the unity of the Church must be maintained. While not abandoning his ecclesiology and church discipline, he declared, "It is necessary that each one of us express his feelings on this issue without judging anyone or cutting him off from communion if he is moved to think in a different way."[4] Thus on a major issue such as church membership Cyprian insisted that divergences of practice should be respected.

Augustine of Hippo was later to resolve the issue of heretical baptism for the West by modifying the North African discipline while not abandoning it totally. He approved of Cyprian's view that one is free to feel differently while preserving communion.[5]

These two examples show the Bishop of Rome opposing particular practices in Asia Minor (the East) and North Africa (a very powerful local church in the West). Bishops of Rome also supported divergence in practice. When Leander of Seville enquired from Pope Gregory the Great (d. 604) whether there should be a single or a triple immersion for baptism, he replied, *"De trina vero mersione baptismatis nil responderi verius potest quam ipsi sensitis, quia in una fide nil officit sanctae ecclesiae consuetudo diversa"* (Concerning the triple baptismal immersion one may indeed follow one's feelings; for, provided there is one faith, diverse customs of the Holy Church are not harmful).[6] The same Gregory is supposed to have encouraged Augustine of Canterbury to choose from various liturgical traditions what he considered suitable for English Christians:

"If you have found something more pleasing to almighty God, either in the Roman or in the Frankish or in any other Church, make a careful choice and institute in the Church of the English — which as yet is new to the Faith — the best usages which you have gathered together from many Churches. . . . Therefore choose from each particular Church what is godly, religious and sound, and gathering all together as it were into a dish, place it on the table of the English for their customary diet."[7]

Even if some may legitimately doubt the authenticity of this letter, the tone is not in dissonance with authentic letters of Gregory.

These different practices pertaining to the sacred liturgy, the divergent usages, the juridical and administrative norms proper to local churches in Asia Minor, Rome, North Africa, etc., cumulatively led to the emergence of what are called liturgical rites. The rite, in this sense, does not simply apply to a single action of, for example, sacramental administration. Rather, it touches all expressions of the faith particular to a local church. The definitive emergence of such rites in the Christian Church depended on a number of factors, including dividing Christian groups into ecclesiastical provinces following the prevailing Roman political outfit, turning some local churches toward more influential metropolitan centers like Rome, Alexandria,

Antioch, and Constantinople, and the geographical location of a given sociocultural group. In addition, political realities, doctrinal controversies, and cultural and linguistic differences contribute in no small way to divergent practices. The crucial factor of the political realities in the Roman empire led to the emergence of two major liturgical blocks: the Western and Eastern liturgies. Within these two major blocks, liturgical families and types developed their own specific rites.

THE PRINCIPAL LITURGIES OF THE WEST AND THE EAST

The Western Church today only recognizes two rites: the Roman rite and the Ambrosian rite. Before the unification of the Roman liturgy, referred to above, the West had, in addition to the two surviving rites, a group known as the Gallic rites. These are the Gallican, the Mozarabic, and the Celtic rites. The dominant position of the Western popes and their ideology of unity (especially from Gregory VII) ensured uniformity in practice. But local conditions continued being imposed until the Council of Trent, when rigid uniformity became the norm (the Missal of Pius V [1570] and the Roman Ritual of 1614).

The overriding concern of the Eastern Church is diversity. Two major groups or families emerged — the Antiochene and the Alexandrian groups — along with subgroups already discernible from the fourth century. The Antiochene group is made up of the West and East Syrian rites. The West Syrian subgroup includes the Syro-Antiochene, the Maronite, the Armenian, and the Byzantine rites. In the East Syrian subgroup, the Nestorian, Chaldean, and Malabar rites are practiced. The liturgies of the Alexandrian group are the Coptic and Ethiopian rites. These Eastern rites are still practiced today. Some have united with Rome (uniates) without abandoning their particular practices.

From merely listing these rites without describing them, one notices the clear option in the East for diversity, as opposed to the Western inclination toward uniform administration and usages. As Congar says:

"The East remained fixed to the idea of local or particular churches in communion one with another in the unity of faith, love, and the Eucharist; unity realised in [mutual] exchange and communication. Then, when it becomes necessary a council is held. Unity of communion! The West, severed from North Africa by Islam, accepts the authority of the Roman see, which in the course of history, occupied more and more place."[8]

The inclination of the West toward uniformity was definitively broken by the Vatican Council II. The Council's document on the liturgy contains a general statement on the decision to move away from the uniformity and rigidity that flowed from the Council of Trent (*Sacrosanctum concilium,* no. 37). This general statement emphasizes the Church's openness to welcome patterns of behavior (gestures, rituals) of diverse groups of peoples, provided these patterns are not in conflict with the faith.

"Even in the liturgy, the Church has no wish to impose a rigid uniformity in matters which do not involve the faith or the good of the whole community. Rather she respects and fosters the spiritual adornments and gifts of the various races and peoples. Anything in their way of life that is not indissolubly bound up with superstition and error she studies with sympathy and, if possible, preserves intact. Sometimes in fact she admits such things into the liturgy itself, as long as they harmonize with its true and authentic spirit."

There is no doubt here that the Council wishes to reaffirm and assume once again the patristic principle of diversity. From the pontificate of the humanist Pope Leo XIII, the attitude of the Roman Church toward the Oriental rites had changed. These rites were once again being respected as an adornment for the Church and an affirmation of the divine unity of the Catholic faith.[9] Vatican II has widened this application of unity in diversity to peoples of the Western rite.

According to the Council's decree on the liturgy the return to diversity is realized in two moments. First of all, there may be an adaptation of the typical editions of the liturgical books of the Roman rite to different groups "provided the unity of the Roman rite is maintained" (nos. 38–39). Second, there may be a more radical adaptation. As the Council Fathers declared:

"In some places and circumstances, however, an even more radical adaptation of the liturgy is needed and entails greater difficulties.

"Therefore:

(1) The competent territorial ecclesiastical authority mentioned in Article 22, par. 2, must, in this matter, carefully and prudently consider which elements from the traditions and genius of individual

peoples might appropriately be admitted into divine worship. Adaptations which are judged to be useful or necessary should then be submitted to the Apostolic See, by whose consent they may be introduced" (no. 40).

It is because this declaration of Vatican II is such a radical shift from previous (post-Tridentine) liturgical discipline that the Fathers of the Council expressed the need for care and study in its application.[10] This radical adaptation is what many refer to today as inculturation. When this process is applied to Africa, the faith becomes culture, Christ in the members of his body becomes African, an African Christianity emerges, and the liturgy becomes a sumptuous cultural experience. This radical adaptation creates a unity in the Church that not only embraces diversity, but is indeed verified in diversity.[11] The emergent liturgies in various parts of sub-Saharan Africa described below are realizations of this radical adaptation or inculturation.

THE LITURGIES OF AFRICA

Successful liturgical inculturation makes the Christian liturgical celebration a cultural experience. When we reviewed experiences of liturgical inculturation in the first chapter, we saw that the move toward truly African Christian liturgies since Vatican Council II has not been impressive. The blame for this slow process rests on the church leadership in Africa. The leaders of the church in Africa (bishops and priests), who are implementing the reforms of Vatican II, were mainly brought up in the monolingual pre-Vatican II liturgy. They faced the onerous task of reconciling the multiplicity of languages and cultures in Africa to the need to celebrate and transmit the liturgy of the universal Church (generally understood by them as the Roman rite). This task required study, knowledge, and courage. Many of the leaders felt safer in prudential compliance with the received typical editions of the Roman liturgy that allowed few adaptations. They therefore ignored the pluriform stance adopted by Vatican II on liturgical matters. Few bishops, like the late Cardinal Malula of Kinshasa, saw the emergence of a truly African and Christian Church in an independent Africa as a viable option. Moves toward this radical direction, when not deliberately obstructed, have been very slow.

Despite the hesitancy of the Church leadership and the slow movement toward African rites, indications are that there is no going back from the emergence of local liturgies in Africa. Certain key gestures adopted in various African regions, thanks to the reforms of Vatican II, have become widespread all over Africa. These include the use of the vernacular language; the adoption of local liturgical hymnody accompanied by drums, gongs and other native instruments, hand clapping, rhythmical swaying, and dancing; and the increasing visibility of local liturgical art and architecture. These elements have started to demarcate liturgical life in the African region.

The rediscovery of the power of the Word of God since the reforms of Vatican II has also made a very powerful impact on Roman Catholic celebrations in Africa. Before the reform, the use of the Bible was associated with Protestant worship, as recitation of the rosary was with Roman Catholic worship. But with the reforms of the council, the love for the Word of God among Africans was predictably extended to the Jewish-Christian Scriptures in African Catholic celebrations. For in Africa:

"The word is everything,
It cuts, flays.
It models, modulates.
It perturbs, maddens.
It heals or kills.
It amplifies or lowers according to its force.
It excites or calms souls."[12]

The celebration and sharing of the Word of God along the patterns of African rhetorics (audience participation, gestures, lyrical interventions) are acquired and practiced all over Africa. Similarly, everyday concerns are integrated into the celebration of the liturgy (Word and Eucharist) in the form of bidding prayers rendered spontaneously. These crucial gains from the liturgical renewal of Vatican II are presupposed in the review of liturgical creativity in the three African regions. They all indicate a point of no return toward emergent local liturgies in Africa.

In critically examining the various directions liturgical creativity is approached by each region, we move from the general concerns of the region to the specific areas where each region has started making contributions. Thus in West Africa, there are particular ways in which the Eucharistic celebration is turning native among the Ashanti, Yoruba, and Igbo groups. But the emerging liturgical contribution of this region to African Christianity and to the universal Church is in developing Christian passage or transition rites. This region has consequently produced a very well-developed adaptation of traditional initiation rites to the received Christian rite of initiation (the Moore ritual in the diocese of Diebougou, Bourkina Faso); a Christianization of traditional naming ceremony (as distinct from baptism) among the Yoruba of Nigeria; and the Christianization of Igbo (Nigerian) patterns of passing through crises in life with adequate rites that heal or enhance relationship (*igba ndu,* ritual covenanting). Also in Central and East Africa afflictions by witches, evil men, and spirits may be resolved by participation in charismatic prayer that is widely diffused in this region. But the emergent liturgies of these areas are concentrating on the Eucharistic celebration and the consecration of virgins. Thus we shall examine the Cameroonian Mass, the Zairean Mass, the Eucharistic Prayers of East Africa, and the ritual for the consecration of virgins in Zaire.

Liturgical Creativity in the West African Region

This region is divided into two linguistic groups: English- and French-speaking. Liturgical experimentation has been going on among the two language groups, but the experimentations among the French-speaking peoples have caught the attention of watchers of liturgical inculturation more than the "quiet revolution" taking place in the English-speaking region. We shall first of all examine the emergent Christian rituals of the English-speaking groups, then discuss the experiments in Francophone West Africa.

The Liturgies of English-speaking West Africa

There is an interterritorial umbrella covering the episcopal conferences of English-speaking West Africa — the Association of Episcopal Conferences of Anglophone West Africa (AECAWA). This association held an important assembly in August 1989 where it studied the theme for the African synod, Evangelization (inculturation, social communications, and priestly formation). Inculturation is thus one of the concerns of this region. The bishops like to pass on to the Catholic Institute of West Africa (CIWA), located in Port Harcourt, Nigeria, the task of helping the local churches of the area make the gospel become fully cultural. In addition to CIWA, seminaries and theological associations in the region are participating in the popular enterprise of making Christianity native in the West African region.[13] While these institutions announce and critique local efforts of inculturation, the real task of creation is done by those who are so gifted and who are in touch with life in each local church.

Experiments geared toward adapting the typical editions of the Roman liturgy are on course in English-speaking West Africa. Some of these adaptations have gone beyond the limits of preserving the unity of the Roman rite. They already chart ways for the emergence of new rites. For example, among the Ashanti of Ghana the Corpus Christi celebration is adapted to the *Odwira* festival (the yearly outing of the *Asantehene,* the Ashanti king). It is a ceremony suffused with color and meaning. The same emergence of the king has been integrated into rituals surrounding the consecration during the Eucharistic Prayer. Among the Igbo of Nigeria, the same Corpus Christi festival is celebrated as *Ofala Jesu* (Jesus' annual outing as king) with fanfare, cannon shots, song and dance, etc. Another rather striking adaptation among the Igbo is the introduction of patterns of cooperative development or improvement unions into the rite of the "presentation of gifts" during the Eucharistic celebration. This may require more detailed description.

The presentation of the gifts or offerings in procession, according to the Roman rite, involves bringing the bread and wine to the altar accompanied by the offertory song. Money or gifts for the poor and the Church may also be collected or brought forward during the preparation of the gifts.[14] Among the Igbo this has been converted into a procession of song and dance by everybody in the assembly to present his or her gift to the Lord. It has become a fundraising strategy to ensure a self-reliant church. Offertory hymns are carefully worked to inspire participation. The procession is accompanied by singing, hand-clapping, and dancing. The minister often stands before the altar to sprinkle holy water on those presenting their gifts. The most dramatic display of this kind of presentation of gifts is on Holy Thursday (Chrism Mass). Parishes, sodalities, religious communities, and organizations within the diocese come forward with gifts of all kinds. Bishops who may have reservations about charismatic hymns, hand-clapping, dancing, and percussion evocative of jazz encourage or allow the free performance of these in order to generate as much revenue as possible. In Nsukka diocese, Holy Thursday 1993, this procession lasted for over two hours in a four-hour Mass. The choir of the charismatic prayer group (distinct from the church choir) held the field for the duration of the procession. There were thirty-two different songs in which the people actively participated. There may be exaggerations (even abuses) in this pattern of prayer,[15] but there is little doubt that there is an integration of local attitudes prevalent in improvement unions into the church discipline and worship. The local attitude toward benevolent spirits and the expression of intensive prayer through sacrifices are also linked to the popularity of this presentation of gifts. This pattern of raising funds for the needs of the church is not limited to Igbo communities, but it is most pronounced among the Igbo. "If the Ibo's highest expression of himself is in finance, then it is no doubt that he should sanctify it in this way."[16]

These adaptations of the typical editions of the Roman rite may not yet be seen as radical. There is, generally, very little encouragement or support of radical adaptation by the clergy, individual bishops, or conferences of bishops. For example, the Mass composed by Bishop Sarpong of Kumasi (Ghana) has not been practiced and it failed to attract the support of his clergy. In a similar way, a liturgical research group, established in the Awka diocese of Nigeria, was not permitted to experiment on a proposed Igbo Mass after three years of research.[17] The interdiocesan liturgical commission for Igbo-speaking areas of Nigeria has published a "Proposed Rite of Marriage," which tries to transform the native patterns of celebrating marriage into a Christian celebration. But this is still on paper. The fundamental characteristic of liturgy or ritual is action (practice). We shall therefore not concern ourselves with compositions that have never been experimented within a given group. Consequently, our critical assessment of radical adaptations of the liturgy in the English-speaking areas of West Africa will be limited to the naming ceremony among the Yoruba Catholics of Nigeria, and the *igba ndu* or ritual covenanting among the Igbo Christians also of Nigeria. The first has received the official approval of the Oyo and Ibadan dioceses and is generally practiced all over Yorubaland. The latter has depended mostly on the initiative of individual pastors for the composition of the liturgical structure, the ritual text, and the place and occasion for its celebration.

The Christianization of the Naming Ceremony among Yoruba Catholics. Each newborn baby is a little creature of its culture. It is born into an established community with patterns of behavior proper to it. Among many sub-Saharan African groups, the naming ceremony, which takes place eight days after the biological birth, is the occasion for the "social birth" of a child. This ceremony makes the child a member of the community. The naming ceremony is the first major (and symbolic) gesture through which African societies begin the socialization of the child — the beginning of his or her social definition as a person. Infant baptism, among Christians, has overshadowed this native African practice. The gesture, when retained among groups, does not enjoy its original importance. However, among the Yoruba of Nigeria, the traditional patterns are not only retained but have been adapted to the changing world and to the Christian faith. It is cherished as a tradition that may be maintained along with Christian baptism. As the general introduction to the ritual says, "We should not see this type of naming ceremony as a new form of baptism, rather it is another form of tradition which is not against our Christian belief."[18]

There are two remarkable features of the naming ceremony among the Yoruba and other African groups like the Igbo. The first is the imposition of a name or names that display the web of relationships through which the individual is defined. The neonate is linked to loved ancestors, to the day of the week, to prayers made to God or spirits, to particular wishes or experiences of the parents, and so on. Normally the Yoruba go to the *Ifa* oracle to find out the neonate's mission in the world; this is reflected in the name. Naturally, Christians are not expected to go to the *Ifa* oracle. As the introduction to the Christianized Yoruba ritual states, "as Christians we have no other *Ifa* than our Lord Jesus Christ." No child is given a name without this close attention to the linkage with the past. This, in a way, already designs the broad outlines of the individual's future (destiny).

Second, the skills necessary for the child to achieve "personhood" are already anticipated in the instruments presented to the newborn. These are the tools that the social group uses to produce competent humans as defined by the culture. We shall see this in detail in the Yoruba text. Nwabuisi has drawn attention to the importance of skills and relevant instruments for acquiring them in the study of native child-rearing. This is an area that has not interested researchers on the socialization of children. According to Nwabuisi:

"Experts researched into how the child is taught how to manage the intake of food, the discharge of waste, and control of sexual and aggressive impulses in most cases. Research on socialization very rarely addressed itself to the acquisition of broad arrays of skills, qualities, habits and motives. It has next to nothing on modes of moral functioning. All these are very necessary for the adequate social operation of any man or woman in the society."[19]

The core of the naming ceremony is precisely the exposure of the neonate to these skills. They are, needless to say, not yet acquired. But they are highlighted in the ritual to underline that the path toward full development as a responsible member of the group is assured. It imposes an obligation of mutual relationship on both the social group (through the family) and the neonate.

THE RITE OF NAMING A YORUBA CHILD. The rite of naming the child among Yoruba Catholics has eleven parts. It begins with (1) an opening song invoking the Holy Spirit or calling to the Lord for mercy, followed by (2) an opening prayer by the leader or any other person so designated. (3) Next, a Scripture passage is read from one of the following suggested texts: Exodus 2:1-10 (birth, adoption, and naming of Moses); 1 Samuel 1:19-28 (birth, naming, and offering of Samuel to God); Mark 10:13-16 (blessing of the children by Jesus); Luke 1:59-66 (naming ceremony of John the Baptist); Luke 2:21-28 (Jesus' naming and presentation in the Temple). This is followed by (4) a short homily, (5) reading of the Magnificat (Luke 1:46-55), (6) naming of the child, (7) blessing of the child with the relevant tools for becoming a person, (8) a song or words of encouragement from any participant, (9) an expression of thanks from the parents of the newborn, (10) prayer and grace, and (11) the presentation of the gifts to the newborn by the guests. The ceremony closes with light refreshments.

The naming ceremony is normally performed in the early hours of the morning (between 5 and 6 A.M.). The local catechist usually presides. The Christianization of the traditional ritual is ensured by placing the core ritual (parts 6 and 7) within the context of readings from the Christian Scriptures and prayers. The text of blessing the child is reproduced after the names are given. This communicates the principal intentions of the rite.

For steps six and seven — naming and blessing the child — the leader of the assembly takes the child from the parents and asks them for the names they have given the child. The leader calls the names and all present repeat them. Then the leader stands the child up and welcomes him or her to this world. This is followed by the blessing with the elements for becoming a person as determined by the social group:

(1) Water: NN (name of the child is called), this is water. Taste and see. No one can do without water. Drink it and eat with it on earth. When you use water may it not bring you sickness. May you drink it and have life; may you not be drowned.

(2) Salt: This is salt. NN, taste and see. The world is full of flavor. Salt is used for preservation. May God preserve your life from your enemies; may you not be rejected in the world.

(3) Honey: NN, this is honey. Taste and see. It is full of sweetness. It gives delight to the body. May you be happy; may your stay in the world be full of pleasures.

(4) Kola nut: This is kola nut. NN, taste and see. Among the trees in the bush, the kola tree is head. May the Lord make you head in your family and community. The kola nut contains many parts. May your way be blessed, and may the Lord drive away all evil from you.

(5) Bitter kola: This is bitter kola. Taste and see. It is a symbol of old age. NN, may you grow old and may you live to see your grandchildren and great-grandchildren.

(6) Alligator Pepper: NN, the alligator pepper built its home in one place (unity). It contains many seeds. May you be fruitful in life and may your children be united and blessed.

(7) Sugar (or sweetened food): NN, the world is full of sweet things. Taste and see. Eat the good things of this world and grow. May the Lord provide for your daily bread. May evil never come your way wherever you work for your daily bread.

(8) Palm oil: The pride of the soup is the oil. NN, this is palm oil. Taste and see. May your life be full of joy, good fortune, and peace; may the Lord care for you and be with you.

(9) Fish: This is fish. Taste and see. The fish never complains of cold. NN, may the cold of this world spare you, and may you be blessed.

(10) Wine: NN, this is wine. Taste and see. A man full of wine is always full of life. May you be respected among your people; may you draw people to your side and share your wealth with them.

(11) Money: This is money. NN, what makes a person is money. Take it in your hands. May you have a lot of it. Use it to help others.

Use it to become a rich person, and may you prosper in all your undertakings.

(12) Pen: Knowledge is power. It is the way to success. NN, take this pen in your hands. May God give you wisdom and knowledge. May you use this wisdom to renew the face of the earth. Use it to help your relatives and others.

(13) White cloth: NN, for our forefathers, the white cloth is a symbol of good behavior and a sign of victory. May the good Lord clothe you with good manners, and may you be victorious in life over all your enemies and those who do evil.

(14) Candle: Where there is light, darkness gives way. NN, take this light in your hands. May your star be bright until your old age and your death. May the light drive away all spirits of evil from you; may the Lord Jesus be with you.

(15) Bible: The fear of God is the source of all wisdom. NN, this is the Bible, the word of God, the holy book. Love your God and serve him. Let his law be in your heart all the days of your life to enlighten you; may your life be blessed.[20]

CRITICAL REMARKS. The Yoruba child is born and introduced into the Yoruba (African) world through this ritual. This is the way toward the emergence of the Yoruba human type. Each child is welcomed as a unique creation. The names imposed on the newborn baby already encapsulate his or her destiny.

The elements used to bless the child are replete with symbolism. This is brought out in the suggested words of blessing that accompany the bestowal of each of the items to the child. These elements come from the culture and speak to the occasion.

One does not miss the insistent refrain "taste and see." The neonate is being introduced into a world, as defined by Yoruba culture, where humans are at ease. They receive with thanks the pleasurable things God created. Their enterprise — note the stress on success, making money, victory over enemies, etc. — ensures the continuation of these good things for the benefit of one's relatives and other inhabitants of this world. One is immersed in a world-affirming rather than a world-denying culture. There is no indication from the ritual that the Yoruba human type wants to escape from this world.

The naming rite gives birth to the child into a world-affirming society. It gives the baby a taste of what it is destined to enjoy, encounter, and achieve as an adult. "The child is the father of a man," as the saying goes. The joys and pleasures of life, the struggles, fears, and pains encountered in living, are all displayed in this naming ceremony. What is of value and what brings honor are reaffirmed by the community that projects the same unto the child. Visitors to Yorubaland may be struck by the lack of distinction between the way children and adults dress. The child is not only a potential adult; he or she has already started experiencing the full adult life from childhood. This is a very optimistic view of the universe. This optimism explains the inclination of the Yoruba toward celebration. The joy and optimism that dominate the ritual birth of the child into the social group is only a foretaste of what punctuates all of life.

This Christian liturgy of naming the child is rooted in the Yoruba ethnic experience. The integration or adoption of such a ritual into Christian practice is made easy by the parallels existing between the African and the Jewish ways of naming the child. It is therefore easy to select passages from the Jewish-Christian Scriptures for the celebration. There is no doubt that the core of the ritual is Yoruba, yet its adoption into Christian practice introduces a shift into this ethnic ritual. The Lord God addressed in the prayers and blessings remains the same Olorun or Olodumare experienced in both the Yoruba and the Jewish-Christian traditions. But the function of the spirit of divination (Ifa or Orunmila) has been suppressed. The names that reveal the mission (destiny) of the child in the world are chosen through the mediatorship of Jesus Christ. God and Christ have assumed the powers attributed to the spirit of divination. In this way a traditional ritual rooted in ethnic experience succeeds in being fully expressed in Christian categories. Consequently, the Yoruba world into which the neonates of Yoruba Christians are introduced becomes enriched thanks to the interpenetration of the Yoruba practice and the Christian faith.

In a seminar held at Awka in November 1992 on the theme "The Naming Rite in Some of Our Cultures, and Implications for Inculturation of the Rite of Baptism," the naming rites in Yoruba and Igbo cultures were discussed. The participants stressed "the need and importance of inculturational catechesis, further research, creative experimentation, and the importance for the Naming Ceremony to be included within the context of the sacrament of Baptism."[21] The integration of the neonate into the Yoruba world through a Christianized rite followed by another integration of the same child into the Christian "commonwealth" through baptism may appear an unnecessary duplication. Both should therefore be merged. Baptism should be inserted at a certain stage in the naming rite, or, alternatively, elements of the naming ceremony should be integrated into the Christian baptism. Both options are possible provided the principal thrust of Christian baptism is maintained, and provided the rich Yoruba naming ceremony does not disappear (as the Igbo ceremony has more or less disappeared).

However, maintaining the two rites as independent segments of an expanded initiation liturgy appears to be a better option. Tertullian's argument that people are made not born Christian has not been faulted despite the fact that neonates from Christian families are born Christian. The rite for child baptism is an adaptation of the rite for the baptism of adults. The rite aims at adult converts. On the other hand, the naming rite given above aims at introducing the child into the world as defined by the Yoruba culture. The rite is made for children. The Christian rite of baptism could learn from the Yoruba naming ritual motifs, like the joy and optimism that inspire the Yoruba worldview. But a radical adaptation of the rite of baptism should not be based only on the rite of naming the child. It should be based principally on the initiation of adults, which inspired the recent reforms of the Roman rite of Christian initiation.

Christianization of the Igba Ndu (Ritual Covenanting) among Igbo Catholics of Nigeria. Igba ndu literally means binding life together. The referent (or ritual anchor) ensuring the effectiveness of the ritual is God and/or the spirits. The visible signs are symbolic objects like kola nut, *ogirisi* leaf (from the life tree, *newbouldia laevis*), the *ofo* (consecrated stick cut from the *detarium senegalense* tree).

The traditional ritual opens with (1) an invocation of God, spirits, and ancestors, (2) a declaration of the points at issue necessitating the ritual, as already agreed upon by the parties, (3) and the commitment of the parties in form of an oath or promise to abide by the terms declared. This is called *inu iyi* (literally, swallowing or drinking *iyi*). *Iyi* is a mystical object imbued with force through contact with God or spirits. *Iyi* is also a generic term for stream. Each stream is guarded by a spirit. Drinking *iyi* leaves one open to the power of the spirit to save or to kill. Thus *igba ndu* ritual brings blessings when the terms are adhered to. But when the terms of the agreement are broken, one becomes the target of the wrath of the spiritual powers. Finally, (4) the kola nut is the principal meal of the ritual. It is broken and placed on *ogirisi* leaf or dipped in palm oil. Each participant consumes a piece of the nut to seal the bond. This symbolizes sharing life together. Among friends or lovers, an incision is made and the nut is dipped in their common blood and eaten by intimate friends. This also shows an intense sharing of life.

The Igbo, like most sub-Saharan African peoples, experience personhood as relationship. They developed the *igba ndu* ritual as a way of enhancing or healing relationships. Situations that give rise to this ritual include crisis in nuclear or extended family relationship, marriage in crisis, disharmony in kindreds or village-groups. Furthermore, setting up small scale businesses involving more than one person, the enhancement of confidence in clubs and similar associations, and any crisis that may arise in places of work may call for such a ritual. Friends and lovers may also strengthen their relationship by going through this ritual. One may think that modernization and the influence of Christianity would have reduced the need for this ritual: the courts handle conflicts between individuals and the sacraments (especially the sacrament of reconciliation) should heal the hurts in interpersonal relationships. Rather, the contrary appears to be the case. The sacrament of reconciliation is based on the Roman juridical concept of person that tends to be individualistic. Individual confession and absolution may not easily resolve public conflicts that are also threatening the internal peace of the individual. They cannot be compared with the type of communal ritual and bonding experienced in *igba ndu*. The courts are not always competent to handle certain conflicts touching families, kindreds, and village-groups. In Nigeria, customary courts of law exist.[22] These, however, do not handle conflicts in a holistic way. Consequently, *igba ndu,* which takes humans as they are fully displayed in relationship (to other humans, the world, and spirits), remains popular. Naturally, it is more in demand in rural areas than in urban centers.

THE ADOPTION OF *IGBA NDU* RITUAL IN CHRISTIAN PRACTICE. It may be rare to find pastors who are not familiar with this ritual in the Igbo-speaking areas of the Onitsha ecclesiastical province. The practice is more widespread in dioceses of the north Igbo country (the old

Onitsha province) than in the south (the old Owerri province). In the south the common traditional ritual for healing relationship is known as *igba oriko* (the parties in conflict put their hands into the same dish signifying the sharing of life). This practice is falling out of use. In its place is the Christianized ritual known as *ala di mma* (that the land may be good). Any person seeking residence in the village-group (a woman being married into the village-group, children born outside the locality, strangers) is presented with the code of conduct guiding the community. He or she declares allegiance to the community's pattern of behavior while holding the Bible. This practice is common in Mbaise, a dominantly Christian area. Our example will be restricted, however, to the *igba ndu* ritual as it is commonly practiced among Christians in the north Igbo country.

First of all we note the way groups and communities take their conflicts and crises to popular Roman Catholic priest-healers for resolution. In such a search for the well being of the group or community, distinctions as to religious affiliation become relative. Roman Catholics, Protestants, and practitioners of ancestral religions may participate in the same ritual of reconciliation. The most frequented priest-healers are Father G. Ikeobi (based in Onitsha, north Igbo) and Father E. Edeh (based in Elele, south Igbo). Both priests originate from the north Igbo country. They devise a Christian liturgy based on the traditional *igba ndu* ritual in order to resolve the conflict and heal relationship. The preference for priest-healers is not unconnected with the way the Igbo patronized popular oracles like Ibiniukpabe of Arochukwu (south Igbo) and Agbala of Awka (north Igbo), which were service centers for the resolution of serious conflicts.

However, the majority of those who request the *igba ndu* ritual to resolve conflicts or strengthen relationships present their cases before their parish priests, catechists, or family heads. These also devise Christian liturgies based on the traditional ritual to meet the needs. Some priests integrate the ritual with the Eucharistic celebration. But the more common practice is to celebrate the *igba ndu* as a separate liturgy.

There is no model text similar to the Yoruba rite for naming the child. Improvisation is the rule. The choice of Scripture readings and the movement of the prayer depend on the type of *igba ndu* and the president's ability to create. Conflicts in families, village-groups, and places of work may require texts different from those used in celebrations to enhance relationships among club members and business associates. While heads of families may simply adopt the traditional ritual structure of *igba ndu*, prefacing and concluding it with the invocation of the Lord Jesus, catechists and priests rarely preside over such rituals without Scripture readings followed by words of exhortation.

I am more familiar with liturgies improvised by priests.[23] The liturgy analyzed below is frequently celebrated in Isienu parish (Nsukka diocese) where *igba ndu* is performed very regularly.[24]

LITURGY OF *IGBA NDU*. We have already stated that the core of the traditional ritual consists of invocation of God, ancestors, and spirits; declaration of the terms of *igba ndu*; commitment to the terms by the parties while calling on God and the spirits as witnesses; and partaking of the kola nut. The improvised liturgies used by Catholic priests adopt the core of this ritual in principle. But necessary modifications are made to ensure the Christian character of the ritual.

The model formula used by the parish priest of Isienu displays the following movement: (1) blessing of holy water; (2) opening prayer; (3) Scripture reading; (4) homily; (5) explanation by the priest of the terms already agreed upon by the parties; (6) individual or collective declaration of commitment (oath or promise) to abide by the terms — this declaration is made barefoot; (7) sprinkling of holy water by the priest; (8) kiss of peace in the form of a handshake or an embrace to seal the relationship. In addition to the above exercise, each participant in the Isienu ritual fasts on the eve of the ritual celebration and is obligated to recite the fifteen decades of the rosary — five in the morning, five in the afternoon, and five in the evening. The kola nut ritual (covenant meal) has been replaced by the kiss of peace, but some pastors retain this ritual.

The text for the blessing of holy water is taken from the Roman ritual. The opening prayer, composed by the presiding priest, emphasizes God's power to know and the strength of the oath/covenant to effect the desired result. The improvised text used for various types of the ceremony in Isienu goes as follows:

"Almighty, everlasting, all knowing and loving God, as we have come together for this ceremony of swearing on oath/of making a covenant, we ask you to make effective our work. As you accepted the sacrifice of your servant Abel and the offerings of your high priest Melchisedech, may you receive this oath/covenant your angels are bringing before you. Grant that through this oath/covenant your children assembled here in your presence may be bound together in love, unity, peace, justice and progress. Through our Lord."

The following passages from Scripture are favored: Deuteronomy 30:15-20; Sirach 23:7-14, Ecclesiastes 5:1-5, Matthew 5:33-37. Deuteronomy 30:15-20 is the most frequently used text. It is an exhortation addressed to the community to choose life instead of death, blessing instead of curse — a choice set before the people through the preacher (or Moses). Such a passage naturally leads the presiding priest to instruct those assembled on the implications of the commitment they make. The other passages caution against the tongue and against swearing. In Isienu any of the other texts is used especially in situations where a group may have attempted to swear before the symbols of a local spirit or may have adopted superstitious patterns of oath-taking. For example, there is a popular practice of placing one's hand on the running engine of a car or on the tarred road and pronouncing an oath after having consumed alligator pepper. The belief is that a backslider or one who swears falsely will be run over by a car. The Scripture texts are consequently interpreted as a caution against such superstitious patterns.

The terms of agreement vary according to types of *igba ndu*. The items aim at facilitating the progress of the group, and the security of life, property, and the good name of individuals. Antisocial activities are highlighted in the terms as patterns to be avoided. We reproduce two samples of such an agreement. The one from the Umuezuguonyeke family aims at enhancing family relationship. The other from the Nsukka Road Vigilante Group, Orba, aims at reestablishing trust among the security agents in the Orba village-group.

THE UMUEZUGUONYEKE FAMILY. On this day, 5 June 1993, all the members of the Umuezuguonyeke family agreed (1) to take an oath of peace, love, and progress of the entire family; (2) that no member of the family should harm any member of the family of Umuezuguonyeke; (3) that no member should obstruct in any form any good thing that is due for any member of the family; (4) that no property or right due for the entire family should be claimed or pledged by any single person; such property include landed property and domestic property like animals.

The document was duly signed by three members of the family and three witnesses. The ritual was performed on 25 June 1993.

NSUKKA ROAD VIGILANTE GROUP, ORBA. In an effort to ensure an efficient performance of duty, solidarity, confidence, unity, and faith among members, we have unanimously resolved to take an oath of solidarity. (1) Whoever among the members attempts to poison or poisons a fellow member or instigates another to do so . . . is liable to the death penalty. (2) Any act of aiding and abetting criminals and theft . . . is liable to death. (3) Any member knowing that one is a person's wife and still engages in sexual dealings with her is liable to the death penalty. (4) Whoever among the group . . . assassinates one's character for no just cause is bound to the death penalty. (5) Whoever . . . conspires against the group to bring about the collapse of the vigilante exercise . . . is liable to the death penalty. (6) Whoever reveals the secrets of the group . . . is bound to the death penalty. (7) Whoever indulges in a dishonest act to gain advantage or profit in matters related to the financial affairs of the vigilante group without notifying the group is liable to the death penalty.

The death penalty referred to is executed by God in whose name the oath is taken. The oath was taken on 28 June 1993.

The listing of the items involved in the *igba ndu* ritual is immediately followed by commitment in the following or similar words:

"I . . . take oath in the name of God and declare that I shall faithfully observe all the items in our agreement. If I fail to observe any one of them, let God take away my life; but if I observe all of them with fidelity, let God bestow on me long life and health."

The parish priest of Isienu insists that this declaration be made barefoot. With the feet touching the ground the earth is also witness: *enu fulu gi ana fu gi,* "heaven sees you and the earth sees you." The earth-spirit is the most powerful spirit-force in Igbo cosmology. She sanctions all laws made for the well being of humans in this world.

After the declaration of commitment to the terms of the agreement, the priest sprinkles holy water on the assembly and invites the participants to exchange the sign of peace. It is often touching to see people who have been in conflict and under suspicion embrace one another and sing songs of joy. Some even shed tears.

CRITICAL REMARKS. The Christianized liturgy of *igba ndu* is a good example of integrating authentic cultural values into Christianity. In this way one can say that Christianity is being rooted into Igbo culture.[25] In the process of transforming this ritual of binding life together into Christian practice, Igbo religious symbols, *ofo,* local spirits, and forces are replaced by the Bible and the invocation of the one God through Jesus Christ. The core of the ritual and its fundamental meaning remain untouched. It still functions as a mechanism for healing or enhancing relationship. This is not only an experience of the ritual patterns of a culture being transformed by the Christian faith, but also the novelty of cultural patterns being introduced into the Christian response.

The present deplorable economic situation in Nigeria and the culture of violence that forms part of the social order on account of more than twenty years of military dictatorship breed conflicts. Husband and wife, family members, business associates, and so on, reap the bitter fruit of this condition. Pastoral counseling helps to defuse the conflict. Wise people of the family or kindred, parish priests, and the courts give advice and adjudicate between the conflicting parties. But the Igbo tradition's tested transition ritual for passing through these crises is the *igba ndu.* The Igbo (Africans) believe that human judgment or settlement has to be validated (sanctioned) by the spirits for a measure of lastingness. Consequently, the adoption of *igba ndu* ritual into Christian practice is a testimony of the relevance of Christianity among the Igbo. "Religious forms can be relevant only when they grow together with the culture in which they find themselves."[26]

Granted the relevance of this covenant ritual, care should be taken that it does not become too frequent.[27] Pastors who preside at these rituals should carefully oversee the terms of agreement. These should neither be too numerous nor trivial as to be easily forgotten or ignored.

The language of the oath/promise does not have to tend toward the extreme, "let God take away my life." This language, needless to say, is based on the cursing verses that accompany most prayers among the Igbo. Particular circumstances even give rise to curses addressed to actual or putative culprits by *ofo*-holders of families and kindreds. Ejizu gives samples of these from Ntueke and Urualla (southern Igbo): "Lightening strike you dead, if not let a car kill you, Or still may you never see your house again." This curse was addressed to an actual malefactor:

"Whoever steals from his kin, let this *Ofo* kill him.
Whoever prevents his kin from prosperity, let this *Ofo* kill him.
Whoever seduces the wife of another, despising the husband, let this *Ofo* kill him.
He who toys with the life of others, let this *Ofo* kill him,
All forms of poison, whoever designs one, let this *Ofo* kill him."[28]

These curses are addressed to putative offenders. Their language is similar to the oath/covenant taken in Isienu.

We are aware that the Bible contains cursing psalms and cursing verses within individual psalms. Christians used these with approval in the Liturgy of Hours. But the reformed Liturgy of Hours of the Roman rite has carefully excluded these cursing verses from the psalms. The gospel of mercy prevails over the vengeance of the curses.

Many who approach the *igba ndu* may insist that if the language of the oath/promise is not strong/violent ("take away my life"), it may not be taken seriously. However, the strength of the oath/promise is the presence of God as supreme witness and judge. Thus it suffices to state, "let God be my witness."

This brings us to the gesture accompanying the commitment to the terms of the agreement — going barefoot. This gesture is common in both African traditional religion and the world religions. Many Christian groups in Africa (especially the new religious movements) integrate it into their practice. Some Catholics also prefer to pray in this mode. But going barefoot at the crucial moment of *igba ndu* commitment would, in terms of African traditional religion, put one in direct contact with the powerful earth-spirit (Ala) and the ancestors.[29] One attracts the blessings of the spirits by walking according to the rhythm established by them in the human world, or one becomes the captive of these spirits (easy victim of disease and destruction) when one abandons the patterns sanctioned by them. In the Christianized ritual, God (on high) assumes the powers and function of the earth-spirit and ancestors to bless the faithful followers of the covenant and punish the evil offenders. The danger of syncretism exists. This danger may diminish with adequate catechesis. Indeed the whole enterprise of inculturation is fraught with the danger of syncretism insofar as it involves identifying and adapting core patterns of one religious practice to another. But successful inculturation demands courage, knowledge, study, and creativity. The adoption of *igba ndu* ritual into Christian practice is a courageous step toward inculturation. Those pastors and experts gifted with the art of discovering and creating beauty will bring the required refinements into this liturgy that heals or enhances relationships by binding life together.

Creativity in Francophone West Africa

French-speaking West Africa is more widely known as a place where inculturation and liturgical creativity thrive than its English-speaking neighbor. The Francophone region has also established firm structures for the task of making the gospel local.

The interterritorial episcopal conference covering this region has Benin, Ivory Coast, Bourkina Faso, Mali, Senegal, and Togo as members. In 1963 this conference established an episcopal commission for the liturgy. One of the achievements of the commission was to set up in 1968 an institute for the study of religious culture (Institut Supérieur de Culture Religieuse). This testifies to the commission's interest in relating the gospel to culture. In 1975 the institute was converted into the Faculty of Theology of Abidjan (Institut Catholique de l'Afrique de l'Ouest). The liturgical commission became merged with the commission on catechesis. It is this commission that publishes *Le Calao,* the principal periodical on inculturation in this region.[30]

Traditional religion flourishes in this region (especially in Togo and Benin), and the traditional rites of initiation are still very popular. Among the Joola of Senegal, the Bobo of Bourkina Faso, and the Guerzé of Guinea (Conakry), these traditional patterns of initiation draw the youth to initiation camps. As a way of integrating these local experiences into Christian life, Diatta proposed a Christology where Jesus Christ, first-born from the dead, is proclaimed the *initiated* who in turn becomes the *initiator.* Sanon and Luneau name him "Master of initiation."[31] Liturgical research in this region has predictably concentrated on the rite of Christian initiation.

The Principles for Inculturating Christian Initiation. The general introduction to the 1972 Rite of Christian Initiation of Adults (nn. 30–31) reminds episcopal conferences of the provisions of Vatican II that "Following the pattern of the new edition of the Roman ritual, particular rituals are to be prepared . . . adapted to the linguistic and other needs of the different regions" (*Sacrosanctum concilium,* no. 63b), and the provision for wider adaptations. Liturgical work in the West

African region goes beyond adapting the Roman ritual to its "linguistic and other needs." Concerning the sacrament of Christian initiation, Vatican II had its eye on non-European cultures when it decided to restore the catechumenate having distinctive steps and to revise the rites of the baptism for adults.[32] As the council states in *Sacrosanctum concilium*, no. 65:

"In mission lands initiation rites are found in use among individual peoples. Elements from these, when capable of being adapted to Christian ritual, may be admitted along with those found in Christian tradition, according to the norm laid down in Articles 37–40 of this Constitution."

When the sub-commission on the liturgy of the Francophone episcopal conference of West Africa met in Koumi (Bourkina Faso) on 7–9 July 1974 to deliberate on the principles for relating the gospel to their various cultures, the members faced the crucial question of what to do with the typical edition of the Roman ritual. They felt that three possibilities were open to them: to make a literal translation, to adapt, or to create. Their choice fell on creating rituals that, nevertheless, take their inspiration from the Roman editions.

The creation of new rituals pays close attention to the way certain sentiments and motifs are expressed within a given culture. It also pays close attention to the liturgical structure or the movement of the various actions within a given celebration. The commission expressed its operative principle as follows: "It is not enough to insert some African rituals into a Roman structure, rather what should be done is to rediscover the Christian inspiration in order to create a rite that is truly African."[33] The option is for what Vatican II calls "radical adaptation"[34] or what is commonly called inculturation today.

It may be easy to enunciate a general principle, but it is another matter to give it flesh in liturgical celebration. To create a new rite of Christian initiation involves examining local rituals of initiation that offer to researchers the motifs, sentiments, ceremonial movements, and core elements that may influence the Christian initiation of adults in three stages. The Moore ritual (for use in the diocese of Diebougou, Bourkina Faso) is an example of such a local liturgy that has emerged in Francophone West Africa.

The Moore Ritual. The Moore ritual is based on the traditions of the Mossi of Bourkina Faso. It is an effort to rediscover the spirit of the reformed Roman rite for Christian initiation of adults (catechumenate in stages and baptism of adults) and to make it turn native in the Mossi country.

The adoption of the catechumenate by stages in the reformed Roman ritual is already an adaptation of Christian initiation to non-Western cultures. It has made easy, for the Mossi, the interpenetration of the liturgical movement of Christian initiation with their various types of traditional rites of initiation. The glaring analogies that exist between Christian and native rites of initiation are now converted into an advantage for inculturation. In the past it was a serious problem for missionaries who evangelized this region. Some of these analogies drawn from the Bobo traditions in Bourkina Faso are palpable in the Moore ritual. For example: the tree of the cross and the tree of initiation; the procession into a large courtyard (of a local chief) and procession into the house of God; imposing new names on the neophytes by both traditions, which makes the initiate live the communion of ancestors or saints; the rhythm of formation in stages to acquire a new kind of knowledge and wisdom; and, finally putting on new clothes or being dressed in white.[35] When neophytes from this region approach the inculturated liturgy of Christian initiation it becomes easy for them to appreciate and appropriate Christianity as ancestral tradition.[36]

The Liturgical Structure of the Moore Ritual. The first stage of becoming a catechumen, according to the revised Roman ritual, is the focus of the creators of the Moore ritual. This has the following principal elements: (1) first instruction and dialogue, (2) exorcism and renunciation of non-Christian worship, (3) entry into the church, (4) celebration of the word, (5) dismissal of catechumens, (6) celebration of the Eucharist.

An array of Mossi rituals (initiation and transition rites) is displayed in order to create a local Christian ritual that sets a native enquirer on the route of being changed into a Christian. These can be summarized under three headings. (1) *Mossi family rituals* include elementary politeness, welcoming a stranger with all the rules of hospitality, the ritual of adopting a stranger into a family, and birth and mortuary rituals. (2) In *social rituals* (initiation rites) one is taught, in the isolation of initiation camp, to face the realities of life. There is moral education (obedience, loyalty, self-mastery, honesty, etc.), social education (solidarity), civic education (learning a job, rights, and duties), sexual education (circumcision, sexual deportment), and mystical education (relationship to ancestors, spirits, and forces). Together these lead the candidates to a new birth and a new status. (3) *Royal ritual* includes the investiture of chiefs and the proclamation of their honorific names and programs and the correct pattern of behavior in a chief's compound by the rank and file of the community.

It is from the above array of Mossi rituals that the artists and liturgists created the Moore ritual by putting it in intimate contact with the inspiring spirit of the Roman rite. The rites of the first stage of entry into the catechumenate are more detailed than the second and third stages that lead into the actual liturgy of baptism. The movement of the first stage, which is dominated by Mossi family rituals, especially the hospitality ritual and the ritual integration of a stranger into a family, structure the development of the later stages.

The first stage in the Moore ritual has nine movements instead of the six movements identified in the Roman ritual. (1) *Dialogue preparatory to welcoming the strangers* (i.e., the postulants): the delegates of the community present the postulants' request to the family chief (i.e., the presiding priest) who, according to Mossi custom, insists that all the members of the family (Church) should be consulted. A spokesperson is designated to treat the question. (2) *Welcoming the strangers:* the spokesperson delegated by the priest greets strangers. (3) *Preliminary interrogation:* the postulants tell why they want to enter the Christian community, followed by the official designation of members of the community to act as guides (i.e., godparents) to the postulants. (4) *Exorcism and signation:* each designated official (godparent) makes a sign of the cross on the forehead of his or her ward, tying a crucifix around his or her neck. (5) *Welcome drink:* consists of salt, water, and flour, and is prepared by the godparents. (6) *Naming:* an indigenous name with a religious meaning is given in addition to the name of a saint. (7) *Entrance procession into the family court:* having secured the consent of the family, the postulants leave the court precincts to enter the family court (the Church); they are new (adopted) children of the family. (8) *Celebration of the Word of God:* in the homily, the catechumens are instructed to observe the gestures and actions but not to speak, and to see and learn, since they are ignorant of the family customs. (9) *Eucharistic celebration:* in the presence of the catechumens the Eucharist is celebrated.

The rites of the second stage are dominated by the presentation of the Gospel, the Creed *(traditio symboli)*, and the Lord's Prayer to the new members of the family. This is compared to the Mossi custom of showing the adopted stranger the location of the family freshwater pot.

Stage three is the final step of the catechumenate. The assembled Christian family is assured that the new members have reached a point of no return in the initiation process. They make an accurate recitation of the Creed *(redditio symboli)* and the Our Father. They reject the devil and swear their loyalty to the Christ — the Elder-Ancestor: each neophyte throws his or her name written on a piece of paper into the tomb-baptistery, similar to the ancestral tomb. They then appropriate the secret family force through the anointing with the oil of warriors.

At this final stage, says Ouedraogo, the catechumens have practically completed their social, family, moral, and civic initiations into the Christian community. On Good Friday, they take part in the solemn funeral of the Elder-Ancestor; they bestride and walk over the wood of the Cross, placed on the floor, like elder sons in the Mossi family who bestride the corpse of their father. This is a symbolic gesture of total commitment to correct family behavior. Finally, on Easter night, during the ceremony of investiture of the risen Christ copied from the Moogo royal ritual, the candidates infused with all the title names and program of Christ go through their new birth in water and the Spirit (i.e., Spirit of the Elder-Ancestor). They have become Christians, anointed with the oil of kings. They emerge from the initiation clad in white, and all marks of the old order used during the initiation are burnt.

Critical Remarks. We have already noted that the catechumenate in distinctive steps as an integral part of the process of Christian initiation according to the Roman rite is already an adaptation of the Roman rite for the benefit of non-Western Christians. For the Fathers of Vatican II, it is a restoration of a practice very popular in their time. But it is a practice, as we have seen, that is very close to the experience of many African sociocultural groups. It was therefore easy for the Mossi to integrate their local rites into the Christian response.

The artists and composers who put together the liturgical structure of the Moore ritual saw the Church as the household of God (cf. Heb

3:6). This ecclesiology made it easy for them to capitalize on the wealth of the local family rituals. It is into the family that a stranger is welcomed and shown hospitality (given water and the local brew to drink). Finally, the stranger is initiated into the family as a member. Young people of the family (in the wider sense) become adult by passing through a series of initiation rites. Consequently, in the process of inculturating Christian initiation in Mossi country, the artists were able to call up diverse elements of initiation and transition rituals that deeply touch the life in the family, because the Church is a family. The most prominent are the hospitality rituals, the rites for adopting a stranger into the family, the naming ceremony performed for a neonate, and the funeral rites. It was also easy for the artists to operate with a Christology that identified Christ with the ancestors — the Elder-Ancestor.

The decision to create the Moore ritual from diverse rituals covering many aspects of life in Mossi society is the strength of this liturgy. Any motif of the received Christian rite of initiation can be dynamically related to a possible Mossi equivalent. Here also lies the weakness of the ritual. Some aspects of Mossi tradition may be preserved in the Christian initiation rite, but the greater part of these rites may never be preserved. The local rituals were called upon by Christians to formulate patterns that would be in harmony with the culture but are predetermined by the received Roman ritual. Just as we argued above for the protection of the Yoruba naming ceremony as an independent ritual through Christianization, we should also retain some of the rich Mossi rituals independent from their function in the Christian initiation rite. Many dioceses in the West African region already try to initiate the young who were baptized as infants through a program adapted to the catechumenate in distinctive steps. The pedagogy of traditional initiation is brought to bear on the young, as opposed to the cerebral schooltype method of the past. However, rituals like the naming ceremony, mortuary rites, rites of hospitality, etc., should either be Christianized or be allowed to guard their independence in order to expand the Christian ritual apparatus and retain crucial cultural values among the Mossi.

Creativity in the Central African Region

In the Central African region we encounter the colorful liturgy developed in the diocese of Yaounde (Cameroon) — the *ndzon-melen*

Mass. This is the first radical attempt made in Africa to reorganize the Roman Mass. Cameroon has developed liturgical art work in consonance with native African symbolism, as is shown below.

It is, however, in Zaire that we meet a local church that has made the greatest impact on Christian life in Africa. This church has tried to demonstrate that "unity not only embraces diversity, but is verified in diversity" (John Paul II in Sweden). But since the episcopal mandate to experiment in creative liturgies after Vatican II was received in Cameroon before Zaire, we shall start the narration of emerging liturgies in this region with Cameroon. It is here that the first Eucharistic liturgy expressing African sentiments was produced. The Cameroonian Mass preceded the Zairean liturgy.

Liturgical Creativity in the Diocese of Yaounde

The liturgical experimentation in the diocese of Yaounde is not limited to the Eucharistic celebration. It also covers the areas of liturgical art and the practice of religious or consecrated life. The recently established Faculty of Theology of Yaounde, which has already constituted its department of social sciences, may soon add its weight to the ongoing determination of the Cameroonian church to become local.

Credit goes to E. Mveng, S.J., for the pioneering works on liturgical art expressive of the African perception of the universe. Preoccupied with the development of an anthropology dominated by the victory of life over death and an initiation into life through death, Mveng capitalizes on the symbolism of the mask to direct the emergence of a local Christian art. Africans see in the mask the tension of human life toward spiritualization (ancestral status). The mask reveals that life must not be taken at its face value — there is more to life than meets the eye.[37] Mveng tried to concretize this imagery in chromatic art. Two examples are the imposing painting of the Virgin and Child dominating the sanctuary in the cathedral of Yaounde and the painting of the Stations of the Cross with an interesting combination of colors — red (for kingship and glory), white (for death and the spiritual), and black (for struggle and suffering).

Furthermore, Mveng, a Jesuit priest who is also a UNESCO consultant, has researched African spirituality. He has visited prominent traditional centers of spirituality like the "pagan" monastery at Bê (Togo) and the "fetish" convents of Benin (Nigeria). He also drew from the ancient Egyptian initiation cults of Isis and Osiris and the cult of Lyangombe practiced in Kivu, Rwanda, and Uganda. These inspired him to elaborate a local pattern of religious life in a congregation that he founded (the Beatitudes). It is an attempt to bring together the call of the gospel and African traditions of initiation. In the experiments of a local practice of religious life, according to Mveng, "The essence of religious life becomes the *imitation of* a *divine model* rather than the practice of a teaching."[38] If the experiments of Mveng are limited to his community and workshop, the *ndzon-melen* Mass attracts participants from all over the country.

The Ndzon-Melen Mass. Research into the *ndzon-melen* Mass started before the publication of the Missal of Paul VI in 1969. The major seminarians in Otele were experimenting in Ewondo hymnody from 1958. Father Pie-Claude Ngumu continued the local compositions after his ordination in 1960. Negative comments made by foreign missionaries such as "cries without piety" did not discourage the composers. In 1968 Father Ngumu was appointed to the parish of Ndzon-melen, diocese of Yaounde, with a mandate to experiment on an appropriate African liturgy.[39] The colorful Cameroonian Mass was ready for use in 1969.

The inspiration of the *ndzon-melen* Mass came from the structure of Beti assembly. The Beti assembly is convoked by a member of the group who has a particular problem. The purpose of the assembly is fully and freely discussed by all the participants. When the matter has been fully discussed, the leader summarizes the points and announces the proposed solutions to the problem. The assembly acclaims. At this stage, as a show of gratitude, the host serves a meal to the assembly. This shared meal brings the meeting to an end. In other words, the *word* and the *meal* are shared. In this sharing everyone participates. The *ndzon-melen* Mass lays strong emphasis on participation by the assembly. The choir connects the assembly and the altar: it accompanies the priest with hymns and dance to enthrone the book of the gospel, it joins the priest to acclaim the Lord after the consecration, it directs the congregation during the celebration and presents its gifts.

The Liturgy of the Word is the part of the Mass in which a lot of creative work has been done. Instead of beginning with the penitential rite, this part of the Mass uses the following arrangement: opening hymn accompanied by dance (while ministers are vesting), entrance procession, enthronement of the book of the gospel, readings and homily, the Creed, penitential rite, and Collect.

The first part of the Eucharistic celebration is dominated by the idea of the word of God. The word is enthroned, in song and dance, amid the acclamation of the assembled community. After the announcement of the theme of the celebration by the commentator, all sit to listen to the readings, during which an instrumentalist plays background music. The homily follows the normal patterns of African rhetoric: audience participation. In it the challenge of the word of God is clarified. During the penitential rite, designated members of the assembly announce intentions that concern areas of life of the community and individuals needing conversion. Each intention is followed by a response of supplication. The concluding prayer is the prayer of the day.

It is important to note the readjustment that the composers of the *ndzon-melen* Mass made in the liturgical structure of the Liturgy of the Word. This readjustment is followed in Zaire and East Africa. The attitude of penitence as a preparation for presenting oneself before God, as practiced by the Roman rite, is full of meaning. Humans are not worthy to appear before God. On the other hand, the Cameroonian gesture capitalizes on the fact that if the Lord is convoking the assembly, participants must be told the reasons for the convocation: they sit down to listen to this; they express their regret in areas where they are found wanting. However, the whole celebration is joyous: the word of God is a word of consolation, the enthronement of the book of the gospel is thus in song and dance. There is evil in the world. But evil is neither the first nor the last word. Joyous celebration of the creator precedes every other gesture.

The sharing of the word is followed by the meal — the Liturgy of the Eucharist. The characteristic motif is again joy. There is an outburst of joy during the offertory procession. The color and brilliance of this part of the celebration try to create the image of a celestial liturgy. At the Holy, Holy, Holy, designated young maidens surround the altar to await the bridegroom. The choir joins after the consecration to sing the hymn of praise, Glory be to God, to welcome Emmanuel. The communion is accompanied by joyful hymns and is concluded with a thanksgiving hymn and dance.

This colorful Cameroonian liturgy was projected onto the international scene in 1981 during the Eucharistic Congress at Lourdes. It may have been the first time the assembled world Church participated in a liturgy suffused with African gestures. The African at prayer displays the totality of his or her person in gestures. There is no shame in having a body, rather the person as a whole is manifest bodily. The Cameroonian Mass shows that the dance forms an integral part of ritual through which communication may be established between humans and God.

The Zairean Liturgy

Zaire is located in the heart of Africa. It has a landmass greater than Western Europe, and it shares borders with nine African states. Events in Zaire naturally spill over its borders. Half of the Zairean population of over twenty-four million is Roman Catholic. It may not be an exaggeration to say that the Zairean local church has the greatest influence all over Africa. Its theological, liturgical, and pastoral activities are geared toward evolving a local and responsible church. Experimentations in these areas have influenced other local African churches. As far back as the fifteenth and sixteenth centuries, when the kingdom of the Kongo was evangelized, a Christianity that was self-supporting, self-ministering, and self-propagating and responsive to the Kongo worldview was in operation. The Portuguese Capuchins welcomed the parallel between sixteenth-century European cosmology and Kongo cosmology. Christian ritual practices paralleled those existing in the Kongo tradition. The one replaced the other. At conversion the Christian priest *(nganga)* supplanted the traditional expert *(nganga)* whose charms *(nkisi)* were replaced by Christian sacramentals like medals *(nkisi)*. However, the Italian Capuchins who were invited by the Kongo king in the seventeenth century were intolerant of this "syncretistic" Christianity. Also, the missionaries of the colonial period did not accept this brand of local Christianity.[40]

Colonialism failed to put Christian practice permanently under tutelage in the Belgian Congo (Zaire). Missionaries who favored the emergence of indigenous Christianity encouraged Zairean artistic productions. In the 1920s Father G. de Pelichy initiated ivory carvers of Kivu to sculpt biblical images. And in 1936, to the stupefaction of the colonizers, the Apostolic delegate inaugurated the "First Exposition of Congolese Religious Art." After this exposition of Kinshasa, a specific Congolese Christian art assumed its place in the

Christian world. It was featured in three expositions in Rome (1942, 1950, and 1952).[41]

The impact of the liturgical movement in Belgium after World War II may partially explain the receptive attitude of some Belgian missionaries to experimentation in the Belgian colony. But it is to the passion and initiative of the Zairean people that one must attribute the persistent demand for appropriate local Christian practice. This passion is clearly expressed by the late Cardinal Malula of Kinshasa who, on the day of his episcopal ordination before independence (20 September 1959), declared his wish to build a Congolese (Zairean) church in an independent African state.

The Zairean episcopal conference had established in 1957 a Faculty of Theology given the mission of training seminary teachers and lecturers for higher institutes of learning. It is a faculty committed to research and reflection on African Christianity. This commitment led to the celebrated debate, within the faculty, on the viability of an African theology (1965). In 1966 the *Centre d'Études des Religions Africaines* was set up in the faculty and was charged with the task of elaborating Christian thought penetrated with the realities of African traditions.

It is not surprising, therefore, to hear from the bishops of Zaire (in 1961) that the liturgy introduced by the missionaries was alien to Africans, and that a return to the sources would open the way to fundamental adaptations. When the preparatory liturgical commission of Vatican II assembled (1961), the only African member of that commission, Joseph Malula, auxiliary bishop of Kinshasa, in response to the prayer of A. Bugnigni, rendered the Our Father in Lingala. That was a foretaste of the new liturgy.[42] When the Missal of Paul VI was published (1969), the Zairean bishops established a research committee to produce a Eucharistic liturgy responding to the sentiments of their sociocultural area.

The Eucharistic celebration is, however, not the only area where inculturation has taken place in this region. There are realizations in lay ministry *(bakambi)*, small Christian communities, the rite of priestly ordination, and the liturgy for the consecration of virgins. We shall limit our analysis to the consecration of virgins and the Eucharistic liturgy.[43]

Religious Profession of Women or Consecration of Virgins. When Cardinal Malula founded the Congregation of the Sisters of St. Theresa, he wanted to form girls into authentic African women religious. They dressed in wrapper like African women, to the shock of other foreign missionary congregations (1966). By 1969 this practice was followed by women religious of any congregation in Zaire. In 1967 the novel practice of ritual blood pact was introduced in the profession of the first four sisters of St. Theresa. This ritual, which was welcomed by the faithful and some congregations, upset the balance in the movement of the rite and the meaning (spirituality) of religious profession. It challenged the focus on marriage as the dominant metaphor of religious profession of women. The idea of a covenant bond of friendship or a sharing of life with Christ comes into prominence instead of the unique imagery of the bride of Christ. There is a renunciation of the love of marriage and a total dedication to God in the Zairean ritual. But the dominant ritual is the incision made on the candidate's finger. Among the Theresian sisters the blood is dropped on a white cloth placed next to the altar stone; at communion the religious partakes of the cup of benediction (the blood of Christ) to conclude the blood pact. After some hesitation, other Zairean congregations copied this practice and carried it forward.

The congregations creatively developed their liturgies. The core of the rite — the three vows — is retained. But the rituals of benediction or consecration have assumed local characteristics. We shall draw our examples from the liturgies created by the Congregation of Sisters of Charity and the Mothers of Bethany (Ngandanjika, Kasai).

THE SISTERS OF JESUS. The rite of benediction is integrated within the Eucharistic celebration. The congregation lays emphasis on the role of parents and elders in their ritual. These bear the weight of tradition and transmit the blessing of the ancestors.[44]

After the homily, all remain seated. The presiding bishop addresses the parents on their indispensable role in the life of their child whom they are offering willingly for the service of God. Then there is a dialogue between the bishop, the religious superior, and the candidate. After this dialogue the parents pronounce a benediction over their child. In the region of Matadi, kola nut and palm wine are used for the benediction, while in the province of Kasai cohise chalk is used. In the Kasai province, the father sprinkles the chalk mixed with water on the fingers of his daughter and says:

"My daughter, our Ancestors say, 'the insect which is inside the beans can destroy it with ease.' I gave life to you; I do not take it back from you. I am in accord with your desires. Go ahead and persevere. Let your route be as white as this chalk. 'Do not step on any scorpion or any serpent so that you may march only on soft earth and tender herbs.'"

The mother imposes the chalk on the arms of her daughter making two parallel lines on each saying, "let the work of your hands fructify and be prosperous." Then she imposes chalk on her forehead and cheeks saying, "Let your thoughts never miss the track; go ahead with your desires; do not go backwards."[45]

At Matadi the young religious goes on her knees before her father who takes her by the hand and explains to her the seriousness of her commitment. He then invokes God and calls on their ancestors by name, asking them to bless his daughter. Taking the kola nut from his wife, he chews it and sprays it on his daughter's palms. Then, raising the palms thrice heaven-wards, he pronounces the blessing "sambuka, kinda, siama" (be blessed, be strong, stand firm). Then taking a mouthful of palm-wine from a glass, he swallows some and sprays the rest on his daughter's hands, raising them again thrice heaven-wards and pronouncing the blessing. The daughter responds, "yobo" (so be it).[46] It is after this blessing from the parents that the religious pronounces her vows, followed by the solemn blessing by the presiding bishop.

THE MOTHERS OF BETHANY. The mothers of Bethany use a lot of symbolic objects drawn from their locality. The presiding bishop explains the meaning of these after the homily. The piece of white cloth stands for the inner garment of a woman *(mukaya)*: she is espoused to Christ. The white cloth is tied to banana leaves, which stand for fertility. Then there is leopard skin, the symbol of the Lordship of Christ. The piece of rope used to tie a goat is a symbol of the obedience of the religious to Christ. And the band of hair and necklace removed indicate her detachment from material things.

After these explanations, the rite starts with the blessing of the parents, the dialogue between the bishop and the religious superior, the interrogation of the candidate, and the profession. The profession is in the form of an oath instead of a vow or promise. The symbolic objects are integrated into the candidate's declaration. Thus instead of the familiar formula "I . . . make the three simple vows of chastity, poverty and obedience," each candidate says:

"In the name of the Father and of the Son and of the Holy Spirit. Lord Jesus Christ, you said 'let your yes be yes, and your no be no.' Aided by your grace, and before your representative, our bishop, Monsignor . . . , and in the presence of the community of the faithful, I . . . testify before you that I do not lie. Freely in my heart and spirit I bind myself by an oath to you, almighty God, and to the blessed Virgin Mary. An oath of union which I make by putting on my 'mukaya' in order to keep myself only for my Lord, 'He, holding the leopard, and I, holding the banana tree' [*Yeye mukuata nkashama, meme mukuata cikondakonda,* formula for oaths among the Luba]; an oath of union which I make by taking my heart off terrestrial things; an oath of union which I make by disposing my heart to obey 'as the goat which never refuses the rope of its master no matter how rough it is' [a Luba saying indicating submission], and according to thy words: 'here I am, I come to do your will'; and all this, according to the rule of the Mothers of Bethany."[47]

When all the candidates have pronounced the vow, the bishop gives them each a cross to wear around their neck and a ring. Then he blesses the candidates. Each candidate gives a drop of her blood into a particular chalice reserved for her. At communion she alone drinks from the chalice. This seals the pact or bond between her and the Lord. Alternatively, the drop of blood is taken during communion and posed on the consecrated host, which the religious consumes sealing the covenant with the Lord.

The rites of these congregations show how creatively the gospel has become part of the culture in the Zairean region. The evolving culture is rooted in the memory of ancestors, which does not exclude adaptation to changing circumstances. This ancestral tradition has brought development to the rite of consecration of virgins. The focus has shifted from marriage, which has been the model of the religious profession of women since the Romano-Germanic pontifical of the tenth century. The powerful symbol of the blood pact makes the rite of consecration a sharing of life with Christ, a friendship with Christ; the religious woman is making a total offering of herself to God by offering her blood (placed beside the altar stone).[48] The type of fidelity required by the blood pact is better expressed in the oath rather than in the vow or promise that may have little meaning in the Zairean sociocultural area.

The Zairean Mass. In Zaire, the Roman Missal for the use of the dioceses of Zaire is normally referred to as the Zairean rite. The rite as it is used here is wider than the Eucharistic celebration. It covers all the liturgical, theological, and disciplinary patterns found in the church of Zaire. Consequently, a Zairean rite is still in the making. But since the Eucharist is the focal point of the Church's life, the officially approved Zairean Mass is a sign of a new rite in an advanced stage. The committee of experts established by the Zairean conference in 1969 to research a local Eucharistic liturgy came from a region where ritual assemblies follow patterns similar to the one recorded among the Beti of Cameroon. The reasons for the convocation of the assembly may be social, political, economic, or purely religious. Religious assemblies in the Kongo region may take the following pattern: convocation and gathering of the community under its leader, libations to the ancestors *(bakulu)*, invocation of the ancestors by the chief, awaiting the answer of the ancestors through dreams or revelations, community response to the answer through festive celebration or reconciliation, as the case may be. Coming from such a background, it was clear to the team of experts that the Eucharistic liturgy they would produce would not follow the prefabricated pattern of the Roman Mass. Rather the constitutive elements of the Eucharist should form the basis of creating a local Eucharistic liturgy.

The liturgy that emerged from the research was presented to the sacred congregation of rites for study and approval on 4 December 1973. This liturgy was in use *ad experimentum* until its definitive approval came on 30 April 1988.[49] Our analysis will follow the normal division into Liturgy of the Word and Liturgy of the Eucharist.

THE LITURGY OF THE WORD. The Liturgy of the Word is made up of the following elements: entrance procession (announced and accompanied with hymns and rhythmic swaying), invocation of the ancestors in the faith, Glory be to God or any other song of joy (during which there is dance around the altar), Collect, readings, Gospel, homily, Creed, penitential rite, kiss of peace, and prayer of the faithful.

The Kongo pattern of assembly rooted in ancestral practice has influenced the liturgical structure, the gestures, and the content of this part of the Mass. As Mpongo says it is an assembly of ritual reintegration. Participants greet one another when they arrive at the place of assembly. The announcer calls for silence and invites the choir to intone the opening hymn. There is a solemn entrance. The celebrant recaptures the image of the chief who is the link between the human and the spiritual world. His hat is made of leopard skin or decorated with precious stones or sacred feathers; the ministers standing on either side of him carry symbolic objects that honor a dignitary (e.g., spears). The full participation of the assembly is expressed in responses and songs, rhythmic swaying, hand-clapping, strident cries, etc., all directed by the choir.

The most innovative part of this liturgy is the invocation of the ancestors. On arrival at the altar, the celebrant greets it by raising his hands in a "V" and touching the altar with his forehead. This gesture is made at the four sides of the altar. The number four, in ancestral memory, is linked to the four cardinal points and symbolizes the base of the universe, cosmic completeness. After the call by the priest for recollection in the presence of "the Sun that one cannot gaze at directly" (God), he declares the assembly's association with the saints and ancestors. The invocation of the ancestors is in the following form:

Celebrant: You, our ancestors pure of heart
All: Stay with us.
Celebrant: Come, together, let us glorify the Lord.
All: With those who are celebrating Mass at this hour.

This invocation arises out of the assurance that the ancestors continue to play an important role in the life of the community. The confession of Christ does not make their role redundant. "They constitute ideals of Bantu life. They are 'with me' as a tree carrying its branch."[50] In the Kongo region where a high premium is set on ancestral cult, the true ancestors are the *bakulu* who practiced the law and manifested all the virtues prized by the community. The *bankita* are also respected as original ancestors despite the fact that they perished through wars, assassinations, and suicide. The worthless *batembo* are abominated because they were witches and could still constitute a danger to the community.[51] When the Zairean liturgy invokes ancestors who are pure of heart this prolongation of ancestral memory into Christianity does not constitute a threat to the Christ. The alternative invocation used in some dioceses brings this out.

Celebrant: And you our ancestors, you whose life we prolong, you who have encouraged communion and understanding among humans, you the example of whose life has marked our society! See, Jesus, Son of God, is come to our home, and we received him! He made our life increase; the life in which you are ever present! So, be with us now that we celebrate this event. Be with all our people who celebrate it at this moment.

All: Be with us, be with them all.[52]

The Zairean practice may be likened to the commemoration of the Jewish ancestors during the feast of Atonement (Yom Kippur). The Jewish ancestors named run from Adam to Aaron. This extensive memorial was copied by the Clementine liturgy into its Eucharistic Prayer (i.e., the eighth book of the Apostolic Constitutions).[53] However, the naming in the Zairean liturgy is corporate, as opposed to the individual list of the Clementine liturgy.

The Liturgy of the Word comes to its climax with the readings, homily, and penitential service. During all the readings (including the gospel) the congregation is seated, the common way to receive an important message. The penitential rite that follows the homily or the Creed becomes "a solemn affirmation of the desire to belong to God and to remain in communion with one's neighbour and with the cosmos."[54] The community, having been confronted by the word, invokes the mercy of God:

Celebrant: Lord our God
as the leech sticks to the skin
and sucks human blood,
evil has invaded us.
Our life is diminished.
Who will save us, if not you,
our Lord?
Lord, have mercy!

All: Lord, have mercy!

The gesture during this invocation is the profound bow with crossed arms resting on the chest. Holy water is sprinkled as a sign of purification, and the conversion-reconciliation is sealed by the exchange of peace, normally a warm handshake. The location of the exchange of peace before the Eucharistic liturgy depends on the placement of the penitential rite. It also rejoins an earlier practice of the Western liturgy to give the peace before the offering.

LITURGY OF THE EUCHARIST. The liturgical structure of the Liturgy of the Eucharist has not been reworked. But like the Liturgy of the Word participation of the assembly through gestures and words is ensured. The text of the prayers has been reworked to respond to sentiments of the sociocultural area when expressing motifs like offering, praise, and thanksgiving.

First of all, participants deposit their gifts or offerings in a designated place when they enter the church. During the presentation of the gifts, those designated bring the offerings in an offertory dance. Gifts other than bread and wine are presented to the celebrant by a designated member in the following words:

"O priest of God,
here are our gifts,
receive them;
they manifest
our spirit of solidarity and sharing
and that we love one another
as the Lord loves us."

The priest receives the gifts with a gesture of thanks. Then, bread and wine are presented in words echoing the normal presentation prayer of the Roman rite. The Zairean rite insists that those who present the gifts pronounce an address, since gifts are rarely presented in Africa unaccompanied by speech (see the corresponding Jewish practice in Deut 26:5-10). The local missals being developed by various dioceses of Zaire have also reworked the presidential prayer over the gifts to embody local sentiments. In the Luba missal the prayer said on the fourth Sunday of the year goes as follows: "*Maweya of Cyame,* tempest which uncovers those who clothe themselves with raphia *[madiba]*, strong wind which makes the grass to tremble! Behold our gift, but where is yours? We are waiting for you, now and in the days to come. Amen."[55] The tenderness of God is expressed in the phrase *Maweya of Cyame*; his power is compared to the hurricane, and at the offering of the first-fruits, the rhetorical "where is yours?" accompanies the presentation. All these local sentiments have become part of the Christian response to God.

The Eucharistic Prayer is also replete with local praise vocabulary. It is a prayer modeled on the third-century prayer of Hippolytus of Rome (which has been adopted as the second canon of the reformed Roman liturgy). In the opening praise of the Zairean prayer (theological part), images characterizing the traditional African experience of God are converted into honorific titles:

"You, the sun that is not gazed at directly,
You, sight itself,
You, the master of human beings,
You, the Lord of life,
You, the master of all things."

This preponderance of traditional imagery is also part of the Christological part of the prayer where God who creates through Christ is praised:

"Through him, you created heaven and earth;
Through him, you created the waters of the world, the rivers, streams, lakes and all the fish which live in them.
Through him, you created forests, plains, savannas, mountains and all the animals which live in them."

Full participation of the assembly is ensured during the Eucharistic Prayer by interspersing the prayer with congregational responses. This is a mark of traditional African communal prayer tradition, which has been given a prominent place in many compositions of African Eucharistic Prayers. In the Lingala version of the Zairean liturgy, the Eucharistic Prayer is sung from the opening praise to the doxology. It is arranged in such a way that the assembly joins the celebrant to chant the concluding phrase of each paragraph of the prayer. This pattern of the whole assembly celebrating its Lord and God in one voice reaches a crescendo in the doxology. The formula most frequently used in Zairean churches reflects traditional African pattern of affirming decisions or taking oaths; it also reflects the pattern of shouting slogans at political rallies in Zaire.

Celebrant:	Lord, may we glorify your name
People:	Amen!
Celebrant:	Your name
People:	Amen!
Celebrant:	Very honourable
People:	Amen!
Celebrant:	Father
People:	Amen!
Celebrant:	Son
People:	Amen!
Celebrant:	Holy Spirit
People:	Amen!
Celebrant:	May we glorify it
People:	Amen!
Celebrant:	Today
People:	Amen!
Celebrant:	Tomorrow
People:	Amen!
Celebrant:	For ever and ever
People:	Amen!

The lyrical arrangement and hearty rendition of this doxology are an eloquent testimony of a liturgy that is purposefully assuming its position among the liturgies of the Church of God (the universal Church). The approved Zairean Mass and the experimentations in lay ministry, priestly ordination, small Christian communities, Christian youth movement, consecration of virgins, and so on, all point to a local church that is passionately committed to being fully African and Christian.

Liturgical Creativity in the Eastern African Region

The Roman Catholic Church in Eastern Africa is grouped around AMECEA (the Association of Member Episcopal Conferences of Eastern Africa). AMECEA is a service organization for the national conferences of Catholic bishops in Ethiopia, Kenya, Malawi, Sudan, Tanzania, Uganda, and Zambia from whom it receives its mandate. This organization has a pastoral institute (Gaba Pastoral Institute) established in Uganda in 1967, which moved to Eldoret in 1976. The institute is the chief research organ in the region. The Catholic Higher Institute of Eastern Africa (now the Catholic University of Eastern

Africa) was established later in Nairobi as a further resource institute for the cushioning of a local church.

AMECEA is totally committed to the localization of the church in the region. A self-ministering, self-supporting, and self-propagating local church is its ambition. The Fifth Triennial AMECEA Plenary Conference in 1976 took as its theme, "Building Christian Communities." It was from this conference that the idea to create small Christian communities all over AMECEA countries was taken. Despite some problems that have been encountered in the realization of this project, it has recorded a measure of success. Christians in those regions where it is established have become more responsible and creative in areas of justice, peace, and inculturation.

In the same Plenary Conference of 1976 decisions were also made on "Worship, the Source and Fullest Expression of Christian Community." The preoccupation was to make worship the affair of the local assembly, the basic community. There should be community-wide education and commissioned research and experiments in order to incarnate worship into the life of the community. The suggested areas of the research are the sacraments of Christian initiation, marriage rites, and new Eucharistic Prayers; the areas of para-liturgy, sacramentals, and devotions are not excluded.[56]

Research and experimentation on Christian initiation have not yielded the expected fruit despite the fact that traditional initiations are popular in many ethnic groups within the region.[57] The dispute over adaptations on initiation and the differences in customs have not encouraged further research into this area. Models of the marriage ritual have been produced, but it is not clear how far these have been implemented in practice.[58] It is in the area of the Eucharistic celebration that more results were recorded. Indeed AMECEA sees the building of the local church as centered on the Eucharist. "The local church is essentially a Eucharistic community that is orientated to the Eucharist, finds its fullest meaning in the Eucharist, and lives from one Eucharist to the next."[59]

Research into the Eucharistic Liturgy

The Gaba Pastoral Institute is the center for most of the research carried out in this region. The Eucharistic texts that were produced at Gaba were also experimented on in the same institute. The results of the Gaba effort have not been received with the same enthusiasm all over the region. In fact in some places they have been viewed with suspicion. Local liturgical research also goes on outside the Gaba Institute. For example, the creative celebrations in Malawi, like those of the community of the Poor Clares (Sisters of St. Francis) under the direction of Father A. Chima, merit attention.[60] Unfortunately, the texts of these are not available to me at the time of writing. Our comments will therefore be limited to the Gaba productions.

The Gaba productions can be viewed in two ways: (1) a general overview of the Eucharistic celebration and (2) the new Eucharistic Prayers of Eastern Africa.

An Overview of the Eucharistic Celebration. In general the celebrations at Gaba are based on themes. Some of these themes include children's Christmas Day, joy, gifts for services, bread of life, simplicity before God, African unity, thanksgiving, and thanksgiving for 1975 at Gaba.[61] The theme may determine the liturgical structure, the kind of readings, and the Eucharistic Prayer to be used. For example, while some of the themes follow the liturgical model of the Roman rite, the celebration of African unity restructures the Liturgy of the Word and uses the all-Africa Eucharistic Prayer. The celebration on African unity begins with opening reflections and exchanges among participants from various African countries on the theme, then two appropriate readings from the Old Testament and the gospel are rendered. The homily follows. Finally, the penitential rite, which concludes the Liturgy of the Word, comes as an acknowledgment by the community of the guilt in the divisions present in Africa.

The Tanzanian Mass, composed in 1977 by Tanzanian students at the Pastoral Institute under the supervision of Father A. Shorter, with the consent of the Tanzanian bishops, is not thematic. It develops a regular liturgical structure and inserts a new Eucharistic Prayer. The liturgical structure is as follows: opening liturgy (comprising of entrance, greeting, announcement of the intention, invocation of the ancestors), Liturgy of the Word (made up of the readings, prayer preceding the readings, blessing of the readers, homily), Liturgy of Reconciliation (there are three models, each of which concludes with the exchange of peace), offertory and prayers (including the offertory procession, washing of hands, receiving and offering the gifts, prayer of the faithful), Eucharistic Prayer, Our Father and embolism, invitation and participation in the Lord's banquet, thanksgiving praise (Gloria may be sung), and the concluding rite.

The Tanzanian liturgical structure is very close to what we have seen in the *ndzon-melen* liturgy and the Zairean Mass. It is certainly dependent on these earlier compositions. One may draw attention to the recognition of the power of the word in these liturgies. The word is the sacred (mystical) patrimony of the community. It is "too large" for the mouth of an individual to pronounce this word, because it belongs to God.[62] It requires the mandate of the community for an individual to proclaim it. Thus in the Tanzanian Mass we have the following rubric:

The First Reading:	The Reader will ask blessings from the priest saying: "I believe in the word of God and I ask you to bless me that I may proclaim it."
Priest:	May the almighty God who sends you to proclaim His word of salvation to His people, bless you and open your eyes and your lips to proclaim His word with sincerity.
Reader:	Amen.

The Eucharistic Prayer. The Gaba Institute has shown a leadership role in the production of Eucharistic Prayers. Although the Sacred Congregation for Divine Worship was not receptive to the wish of episcopal conferences to compose their own Eucharistic Prayers, it left the door open to provide more prayers.[63] This led to the creation of the Eucharistic Prayers for reconciliation and for celebrations with children, which have been in use since 1974. The AMECEA institute composed the "all-Africa" Eucharistic Prayer in 1969. In 1973 the Kenyan, Tanzanian, and Ugandan Eucharistic Prayers were put together. The Tanzanian Mass composed in 1977 had a provision for two Eucharistic Prayers, one explaining African values and the other explaining the relational unity of the Holy Trinity.

The all-Africa prayer is dominated by motifs of thanksgiving and festive meals. It was created with the structure of the Eucharistic Prayers of the historic liturgies as background: opening praise, thanksgiving for creation and/or redemption, epiclesis, institution narrative, *anamnesis,* second epiclesis, intercessions, and doxology. This also forms the background of the 1977 Tanzanian Eucharistic Prayer, which highlighted the following African values: the meaning of creation and the creator, the beauty of creation, humans in creation and as created in God's image, sin (its antiquity and results) and reconciliation, service and generosity in society, equality of human beings, our ancestors and our relationship with them, Christ as our brother (Ancestor of ancestors), faith in the life to come, faith in leadership and respect for leaders and all people, faith and hope in the future generations, faith in and respect for elders, who are the foundation of wisdom.

On the other hand, the three other prayers (from Kenya, Tanzania, and Uganda) composed in 1973 follow a more radical pattern. While maintaining the liturgical structure of the Eucharistic Prayer, the various parts of the prayer adapt or simply adopt suitable prayers drawn from African traditional religion. The Kenyan Eucharistic Prayer is very striking, and we give the full text. We add the subtitles to demarcate the paragraphs as they are named in the historic liturgies.

A Kenyan Eucharistic Prayer

(1) *Opening Praise* (based on a Kikuyu Prayer):

Principal Celebrant (PC): O Father, Great Elder, we have no words to thank you,
But with your deep wisdom
We are sure that you can see
How we value your glorious gifts.
O Father, when we look upon your greatness,
We are confounded with awe.
O Great Elder,
Ruler of all things earthly and heavenly,
We are your warriors,
Ready to act in accordance with your will.

(1.1) *Congregational Response* (based on a Galla Prayer):

ALL: Listen to us, aged God,
Listen to us, ancient God,
Who has ears.
Look at us, aged God,
Look at us, ancient God,

Who has eyes.
Receive us, aged God,
Receive us, ancient God,
Who has hands.

(2) *Epiclesis* (based on a Kikuyu Prayer):

Concelebrants (CC): You, the Great Elder,
Who dwells on the shining mountain,
Your blessing allows our homesteads to spread.
Your anger destroys them.
We beseech you,
And in this we are in harmony
With the Spirits of our ancestors;
We ask you to send the Spirit of life *(hands outstretched)*
To bless and sanctify our offerings,
That they may become for us the Body and Blood
Of Jesus, our Brother and your Son.

(3) *Institution Narrative:*

CC: On the night of his suffering,
He gave thanks for the bread which he held in his hands.
This bread he shared among his friends, saying:
All of you, take this, eat this.
It is my Body which will be handed over for you.

ALL: Amen. We believe that this is truly your body!

CC: Then he shared drink with them, saying:
All of you, take this, drink this.
It is my Blood, the Blood of the pact of brotherhood,
Which begins today and lasts forever.
This Blood will be poured out for you,

And for all,
So that sins may be taken away.
Do this and remember me.

ALL: Amen. We believe that this is truly your blood!

(4) *Acclamation:*

PC: Let us proclaim the mystery of Faith.

(4.1) *Congregational Response* (based on a Luyia Prayer):

ALL: O Sun of Justice,
You rise in the east through God's leadership and power.
Wash away all our evils.
Bring us, through this mystery,
A share in your death and resurrection,
As the sun sets and rises again.

(5) *Prayer of Offering* Anamnesis, *Prayer for Fruitful Effects of Communion* (based on a Meru Prayer):

CC: Owner of all things,
We offer you this Cup in memory of your Son.
We beg you for life,
For healthy people with no disease,
May they bear healthy children.
And also women who suffer because they are barren,
Open the way by which they may see children.
Give the good life to our parents and kin
Who are with you.

(6) *Intercession* (based on a Kikuyu Prayer):

PC: Say you, the elders may have wisdom and speak with one voice.

ALL: Praise be to God. Peace be with us!

PC: Say you, the people may have peace and fellowship

	With Mary, the Great Mother, And all the Holy Ones.
ALL:	Praise be to God. Peace be with us!
PC:	Say that our chief Bishop . . . And our Bishop . . . May have wisdom and life.
ALL:	Praise be to God. Peace be with us!
PC:	Say that the peoples, the herds, and the fields may prosper.
ALL:	Praise be to God. Peace be with us!

(7) *Doxology:*

ALL:	O Father, your power is greater than all powers. O Son, under your leadership we cannot fear anything. O Spirit, under your protection there is nothing we cannot overcome. Amen.

Critical Remarks. The composers of the Kenya prayer used the prayer traditions of the Kikuyu, Galla, Luyia, and Meru ethnic groups as sources. This orientation naturally plants the Kenyan church at prayer in its familiar context. There is consequently a preference for concrete imagery, accentuation, or repetition of key phrases or words, and a high degree of participation by the assembly. This is the characteristic of these Eucharistic Prayers from East Africa; it also characterizes African prayers. The composers have carefully merged prayers from different traditions to ensure a harmonious flow from one section of the Eucharistic Prayer to another. For example, the opening praise drawn from the Kikuyu tradition ("Father, Great Elder") blends naturally with the congregational response ("Listen to us aged God").

The novelty of these prayers is the facility with which texts of the ancestral tradition expressing sentiments and motifs that characterize the Eucharistic Prayer are adopted for use in the new Christian Eucharistic Prayer. For example, the opening praise of the Kenya prayer is a slight adaptation of a Kikuyu prayer of thanksgiving. The original Kikuyu text is as follows:

"O, my Father, great Elder, I have no words to thank you, but with your deep wisdom I am sure that you can see how much I prize your glorious gifts. O my Father, when I look upon your greatness, I am confounded with awe. O great Elder, ruler of all things both on heaven and on earth, I am your warrior, and I am ready to act in accordance with your will."[64]

Mbiti, in his collection of prayers of African religion, notes that the above prayer was said by the eponymous ancestor of the Kikuyu. The Kenyan Christians have transformed an individual thanksgiving into a community giving thanks. The thanksgiving is a suitable attitude of a favored community. From its ancestral memory, which now includes the memory of redemption in the Christ, the favored community is ready to carry out the command of the Great Elder.

The lyrical congregational response to the opening praise displays a two-way intimate conversation between God and the favored Christian community. Taken from the Galla tradition, the response plucks at the chords of the divine heart and draws God's attention to the pleading of the displayed community. The Great Elder hears, looks with kindness on his children, and gathers them in his hands. This is a thanksgiving praise that, by recalling the favors for which God is thanked, realizes greater favors.

The institution narrative is not taken from any particular prayer tradition. It is a well-composed narrative based on the African values of sharing life and making a blood covenant. This narrative is the same as the one used in the all-Africa Eucharistic Prayer. There is a lack of symmetry in the actions of Jesus narrated. About the bread, it is, "He gave thanks for the bread." There is no corresponding thanksgiving over the drink. It is also to be noted that the seven actions of Jesus at the Last Supper — took, blessed, broke, gave (for the bread), and took, blessed, gave (for the wine) — have been reduced to three actions in the Kenya prayer. In the Kenya prayer Jesus gave thanks, shared (the bread), and shared (the wine). The verb share does not appear to have the same implication when used about the bread and the drink: "This bread he shared among his followers," indicating breaking and distributing the bread among the disciples. While, "he shared drink with them" may indicate that he drank the wine with them. Whether or not Jesus would taste the elements that carry his person (body and blood) is open to question.[65] However, the idea of "sharing the drink" is intimately tied to the perception of the Eucharistic celebration as a blood pact. We already saw the operation of this symbolism in the consecration of virgins in Zaire. And insofar as Jesus offers himself as food and drink — implying mutual assimilation — the experience of blood pacts or covenants (in which both parties mutually taste one another's blood) becomes a powerful imagery to localize the understanding of the Eucharist. It is interesting that only in Egypt and Ethiopia do we encounter Eucharistic Prayers of the historic liturgies that refer to Jesus as tasting the bread and wine. The African experience of the intimate sharing of life as expressed in the blood covenant may lend itself to a deep but contextual appropriation of the Eucharist.

The rest of the prayer is drawn from various traditions as indicated. The acclamation plays on solar symbolism; it draws a beautiful picture of death and resurrection as sunset and sunrise. The prayer of offering and *anamnesis* are drowned by the presentation of the desired effects for fruitful communion. These effects are typically local and African: life, health, fertility. The intercession prays for the local elders and the Church elders, and associates the whole community with Mary and the saints. And the doxology is a proclamation of the community's security under the father's power, the son's leadership, and the Spirit's protection.

In conclusion, we must emphasize that the decision of the AMECEA research group to adopt or adapt existing local prayer traditions in the composition of Christian Eucharistic Prayers is justified. From our study of the Jewish and Western Christian traditions in the previous chapters, we have encountered many instances of the conversion of local religious practices to express the Christian faith. Christians in East Africa, therefore, draw the resources to express their faith in Christ from their ancestral heritage. This exercise introduces development into the ancestral tradition. It becomes an opportunity for the African Christians to display what is stored in the ancestral memory for the service of a wider group. The faith experience in Christ directs what is adopted, adapted, transformed, or rejected in the tradition to express and serve the same faith. But the Christian faith has also received development. It has become enriched in being expressed in categories peculiar to Africans. In being introduced into the store house of African ancestral memory and into the concerns of present-day Africans, it is made to devise creative patterns of responding to the concerns and of expressing fulfillment of our needs.

NOTES

1. An illuminating study of the history of unity in difference in the various liturgical traditions of the Eastern and Western Churches is contained in the collective work *Liturgie de l'Eglise particulière et Liturgie de l'Eglise universelle*, Conférence Saint Serge, XXIIe Semaine d'Etudes liturgiques, Paris, 30 June–3 July 1975 (Roma: Edizioni Liturgiche, 1976).

2. Here I draw from my former study "Africa's Right to Be Different: Christian Liturgical Rites and African Rites," *Bulletin of African Theology* IV/7:1982, 87–109; IV/8:1982, 243–76. This has also been published as *Liturgy: Truly Christian, Truly African*, Spearhead no. 74 (Eldoret: Gaba Publications, 1982). See also my "African Cultures and the Christian Liturgy," *West African Journal of Ecclesial Studies* 2/1:1990, 59–83.

3. Eusebius, *Church History* 5.24.

4. Cyprian's views are expressed in *Letters* 69–74, and also in his *The Unity of the Catholic Church*, no. 6. See Saint Cyprian, *The Lapsed: The Unity of the Catholic Church*, trans. and annotated by M. Benevot (Westminster, Md.: Newman Press; London: Longman, Green & Co., 1957).

5. See Congar, *Diversités et Communion*, 38; Augustine, *De Baptismo* 3.3–5.

6. *Ep.* 1.43; *PL* 11.497. See J. A. Jungmann, *The Mass of the Roman Rite*, revised by C. K. Riepe (Westminster: Christian Classics, 1978) 74. A. Bouley, *From Freedom to Formula: The Evolution of the Eucharistic Prayer from Oral Improvisation to Written Texts* (Washington, D.C.: The Catholic University of America Press, 1981) 180, n. 74.

7. *Ep.* 2.64.3; *PL* 77.1187; cited by Jungmann, *Missarum Sollemnia* (Paris: Aubier, 1956) 133, n. 35. Bouley, *From Freedom to Formula*, 184, 196–7.

8. Congar, *Diversités et Communion*, 42–43. See also his *L'Ecclésiologie du Haut Moyen Age: De St. Grégoire le Grand à la Désunion entre Byzance et Rome* (Paris: Cerf, 1968) 19.

9. See Leo XIII's *Orientalium Dignitas Ecclesiarum* of 1894.

10. See the studies of Chupungco, *Liturgies of the Future: The Process and Methods of Inculturation* (New York: Paulist Press, 1989) ch. 1; Bugnini, *The Reform of the Liturgy: 1948–1974*, trans. M. J. O'Connell (Collegeville: The Liturgical Press, 1990) ch. 4.

11. The above expressions are drawn from the teachings of Popes Paul VI and John Paul II. See, for example, Paul VI's *Africae terrarum* in *Docu-*

mentation Catholique 1505, 19 Nov. 1967, 1937–55, and his address to the African bishops gathered in Kampala, Uganda, in 1969 published in *African Ecclesial Review* XX/6:1978, 322–6. See also John Paul II's address to Kenyan and Zairean bishops during his visit to Africa (2–12 May 1980), *Documentation Catholique* 1787:1980; *African Ecclesial Review* XXII/4:1980, and his address during his visit to Sweden in 1989.

12. A song of Komo (Malian) initiation society, cited by L. V. Thomas and R. Luneau, *Les Religions d'Afrique noire*, vol. 1 (Paris: Stock and Plus, 198) 28.

13. See the publications in the following periodicals of the region: *West African Journal of Ecclesial Studies, Nigerian Journal of Theology, Bulletin of Ecumenical Theology,* and many other journals of individual seminaries in the region. See also Acts of Conferences like: *Evangelization in Africa in the Third Millennium: Challenges and Prospects* (CIWA, Port Harcourt, 1992), *Healing and Exorcism: The Nigerian Experience* (Spiritan International School of Theology Attakwu, Enugu, 1992).

14. See the *General Instruction on the Roman Missal,* nn. 49–53.

15. Some worshipers leave the assembly as soon as they make their offering.

16. S. Leith-Ross, *African Women* (London: Faber, 1934) 123.

17. See E. E. Uzukwu, "Liturgical Creativity in Igbo Christian Communities," *Cahiers des Religions Africaines* XX–XXI/39–42:1986–87, 523–34.

18. See T. M. Ilesanmi, "Eto Ati Adura Isomolorukoi," *Adura Onigbagbo* (Ilesha: Iranoo-Owuro Press, 1978).

19. E. M. Nwabuisi, "Socialization and the Nigerian Child: A Case Study of Ebe Child-rearing," *Religion and African Culture: I. Inculturation — A Nigerian Perspective,* ed. E. E. Uzukwu (Enugu: Spiritan Publications, 1988) 10–21, esp. 14.

20. Original Yoruba text translated by Jerome Otitoyomi Dukiya of Spiritan School of Philosophy Isienu, Nsukka, Nigeria.

21. See E. S. Obot, "Nigeria: The Naming Rite," *Church and Culture* 19:1993, 11.

22. See B. O. Okere, "Nigerian Customary Law and the Received English Law: Confrontation and Harmonization," *Religion and African Culture,* 22–45.

23. I analyzed one such liturgy in my "African Personality and the Christian Liturgy," *African Christian Studies* 3/2:1987, 61–74.

24. Since the ritual is in high demand in this parish, the parish priest presides over its celebration once or twice a month. Groups who participate listen to the Scripture reading together and then make their commitments according to families or associations. In the six months I have worked as associate pastor in this parish (January–June 1993) a minimum of four such rituals have been celebrated each month.

25. See the definition of inculturation by the Extraordinary Assembly of Bishops, Final report, 7 December 1985.

26. H. Mol, *Identity and the Sacred: A Sketch for a New Social-Scientific Theory of Religion* (Oxford: Basil Blackwell, 1976) 73; cited by F. M. Mbon, "The Quest for Identity in African New Religious Movements," *New Religious Movements and Society in Nigeria,* Bayreuth African Studies Series 17, ed. G. Ludwar-Ene (West Germany: Bayreuth University, 1991) 22.

27. Observers of the Nsukka region note the frequency with which the *igba ndu* ritual is celebrated.

28. C. I. Ejizu, *OFO: Igbo Ritual Symbol* (Enugu: Fourth Dimension Publishers, 1986) 106–11.

29. See Mbon, "The Quest for Identity," 20.

30. See *Le Calao* 29/1:1975, 9, for the process of establishing these commissions.

31. N. Diatta, "Et si Jésus-Christ, Premier-né d'entre les Morts, était l'initié," *Telema* 57/1:1989, 49–72; "Jésus-Christ: Initié et Initiateur," *Théologie Africaine Bilan et Perspectives,* Actes de XVIIe Semaine Theologique de Kinshasa 2–8 April 1989 (Kinshasa: Facultes Catholiques de Kinshasa, 1989) 137–54; A. T. Sanon and R. Luneau, *Enraciner l'Evangile: Initiations Africaines et Pédagogie de la Foi* (Paris: Cerf, 1982) 11. These Christological titles are suggested by Heb 7:11 where Jesus is said to be perfected *(teleiôsis),* and Heb 12:2 where he is called the perfecter *(teleiôtês).*

32. See *Sacrosanctum concilium,* nos. 64, 66.

33. *Le Calao* 29/1:1975, 29–30.

34. *Sacrosanctum concilium,* no. 40.

35. See Sanon and Luneau, *Enraciner l'Evangile,* 132–3.

36. See R. Ouedraogo, "Rituel Moore," *Le Calao* 51/3:1980, 34–47; see also E. Uzukwu, "Africa's Right to Be Different: Part II: African Rites in the Making," *Bulletin of African Theology* IV/8:1982, 263–7; idem, *Liturgy: Truly Christian, Truly African* (Eldoret: Gaba Publications, 1982) 50–55.

37. N. Tshiamalenga, "L'Art comme Langage et comme Verbe," *Cahiers des Religions Africaines* XVI/31–32:1982, 65; E. Mveng, *L'Art d'Afrique noire, Liturgie cosmique et Langages religieux* (Yaounde: Cle, 1974); idem, *L'Art et l'Artisanat Africains* (Yaounde: Cle, 1980); idem, *L'Afrique dans l'Eglise, Paroles d'un Croyant,* (Paris: l'Harmattan, 1985) ch. 1.

38. E. Mveng, "L'Expérience de la Communauté des Béatitudes du Cameroun," a paper presented at the Colloque International *Vie Monastique et Inculturation á la Lumière des traditions et Situations africaines,* Kinshasa, 19–25 Feb. 1989.

39. For the literature on this liturgy see P. Abega, "La Liturgie camerounaise," *Mediations Africaines du Sacre,* Actes du 2e Colloque International, Kinshasa, 16–22 Nov. 1986, *Cahiers des Religions Africaines* XX–XXI/39–42:1986–87; idem, "L'Experience liturgique de Ndzon-Melen," *Telema* 16/4:1978, 41–50; idem, "Liturgical Adaptation," *Christianity in*

Independent Africa, ed. E. Fashole-Luke (Indianapolis: Indiana University Press, 1978) 597–605. I analyzed this liturgy in previous publications: *Liturgy: Truly Christian, Truly African*, 56–58; "Africa's Right to Be Different: Part II: African Rites in the Making," 268–9; "African Cultures and the Christian Liturgy," 67–69.

40. J. Thornton, "The Development of an African Catholic Church in the Kingdom of the Kongo, 1491–1750," *Journal of African History* 25/2:1985, 147–67, esp. 156–9.

41. See Badi-Banga Ne-Nwime, "Expression de la Foi chrétienne dans l'Art plastique zaïrois," *Cahiers des Religions Africaines* XVI/31–32:1982, 135–67, esp. 148–50.

42. See Malula's preface to L. Kabasele's book, *Alliances avec le Christ en Afrique* (Athens: Editions Historiques S. D. Basilopoulos, 1987) 13.

43. For the literature on the liturgical creativity in Zaire see Kabasele, *Alliances avec le Christ en Afrique*; idem, "Nouveaux Rites, Foi Naissante," *Lumière et Vie* 159:1983, 61–73; idem, "L'inculturation sacramentelle au Zaïre," *Lumen Vitae* XLII/1:1987, 75–84. See also L. Mpongo, "Le Rite zaïrois de la Messe," *Spiritus* 19 (n. 73):1978, 436–41; B. Hearne, "The Significance of the Zaire Mass," *African Ecclesial Review* 17:1975, 243–8; B. Luykx, *Culte chrétien en Afrique après Vatican II* (Fribourg: Nouvelle Revue de Science Missionaire, 1974) esp. 93–94. See also my essay on African rites cited above.

44. See Kabasele, "Nouveaux Rites, Foi Naissante," 69.

45. Kabasele, *Alliances avec le Christ en Afrique*, 96.

46. Oral narration of a professed sister in Kabasele, *Alliances avec le Christ en Afrique*, 99–100; see also idem, "Nouveaux Rites, Foi Naissante," 69–70.

47. Kabasele, *Alliances avec le Christ en Afrique*, 104.

48. See the analysis of the symbolic objects at the consecration of virgins by Kabasele in his *Alliances avec le Christ en Afrique*, part 2, ch. 3, esp. 216–26. Kabasele also has a brief history of the development of the rite of consecration of virgins from the fourth century to the reform of Vatican II on 113–26.

49. See Congregation for Divine Worship, "Zairensium Dioecesium," *Notitiae* 264:1988, 457; Conférence Episcopale du Zaïre, *Missel Romain pour les Dioceses du Zaïre* (Kinshasa: Conférence Episcopale du Zaïre, 1988).

50. Kabasele, "L'inculturation sacramentelle au Zaïre," 81, n. 14.

51. See C. M. Mulago, *La Religion traditionnelle des Bantu et leur Vision du Monde* (Kinshasa: Faculté de Théologie Catholique, 1980); N. Mujynya, *L'Homme dans l'Univers des Bantu* (Kinshasa: Presses Universitaires du Zaïre, 1978); B. Bujo, "Nos Ancêtres, ces Saints inconnus," *Bulletin of African Theology* 1/2:1979, 165–78; A. M. Ngindu, "Propos et Problèmes Concernant le Culte des Morts ches les Baluba du Kasayi," *Cahiers des Religions Africaines* 3/5:1969, 79–109.

52. From Kabasele, "Nouveaux Rites, Foi Naissante," 65.

53. For the liturgy of the Apostolic Constitutions see A. Hanggi and I. Pahl, *Prex Eucharistica* (Fribourg: Editions Universitaires, 1968) 82ff.

54. L. Mpongo, "Le Rite zaïrois de la Messe," 438.

55. Taken from Kabasele, "Nouveaux Rites, Foi Naissante," 66.

56. The works of the Fifth Triennial Plenary Conference are published in *African Ecclesial Review* 18/5:1976. The decisions on worship are found on 251–2. See my "African Liturgical Rites in the Making," 254–61; and also my *Liturgy: Truly Christian, Truly African*, 39–48, for analysis of liturgical creativity in the Eastern African region.

57. See the works of V. Turner among the Ndembu of Zambia like *The Forest of Symbols: Aspects of Ndembu Ritual* (Ithaca, N.Y.: Cornell University Press, 1967) and *The Drums of Affliction* (Oxford: Clarendon Press, 1968).

58. See A. Shorter, "Liturgical Creativity in East Africa," *African Ecclesial Review* 19/5:1977, 258–67.

59. Fifth Triennial AMECEA Plenary Conference, "Building Christian Communities," *African Ecclesial Review* 18/5:1976, 25.

60. The video recording of some of these celebrations is contained in Thomas A. Kane, *The Dancing Church* (Mahwah, N.J.: Paulist Press, 1991).

61. See B. Hearne and N. Mijere, *Celebration II*, Spearhead 42 (Eldoret: Gaba Publications, 1976).

62. The expression is from the Bambara of Mali. See L. V. Thomas and R. Luneau, *Les Religions d'Afrique noire*, vol. 1 (Paris: Editions stock, 1981) 28; M. Griaule, *Conversation with Ogotemmeli* (London: Oxford University Press, 1965) 138ff.

63. See *Eucharistiae Participationem* of 27 April 1973, nos. 5 and 6, in *Documents of the Liturgy (1963–1979)* (Collegeville: The Liturgical Press, 1982).

64. J. S. Mbiti, *The Prayers of African Religion* (London: SPCK, 1975) 151.

65. See J. Jeremias, *The Eucharistic Words of Jesus* (London: SCM Press, 1973) 207–18 for a full discussion.

Summary and Conclusion

This book has argued that the rhythm of our gestures is meaningful within an ethnic group. Body motions and attitudes adopted toward the body reveal group assumptions. The Greco-Roman world and Latin patristic Christianity held the body suspect. The result is the adoption of minimal gestures in the liturgy. On the other hand, Africans tune into the rhythm of life in the world bodily; the self in all its complexity is manifest bodily. Life in the world, as a result, explodes in the dance and other adequate gestures. Consequently, the emerging Christian liturgies of Africa emphasize intense community participation with appropriate gestures.

Second, ritual performance, as anthropological research shows, reveals the beliefs and structures of any social group. Communities reaffirm and express their core experiences through ritual. In the New Testament community, for example, the (Eucharistic) meal ritual was the center for the proclamation and reliving of the experience of Jesus' paschal mystery until he comes again. Through the Eucharistic rite Christians display a pattern of relationship that excludes all discrimination. On the other hand, the native African community is convoked in assembly to deliberate on matters affecting the life of the community or any of its members. In such an assembly, the problem is fully discussed and ritually presented before the anchor. All participate fully. In the emergent Eucharistic liturgies and other types of Christian assembly in Africa community participation is highlighted. Furthermore, some native rituals that accompany individuals and groups in their passage through life are being Christianized.

Third, we emphasized that the foundation story of any group carries the faith of the group. This sacred history may be narrated in ritual context or expressed through group or individual ritual display. Among the Igbo of Nigeria the story is not only relived by a new priest-king, but it is ritualized in interpersonal relationships (the ethics of politics and economy). The prevailing practice of the ancient near east (Mesopotamia and Israel) is also to display in life what is narrated in the foundation stories. The Christian principle that the rule of faith is intimately connected with the rule of prayer is not new. The value of each narrative lies in its power to sustain a group inserted in the world. This power is felt through participation ritual and ethical behavior.

Fourth, we showed that passage or transition rites were and are very popular in Africa. As societies become more complex, they may require fewer rituals, but no group can do without rites as members pass from birth through adolescence and adulthood to death. The reformed Roman Rite of Christian Initiation of Adults adopted the catechumenate by stages. This offers African Christians of the Roman rite an opportunity to adopt the received Roman text of Christian initiation or to radically modify it. Its adaptation has been realized in French-speaking West Africa. But the need for adequate transition or life crises rituals is very much felt today in Africa. These may no longer be ignored if the faith must become culture.

Finally, our samples of emergent African liturgies are not exhaustive. They indicate to us some practical realizations in the creative encounter between African cultures and the Christian gospel. They show a growing confidence in the way Roman Catholic Christians in Africa accept their environment. Christianity, which in its history moved from a predominantly Jewish background to one that is Hellenistic, has the experience of a multiplicity of rites. This experience supports liturgical inculturation in Africa as an obligatory enterprise. Africans must maintain and work toward such a legitimate pluralism not only in cult and discipline, but also in the theological expression of the received Christian faith.

Bibliography

Abega, P. "La Liturgie camerounaise." *Médiations Africaines du Sacré.* Actes du 2e Colloque International, Kinshasa (Nov. 16–22, 1986). *Cahiers des Religions Africaines* 20–21 (1986–87) 39–42.

_________. "L'Expérience liturgique de Ndzon-Melen." *Telema* 16:4 (1978) 41–50.

_________. "Liturgical Adaptation." *Christianity in Independent Africa.* Ed. E. Fashole-Luke, 597–605. Indianapolis: Indiana University Press, 1978.

Achebe, C. "Chi in Igbo Cosmology." *Morning Yet on Creation Day.* London: Heinemann, 1975.

_________. *Things Fall Apart.* London: Heineman, 1958.

Achtemeier, P. J. "The Origin and Function of the Pre-Marcan Miracle Catenae." *Journal of Biblical Literature* 91 (1972) 198–221.

Ackroyd, P. R. *Exile and Restoration.* Philadelphia: Westminster Press, 1968.

Acta Conciliorum et Epistolae Decretales ac Constitutiones Summorum Pontificum. Vol. 1. Parisiis: 1715.

The Acts of the Christian Martyrs. Introduction, texts, and translations by H. Musurillo. Oxford: Clarendon Press, 1972.

Afigbo, A. E. "Prolegomena to the Study of the Culture History of the Igbo-Speaking Peoples of Nigeria." *Igbo Language and Culture.* Ed. F. C. Ogbalu and E. N. Emenajo. Ibadan: Oxford University Press, 1975.

Alberigo, G., and A. Ngindu Mushete. *Concilium* 1992/1: *Towards the African Synod.*

Albrektson, B. *History and the Gods: An Essay on the Idea of Historical Events as Divine Manifestations in the Ancient Near East and in Israel.* Lund: CWK Gleerup, 1967.

Alderink, L. J. "The Eleusinian Mysteries in Roman Imperial Times." *Aufstieg und Niedergang der Römischen Welt.* 2.18.2. Ed. H. Temporini and W. Haase, 1457–97. Berlin and New York: W. de Gruyter, 1989.

Alexander, J., and D. G. Coursey. "The Origins of Yam Cultivation." *The Domestication and Exploitation of Plants and Animals.* Ed. P. J. Ucko and G. W. Dimbley, 405–25. London: Gerald Duckworth and Co., 1969.

Amalorpavadass, D. S. "Theological Reflections on Inculturation." *Studia Liturgica* 20:1 (1990).

Ancient Near Eastern Texts (ANET). Ed. J. B. Prichard. 3d ed. Princeton, N.J.: Princeton University Press, 1969.

Andrieu, M. *Les Ordines du Haut Moyen Age. I. Les Manuscrits.* Louvain: Spicilegium Sacrum Lovaniense, 1931.
Anifowose, R. *Violence and Politics in Nigeria: The Tiv and Yoruba Experience.* New York: Nok, 1982.
Anyanwu, K. C. "The Meaning of Ultimate Reality in Igbo Cultural Experience." *Ultimate Reality and Meaning* 7:2 (1984) 84–101.
__________. "A Response to A.G.A. Bello's Methodological Preliminaries." *Ultimate Reality and Meaning* 14 (1991) 61–9.
__________. "Sound as Ultimate Reality and Meaning: The Mode of Knowing Reality in African Thought." *Ultimate Reality and Meaning* 10 (1987) 29–38.
Arinze, F. A. *Sacrifice in Ibo Religion.* Ibadan: Ibadan University Press, 1970.
Armstrong, R. "Glottochronology and West African Linguistics." *Journal of African History* 3 (1962).
__________. *The Study of West African Languages.* Ibadan: Ibadan University Press, 1964.
Arranz, M. "Les Rôles dans l'Assemblée chrétienne d'après le 'Testamentum Domini.'" *L'Assemblée Liturgique et les Différents Rôles dans l'Assemblée.* Conférences Saint-Serge, XXIIIe Semaine d'Etudes Liturgiques, Paris, June 28–July 1, 1976. Rome: Edizioni Liturgiche, 1977.
Ashamani, C. B. "The Orthodox Liturgy and the Apocalypse." *Patristic and Byzantine Review* 9:1 (1990) 30–7.
Atado, J. C. *Welcome Jesus, Bye Bye Satan: Spiritual Pills to Overcome Your Problems.* Sokoto, 1990.
Audet J. P. *La Didaché. Instruction ces Apôtres.* Paris: Librairie Lecoffre, 1958.
Augustine, Saint. *Against Two Letters of Pelagius.* 4.7. *Nicene and Post-Nicene Fathers.* Vol. 5. Ed. P. Schaff. Peabody, Mass.: Hendrickson Publishers, 1994.
__________. *Confessions. The Fathers of the Church: A New Translation.* Vol. 21. Trans. V. J. Bourke. New York: Fathers of the Church, Inc., 1953.
__________. *Letters.* Vol. 2. *The Fathers of the Church: A New Translation.* Vol. 18. Trans. V. J. Bourke. New York: Fathers of the Church, Inc., 1953.
Aune, D. E. "The Influence of Roman Imperial Court on the Apocalypse of John." *Biblical Research* 28 (1983) 5–26.
Ayendele, E. A. *The Missionary Impact of Modern Nigeria.* London: Longmans, 1966.
Babour, I. *Myth, Models and Paradigms.* San Francisco: Harper and Row, 1974.
Badi-Banga, Ne-Nwime. "Expression de la Foi Chrétienne dans l'Art plastique zaïrois." *Cahiers des Religions Africaines* 26:31–2 (1982) 135–67.
Bainbridge, W. S., and R. Stark. "Cult Formation: Three Compatible Models." *Religion and Religiosity in America.* Ed. J. K. Hadden and T. E. Long, 35–53. New York: Crossroad, 1983.
Banks, R. *Paul's Idea of Community: The Early House Churches in Their Historical Setting.* Grand Rapids, Mich.: Eerdmans, 1980.
Barr, J. "Story and History in Biblical Theology." *Theology Digest* 24 (1976) 265–7.

Barret, D. *Schism and Renewal in Africa.* Nairobi: Oxford University Press, 1968.

Beeck, F. J. van. *God Encountered: A Contemporary Catholic Systematic Theology.* Vol. 1, *Understanding the Christian Faith.* New York: Harper and Row, 1989.

Beidelman, T. O. "Swazi Royal Ritual." *Africa* 36:4 (1966) 373–405.

Bellinger, W. H. "Maker of Heaven and Earth: The Old Testament and Creation Theology." *Southwestern Journal of Theology* 32 (1990) 27–35.

Benko, S. "The Libertine Gnostic Sect of the Phibionites According to Epiphanius." *Vigiliae Christianae* 21 (1967) 103–19.

__________. "Pagan Criticism of Christanity During the First Two Centuries A.D." *Aufstieg und Niedergang der Römischen Welt.* 2.23.2. Ed. H. Temporini and W. Haase, 1055–118. Berlin: Walter der Gruyter, 1980.

Bentzen, A. "On the Ideas of 'the Old' and 'the New' in Deutero-Isaiah." *Studia Theologica* 1 (1948) 183–7.

Berger, P. L. *The Sacred Canopy.* Garden City, N.Y.: Doubleday, 1967.

Bimwenyi-Kweshi, O. *Discours théologique négro-africain.* Paris: Présence Africaine, 1981.

Birdwhistell, R. *Kinesics and Context.* Philadelphia: University of Pennsylvania Press, 1970.

Bishop, E. *Liturgica Historica.* Oxford: Clarendon Press, 1918.

Black, J. A. "The New Year Ceremonies in Ancient Babylon: 'Taking Bel by the Hand' and a Cultic Picnic." *Religion* 11 (1981) 39–59.

Blair, E. P. "An Appeal to Remembrance: The Memory Motif in Deuteronomy." *Interpretation* 15 (1961) 41–7.

Bloch, M. *Ritual, History and Power: Selected Papers in Anthropology.* London: Athlone Press, 1989.

The Book of Jubilees or the Little Genesis. Translated from the Ethiopic text by R. H. Charles, with an introduction by C. H. Box. London: SPCK, 1917.

Boman, T. *Hebrew Thought Compared with Greek.* London: SCM, 1960.

Booth, N. S. "Time and Change in African Traditional Thought." *Journal of Religion in Africa* 7 (1975) 81–91.

Bornkamm, G. "Mysterion." *Theological Dictionary of the New Testament.* Vol. 4. Ed. G. Kittel, 802–27. Grand Rapids, Mich.:Eerdmans, 1967.

Botte, B. *La Tradition Apostolique de Saint Hippolyte.* Münster: Aschendorffsche Verlagsbuchhandlung, 1963.

Bottero, J. "Les Noms de Marduk, l'Ecriture et la 'logique' en Mésopotamie." *Essays in the Ancient Near East in Memory of Jacob J. Finkelstein.* Ed. M. de Jong Ellis, 5–28. Hamden, Conn.: Archon Books, 1977.

Bouley, A. *From Freedom to Formula: The Evolution of the Eucharistic Prayer from Oral Improvisation to Written Texts.* Washington, D.C.: Catholic University of America Press, 1981.

Bouyer, L. *Eucharist, Theology and Spirituality of the Eucharistic Prayer.* Notre Dame, Ind.: University of Notre Dame Press, 1968.

Brandon, S.G.F. "The Propaganda Factor in Some Ancient Near Eastern Cosmogonies." *Promise and Fulfillment.* Essays presented to

Professor S. H. Hooke. Ed. F. F. Bruce, 20–35. Edinburgh: T. and T. Clark, 1963.

Brown, K. McCarthy. "'Plenty of Confidence in Myself': The Initiation of a White Woman Scholar into Haitian Vodou." *Journal of Feminist Studies in Religion* 3:1 (1987) 67–76.

Brown, P. *The Body and Society.* New York: Columbia University Press, 1988.

__________. *The World of Late Antiquity.* London: Thames and Hudson, 1971.

Brown, R. *The Churches the Apostles Left Behind.* New York: Paulist Press, 1984.

__________. "New Testament Background for the Concept of Local Church." *Proceedings of the 36th Annual Convention of the Catholic Theological Society of America,* June 10–13, 1981. 36 (1982) 1–14.

__________. "The Semitic Background to the New Testament Mysterion." *Biblica* 39 (1958) 426–48; 40 (1959) 70–87.

Bugnini, A. *The Reform of the Liturgy, 1948–1974.* Trans. M. J. O'Connell. Collegeville: The Liturgical Press, 1990.

Bujo, B. "Nos Ancêtres, ces Saints inconnus." *Bulletin of African Theology* 1:2 (1979) 165–78.

Burns, R. "The Book of Exodus." *Concilium* 189:1 (1987) 11–21.

Campbell, J. *The Masks of God: Creative Mythology.* New York: Penguin, 1976.

__________. *Myths to Live By.* New York: Bantam Books, 1972.

Cassian. *Institutes.* Books II and III. *Nicene and Post Nicene Fathers of the Church.* Ed. P. Schaff. Grand Rapids, Mich.: Eerdmans, 1963.

Cassirer, E. *The Philosophy of Symbolic Forms.* Vol. 2, *Mythical Thoughts.* New Haven, Conn.: Yale University Press, 1955.

Castoriadis, C. "Time and Creation." *Chronotypes: The Construction of Time.* Ed. J. Bender and D. E. Wellbery, 38–64. Stanford, Calif.: Stanford University Press, 1991.

Cazelles, H. "L'Assemblée liturgique et les différents Rôles dans l'ancien Testament." *L'Assemblée liturgique et les différents Rôles dans l'Assemblée.* Conférences Saint-Serge, XXIIIe Semaine d'Etudes Liturgiques, Paris, June 28–July 1, 1976. Rome: Edizioni Liturgiche, 1977.

Cazeneuve, J. *La Sociologie du Rite.* Paris: Presses Universitaires de France, 1971.

Chadwick, H. "Prayer at Midnight." *Epektasis. Mélanges Patristiques offerts au Cardinal Jean Daniélou.* Ed. J. Fontaine and C. Kannengiesser, 47–9. Paris: Beauchesne, 1972.

Chauvet, L. M. *Du Symbolique au Symbole.* Paris: Cerf, 1979.

Childs, B. S. *Memory and Tradition in Israel.* London: SCM, 1962.

__________. "A Traditio-Historical Study of the Reed Sea Tradition." *Vetus Testamentum* 20 (1970) 406–18.

Chupungco, A. J. *Liturgies of the Future: The Process and Methods of Inculturation.* New York: Paulist Press, 1989.

Clark J. D., ed. *Cambridge History of Africa.* Vol. 1, *From the Earliest Times to c. 500 B.C.* Cambridge: Cambridge University Press, 1982.

_________. "The Pre-Historic Origin of African Cultures." *Journal of African History* 5:2 (1964) 161–83.

Clement of Alexandria. *Exhortation to the Heathens,* esp. ch. 2. *The Ante-Nicene Fathers.* Vol. 2. Trans. A. Roberts and J. Donaldson. Grand Rapids, Mich.: Eerdmans, 1989.

Clerck, P. de. "Un Seul Baptême des Adultes et Celui des petits Enfants." *La Maison Dieu* 185 (1991) 7–33.

Clifford, R. J. *Fair Spoken and Persuading: An Interpretation of Second Isaiah.* New York: Paulist Press, 1984.

_________. "The Hebrew Scriptures and Theology of Creation." *Theological Studies* 46 (1985).

Clinton, K. "The Eleusinian Mysteries: Roman Initiates and Benefactors, Second Century B.C. to A.D. 267." *Aufstieg und Niedergang der Römischen Welt.* 2.18.2. Ed. H. Temporini and W. Haase. Berlin: Walter de Gruyter, 1989.

Chrysostom. *Homily in Acts of the Apostles.* I. *Nicene and Post-Nicene Fathers.* Vol. 6. Ed. P. Schaff. Peabody, Mass.: Hendrickson Publishers, 1994.

Cole, S. G. "The Mysteries of Samothrace during the Roman Period." *Aufstieg und Niedergang der Römischen Welt.* 2.18.2. Ed. H. Temporini and W. Haase, 1565–98. Berlin: W. de Gruyter, 1989.

Conflict at Colossae: A Problem in the Interpretation of Early Christianity Illustrated by Selected Modern Studies. Sources for Biblical Studies 4. Ed. and trans. with introduction and epilogue by F. O. Francis and W. A. Meeks. Missoula, Mont.: Society of Biblical Literature, 1973.

Conford, F. M. *The Unwritten Philosophy and Other Essays.* Cambridge, Mass.: University Press, 1967.

Congar, Y. M. *Diversités et Communion.* Paris: Cerf, 1982.

_________. *L'Ecclésiologie du Haut Moyen Age. De St. Gregoire le Grand à la Désunion entre Byzance et Rome.* Paris: Cerf, 1968.

_________. "Le Monothéisme politique et le Dieu Trinité." *Nouvelle Revue Thélogique* 103:1 (1981) 3–17.

Connolly, R. H. *The So-Called Egyptian Church Order and Derived Documents.* Cambridge: University Press, 1916.

Cothenet, E. "Liturgie terrestre et Liturgie céeste d'après l'Apocalypse." *L'Assemblée Liturgique et les Différents Rôles dans l'Assemblée.* Conférences Saint-Serge, XXIIIe Semaine d'Etudes Liturgiques, Paris, June 28–July 1, 1976. Rome: Edizioni Liturgiche, 1977.

Coursey, D. G. "The Origins and Domestication of Yams in Africa." *Origins of African Plant Domestication.* Ed. J. Harlan et al., 383–408. Hague: Mouton Publishers, 1976.

Cross, F. M. *Canaanite Myth and Hebrew Epic.* Cambridge, Mass.: Havard University Press, 1973.

Cyprian. *Letter.* 5.2.1. *The Letters of Cyprian of Carthage.* Vol. 1, *Letters 1–27.* Ancient Christian Writers, no. 43. Trans. and annotated by G. W. Clarke. New York: Newman Press, 1984.

———. *The Letters of Cyprian of Carthage.* Vol. 3, *Letters 55–66.* Ancient Christian Writers, no. 46. Trans. and annotated by G. W. Clarke. New York: Newman Press, 1986.

———. *The Unity of the Catholic Church.* Ancient Christian Writers, no. 25. Ed. J. Quasten and J. C. Plumpe. New York: Newman Press, 1956.

Cyril of Jerusalem. *Five Catechetical Lectures.* Catechetical Lectures 19.1. *Nicene and Post-Nicene Fathers of the Christian Church.* 2d series, vol. 7. Ed. P. Schaff and H. Wace. Grand Rapids, Mich.: Eerdmans, 1983.

Daget, S. *De la Traite à l'esclavage.* Actes du Colloque international sur la traite des Noirs, Nantes 1985. Paris: Société Française d'Histoire d'Outre-Mer; Nantes: Centre de Recherche sur l'Histoire du Monde Atlantique, 1988.

Daniel, S. *Recherches sur le Vocabulaire du Culte.* Paris: Librairie C. Klincksieck, 1966.

Danielou, J. *The Bible and the Liturgy.* Notre Dame, Ind.: University of Notre Dame Press, 1966.

Deiss, L. *Vivre la Parole en Communauté.* Paris: Desclée de Brouwer, 1974. English translation: *God's Word and God's People.* Collegeville: The Liturgical Press, 1976.

Delcor, M. "Commémorer à Qumran: L'Historicisation des Fêtes." *La Commémoration.* Colloque du Centenaire de la Section des Sciences Religieuses de l'Ecole pratique des Hautes Etudes. Ed. P. Gignoux. Louvain-Paris: Peeters, 1988.

Delumeau, J. Leçon inaugurale au College de France, Feb. 13, 1975. Reprinted as annex I in his *Le Christianisme va-t-il Mourir?* Paris: Hachette, 1977.

Diatta, N. "Et si Jésus-Christ, Premier-né d'entre les Morts, était l'initié." *Telema* 57:1 (1989) 49–72.

———. "Jésus-Christ: Initié et Initiateur." *Théologie Africaine Bilan et Perspectives.* Actes de XVIIe Semaine Thélogique de Kinshasa, April 2–8, 1989. Kinshasa: Facultes Catholiques de Kinshasa, 1989.

Dibelius, M. "The Isis Initiation in Apuleius and Related Initiatory Rites." *Conflict at Colossae,* 61–121.

Dieterlen, G. "L'image du Corps et les Composantes de la Personne chez les Dogon." *La Notion de Personne en Afrique Noire.* Colloques intem-ationaux de CNRS, no. 544. Paris: CNRS, 1981.

Dix, G. *The Shape of the Liturgy.* 1945. Reprint, London: Dacre, 1975.

———. *The Treatise on the Apostolic Tradition of St. Hippolytus of Rome.* London: SPCK, 1937.

Documents of the Christian Church. 2d ed. Selected and edited by H. Battenson. London: Oxford University Press, 1963.

Dodds, E. R. *Pagan and Christian in an Age of Anxiety.* Cambridge, Mass.: Harvard University Press, 1965.

Dorjahn, V. R. "The Initiation and Training of Temne *Poro* Members." *African Religious Groups and Beliefs.* Papers in Honor of William R. Bascom.

Ed. S. Ottenberg, 35–62. Meerut, India: Archana Publications for Folklore Institute, 1982.

Durkheim, E. *The Elementary Forms of the Religious Life.* 2d ed. London: George Allen and Unwin, 1976.

Dussel, E. "The Real Motives of the Conquest, 1492–1992: The Voice of the Victims." *Concilium* 6 (1990) 30–46.

Eboussi-Boulaga, F. *A Contretemps. L'Enjeu de Dieu en Afrique.* Paris: Karthala, 1991.

Echeruo, M.J.C. *A Matter of Identity.* 1979 Ahiajoku Lecture. Owerri: Ministry of Information, Culture, Youth and Sports, 1979.

Ejizu, C. I. *OFO: Igbo Ritual Symbol.* Enugu: Fourth Dimension Publishers, 1986.

__________. "Ritual Enactment of Achievement: *Ikenga* Symbol in Igboland." *Paideuma* 37 (1991) 233–51.

Ela, J. M. *The African Cry.* Maryknoll, N.Y.: Orbis Books, 1986.

__________. *De l'Assistance à la Libération. Les Tâches actuelles de l'Eglise en milieu africain.* Paris: Centre Lebret, 1981.

Eliade, M. *Cosmos and History: The Myth of Eternal Return.* New York: Harper and Row, 1959.

__________. *Myths, Dreams and Mysteries.* London: Collins, 1960.

__________. *Rites and Symbols of Initiation.* New York: Harper and Row, 1958.

Equiano, Olaudah. *Equiano's Travels: His Autobiography: The Interesting Narrative Life of Olaudah Equiano or Gustavus Vassa the African.* Abridged and edited by P. Edwards. London: Heinemann, 1969.

Eusebius. *Church History. Nicene and Post-Nicene Fathers of the Church.* 2d series, vol. 1. Ed. P. Schaff and H. Wace. Grand Rapids, Mich.: Eerdmans, 1986.

__________. *The History of the Church from Christ to Constantine.* 7.22.4. Trans. with introduction by G. A. Williamson. New York: New York University Press, 1966.

Faivre, A. "La Documentation canonico-liturgique de l'Eglise ancienne. II. Les 'Unités littéraires' et leurs Relectures." *Revue des Sciences Religieuses* 206:4 (1990) 273–97.

Farby, H. J. "Gedenken und Gedàchtnis im alten Testament." *La Commémoration.* Colloque du Centenaire de la Section des Sciences Religieuses de l'Ecole pratique des Hautes Etudes. Ed. P. Gignoux. Louvain-Paris: Peeters, 1988.

Ferguson, E. "Spiritual in Early Christianity and Its Environment." *Aufstieg und Niedergang der Römischen Welt.* 2.23.2. Ed. H. Temporini and W. Haase, 1151–89. Berlin and New York: W. de Gruyter, 1980.

Fiala, V. "Les Prière d'Acceptation de l'Offrande et le Genre littéraire du Canon romain." *Eucharisties d'Orient et d'Occident.* Vol. 1. Ed. B. Botte et al., 117–33. Paris: Cerf, 1970.

Finkelstein, L. "The Development of the Amidah." *Jewish Quarterly Review* 16 (1925–26) 1–43, 127–70.

Finn, T. M. "It Happened One Saturday Night: Ritual and Conversion in Augustine's North Africa." *Journal of the American Academy of Religion* 58:4 (1990) 591.

Fiorenza, E. S. *The Book of Revelation: Justice and Judgment.* Philadelphia: Fortress Press, 1985.

__________. *In Memory of Her: A Feminist Theological Reconstruction of Christian Origins.* New York: Crossroad, 1988.

Firth, R. *Symbols, Public and Private.* London: George Allen and Unwin, 1973.

Fisher, L. R. "Creation at Ugarit and in the Old Testament." *Vetus Testamentum* 15 (1965) 313–24.

Fossaert, R. *Le Monde au 21e Siècle. Une Théorie des Systemes Mondiaux.* Paris: Fayard, 1991.

Fourrez, G. *Sacraments as Passages: Celebrating the Tensions of Modern Life.* Notre Dame, Ind.: Ave Maria Press, 1983.

Frend, W.H.C. *Martyrdom and Persecution in the Early Church: A Study of a Conflict from the Maccabees to Donatus.* Oxford: Basil Blackwell, 1965.

__________. *The Rise of Christianity.* London: Darton, Longman, and Todd, 1984.

Gaba, C. R. *Scriptures of an African People.* Maryknoll, N.Y: Orbis Books, 1973.

Gager, J. G. *Kingdom and Community: The Social World of Early Christianity.* Englewood Cliffs, N.J.: Prentice-Hall, 1975.

Gallant, C. "A Jungian Interpretation of the Eleusinian Myths and Mysteries."*Aufstieg und Niedergang der Römischen Welt.* 2.18.2. Ed. H. Temporini and W. Haase, 1540–63. Berlin and New York: W. de Gruyter, 1989.

Garnsay, P. "Religious Toleration in Classical Antiquity." *Persecution and Toleration.* Ed. W. J. Sheils. Oxford: Basil Blackwell, for the Ecclesiastical History Society, 1984.

Gbuji, A. O. *Pastoral on Title-Taking and Traditional Funeral Ceremonies.* Isseleuku, Nigeria: 1984.

Gennep, A. van. *The Rites of Passage.* London: Routledge and Kegan Paul, 1960.

George, A. R. "Sennacherib and the Tablet of Destinies." *Iraq* 48 (1986) 133–46.

Girard, R. *Des Choses cachées depuis la Fondation du Monde.* Written in collaboration with J. M. Oughourlian and G. Lefort. Paris: Grasset, 1978.

__________. *The Scapegoat.* Trans. Y. Freccero. Baltimore: Johns Hopkins University Press, 1986.

__________. *La Violence et le Sacré.* Paris: Grasset, 1972.

Goffman, E. *Interaction Ritual.* New York: Pantheon Books, 1967.

__________. *The Presentation of Self in Everyday Life.* New York: Doubleday, 1959.

Goodenough, E. R. *By Light Light.* New Haven, Conn.: Yale University Press, 1935.

Goody, J. "The Time of Telling and the Telling of Time in Written and Oral Cultures." *Chronotypes: The Construction of Time.* Ed. J. Bender and D. E. Wellbery, 77–96. Stanford, Calif.: Stanford University Press, 1991.

Gossiaux, P. P. "Mythe et Pouvoir. Le Culte de Ryangombe-Kiranga (Afrique équatoriale de l'Est)." *Le Mythe. Son Langage et son Message.* Actes du colloque de Liège et Louvain-la-Neuve 1981. Ed. H. Limet and J. Ries, 337–72. Louvain-la-Neuve: Centre d'Historie des Religions, 1983.

Gottwald, N. K., ed. *The Bible and Liberation: Political and Social Hermeneutics.* Maryknoll, N.Y.: Orbis Books, 1983.

———. *The Tribes of Yahweh: A Sociology of the Religion of Liberated Israel 1250–1050 B.C.E.* 1979. Reprint, Maryknoll, N.Y.: Orbis Books, 1985.

Gougaud, L. "La Danse dans les Église." *Revue d'Histoire Ecclesiastique* 15 (1914) 5–22, 229–45.

Grainger. *The Language of the Rite.* London: Darton, Longman and Todd, 1974.

———. *The Message of the Rite: The Significance of Christian Rites of Passage.* Cambridge, Mass.: Lutterworth Press, 1988.

Grassi, J. A. "The Liturgy of Revelation." *Bible Today* 24:1 (1986) 30–7.

Gray, R., ed. *The Cambridge History of Africa.* Vol. 4, *From 1600 to c. 1790.* Cambridge, Mass.: Harvard University Press, 1975.

Greenberg, J. *The Languages of Africa.* Bloomington: Indiana University Press, 1966.

Grelot, P. "Du Sabbat juif au Dimanche chrétien." *La Maison Dieu* 124 (1975) 14–54.

Griaule, M. *Conversations with Ogotemmeli.* London: Oxford University Press, 1965.

Griffin, D. R., ed. *Archetypal Process: Self and Divine in Whitehead, Jung, and Hillman.* Evanston, Ill.: Northwestern University Press, 1989.

Groenbaek, J. "Baal's Battle with Yam: A Canaanite Creation Fight." *Journal for the Study of the Old Testament* 33 (1985).

Guillet, J. "Le Langage spontané de la Bénédiction dans l'ancien Testament." *Recherches des Sciences Religieuses* 57 (1969) 163–204.

Gunkel, H. *The Psalms: A Form-Critical Introduction.* Philadelphia: Fortress Press, 1967.

Gy, P.-M. *La Liturgie dans l'Histoire.* Paris: Cerf, 1990.

Hackett, R.I.J., ed. *New Religious Movements in Nigeria.* Lewinston/ Queenston: Edwin Mellen Press, 1987.

Hadden, J. K. "Religion and the Construction of Social Problems." *Religion and Religiosity in America.* Ed. J. K. Hadden and T. E. Long, 17–30. New York: Crossroad, 1983.

Hamman, A. "La Prière chrétienne et la Prière Païenne, Formes et Différences." *Aufstieg und Niedergang der Römischen Welt.* 2.23.2. Ed. H. Temporini and W. Haase, 1199–212. Berlin and New York: W. de Gruyter, 1980.

Hanggi, A., and I. Pahl. *Prex Eucharistica.* Fribourg Suisse: Editions Universitaires, 1968.

Hanson, R.P.C. "The Christian Attitude to Pagan Religions up to the Time of Constantine the Great." *Aufstieg und Niedergang der Römischen Welt.* 2.23.2. Ed. H. Temporini and W. Haase, 910–73. Berlin and New York: W. de Gruyter, 1980.

Hayes, J. H., and J. M. Miller, eds. *Israelite and Judaean History.* Philadelphia: Westminster Press, 1977.
Healey, J. C. "Four Africans Evaluate SCCs in East Africa." *African Ecclesial Review* 29:5 (1987) 266–77.
Hearne, B. "The Significance of the Zaire Mass." *African Ecclesial Review* 17 (1975) 243–8.
__________, and N. Mijere. *Celebration II.* Spearhead 42. Eldoret: Gaba Publications, 1976.
Hebga, M. "Worthy and Unworthy Churches." *Concilium* 130:10 (1979) 105–12.
Hedegard, R. *Seder Rav Amram Gaon.* Part I. Hebrew texts with critical apparatus; translation with notes and introduction. Lund: a.-B.Ph. Lindestedts Universitets-Bokhandel, 1951.
Helgeland, J. "Time and Space: Christian and Roman."*Aufstieg und Niedergang der Römischen Welt.* 2.23.2. Ed. H. Temporini and W. Haase, 1285–305. Berlin and New York: W. de Gruyter, 1980.
Henrichs, A. "Pagan Rituals and the Alleged Crimes of the Early Christians: A Reconstruction." *Kyriakon.* Festschrift Johannes Quasten. Vol. 1. Ed. P. Granfield and J. A. Jungmann, 18–35. Münster: Verlag Aschendorff, 1970.
Henderson, R. N. *The King in Everyman: Evolutionary Trends in Onitsha Ibo Society and Culture.* New Haven, Conn.: Yale University Press, 1972.
Hick, J. "The Non-Absoluteness of Christianity." *The Myth of Christian Uniqueness.* Ed. J. Hick and P. F. Knitter. Maryknoll, N.Y.: Orbis Books, 1987.
Hochegger, H. *Le Langage des Gestes Rituels.* Vol. 1. Bandundu: Ceeba, 1981.
Hollenbach, P. W. "The Constitution of Human Community in Two Ancient Civilizations." *Biblical Literature: 1974 Proceedings.* Compiled by F. O. Francis. Florida: American Academy of Religion, 1974.
Horton, R. "African Conversion." *Africa* 41:2 (1971) 85–108.
__________. "African Traditional Thought and Western Science: Part I: From Tradition to Science." *Africa* 37 (1967) 50–71. "Part II: The 'Closed' and 'Open' Predicaments." *Africa* 37 (1967) 153–87.
__________. "Judaeo Christian Spectacles: Boon or Bane to the Study of African Religions." *Cahiers d'Etudes Africaines* 96:24 (1984) 391–436.
__________. "Ritual Man in Africa." *Africa* 34 (1964) 85–103.
Horton, W.R.G. "God, Man, and the Land in a Northern Ibo Village-group." *Africa* 26 (1956).
Hruby, K. "La Fête des Tabernacles au Temple, à la Synagogue et dans le nouveau Testament." *L'Orient Syrien* 7 (1962) 163–74.
__________. "Les Heures de Prière dans le Judaisme à l'Epoque de Jésus." *La Prière des Heures.* Ed. Mgr. Cassien and B. Botte, 59–84. Paris: Cerf, 1963.
Huizinga, J. *Homo Ludens.* Boston: Beacon Press, 1953.
Hurbon, L. *Dieu dans le Vaudou Haïtien.* Paris: Payot, 1972.

Idelsohn, A. Z. *Jewish Worship and Its Developments.* New York: Schocken Books, 1972.
Ignatius of Antioch. *Epistle to the Romans. Early Christian Writings: The Apostolic Fathers.* Trans. M. Stanforth. 1968. Reprint, Middlesex: Penguin, 1975.
Ilesanmi, T. M. "Eto Ati Adura Isomolorukoi." *Adura Onigbagbo.* Ilesha: Iranoo-Owuro Press, 1978.
Isichei, E. *A History of the Igbo People.* London: MacMillan, 1976.
__________. *Igbo Worlds: An Anthology of Oral Histories and Historical Descriptions.* Philadelphia: Institute for the Study of Human Issues, 1978.
Jahn, J. *Muntu: An Outline of Neo-African Culture.* London: Faber and Faber, 1961.
Jasper, R.C.D., and G. J. Cuming. *Prayers of the Eucharist: Early and Reformed Texts.* Trans. and ed. with commentary. 3d ed., revised and enlarged. New York: Pueblo, 1987.
Jedin, H. *History of the Church.* London: Burns and Oates, 1981.
Jeffreys, M.D.W. "Additional Steps in Umundri Coronation Ceremony." *Africa* 9 (1936) 403–6.
__________. "The Divine Umundri King." *Africa* 8 (1935) 346–54.
Jeremias, J. *The Eucharistic Words of Jesus.* London: SCM, 1973.
Jerome, Saint. *Letter.* 107.2. *Nicene and Post-Nicene Fathers of the Christian Church.* 2d series, vol. 6. Ed. P Schaff and H. Wace. Grand Rapids, Mich.: Eerdmans, 1983.
Johnson, P. *A History of Christianity.* New York: Penguin, 1976.
Jones, G. I. "Ibo Land Tenure." *Africa* 19 (1949) esp. 316–21.
Jousse, M. *L'Anthropologie du Geste.* Paris: Resma, 1969.
Jung, C. *Memories, Dramas, Reflections.* New York: Random House, 1963.
Jungmann, J. A. *The Mass of the Roman Rite.* Revised by C. K. Riepe. Westminster, Md.: Christian Classics, 1978.
__________. *Pastoral Liturgy.* London: Challoner, 1962.
Kabasele, L. *Alliances avec le Christ en Afrique.* Athens: Editions Historiques S. D. Basilopoulos, 1987.
__________. "L'inculturation sacramentelle au Zaïre." *Lumen Vitae* 42:1 (1987) 75–84.
__________. "Nouveau Rites, Foi Naissante." *Lumière et Vie* 159 (1983) 61–73.
Kairos Theologians. *The Kairos Document: Challenge to the Church: A Theological Comment on the Political Crisis in South Africa.* Grand Rapids, Mich.: Eerdmans, 1986.
__________. "The New Kairos." *Voices from the Third World* (EATWOT) 13:2 (1990) 142–3.
Kalu, O. U., ed. *The History of Christianity in West Africa.* London: Longman, 1980.
__________. "Precarious Vision: The African's Perception of His World." *Readings in African Humanities: African Cultural Development.* Ed. O. U. Kalu, 37–44. Enugu: Fourth Dimension, 1980.

Kapelrud, A. S. "Creation in the Ras Shamra Texts." *Studia Theologica* 34 (1980) 1–11.
Kaumba, L. "Impasses d'une Théologie de l'Inculturation." *Philosophie Africaine face aux Libérations religieuses.* Actes de la Xie Semaine Philosophique de Kinshasa. Nov. 27–Dec. 3, 1988. Facultés Catholiques de Kinshasa, 1990.
Keifer, R. A. "The Unity of the Roman Canon: An Examination of Its Unique Structure." *Studia Liturgica* 11 (1976) 39–58.
Kelly, J.N.D. *Early Christian Doctrines.* New York: Harper and Row, 1978.
King, L. W. *The Enuma Elish: The Seven Tablets of Creation.* Vol. 1. 1902. Reprint, New York: AMS Press, 1976.
Kirk, G. S. *Myth: Its Meaning and Function in Ancient and Other Cultures.* Cambridge, Mass.: Harvard University Press, 1970.
__________. "On Defining Myths." *Sacred Narrative: Readings in the Theory of Myth.* Ed. A. Dundes. Berkeley: University of California Press, 1984.
Kloppenberg, J. S. *The Formation of Q: Trajectories in Ancient Wisdom Collections.* Philadelphia: Fortress Press, 1987.
Kragerud, A. "The Concept of Creation in Enuma Elish." *Ex Orbe Religionum. Studia Geo Widengren.* Lugduni Batavorum: Brill, 1972.
Kraus, H. J. *Worship in Israel: A Cultic History of the Old Testament.* Oxford: Basil Blackwell, 1966.
Kucharek, C. A. *The Byzantine-Slav Liturgy of St. John Chrysostom.* Allendale, N.J.: Alleluia Press, 1971.
__________. *The Sacramental Mysteries: A Byzantine Approach.* Allendale, N.J.: Alleluia Press, 1976.
Kuper, H. "A Ritual Kingship among the Swazi." *Africa* 14:255–6.
La Fontaine, J. S. *Initiation: Ritual Drama and Secret Knowledge Across the World.* Middlesex: Penguin, 1985.
Lambert, W. G. "A New Look at the Babylonian Background of Genesis." *Journal of Theological Studies* 16 (1965).
__________. "Ninurta Mythology in Babylonian Epic of Creation." *Keilschrifliche Literaturen.* Ed. K. Hecker and W. Sommerfeld, 55–60. Berlin: Dietrich Reimer Verlag, 1986.
__________. "The Reign of Nebuchadnezzar I: A Turning Point in the History of Ancient Mesopotamian Religion." *The Seed of Wisdom.* Essays in Honor of T. J. Meek. Ed. W. S. McCullough, 3–13. Toronto: University of Toronto Press, 1964.
__________. Review of W. Sommerfeld's thesis *Der Aufstieg Marduks* (Kevelaer: Butzon und Bercker, l982), in his "Studies in Marduk," 1–9.
__________. "Studies in Marduk." *Bulletin of the School of Oriental and African Studies* 47 (1964).
Langer, S. *Philosophy in a New Key: A Study in the Symbolism of Reason, Rite, and Art.* 3d ed. Cambridge, Mass., and London: Harvard University Press, 1957.

Lawuyi, O. B. "Self-Potential as a Yoruba Ultimate: A Further Contribution to URAM Yoruba Studies (URAM 7:173–200; 11:233–242)." *Ultimate Reality and Meaning* 14 (1991) 21–9.

Lease, G. "Mithraism and Christianity: Borrowings and Transformations." *Aufstieg und Niedergang der Römischen Welt.* 2.23.2. Ed. H. Temporini and W. Haase, 1306–32. Berlin and New York: W. de Gruyter, 1980.

Ledogar, R. J. *Acknowledgment: Praise Verbs in the Early Greek Anaphoras.* Rome: Herder, 1968.

Leithross, S. *African Women.* London: Faber, 1934.

Leo the Great. *Sermo.* 27. *Nicene and Post-Nicene Fathers of the Christian Church.* 2d series, vol. 12. Ed. P Schaff and H. Wace. Grand Rapids, Mich.: Eerdmans, 1983.

Leonard, A. G. *The Lower Niger and Its Tribes.* London: Frank Cass, 1906.

Levinson, H. S. "Traditional Religion, Modernity and Unthinkable Thoughts." *Journal of Religion* 41 (1981) 37–58.

Lévi-Strauss, C. *Totemism.* Boston: Beacon Press, 1963.

Liber, M. "La Récitation du Schema et des Bénédictions." *Révue d'Etudes Juives* 57 (1909) 161–93.

__________. "Structure and History of the Tefillah." *Jewish Quarterly Review* 40 (1949–50) 331–57.

Lietzmann, H. *Mass and Lord's Supper.* Introduction and supplementary essay by R. D. Richardson. Leiden: Brill, 1953.

Linden, I. "Chewa Initiation Rites and *Nyau* Societies: The Use of Religious Institutions in Local Politics at Mua." *Themes in the Christian History of Central Africa.* Ed. T. O. Ranger and J. Weller, 30–44. London: Heinemann, 1975.

Liturgie de l'Eglise particulière et Liturgie de l'Eglise universelle. Conférence Saint Serge. XXIe Semaine d'Etudes Liturgiques, Paris, June 30–July 3, 1975. Roma: Edizioni Liturgiche, 1976.

Loza, J. "Les Catéchèses Etiologiques dans l'ancien Testament." *Revue Biblique* 78 (1971) 481–500.

Luykx, B. *Culte chrétien en Afrique après Vatican II.* Fribourg: Nouvelle Revue de Science Missionaire, 1974.

MacAloon, J. J. "Sociation and Sociability in Political Celebrations." *Celebration: Studies in Festivity and Ritual.* Ed V. Turner, 255–71. Washington, D.C.: Smithsonian Institution Press, 1982.

Machinist, P. "Literature as Politics: The Tukulti-Ninurta Epic and the Bible." *Catholic Biblical Quarterly* 38 (1976) 455–82.

Malefijt, A. de Waal. *Religion and Culture: An Introduction to the Anthropology of Religion.* New York: Macmillan Co., 1968.

Malinowski, B. *Magic, Science and Religion.* Garden City, N.Y.: Anchor Books, 1954.

Martin-Achard, R. *Essai biblique sur les Fêtes d'Israel.* Genève: Labor et Fides, 1974.

"Martus, Marturéô, marturia, marturion." *Theological Dictionary of the New Testament.* Vol. 4. Ed. G. Kittel, 474–508. Grand Rapids, Mich.: Eerdmans, 1967.
Marty, F. "Signe, Symbole, Sacrement." *Recherches de Science Religieuse* 75:2 (April–June 1987).
Mbembe, A. *Afriques Indociles.* Paris: Karthala, 1988.
Mbiti, J. S. *African Religions and Philosophy.* London: Heinemann, 1969.
__________. *New Testament Eschatology in an African Background.* London: Oxford University Press, 1971.
__________. *The Prayers of African Religion.* London: SPCK, 1975.
Mbon, F. M. "The Quest for Identity in African New Religious Movements." *New Religious Movements and Society in Nigeria.* Bayreuth African Studies Series 17. Ed. G. Ludwar-Ene, 71–82. West Germany: Bayreuth University, 1991.
McCarthy, D. J. "Creation Motifs in Ancient Hebrew Poetry." *Creation in the Old Testament.* Ed. B. W. Anderson, 74–89. Philadelphia: Fortress Press, 1984.
__________. *Treaty and Covenant: A Study in Form in the Ancient Oriental Documents and in the Old Testament.* Rome: Pontifical Biblical Institute, 1963.
Medebielle, A. "Eglise." *Dictionnaire de la Bible.* Supplement II. Ed. L. Pirot. Paris: Letouzey et Ane, 1934.
Meek, C. K. *Law and Authority in a Nigerian Tribe.* London: Oxford University Press, 1937.
Meeks, W. A. *The First Urban Christians: The Social World of the Apostle Paul.* New Haven, Conn., and London: Yale University Press, 1983.
Meslin, M. *Le Christianisme dans l'Empire Romain.* Paris: Presses Universitaires de France, 1970.
__________. "Vases Sacré, et Boissons d'Eternité dans les Visions des Martyrs africains." *Epektasis.* Mélanges Patristiques Offerts au Cardinal Jean Daniélou. Ed. J. Fontaine and C. Kannengiesser, 139–53. Paris: Beauchesne, 1972.
Messi Metogo, E. *Théologie africaine et Ethnophilosophie.* Paris: l'Harmattan, 1985.
Metuh, E. I. *African Religion in Western Conceptual Schemes.* Ibadan: Pastoral Institute, 1985.
Michalowski, P. "Presence at Creation." *Lingering Over Words.* Studies in Ancient Near Eastern Literature in Honor of William L. Moran. Ed. T. Abusch et al. Atlanta: Scholars Press, 1990.
Milgrom, J. *Studies in Cultic Theology and Terminology.* Leiden: Brill, 1983.
Minutes of Meeting of the Inculturation Commission of the Catholic Diocese of Nsukka held on January 2, 1993, at St. Theresa's Cathedral, Nsukka.
Mofokeng, T. A. "Popular Religiosity: A Liberative Source and Terrain of Struggle." *Popular Religion, Liberation and Contextual Theology.* Ed. J.

van Nieuwenhove and B. K. Goldewijk. Nijmegen: J. H. Kok-Kampen, 1991.
Mol, H. *Identity and the Sacred: A Sketch for a New Social-Scientific Theory of Religion.* Oxford: Basil Blackwell, 1976.
Moore, R. L. "Ritual Process, Initiation and Contemporary Religion." *Jung's Challenge to Contemporary Religion.* Ed. M. Stein and R. L. Moore, 152–3. Wilmette, Ill.: Chiron Publications, 1987.
Moreton, M. J. "Eis Anatolâs Blépsate: Orientation as a Liturgical Principle." *Studia Patristica* 17:2 (1982) 575–90.
Mowinckel, S. *The Psalms in Israel's Worship.* New York: Abingdon Press, 1962.
Mpongo, L. "Le Rite zaïrois de la Messe." *Spiritus* 19:73 (1978) 436–41.
Mudimbe, V. Y. *The Invention of Africa: Gnosis, Philosophy, and the Order of Knowledge.* Bloomington and Indianapolis: Indiana University Press, 1988.
Mujynya, N. *L'Homme dans l'Univers des Bantu.* Kinshasha: Presses Universitaires du Zaïre, 1978.
Mulago, V. *La Religion traditionelle des Bantu et leur Vision du Monde.* Kinshasa: Faculté de Théologie Catholique, 1980.
Murtonen, A. "The Use and Meaning of the Words leBarek and Berakah in the Old Testament." *Vetus Testamentum* 9 (1959) 158–77.
Musurillo, H. *The Acts of the Christian Martyrs.* Introduction, texts, and translations. Oxford: Clarendon Press, 1972.
Mveng, E. *L'Afrique dans l'Eglise. Parole d'un Croyant.* Paris: Harmattan, 1985.
__________. *L'Art d'Afrique noire. Liturgie cosmique et Langage religieux.* Yaoundé: Clé, 1974.
__________. "L'Expérience de la Communauté des Béatitudes du Cameroun." Paper presented at the Colloque International *Vie Monastique et Inculturation à la Lumière des traditions et Situations africaines.* Kinshasha, Feb. 19–25, 1989.
Myerhoff, B. "Rites of Passage: Process and Paradox." *Celebration: Studies in Festivity and Ritual.* Ed V. Turner. Washington, D.C.: Smithsonian Institution Press, 1982.
Ndiokwere, N. I. *Search for Security.* Benin City, Nigeria: AMBIK, 1990.
Neusner, J. *The Mishnah: A New Translation.* New Haven, Conn., and London: Yale University Press, 1988.
Ngindu, A. M. "Propos et Problèmes Concernant le Culte des Morts ches les Baluba du Kasayi." *Cahiers des Religions Africaines* 3:5 (1969) 79–109.
Niangoran-bouah, G. "La Drummologie et la Vision négro-africaine du sacre." *Médiations Africaines du Sacré.* Actes du 3e Colloque International du CERA. Kinshasha, Feb. 16–22, 1986.
Nock, A. D. *Conversion: The Old and the New in Religion from Alexander the Great to Augustine of Hippo.* 1933. Reprint, Oxford: University Press, 1961.

Noth, C. R. "The 'Former Things' and the 'New Things' in Deutero-Isaiah." *Studies in Old Testament Prophecy.* Ed. H. H. Rowley, 111–26. New York: Scribner, 1950.

La Notion de Personne en Afrique noire. Colloques internatiounaux de CNRS, no. 544. Paris, Oct. 11–17, 1971. Paris: CNRS, 1981.

Nwabueze, B. O. *The Igbo in the Context of Modern Government and Politics in Nigeria: A Call for Self-Examination and Self-Correction.* Owerri: Ministry of Information, Culture, Youth and Sports, 1985.

Nwoga, D. I. *The Supreme Being as Stranger in Igbo Religious Thought.* Ekwerazu, Mbaise: Hawk Press, 1984.

Nwokocha, C. C. "The Kola: Igbo Symbol of Love and Unity: A Valuable Starting Point for the Study of the Eucharist." Th.D. dissertation. Universitas Urbaniana Rome, 1969.

Obi, C. "Town Where Widows Sleep with Their Dead Husbands." *Vintage People.* Lagos (Feb. 19–25, 1993) 7.

Obi, C. A., et al. *A Hundred Years of the Catholic Church in Eastern Nigeria 1885–1985.* Onitsha: Africana Fep, 1985.

Obiefuna, A. K. *The Church and Culture.* A case study in Awka. 1990.

Odey, J. *Ritual Circumcision in Ezza and the Christian Faith.* Ibadan: Claverianum Press, 1986.

Ofodile, F. "The Right of Women in Nigeria (State and Church)." *Human Rights in Nigerian Society and Church.* The Second SIST Missiology Symposium, Nov. 29–Dec. 1, 1990.

Okeke, D. C. "African Concept of Time." *Cahiers des Religions Africaines* 7:14 (1973) 207–301.

Okigbo, P.N.C. *Towards a Reconstruction of the Political Economy of Igbo Civilization.* Owerri: Ministry of Information, Culture, Youth and Sports, 1986.

Okpewho, I. *Myth in Africa: A Study of Its Aesthetic and Cultural Relevance.* Cambridge: Cambridge University Press, 1983.

Olshewsky, T. M. "Between Science and Religion."*Journal of Religion* 62:3 (1982).

Onaiyekan, J. "State Secularity and the Nigerian Church." *Bulletin of Ecumenical Theology* 2:1, 75–83.

Onwuejeogwu, M. A. *An Igbo Civilization: Nri Kingdom and Hegemony.* London: Ethnographica and Ethiope, 1981.

Origen. *Commentary on John.* 6.36. *The Ante-Nicene Fathers.* Vol. 9. Ed. A. Menzies. New York: Charles Scribner's Sons, 1906.

__________. *Exhortation to Martyrdom.* In his *Prayer: Exhortation to Martyrdom.* Trans. and annotated by J. J. O'Meara. Westminster, Md.: Newman Press, 1954.

Oriji, J. N. *Traditions of Igbo Origin: A Study of Pre-colonial Population Movements in Africa.* New York: Peter Lang, 1990.

Ottenberg, S. "Ibo Receptivity to Change." *Continuity and Change in African Cultures.* Ed. W. R. Bascom and M. J. Herskovits, 130–59. Chicago: University of Chicago Press, 1959.

Ouedraogo, R. "Rituel Moore." *Le Calao* 51:3 (1980) 34–47.
Pagels, E. "Christian Apologists and the 'Fall of the Angels': An Attack on Roman Imperial Power." *Harvard Theological Review* 78:3–4 (1985) 301–25.
The Passover Haggadah. Based on the Haggadah Studies of E. D. Goldschmidt. Ed. N. N. Glatzer. New York: Schocken Books, 1969.
Paul VI, Pope. *Africae Terrarum* in *Documentation Catholique,* 1505. Nov. 19, 1967, pp. 1937–55.
Polanyi, M., and H. Prosch. *Meaning.* Chicago: University of Chicago Press, 1975.
Prigent, P. *Apocalypse et Liturgie.* Neuchatel: Delachaux et Niestlé, 1964.
"Qahal." *A Hebrew and English Lexicon of the Old Testament.* Ed. F. Brown, S. R. Driver, and C. A. Briggs, 874–5. 1907. Reprint, Oxford: Clarendon, 1972.
Quasten, J. *Patrology.* Vol. 1. Westminster, Md.: Newman Press, 1950.
Quispel, G. "The Origin of the Gnostic Demiurge." *Kyriakon.* Festschrift Johannes Quasten. Vol. 1. Ed. P. Granfield and J. A. Jungmann, 271–6. Münster: Verlag Aschendorff, 1970.
Rad, G. von. *Old Testament Theology.* Vol. 1. New York: Harper and Row, 1962.
__________. *Old Testament Theology.* Vol. 2. London: Oliver and Boyd, 1965.
__________. *The Problem of the Hexateuch.* Edinburgh: Oliver and Boyd, 1966.
Rahmani, I. E. *Testamentum Domini Nostri Jesu Christi.* Hildesheim: 1968.
Richards, D. "The Ideology of European Dominance." *Présence Africaine* 111 (1979) 3–18.
Ricoeur, P. *The Symbolism of Evil.* Boston: Beacon Press, 1967.
Ringgren, H. "Bara." *The Theological Dictionary of the Old Testament.* Vol. 2. Ed. G. J. Botterwech and H. Ringgren, 246–7. Grand Rapids, Mich.: Eerdmans, 1974–75.
The Rites of the Catholic Church as Revised by the Second Vatican Ecumenical Council. New York: Pueblo, 1976.
Rodopoulos, R. "Irenaeus on the Consecration of the Eucharistic Gifts." *Kyriakon.* Festschrift Johannes Quasten. Vol. 2. Ed. P. Granfield and J. A. Jungmann. Münster: Verlag Aschendorff, 1970.
Rordorf, W. "La 'Diaconie' des Martyrs selon Origène." *Epektasis. Mélanges Patristiques offerts au Cardinal Jean Daniélou.* Ed. J. Fontaine and C. Kannengiesser, 395–402. Paris: Beauchesne, 1972.
Rossi, M. A. "The Passion of Perpetua, Every Woman of Late Antiquity." *Pagan and Christian Anxiety: A Response to E. R. Dodds.* Ed. R. C. Smith and J. Lounibos, 53–86. London: University Press of America, 1984.
Rousseau, O. *The Progress of the Liturgy.* Westminster, Md.: Newman Press, 1951.
Saggs, H.S.F. *The Encounter with the Divine in Mesopotamia and Israel.* London: Athlone Press, 1978.
Sanneh, L. *West African Christianity.* Maryknoll, N.Y.: Orbis Books, 1983.

Sanon, A. T., and R. Luneau. *Enraciner l'Evangile. Initiations Africaines et Pédagogie de la Foi.* Paris: Cerf, 1982.
Sassier, P. *Du Bon Usage des Pauvres. Histoire d'un Thème Politique (XVIe–XXe Siècle).* Paris: Fayard, 1990.
Scharbert, J. "Brk, Berakah." *The Theological Dictionary of the Old Testament.* Vol. 2. Ed. G. J. Botterwech and H. Ringgren, 279–80. Grand Rapids, Mich.: Eerdmans, 1974–75.
Scheflen, A. E., and A. Scheflen. *Body Language and Social Order.* Englewood Cliffs, N.J.: Prentice-Hall, 1972.
Schillebeeckx, E. *Christ: The Experience of Jesus as Lord.* New York: Seabury, 1980.
__________. *The Church: The Human Story of God.* New York: Crossroad, 1990.
Schmid, H. H. "Creation, Righteousness, and Salvation: 'Creation Theology' as the Broad Horizon of Biblical Theology." *Creation in the Old Testament.* Ed. B. W. Anderson. Philadelphia: Fortress Press, 1984.
Schmitt, J.-C. *La Raison des Gestes dans l'Occident Médiéval.* Paris: Gallimard, 1990.
Schoffeleers, M. "The Interaction of the M'Bona Cult and Christianity, 1859–1963." *Themes in the Christian History of Central Africa.* Ed. T. O. Ranger and J. Weller, 14–29. London: Heinemann, 1975.
Segal, J. B. *The Hebrew Passover: From the Earliest Times to A.D. 70.* London: Oxford University Press, 1963.
Shank, H. "Israel's Emergence in Canaan: *BR* Interviews Norman Gottwald." *Bible Review* 5:5 (Oct. 1989) 26–34.
Shaw, T. *Igbo-Ukwu: An Account of Archaeological Discoveries in Eastern Nigeria.* 2 vols. London: Faber and Faber, 1970.
Shepherd, M. H. *The Paschal Liturgy and the Apocalypse.* London: Lutterworth Press, 1960.
Shorter, A. "Liturgical Creativity in East Africa." *African Ecclesial Review* 19:5 (1977) 258–67.
Smith, D. E., and H. E. Taussig. *Many Tables: The Eucharist in the New Testament and Liturgy Today.* London and Philadelphia: SCM and Trinity Press International, 1990.
Smith, J. Z. "A Pearl of Great Price and a Cargo of Yams: A Study in Situational Incongruity." *History of Religions* 16:1 (1976) 1–19.
__________. "A Slip in Time Saves Nine: Prestigious Origins Again." *Chronotypes: The Construction of Time.* Ed. J. Bender and D. E. Wellbery, 67–76. Stanford, Calif.: Stanford University Press, 1991.
__________. *To Take Place: Toward Theory in Ritual.* Chicago: University of Chicago Press, 1987.
Smith, M. "The Common Theology of the Ancient Near East." *Journal of Biblical Literature* 71 (1952) 135–47.
__________. "On the Difference Between the Culture of Israel and the Major Cultures of the Ancient Near East." *Journal of Ancient Near Eastern Society* 5 (1973) 389–95.

Soyinka, W. *Myth, Literature and the African World.* Cambridge, Mass.: Cambridge University Press, 1976.
Spriggs, D. G. *Two Old Testament Theologies.* London: SCM, 1974.
Stevenson, W. B. "Hebrew ʿOlah and Zebah Sacrifices." *Festschrift Albert Bertholet.* Ed. V. Baumgartner et al., 488–97. Tubingen: J.C.B. Mohr, 1950.
Stevenson W. T. "Myth and the Crisis of Historical Consciousness." *Myth and Crisis of Historical Consciousness.* Ed. L. W. Gibbs and W. T. Stevenson. Missoula, Mont.: Scholars Press, 1975.
Stewart, Z. "Greek Crowns and Christian Martyrs." *Antiquité Païenne ef Chrétienne.* Ed. E. Lucchesi and H. D. Saffery, 119–24. Genève: Patrick Cramer, 1984.
Sundkler, B.G.M. *Bantu Prophets in South Africa.* Oxford: Oxford University Press, 1961.
Taft, R. *The Liturgy of the Hours in East and West.* Collegeville: The Liturgical Press, 1986.
Talbot, P. A. *The Peoples of Southern Nigeria.* Vol. 2. London: Cass, 1926.
__________. *Some Nigerian Fertility Cults.* London: Oxford University Press, 1927.
__________. *Tribes of the Niger Delta.* 1932. Reprint, London: Cass, 1967.
Talley, T. J. *The Origins of the Liturgical Year.* New York: Pueblo, 1986; Collegeville: The Liturgical Press, 1991.
Tempels, P. *Bantu Philosophy.* Paris: Presence Africaine, 1959.
Tertullian. *Apology.* 7. *The Ante-Nicene Fathers.* Vol. 3. Ed. A. Roberts and J. Donaldson. Edinburgh: T. and T. Clark, 1989.
Theissen, G. *Studien zur Soziologie des Urchristentums.* Tübingen: Mohr (Siebeck), 1979.
Thomas, L. V. "Mort symbolique et Naissance initiatique." *Cahiers des Religions Africaines* 7 (1970) 41–73.
__________, and R. Luneau. *Les Religions d'Afrique noire.* 2 vols. Paris: Editions Stock, 1981.
Thomas, N. W. *Anthropological Report on the Ibo-Speaking Peoples of Nigeria.* Part I. London: Harrison, 1913–14.
Thompson, L. L. *The Book of Revelation: Apocalypse and Empire.* New York and Oxford: Oxford University Press, 1990.
Thornton, J. "The Development of an African Catholic Church in the Kingdom of the Kongo 1491–1750." *Journal of African History* 25:2 (1984) 147–67.
Thureau-Dangin, F. *Rituels accadiens.* Paris: E. Leroux, 1921.
Tihon, P. "Theology of the Eucharistic Prayer." *The New Liturgy.* Ed. L. Sheppard. London: Darton, Longman and Todd, 1970.
Tracy, D. *Blessed Rage for Order.* New York: Seabury, 1975.
Trompf, G. W. *The Idea of Historical Recurrence in Western Thought: From Antiquity to the Reformation.* Berkeley: University of California Press, 1979.

Tshiamalenga, N. "L'Art comme Langage et comme Verbe." *Cahiers des Religions Africaines* 16 (1982) 31–2.
Turner, V. *Dramas, Fields and Metaphors: Symbolic Action in Human Society.* Ithaca, N.Y., and London: Cornell University Press, 1974.
__________. *The Drums of Affliction.* Oxford: Clarendon Press, 1968.
__________. *The Forest of Symbols: Aspects of Ndembu Ritual.* Ithaca, N.Y.: Cornell University Press, 1967.
__________. *The Ritual Process: Structure and Anti-Structure.* Chicago: Aldine, 1969, 1973.
Tutu, D. "Black Theology and African Theology: Soulmates or Antagonists." *A Reader in African Theology.* Ed. J. Praratt, 46–57. London: SPCK, 1987.
Uchendu, V. C. *The Igbo of Southern Nigeria.* New York: Rinehart and Winston, 1965.
__________. "'Kola Hospitality' and Igbo Lineage Structure." *Man* 64 (1964) 47–50.
Uzukwu, E. E. "African Cultures and the Christian Liturgy." *West African Journal of Ecclesiastical Studies* 2:1 (1990) 59–83.
__________. "African Personality and the Christian Liturgy." *African Christian Studies* 3:2 (1987) 61–74.
__________. "African Symbols and Christian Liturgical Celebration." *Worship* 65:2 (1991).
__________. *Anamnesis in Africa: The Jewish-Christian Concept of Memorial and the Igbo of Southern Nigeria.* Unpublished M.Th. thesis. St. Michael's College, 1976.
__________. "The Birth and Development of a Local Church: Difficulties and Signs of Hope." *Towards the African Synod Concilium* 1 (1992) 17–23.
__________. *Blessing and Thanksgiving among the Igbo: Towards a Eucharistia Africana.* Toronto: University of St. Michael's College, 1978.
__________. "Igbo World and Ultimate Reality and Meaning." *Ultimate Reality and Meaning* 5:3 (1982) 18–209.
__________. "Liturgical Creativity in Igbo Christian Communities." *Cahiers des Religions Africaines* 20–21:39–42 (1986–87) 523–34.
__________. *Liturgy: Truly Christian, Truly African.* Spearhead no. 74. Eldoret: Gaba Publications, 1982.
__________. "Nri Myth of Origin and Its Ritualization: An Essay in Interpretation." *Religion and African Culture.* Vol. 1, *Inculturation: A Nigerian Perspective.* Ed. E. E. Uzukwu, 92–101. Enugu: Spiritan Publications, 1988.
Vallely, P. *Bad Samaritans: First World Ethics and Third World Debt.* Maryknoll, N.Y.: Orbis Books, 1990.
Vanni, U. "The Ecclesial Assembly 'Interpreting Subject' of the Apocalypse." *Religious Studies Bulletin* 4:3 (1984) 79–85.
Vaux, R. de. *Ancient Israel: Its Life and Institutions.* London: Darton, Longman and Todd, 1961.
Vergote, A. *Dette et Désir.* Paris: Seuil, 1978.

Vidal, J. "Aspects d'une Mythique." *Le Mythe: Son Langage et son Message.* Actes du colloque de Liège et Louvain-la-Neuve. Ed. H. Limet and J. Ries. Louvain-la-Neuve: Centre d'Histoire des Religions, 1983.

Weiser, A. *The Psalms.* London: SCM, 1962.

Westermann, C. *Genesis 1–11: A Commentary.* Trans. J. J. Sullivan. Minneapolis: Augsburg Publishing House, 1984.

__________. *Praise and Lament in the Psalms.* Atlanta: John Knox Press, 1981.

Wiens, D. H. "Mystery Concepts in Primitive Christianity and in Its Environment." *Aufstieg und Niedergang der Römischen Welt.* 2.23.2. Ed. H. Temporini and W. Haase, 1248–84. Berlin and New York: W. de Gruyter, 1980.

Wilken, R. L. *The Christians as the Romans Saw Them.* New Haven, Conn.: Yale University Press, 1984.

Yerkes, R. K. *Sacrifice in Greek and Roman Religions and Early Judaism.* London: Adam and Charles Black, 1953.

Yerushalmi, Y. *Zakhor.* Seattle and London: University of Washington Press, 1982.

Zeitlein, S. "The Morning Benedictions and the Readings in the Temple." *Jewish Quarterly Review* 44 (1953–54) 330–3.

Zeusse, E. M. *Ritual Cosmos: The Sanctification of Life in African Religions.* Athens: Ohio University Press, 1979.

Index